**ABSOLUTE OpenBSD
UNIX for the Practical Paranoid**

ABSOLUTE OpenBSD

UNIX for the Practical Paranoid

by Michael W. Lucas

NO STARCH
PRESS

San Francisco

Publisher: William Pollock
Managing Editor: Karol Jurado
Cover and Interior Design: Octopod Studios
Copyeditor: Kenyon Brown
Compositor: Wedobooks
Proofreader: Stephanie Provines

Distributed to the book trade in the United States by Publishers Group West, 1700 Fourth Street, Berkeley, CA 94710; phone: 800-788-3123; fax: 510-658-1834.

Distributed to the book trade in Canada by Jacqueline Gross & Associates, Inc., One Atlantic Avenue, Suite 105, Toronto, Ontario M6K 3E7 Canada; phone: 416-531-6737; fax 416-531- 4259.

For information on translations or book distributors outside the United States, please contact No Starch Press, Inc. directly:

No Starch Press, Inc.
555 De Haro Street, Suite 250, San Francisco, CA 94107
phone: 415-863-9900; fax: 415-863-9950; info@nostarch.com; http://www.nostarch.com

Library of Congress Cataloguing-in-Publication Data

Lucas, Michael W., 1967-
        Absolute OpenBSD: UNIX for the practical paranoid / Michael W. Lucas.
        p. cm.
Includes index.
        ISBN 1-886411-99-9
1. OpenBSD (Electronic resource) 2. Operating systems (Computers) 3. UNIX (Computer file) I. Title.
        QA76.9.O63L835 2003
        005.4'32--dc21
                                        2003000473

For Elizabeth,
who brings spring's rich warm sunlight
into darkest night

ACKNOWLEDGMENTS

OpenBSD is quite a trip, and the OpenBSD community even more so. Since starting this book, I've talked with more practical and professional paranoids than I knew existed outside of politics. It's been my privilege to work with some of the best computer security people in the world. Best of all, these people care about their work, and the impact it has on average people such as our parents and friends.

The following people all provided feedback on one or more chapters of this book, or answered specific questions on frequently-misunderstood aspects of OpenBSD, and as such deserve my heartfelt thanks. Some of them are OpenBSD crown princes, and others are just users who were trying to figure out what their computer was actually doing. What I've done right is thinks to them, and what I've done wrong is my own fault. They are, in alphabetical order: Shawn Carroll, Chris Cappuccio, Dave Feustel, Thorsten Glaser, Daniel Hartmeier, Jason Houx, Volker Kindermann, Anil Madhavapeddy, U.N. Owen (aka dreamwvr), Francisco Luis Roque, Srebrenko Sehic, Matt Simonsen, Sam Smith, Duncan Matthew Stirling, Peter Werner, and Jason Wright.

A special thanks goes out to Theo de Raadt, for taking time out of his fiendishly busy schedule to provide special insight into the innards of OpenBSD, for not holding back when I goofed, and especially for sticking to his standards of freedom, despite everything the world has to say on that subject.

When an author says something like, "Hold the presses! OpenBSD just added a whole slew of functionality and I have to rewrite huge sections of the book you were planning to ship out tomorrow," the editor is supposed to respond with dire threats involving chainsaws. The folks at No Starch just say, "Well, get to work then." I have been forced to report to the Secret Author Cabal that Bill and Karol are patient, kind, and thoughtful enough to resist our best techniques for driving publishers into Lovecraftian madness.

Then there's Sifu Brown and the fine staff and volunteers of the School of Chinese Martial Arts in Berkley, Michigan (http://www.ZenMartialArts.com). They have absolutely nothing to do with computers, but they have an awful lot to do with me not making dire threats involving chainsaws. Somehow, the Five Ways to Become a Great Martial Artist turned out to be the same as the Five Ways to Write a Great Computer Book — I just never knew it before.

And finally, for Liz, and not just for catching the pet rats before they can stash seeds in server cases.

Michael Lucas
Saint Clair Shores, MI
May 2003

BRIEF CONTENTS

CONTENTS IN DETAIL

0
INTRODUCTION

1
ADDITIONAL HELP

2

INSTALLATION PREPARATIONS

3

DEDICATED INSTALLATION

4
MULTIBOOT INSTALLATION

5
POST-INSTALL SETUP

6
STARTUP AND BOOTING

7
MANAGING USERS

8
NETWORKING

9
INTERNET CONNECTIONS

10
ADDITIONAL SECURITY FEATURES

11
BASIC KERNEL CONFIGURATION

12
BUILDING CUSTOM KERNELS

13
ADD-ON SOFTWARE

14
/ETC

15
DISK AND FILE SYSTEM MANAGEMENT

16
UPGRADING OPENBSD

17
BASIC PACKET FILTERING

18
MORE PACKET FILTERING

19
MANAGING PF

A
i386 KERNEL CONFIGURATION CHOICES

B
PF EXAMPLE CONFIGURATIONS

AFTERWORD
463

INDEX
465

0

INTRODUCTION

*The very quick path
to a quiescent pager?
OpenBSD.*

 Welcome to *Absolute OpenBSD*! This book is an introductory text to general management of the OpenBSD server operating system. OpenBSD is a member of the BSD family of operating systems and is widely regarded as the most secure operating system available anywhere, under any licensing terms. It's widely used by Internet service providers, embedded systems manufacturers, and anyone who needs security and stability. If you're an experienced UNIX systems administrator who wants to add OpenBSD to your repertoire, this book is for you!

By the time you finish this book you should be comfortable on an OpenBSD system. You will understand how to manage, upgrade, and patch computers running OpenBSD. You'll also have a basic understanding of OpenBSD's software, security, and network management features.

What Is BSD?

AT&T employees created UNIX in the early 1970s. At the time, the monster telephone company was forbidden to compete in the computer industry. The telecommunications company used UNIX internally, but could not transform it into a commercial product. As such, AT&T was willing to license the UNIX software and its source code to universities for a nominal fee. This worked well for all parties: AT&T got a few pennies and a generation of computer scientists who cut their teeth on AT&T technology, the universities avoided high operating system license fees, and the students were able to dig around inside the source code and see how computers really worked.

Compared to some of the other operating systems of the time, the original UNIX wasn't very good. But all these students had the source code for it and could improve the parts that they didn't like. If an instructor found a certain bug particularly vexing, he could assign his students the job of fixing it. If a university network engineer, professor, or student needed a feature, he could use the source code to quickly implement it. As the Internet grew in the early 1980s, these additions and features were exchanged between universities in the form of patches. The Computer Science Research Group (CSRG) at the University of California, Berkeley, acted as a central clearinghouse for these patches. The CSRG distributed these patches to anyone with a valid AT&T source code license. The resulting collection of patches became known as the Berkeley Software Distribution, or BSD.

This continued for a long, long time. If you look at the copyright for any BSD-derived code, you will see the following text.

```
Copyright 1979, 1980, 1983, 1986, 1988, 1989, 1991, 1992, 1993, 1994
         The Regents of the University of California. All rights reserved.
```

Fifteen years of continuous development by the brightest students of the best computer science programs in the world, moderated by the faculty of one of the top technical schools in the country. That's more than a lifetime in software development. As you might imagine, the result was pretty darn good — almost everyone who used UNIX was really using BSD. The CSRG was quite surprised, near the end of these years, when it found that it had replaced almost all of the original AT&T code!

BSD Goes Public

In the early 1990s, the CSRG's funding started to run out. The University of California had to decide what to do with all this wonderful source code it owned. The simplest thing would have been to drop the original tapes down a well and pretend that the CSRG had never happened. In keeping with the spirit of academic freedom, however, it released the entire BSD collection to the public under an extremely liberal license. The license can be summarized like this:

- Don't claim you wrote this.
- Don't sue us if it breaks.
- Don't use our name to promote your product.

Compare this with the software license found on almost any commercial operating system. The BSD license is much easier to understand and unobjectionable to almost anyone. Anyone in the world can take the BSD code and use it for any purpose they like, from desktop computers to self-guided lawnmowers. Not surprisingly, many computer manufacturers jumped right on BSD. Not only was the code free, but also every computer science graduate for the last 15 years was familiar with it.

AT&T UNIX

As the CSRG was merrily improving AT&T's product, AT&T was doing its own UNIX development work to meet its internal needs. As AT&T developers implemented features, they also evaluated patches that came from the CSRG. When they liked a chunk of BSD code, they incorporated it wholesale into AT&T UNIX, then turned around and relicensed the result back to the universities, who used it as the basis for their next round of work.

This somewhat incestuous relationship kept going for many years, until the grand AT&T breakup. Suddenly, the telecommunications giant was no longer forbidden to dabble in commercial computing. Thanks to years of development, and that generation of computer scientists who knew it, UNIX abruptly looked like a solidly marketable product. Berkeley's release of the BSD code met with great displeasure from AT&T and instigated one of the most famous computer-related lawsuits of all time.

After some legal wrangling, the case was settled out of court. The Berkeley lawyers proved that most of the code in dispute originated in BSD, not in original AT&T UNIX. Only a half-dozen files were original AT&T property, while the rest of the operating system belonged to the CSRG and its contributors. As if that wasn't bad enough, AT&T had even removed the original Berkeley copyright statement from the files it had appropriated from the CSRG! AT&T went away and sulked for a while, finally releasing System V UNIX. The CSRG removed disputed files and released BSD 4.4-Lite2, a complete collection of CSRG code utterly unencumbered by any AT&T copyrights.

BSD 4.4-Lite2, also known just as "Lite 2," is the grandfather of all modern BSD software. This code was not usable out of the box, and it required some tweaks and additions to function. Various groups of programmers, such as BSDi, the NetBSD Project, and the FreeBSD Project, took it on themselves to make this code usable and to maintain it. Each project was independently managed.

What Is OpenBSD?

OpenBSD's founder, Theo de Raadt, started as a NetBSD developer several years ago. He had several strong disagreements, on many fronts, with the NetBSD developers about how the operating system should be developed. Eventually, he went out on his own and founded the OpenBSD Project, attracting quite a few like-minded developers to work with him. The OpenBSD team introduced several ideas into the open-source OS world that are now taken for granted, such as public access to the CVS repository and commit logs.

The OpenBSD team quickly established an identity of its own as a security-focused group and is now one of the best-known types of open-source BSD. Today, major companies such as Adobe Systems rely on OpenBSD to provide a reliable, secure operating system.

Today, OpenBSD is a BSD-based UNIX-like operating system with a fanatical attention to security, correctness, usability, and freedom. It runs on many different sorts of hardware including the standard "Intel PC" (i386), the Macintosh (mac68k and macppc), Sun's Sparc (sparc and sparc64), Compaq's Alpha (alpha), and more. OpenBSD puts almost all its efforts into security features, security debugging, and code correctness. The OpenBSD folks have demonstrated that correct code has a much lower chance of failing, and hence greater security. While some other BSDs focus on different goals, OpenBSD strives to be the ultimate secure operating system.

The OpenBSD team continually improves the operating system to enhance its security, stability, and freedom. This includes everything from the actual code in the operating system, to the online manual (which has a nearly legendary quality in the free software community), to the debugging and development environment, to the continuous software license auditing.

Other BSDs

So, what are these other versions of BSD, anyway? The main variants are NetBSD, FreeBSD, Mac OS X, and BSD/OS.

NetBSD

NetBSD is the direct ancestor of OpenBSD and was written to run on as many different types of hardware as possible. OpenBSD maintains much of this platform-independent design, but doesn't support all of the platforms NetBSD does.

FreeBSD

FreeBSD is the most popular open-source BSD. While the FreeBSD team considers security important, security is not its reason for eating, sleeping, and breathing as it is for the OpenBSD folks.

Mac OS X

The latest version of the Macintosh operating system is based on BSD. OpenBSD makes a comfortable and full-featured desktop for a computer professional, but may scare your grandparents. If you want a very friendly, candy-coated desktop that you can put down in front of grandma, but want power and flexibility under the hood, you might check it out. The source code for the graphic interface of Mac OS X is not available, but you can get the source code for the BSD layer and the Mach kernel from Apple.

BSD/OS

BSD/OS is a commercial, closed-source operating system produced by Wind River that greatly resembles the open-source BSDs. Some hardware manufacturers will not release specifications for their hardware unless the recipient signs a non-disclosure agreement (NDA). These NDAs are anathema to any open-source development project. Wind River will sign these NDAs and include reliable drivers for this hardware in BSD/OS.

If you need to run particular server-grade hardware, and it isn't supported under OpenBSD or any other open-source BSD, you might investigate BSD/OS.

OpenBSD Users

OpenBSD is more than just a collection of bits on CD-ROM. It's also a community of users, developers, and contributors. This community can be a bit of a culture shock for anyone who doesn't know what to expect.

Many other open-source operating systems place large amounts of effort into growing their user bases and bringing new people into the UNIX fold. The OpenBSD community doesn't. Most open-source UNIX-like operating systems do a lot of pro-UNIX advocacy. Again, OpenBSD doesn't. Some of the communities that have grown up around these operating systems actively welcome new users and do their best to make newbies feel welcome. OpenBSD does not. They are not trying to be the most popular operating system, just the best at what they do. The OpenBSD developers know exactly who their target market is: themselves.

The OpenBSD community generally expects users to be advanced computer users. They have written extensive documentation about OpenBSD, and expect people to be willing to read it. They're not interested in coddling new UNIX users and will say so if pressed. They don't object to new UNIX users using OpenBSD, but do object to people asking them for basic UNIX help just because they happen to be running OpenBSD. If you're a new UNIX user, they will not hold your hand. They will not develop features just to please users. OpenBSD exists to meet the needs of the developers, and while others are welcome to ride along the needs of the passengers do not steer the project.

OpenBSD Developers

So, how can a group of volunteers scattered all over the world actually create, maintain, and develop an operating system? Almost all discussion takes place via email and online chat. This can be slower than a face-to-face meeting, but is the only means by which people everywhere in the world can openly and reasonably communicate. This also has the advantage of providing a written record of discussions.

OpenBSD has three tiers of developers: the contributors, the committers, and the coordinator.

Contributors

Contributors are OpenBSD users who have the skills necessary to add features to the operating system, fix problems, or write documentation. Almost anyone can be a contributor. Problems range from a typographical error in the documentation to a device driver that crashes the system under particular circumstances. Every feature that is included in OpenBSD is there because some contributor took the time to sit down and write the code for it. Contributors who submit careful, correct fixes are welcome in the OpenBSD group.

If a contributor submits enough fixes of high enough quality, he may be offered the role of committer.

Committers

Committers are people who have direct access to the central OpenBSD source code repository. Most committers are skilled programmers who work on OpenBSD in their own time, as a hobby. They can make whatever changes they deem necessary for their OpenBSD projects, but are answerable to each other and to the project coordinator. They communicate via a variety of mailing lists, which are available for reading by interested parties. As these mailing lists are meant for developers to discuss coding and implementation details on, users asking basic questions are either ignored or asked to be quiet.

A committer's work is frequently available on websites and mailing lists before being integrated into the main OpenBSD source code collection, allowing interested people to preview their work. While being a committer seems glamorous, these people also carry a lot of responsibility — if they break the operating system or change something so that it conflicts with the driving "vision" of the Project, they must fix it. All OpenBSD committers answer to the project coordinator.

Coordinator

Theo de Raadt started OpenBSD in 1995 and still coordinates the project. He is the final word on how the system works, what is included in the system and who gets direct access to the repository. He resolves all disputes that contributors and committers cannot resolve amongst themselves. Theo takes whatever actions are necessary to keep the OpenBSD Project running smoothly.

Many people have very specific coordination roles within OpenBSD — quite a few architectures have a "point man" for issues that affect that hardware, the compiler has a maintainer, and so on. These are people who have earned that position of trust within the community. The only time that Theo acts as the final word is when someone has broken one of OpenBSD's few rules, such as bringing bad licenses into the source tree or behaving poorly with other committers.

This style of organization, with a central benevolent dictator, avoids a lot of the problems other large open-source projects have with management boards, core teams, or other structures. When someone decides to work on OpenBSD, they can either accept Theo's decisions as final or risk conflicting with the main OpenBSD Project. Thanks to the cooperative nature of OpenBSD development, Theo doesn't have to use that Big Stick nearly as often as one might think.

OpenBSD's Strengths

So, what makes OpenBSD OpenBSD? Why bother with another open-source UNIX-like operating system when there are many out there, many closely related to OpenBSD? What makes this OS worth a computer, let alone entrusting with your corporate firewall?

Portability

OpenBSD is designed to run on a wide variety of popular processors and hardware platforms. These platforms include, but are not limited to: Intel (80386 and compatibles), Alpha, Macintosh (both PowerPC and 68000 models), almost everything from Sun, and a variety of more obscure platforms. Chances are, any computer you will come across can run OpenBSD. The OpenBSD team wants to support as many interesting hardware architectures as they have the hardware and skills to maintain, so more are being added regularly.

Power

OpenBSD runs on hardware that's been obsolete for ten years. This isn't a deliberate design decision — the hardware was in popular use when OpenBSD was started, and the developers try to maintain speed and compatibility when they can. People who are running OpenBSD on an ancient VAX quickly catch changes that badly affect system performance on 486s, while people running modern Pentium 4s would probably never notice. Some of these changes are required by the advancing nature of the Internet, changes in the tools used to build OpenBSD, and added functionality in the system, but those that are the result of programming errors or misunderstandings are caught quickly.

OpenBSD leaves you every scrap of computing power possible to run your applications. In the end, people use applications and not operating systems. This means that a system with a one-gig disk and a 486 CPU can still make a solid web server once you install OpenBSD! A low-footprint operating system gives the most bang out of hardware.

Documented

Many free software projects are satisfied with releasing code. Some think that they're going above and beyond by including a help function in the program itself, available by typing some command-line flag. Others really go all out and provide a grammatically incorrect and technically vague manual page.

OpenBSD's documentation is expected to be both complete and accurate. The manual pages for system and library calls are extensive, even when compared to the other BSDs, and include discussions on usage and security. In its audit of the OpenBSD source code tree, the OpenBSD team found any number of circumstances where people had used the library interface as the manual page said they should, but the manual page was incorrect! This created both potential and actual security problems. As such, a documentation error is considered a serious bug and treated as harshly as any other serious bug.

Free

In keeping with the spirit of the original BSD license, OpenBSD is free for use in any way by anyone. You can use it in any tool you like, on any computer, for any purpose. Most of today's free software is licensed under terms that require distributors of software to return any changes back to the project owner. OpenBSD doesn't come with even that minor requirement. You can take OpenBSD, modify it, and embed it in refrigerators that order replacement food over the Internet, without ever paying the developers a dime.[1]

OpenBSD is perhaps the freest of the free operating systems. Like every other free UNIX-like operating system, the source code tree inherited from OpenBSD originally contained a wide variety of programs that shipped under conditional licenses. Some were free for non-commercial use; some were free if you changed the name once you made a change to the code; others had a variety of obscure licensing terms, such as indemnifying a third party against lawsuits. These have been either ripped out or replaced with freely licensed alternatives.

Theo de Raadt said on a mailing list during a discussion of licensing terms:

```
We know what a free license should say.
   It should say
 * Copyright foo
 * I give up my rights and permit others to:
                distribute
                sell
                give
                modify
                use
 * I retain the right to be known as the author/owner
```

---

[1] If you work at a company implementing such technology, please base it on OpenBSD. I do not want my refrigerator to be hacked and find 4,000 gallons of sour cream on my doorstep the next day!

```
When it says something else, ask this:
* - is it 100% guaranteed fluff which cannot ever affect anyone?
* - is it giving away even more rights (the author right)?
If not, then it must be giving someone more rights, or by the same token -
taking more rights away from someone else!
Then it is _less_ free than our requirements state!
```

The OpenBSD Project does a lot of work to guarantee that its licensing is as stringently free as its code is correct.

Correctness

OpenBSD developers strive to implement solutions correctly. This means that they follow UNIX standards such as POSIX and ANSI in their implementations. They make it a strict rule to write programs in a reliable and secure manner, following programming's best current practices. Every skilled programmer knows that programs written correctly are more reliable, predictable, and secure. Many free software producers are satisfied if it compiles and seems to work, however, and quite a few commercial software companies don't give their programmers time to write code that correctly. Code in OpenBSD has been made correct by dint of much hard work, and anyone who tries to introduce incorrect code will be turned away — generally politely, and often with constructive criticism, but turned away nonetheless. And that brings us to OpenBSD's most well-known claim to fame.

Security

OpenBSD strives to be the most secure operating system in the world. While it can reasonably make that claim now, it's a position that requires a constant struggle to maintain. People who break into systems are constantly trying new ways to penetrate computer systems, which means that today's feature may be tomorrow's security hole. As OpenBSD developers learn of new classes of programming errors and security holes, they scan the entire source tree for that class of problem and fix them before anyone even knows how they *might* be exploited. The history of computer security shows that users cannot be expected to patch or maintain their own systems; those systems must be secure out of the box. OpenBSD's goal is to eliminate those problems before they exist.

OpenBSD Security

Even though OpenBSD is tightly secured, computers running OpenBSD are still broken into. That might seem contradictory, but in truth it means that the person running the computer didn't understand computer security.

OpenBSD has many integrated security features, but people frequently assume that these features handle security for everything that can be installed on the computer. A moment's thought will show that this really isn't possible. No operating system can protect itself from the computer operator's mistakes. An OS can protect itself from problems in installed software to a limited extent, but ultimately the responsibility for security is in the hands of the administrator.

Consider a web server program running on OpenBSD. OpenBSD will provide the server with a stable, reliable platform, and will do as the server program asks, within the permissions the systems administrator has assigned to it. If the systems administrator has set up the server in a careful and correct manner, something going wrong with the web server will not endanger the operating system. If the sysadmin has integrated the web server with OpenBSD or has chosen to let the web server run with unrestricted privileges, the web server can inflict almost unrestricted damage to the computer software. If an intruder breaks into such a web server, they can use that integration and high permissions setting to lever their way into the operating system itself.

If such a break-in happens, is it OpenBSD's fault? Obviously not. The systems administrator is expected to follow basic security precautions when installing and configuring programs. No operating system can protect itself from an ignorant or careless sysadmin.

Ultimately, security is the responsibility of the systems administrator. Throughout this book, we will discuss some of the basic security precautions you should be taking when installing and running programs. We will also discuss the advanced security features OpenBSD offers in order to protect itself and help in your systems administration duties.

OpenBSD's Uses

So, OpenBSD has all these nifty features, abilities, and strengths. Where does it fit into your "computing strategy"? That ultimately depends on what your strategy is and where you need it. OpenBSD can be used anywhere you need a solid, reliable, and secure system. I recommend OpenBSD for any of three different uses: on the desktop, as a server, or as a network management device.

Desktop

If you need a powerful desktop with all the features you'd expect from a complete UNIX-like workstation, OpenBSD will do nicely. Desktop GUIs, office suites, web browsers, and other programs an average user likes on a computer are available. OpenBSD supports a variety of development tools, application environments, network servers, and other features needed by programmers and web developers. If you're a network administrator OpenBSD supports packet sniffers, traffic analyzers, and all the other programs you might have come to rely upon.

Server

If you're serving web pages, handling email, providing LDAP services, or offering any sort of network services to clients, OpenBSD can help you. It's a cheap and reliable platform. Once it's set up, it just works. Web servers, database servers, and more all work under OpenBSD. And, of course, it's secure, which you cannot underestimate on today's Internet.

Network Management

OpenBSD makes an excellent firewall, bridge, or traffic shaper. You can use it to support intrusion detection software, web proxies, or traffic monitors. The integrated PF firewall provides state-of-the-art network connection management and control and strips out many dangerous types of traffic before they even reach your servers. Of course, OpenBSD can do all this as cheaply and reliably as it can do anything else.

Who Should Read This Book?

This book is written for an experienced UNIX user or system administrator who is interested in adding OpenBSD mastery to his repertoire. It assumes you're familiar with programs and commands such as tail(1), chmod(1), ping(8), and so on. In many cases we'll discuss programs that you may be familiar with, but might be slightly different on OpenBSD.

For maximum benefit, you should have a system on which to install Open-BSD. OpenBSD will coexist with another operating system, if properly installed. While this is excellent for learning purposes, if you're going to use OpenBSD in a production environment you should dedicate a machine to it. We'll discuss both installation methods. Our installation examples will be written for the i386, or "standard PC," but will work almost identically on any hardware platform. (You may need to look at hardware-specific resources for information on how to handle your hardware, however; for example, the method for booting off of CD-ROM varies from platform to platform.)

Most people think that OpenBSD is not the easiest UNIX-like operating system, or the easiest version of BSD, or even the easiest version of open-source BSD. It doesn't have handy "wizards" that walk you through each stage of the configuration process. It has very few menu-driven front ends. Once you're familiar with how the system works, though, such wizards only get in the way. The OpenBSD developers and support groups are not really interested in helping rank UNIX beginners and usually refuse to answer basic UNIX questions.

To really understand OpenBSD you need to be willing to learn, experiment, and spend some time accumulating understanding. The good news is, OpenBSD merely shows you what other operating systems conceal. Much of this knowledge can be directly applied to other versions of BSD, other UNIX-like operating systems, and even completely foreign operating systems such as Microsoft's Windows platforms.

Contents Overview

Here's a brief description of what you'll find in the next several chapters.

Chapter 1, *Additional Information Resources*, discusses the system documentation available both in the installed system and on the World Wide Web. You might need this information to complete your installation tasks, so we present it up front.

Chapter 2, *Installation Preparations*, discusses the steps necessary to install OpenBSD on an i386 (aka "standard PC"). We will discuss both standalone and shared-system installs, as well as some basic tasks you should take care of when you finish the install.

Chapter 3, *Installation Walkthrough*, carries you through every step of the installation process. While the installer is very simple and powerful, it assumes a certain level of knowledge about computer hardware and about OpenBSD that you may not yet possess. You will get all the skills you need to install OpenBSD here.

Chapter 4, *Multiboot Installation*, teaches you how to install OpenBSD on a system with another operating system such as Linux, FreeBSD, or any version of Microsoft Windows. With this information, you should be able to install OpenBSD with any operating system of your choice.

Chapter 5, *Post-Install Configuration*, discusses some of the steps experienced systems administrators probably want to take once after installing an OpenBSD system. We also discuss the main system configuration settings found in /etc/ rc.conf.

Chapter 6, *System Startup*, covers the OpenBSD booting process. The various files used by the booting process are documented, and management of the boot process.

Chapter 7, *Managing Users*, discusses how to add, remove, and restrict users in OpenBSD, as well as giving them basic privileges with the integrated sudo tool.

Chapter 8, *Networking*, reviews some of the basics of the Internet standard TCP/IP protocol and cover some of OpenBSD's tools for examining and trouble-shooting the network.

Chapter 9, *Network Connections*, teaches you how to connect to the Internet via dialup and via Ethernet.

Chapter 10, *Additional Security Features*, describes general OpenBSD security tools such as securelevels and systrace.

Chapter 11, *Basic Kernel Configuration*, describes the various tools available to configure your kernel. Unlike many other free UNIX-like operating systems, OpenBSD does not require the administrator to recompile the kernel. Instead, a variety of other tools are available for kernel tweaking.

Chapter 12, *Kernel Compilation*, discusses how to recompile the kernel in those rare incidents when you must.

Chapter 13, *Additional Software*, describes OpenBSD's add-on software management tools. We learn how to compile your own software in a manner consistent with OpenBSD's tools and how to check and remove installed software.

Chapter 14, *Upgrading OpenBSD*, describes the various methods an administrator can use to upgrade an installed OpenBSD system.

Chapter 15, *Disks*, discusses OpenBSD's disk management systems and routines, including mounting disk images and encrypted file systems.

Chapter 16, */etc*, describes each of the major files in /etc that have not been covered earlier in the book and how you might want to use each.

Chapter 17, *Packet Filtering*, documents OpenBSD's integrated packet filtering engine, PF. We present real-world traffic filtering situations and how they should be handled.

Chapter 18, *More Packet Filtering*, covers network address translation, bandwidth management, and a variety of other nifty tricks that can the PF engine can perform for you.

Chapter 19, *Managing PF*, introduces the tools you can use to control the PF system and other tools that work with PF to allow a network administrator a great deal of control over a network.

Appendix A discusses the common kernel features available for x86 (standard PC) hardware.

Finally, Appendix B gives several examples of PF usage in a variety of network types.

Okay, enough boring stuff. On to OpenBSD!

1

ADDITIONAL HELP

Countless documents:
man pages, web, and HOWTOs:
If you can find them.

So, now that you've bought this book, you might think that you possess all the information you will ever need about OpenBSD. You hold in your hands the ultimate repository of all OpenBSD wisdom and acumen, and once you master its contents you will be lord and master of all that OpenBSD has to offer. Right?

Sorry, no. Even if you could find a book prepared by someone with a thorough and total mastery of OpenBSD, he could not possibly cover everything there is to know in a single book. OpenBSD may be less than a decade old, but UNIX has been kicking around the block for 30 years. BSD has been around for 25 years. OpenBSD builds on three decades of tradition, knowledge, and power. You won't master it with *any* single book. You might master it with a room full of books and a few years time, if you give up trivial things like friendship and bathing in favor of study. (Actually, if you give up bathing, friendship will give itself up.)

The OpenBSD community maintains a wide variety of information sources. Some are integrated with OpenBSD itself, such as the man pages. The OpenBSD Project, such as the main OpenBSD website and the various mailing lists hosted at OpenBSD.org, maintains others. Still more users and devotees of OpenBSD maintain other websites, mailing lists, and documentation projects. The flood of available information can be overwhelming to experienced users, let alone new users. The goal of this chapter is to take you by the hand and lead you through some of it.

OpenBSD Community Support

If you have only worked with commercial UNIX before, you might find OpenBSD's support process a little surprising. There is no toll-free number to call and no vendor to escalate within. No, you may *not* speak to a manager. There isn't one. And there's a good reason for that; the management is you.

Commercial operating systems, such as those provided by Microsoft, conceal their inner workings. The only access you have to the operating system is the options presented by the GUI, plus a few command-line tools that are almost an afterthought. If you want to learn more about how your operating system works, you *cannot*. When something breaks, you can either live with it or make offerings to the vendor to make the problem go away. Even if you do pay for help, the people on the other end of the phone frequently know little more than you do.

OpenBSD, on the other hand, is completely open. You can view the source code. You can view object code, if you want to. You have manual pages, and FAQs, and all sorts of instructions and documentation that enable you to help yourself. You also have access to the CVS logs via the Web and via CVS itself. These logs describe every change that has ever been made to every part of the system so you can back out changes, understand the motivations behind changes, and even contact the people who have most recently updated the component you're interested in and ask them why a particular change was made. You have the opportunity to learn about the operating system in exquisite, excruciating detail. The OpenBSD developers have gone to a lot of trouble to answer basic questions for you in their existing documentation — and they expect you to use it.

If you want to learn about OpenBSD, you need to make the jump from eating what you're served to reading the cookbook and creating your own dinner. If you're willing to learn from what is provided, you will develop skills both in solving problems and in OpenBSD, and you'll make some friends in the OpenBSD community in the process. If you want to use OpenBSD and don't have the time or inclination to learn, invest in a commercial support contract. Many different vendors support OpenBSD; check the OpenBSD website for details.

If you aren't interested in learning or buying a support contract, then OpenBSD is simply not for you.

"The Code Is Fine; What's Wrong with You?"

In most cases, people do not have problems with OpenBSD itself. The software runs, and it runs well. Most problems people have with OpenBSD come from their own understanding, or lack thereof. When a program behaves unexpectedly, you probably have a gap in your own comprehension of how things work. Your goal in resolving problems should be to improve your knowledge so you can make the system behave, as you require. Other people make OpenBSD work correctly, and you can too.

You might find that a problem is quite real, however. You might uncover a bug in OpenBSD, or learn that you have bad hardware, or discover that a third-party tool really does crash under particular circumstances. You cannot be certain you've found a bug until you understand correct behavior — not just how you think the system works, but how it really does work. You must learn how the system should behave and why, so you can identify real bugs when you find them.

For example, before writing this book I had never used an OpenBSD machine to display a serial console. All of my UNIX boxes are hooked up to a rusty old Livingston terminal server. Most people aren't stuck with that many serial consoles, however, and want to use a null modem cable between two OpenBSD machines and have each serve as the terminal for the other's console. (We cover serial consoles in Chapter 6.) From reading the manual page, it seemed simple enough; once the cable is attached and the test machine is configured to dump its console out the serial port, become root on your display machine and type "tip tty00," and the other machine's console should appear in the terminal window. This didn't work.

The question then became, "Am I doing it wrong, or is something wrong with my hardware, or is there a bug in OpenBSD?" Swapping systems around showed that the command worked on other OpenBSD machines, just not on this test box. Further tests with a serial mouse and a modem showed that the serial port on the test machine was bad. I originally planned to do all of the tests for this book on a Pentium 166 to make the point that OpenBSD works well on older hardware[1], but wound up purchasing a brand-new AMD 1800 instead.

Had the serial port not been bad, and if I had taken the correct steps, I might have actually found an OpenBSD bug. Once you have confirmed that an actual bug exists, and have narrowed down the bug to a precise problem, be sure to notify the OpenBSD development team with sendbug(1). A good bug report includes all possible information about the problem, a description of the problem, a way to replicate the problem on other systems, and a suggested fix with source code.

OpenBSD has three main information sources: man pages, websites, and mailing lists. To understand why your system behaves a certain way in particular circumstances, you may need to check all three.

---

[1] That point has now become, "OpenBSD runs well on older hardware that hasn't been burned out after years of abuse."

Man Pages

Man pages, short for "manual," are the original way of presenting UNIX documentation. While man pages have a reputation for being obtuse, difficult to read, or incomplete, the OpenBSD manual pages are quite informative.

The OpenBSD team considers man pages to be the final word in system documentation. They are expected to be correct. Errors in man pages are considered serious bugs and are dealt with as quickly as possible and as forcefully as necessary. As such, you can expect that the man page will be correct and complete. Man pages should be your first line of attack in learning how something works.

A man page is *not* a tutorial. It explains how something works, not what to type to make particular effects happen. You need to be able to assemble the pieces given by the man page into the tool that you want. If you want a tutorial you need to look at the FAQ, articles on third-party websites, and this book. If you find a tutorial that does exactly what you want, be sure to understand what you're doing as well as what you're typing; otherwise, you'll be stuck when something breaks.

Manual Sections

The OpenBSD manual is divided into nine sections. Each man page appears in only one section. These sections are sometimes called volumes, a relic of the day when the manual was small enough to realistically be printed and distributed. Roughly speaking, these sections are:

1	General Commands
2	System Calls and Error Numbers
3	C Libraries
3p	Perl Libraries
4	Devices and Device Drivers
5	File Formats and Configuration Files
6	Game Instructions
7	Miscellaneous Information
8	System Maintenance Commands
9	Kernel Internals

When reading man pages, you'll usually see the section number in parenthesis after the command, like this: panic(9). This represents both the name of the command, library, or interface (panic) and the section where the man page for that can be found (9). When you see something in this format, you can check the man page for detailed information. Almost every topic has a man page. Some commands or topics have multiple man pages of the same name, in different sections.

You can view man pages with man(1). If you know the section number, give it and then the name of the program. For example, to see the manual page for the standard network utility ping(8), enter:

```
# man ping
```

In response, you should see something like this:

```
PING(8)              OpenBSD System Manager's Manual          PING(8)

NAME
    ping - send ICMP ECHO_REQUEST packets to network hosts

SYNOPSIS
    ping [-DdfLnqRrv] [-c count] [-I ifaddr] [-i wait] [-l preload] [-p
      pattern] [-s packetsize] [-t ttl] [-w maxwait] host

DESCRIPTION
    ping uses the ICMP protocol's mandatory ECHO_REQUEST datagram to elicit
    an ICMP ECHO_REPLY from a host or gateway. ECHO_REQUEST datagrams
    (``pings'') have an IP and ICMP header, followed by a ``struct timeval''
    and then an arbitrary number of ``pad'' bytes used to fill out the pack-
    et. The options are as follows:

    -c count
        Stop after sending count ECHO_REQUEST packets.

    -D  Set the Don't Fragment bit.

    -d  Set the SO_DEBUG option on the socket being used.
```

You can now learn huge amounts about pinging hosts on the Internet, just by understanding this document. If you need more information, you can look at some of the other man pages referenced by ping(8) to build an in-depth picture of the system.

Navigating Man Pages

Once you're in a man page, hitting the space bar will take you forward one full screen. If you don't want to go that far, hitting the ENTER key will scroll down one line. If you go to far, and want to back up, hitting "b" will take you back one screen. To search within a man page for a word, type / followed by the word. You'll jump down to the first appearance of that word. Typing n subsequently will jump you to the next occurrence of that word.

This assumes that you're using the default OpenBSD pager, more(1). If you're using a different pager, you'll have to use the syntax that pager requires. If you don't know what a pager is, then don't worry about it.

Finding Man Pages

One frequent complaint about man pages is that it's difficult to find a man page that covers a topic you're interested in. There's certainly truth to this — many OpenBSD questions can be answered by a simple "read man such-and-such." The problem is finding the correct such-and-such for what you want to know. You can perform basic keyword searches with apropos(1) and whatis(1). Apropos(1) searches for any man page name or description that includes the word you're interested in. Whatis(1) only matches whole words. For example, if you are interested in the ping command, you might try:

```
# apropos ping
Net::Ping (3p) - check a remote host for reachability
Text::Wrap (3p) - line wrapping to form simple paragraphs
boot (8/Alpha) - Alpha system bootstrapping procedures
boot (8/Amiga) - amiga-specific system bootstrapping procedures
...
```

Well, the first command looks somewhat like the standard ping command, but it's in section 3p of the manual — it's a Perl library! The next three matches have nothing to do with ping, but if you examine them closely you'll see that the letters "ping" appear in each of them, encapsulated within the words "wrap*ping*" and "bootstrap*ping*." Depending on the term you're looking for, apropos can give you far too much irrelevant information.

A similar search with whatis(1) gives the following.

```
# whatis ping
ping (8) - send ICMP ECHO_REQUEST packets to network hosts
#
```

That's more like it! You may find that such a narrow search isn't enough for some terms, however. Experiment with apropos(1) and whatis(1) until you're comfortable with them, and you should be able to find just about any topic you like. Between the search functions, and the SEE ALSO sections within man pages (see "Man Page Contents"), you can generally find the information you need.

NOTE *The apropos command is the same as "man -k" (for "keyword search"), and the whatis command is the same as "man -f" (for "full word search").*

Section Numbers and Man

You might find cases where the man page you want has the same name as a man page in some other section of the manual, especially as you add additional software to your OpenBSD machines. In those cases, specifying the section number is the only way to get the exact page you want. Without giving a section number, you'll get the man page of that name with the lowest section number. You can specify a section number before the name of the command, i.e.:

```
# man 8 ping
```

While this example is rather trivial (a "ping" man page only appears in one section of the manual), we'll look in some other cases where it isn't.

Man Page Contents

Man pages have a variety of section headers. While just about any subsection can appear in a man page, several are standard. (See mdoc(7) for a partial list of standard section names, as well as other man page standards.) Like book authors, man page authors try to arrange their content in a manner that makes sense for the program they're describing. Still, you will see some standard headings.

- NAME tells you the names of a program or utility. Some programs have multiple names — for example, the vi(1) text editor is also available as view(1) or ex(1). The man page lists all of these names.

- SYNOPSIS lists the possible command-line options and their arguments, or how a library call is accessed. Frequently, you'll find that this header is enough to spark your memory and remind you of a flag you've used before that caused the program to behave appropriately.

- DESCRIPTION contains a brief synopsis of the program or feature. The contents of this section vary depending on the topic, as programs, files, and interfaces all have very different documentation requirements.

- OPTIONS describes a program's command-line options and their effects.

- BUGS describes known failure conditions, weird behavior, and how to make the program fail in general. This is a great time-saver. Many times I've had a problem with a command only to find that behavior, and sometimes a workaround, listed in the BUGS section. Honesty is a wonderful thing in computing products.

- SEE ALSO is traditionally the last section in a man page. OpenBSD is an interrelated whole; every command has ties to other commands. In an ideal world you would read every man page and be able to hold an integrated image of the system in your head. Because most of us cannot do that, this section provides directions to related man pages.

You now know what you need to navigate the integrated help system. Now let's look at some information resources elsewhere than your computer.

Man Pages on the Web

The manual pages are also available on www.OpenBSD.org and its mirrors. While your system has only the man pages for your release and architecture of OpenBSD, the manual available on the website includes all previous versions of OpenBSD and all architectures. If you want to see differences in the boot process between i386 and Alpha platforms, you can easily compare the manual pages on the website. Similarly, you can see which release certain commands were first documented in and how those commands have changed over time.

www.OpenBSD.org

The OpenBSD website contains a variety of information useful for general OpenBSD administration, installation, and management. The most useful portions are the FAQ and the platform-specific hardware support documents, but the site as a whole contains much useful information. From the front page you see links describing how to access the source code, the CVS repository, the bug reporting system, and other documentation. Information is added regularly, so take a look, and see what they have!

Website Mirrors

Many people mirror the OpenBSD website across the world. In most cases, you can find a mirror for a country by using the format www.*countrycode*.OpenBSD. org. For example, the main British mirror is located at http://www.uk. OpenBSD.org/. There are many exceptions to this rule, however; for example, the main United States mirror is at http://www.usa.OpenBSD.org/. Other mirrors have completely different URLs.

The website mirrors are linked off the bottom of the main OpenBSD website, and hence at the bottom of each mirror site. I recommend that you pick a mirror that responds quickly for you, and bookmark it. The mirror sites are generally underused, while the main site is quite heavily accessed.

The OpenBSD FAQ

The OpenBSD FAQ is the repository of frequently asked questions about OpenBSD. While much of the information in there is duplicated in the manual pages, the FAQ presents the knowledge in an easier-to-follow format. Unlike many other FAQs you might be familiar with, the OpenBSD FAQ includes extensive tutorial information. For example, Chapter 4 of the FAQ contains the full, detailed installation process. Other chapters discuss other features of the system or problems you may encounter. If you're having a problem, or want to know how some major port of OpenBSD works, definitely check the FAQ!

Other Websites

Many people maintain websites dedicated to OpenBSD, or related to OpenBSD, or generally useful to the OpenBSD Project. Any time you have a problem or are trying to understand something, check out these sites for more information. Read third-party documentation carefully and skeptically, however. Anyone can put up a website, and that person can say anything on that site. Tutorials and articles outside of the OpenBSD Project may contain erroneous information, or tutorials that only work in the author's particular situation.

Here are a few popular ones at the time I write this.

- Google BSD (http://www.google.com/bsd/): The Google search engine is one of the most powerful support tools for OpenBSD — or for any piece of software, actually. Google has indexed not only the main OpenBSD website, but also a variety of OpenBSD mailing list archives, third-party websites, and newsgroups. Google is your friend. If you ask someone for help, they will almost always point you to Google. Use it.

- Monkey.org (http://www.monkey.org/openbsd/): This is one of the oldest OpenBSD sites, and a fair chunk of the material here is somewhat dated as of this writing. It contains searchable archives of the OpenBSD mailing lists, which are very valuable. We'll discuss the mailing lists a little later.

- Daemon News (http://www.daemonnews.org/): Daemon News provides a daily news board and monthly ezine devoted to all things BSD, including OpenBSD. Much of the information presented at Daemon News is quite applicable to OpenBSD.

- BSD Forums (http://www.bsdforums.org/): BSD Forums indexes news stories about all sorts of BSD and hosts discussion threads about the articles.

- The OpenBSD Journal (http://www.deadly.org/): This website contains articles, comments, and questions related to OpenBSD. It is an excellent resource for all things OpenBSD.

- O'Reilly Network BSD Developer Center (http://www.onlamp.com/bsd/): This O'Reilly-sponsored site hosts a variety of OpenBSD and general BSD articles, including the column *Big Scary Daemons* by yours truly.

Mailing Lists

You can find a variety of mailing lists dedicated to OpenBSD, run by both the official OpenBSD project and various third parties. We'll discuss what lists exist and how to use them to best advantage.

The Main Mailing Lists

OpenBSD has quite a few mailing lists for public use. All mailing lists are accessible to the public. Some of the lists are a little more private than others, however. Each major hardware platform has a mailing list, but discussion on those lists is strictly limited to people who are either actively developing that platform or sending bug reports for that platform. They aren't of much use to the average OpenBSD user, unless you're tracking problems in a development version of OpenBSD. Here, we're just going to cover the mailing lists that are useful for the average user.

- announce@OpenBSD.org: This is a very low-volume, moderated list that only has important news about the OpenBSD Project. This list receives at least one message every six months, when a new version of OpenBSD comes out.

- security-announce@OpenBSD.org: This mailing list contains security announcements for OpenBSD. When the OpenBSD team learns of a security flaw in OpenBSD, they post a notification and a fix to this mailing list. If you are running an OpenBSD machine plugged into the Internet, you *must* subscribe to this list. We'll see more about this in Chapter 14.
- misc@OpenBSD.org: This list is for general OpenBSD discussion and user questions. While this is the "miscellaneous" list, it still has strict rules for acceptable messages. We'll discuss how to usefully post to an OpenBSD mailing list later this chapter.
- tech@OpenBSD.org: This list is for in-depth technical discussions, such as code discussion and protocol analysis. This is a useful list to subscribe to, but you probably don't want to post here unless you are a developer. As a good rule of thumb, if your post to tech@OpenBSD.org doesn't contain a code diff, you're on the wrong mailing list.

Subscribing to a Mailing List

OpenBSD uses the Majordomo mailing list manager. To subscribe to a mailing list, send a message to majordomo@OpenBSD.org containing the following:

```
subscribe mailing-list-name
```

For example, to subscribe to the misc list, you would send

```
subscribe misc
```

OpenBSD's majordomo requires that all subscription requests be verified. You will receive a message of instructions back. Be sure to follow those instructions to complete your subscription!

Other Official Lists

If you want to become more deeply involved in the OpenBSD community, you might well wonder what other official OpenBSD mailing lists exist. The best way to learn about the lists that currently exist is to ask the mailserver; it'll tell you. Just send a message to majordomo@OpenBSD.org containing the single word:

```
lists
```

You will receive a reply giving the name of each OpenBSD mailing list and its purpose.

NOTE *If you want to learn more about the OpenBSD mailing list manager and what other information you can get, send the single word "help" to majordomo@OpenBSD.org.*

Non @OpenBSD.org Mailing Lists

You can find a fairly complete list of all OpenBSD-related mailing lists hosted by third parties at http://www.OpenBSD.org/mail.html. This includes a variety of lists in languages other than English, as well as some very narrow, special-purpose lists. One particular mailing list I highly recommend for less experienced UNIX administrators is the OpenBSD Newbies list. To subscribe, send a message to openbsd-newbies-subscribe@sfobug.org.

Using the Mailing Lists

Now that you have a subscription to an appropriate OpenBSD mailing list (hopefully misc, and definitely security-announce), you can go and ask all your questions on that mailing list. You won't make any friends, though, and you may even be told to shut up and go away. That's mainly for two reasons: discussion topics are permitted only within a narrow range, and the lists are there to be read and not posted to.

Unless you're in a truly unique situation or really on the bleeding edge of OpenBSD development, someone has probably struggled with your problem before. They've probably posted a message to the mailing lists before. They probably got an answer. That answer probably hasn't changed. The quickest way to get an answer to your question is to find that previous message. That's where the mailing list archives come in.

You can find a variety of mailing list archives on the Net at places such as Geocrawler (http://www.geocrawler.com/). By far, the easiest way to get access to the mailing list archives is to use a powerful search engine such as Google. Carefully choosing your search terms will get results very quickly.

Using OpenBSD Problem-Solving Resources

Let's pick a common question and use the OpenBSD resources to solve it. We'll use several different methods to find an answer. One topic that comes up frequently is that of hardware-accelerated cryptography: how does it work, and what does OpenBSD do to support it? Here's how you find information on this topic from each of the information sources the OpenBSD Project provides.

www.OpenBSD.org

If you look at the main page of the OpenBSD website, you'll find a link pointing to "Integrated Crypto." That leads you in turn to "Cryptographic Hardware Support." Read, learn, and enjoy.

Man Pages

If you just type "man cryptography" you won't get any matches; there is no "cryptography" man page. It's frequently called "crypto," however, and if you try "man crypto" you'll get something.

```
NAME
    crypto - OpenSSL cryptographic library

SYNOPSIS
DESCRIPTION
    The OpenSSL crypto library implements a wide range of
    cryptographic algorithms used in various Internet stan-
    dards. The services provided by this library are used by
    the OpenSSL implementations of SSL, TLS and S/MIME, and
    they have also been used to implement SSH, OpenPGP, and
    other cryptographic standards.

OVERVIEW
    libcrypto consists of a number of sub-libraries that
...
```

Well, that's not what we want. It's nice to have OpenSSL documentation on a
system that includes OpenSSL, but it doesn't answer our question. You might
give up here, but that's not what you want to do either. Notice that this manual
this page falls in Section 3. Information on hardware belongs in Section 4 of the
manual. When multiple man pages share a name, and you don't give man(1) a
section number, the page in the lowest section number is displayed. Try "apropos
crypto" to look for all the man pages that include the word "crypto." You'll notice
the following.

```
...
crypto (3) - OpenSSL cryptographic library
crypto (4) - hardware crypto access driver
crypto (9) - API for cryptographic services in the kernel
...
```

There are three different crypto man pages, each in a different section.
Crypto(3) is for programmers who want to use the OpenSSL cryptographic
interface; crypto(9) is for programmers who want to access crypto routines
within the kernel; and crypto(4) is for cryptographic accelerator hardware. Type
"man 4 crypto" and you'll see what you want.

```
CRYPTO(4)          OpenBSD Programmer's Manual          CRYPTO(4)

NAME
    crypto - hardware crypto access driver

SYNOPSIS
    pseudo-device crypto [count]

DESCRIPTION
    The crypto driver provides userland applications access to hardware cryp-
    to support via the kernel. The /dev/crypto device node primarily oper-
    ates in an ioctl(2) based model, permitting a variety of applications to
    query device capabilities, submit transactions, and get results.

    If count given in the specification, and is greater than 0, a maximum of
...
```

You may have to wade through some dense technical information, but everything you need to know is right here.

Checking the Internet

Go to Google and enter "OpenBSD crypto hardware support." On the day I wrote this, the first page of results gave me a direct link to the relevant OpenBSD web page, a link to a mailing list archive result, and a couple of third-party web pages discussing OpenBSD's hardware crypto support.

Mailing for Help

If the mailing list archives, a web search, the OpenBSD FAQ, the OpenBSD website, man pages, and other assorted resources do not answer your question, you can ask for help. The OpenBSD mailing lists are read by a variety of very knowledgeable and skilled computer professionals. Many of these people enjoy working with OpenBSD and want to help new users. These same people have also frequently spent a great deal of time making OpenBSD information available on the Internet and even answering the same question dozens or hundreds of times.

Look at all the ways we just explored to get information on cryptographic hardware support in OpenBSD. Most topics have information readily available in the same manner. People who read the OpenBSD mailing lists, and answer questions on them, spent their time writing and distributing all that information. Documenting all this was a lot of work. Now imagine their reaction when they receive a piece of email asking about cryptographic hardware support. The people who write those emails have just confirmed that they want their hand held, or they're either unwilling or unable to read the available documentation, or they have the intelligence of a brick. The writer is obviously not ready to use Open-BSD. At best, he will be ignored. At worst, some experienced OpenBSD person who wrote all those docs would probably take offense at his hard work being so utterly discounted and flame the questioner badly enough that his monitor will need three months in the Mayo Clinic Burn Unit.

Keep that in mind before you send an email. Have you really checked everywhere? Are there any other words you can search under? Performing a few extra searches with different keywords is much faster than composing a useful piece of email and has a very good chance of returning an answer.

Discussion Topics

If you are familiar with another free UNIX, you might find OpenBSD's mailing lists a little shocking. OpenBSD users are advanced computer users, almost by definition. If an advanced UNIX user tries to debug a problem with a piece of software, he is generally expected to know enough to ask the responsible party. On support lists for other free UNIX-like operating systems, users are welcome to ask questions on dang near any topic about any piece of software that runs on their chosen platform. The people on these support lists do their best to help out. These support lists, manned by volunteers and dedicated to providing around-the-clock response to whatever question you might ask, are provided by projects that are interested in taking over the world. Remember, though, that isn't the OpenBSD Project's goal.

The OpenBSD folks will happily assist you with problems with OpenBSD, but software that happens to be running on OpenBSD is another matter. You may be able to get help from an OpenBSD list, if someone on that list happens to use the same software you're having trouble with, but you shouldn't count on it. If you're having trouble porting your preferred window manager to OpenBSD because of some differences in OpenBSD's libc, the OpenBSD people would love to talk to you. If you can't configure your window manager the way you'd like, then you need to talk to the people responsible for your window manager.

Contents of Help Requests

Before you send an email, think about the problem you are trying to solve. What question should you actually be asking here? Define the problem as narrowly as possible. Suppose you cannot connect to your Internet service provider. Is the problem that the internal modem dials, but the ISP rejects your connection requests? Does your modem not dial? Is it detected at all? Each of these is a very different problem, with a different solution. That's the problem you want to solve.

Now that you know what the problem is, you need to gather any and all the information related to the problem. You will include this information in your email. This should include:

- The version of OpenBSD you are running.
- Your hardware platform.
- Any error output. Be sure to check in /var/log/messages as well as your terminal.

- /var/run/dmesg.boot
- A complete, but *narrow*, problem description.

Formatting Help Requests

Quite a few OpenBSD users[2] use a text-based email reader such as mutt. (Quite a few also use graphic-friendly mail readers, mind you.) These are very powerful programs for handling large amounts of email, but they do not display HTML messages. If you are using a graphic mail client such as Microsoft Outlook, send your mail in plain text. What's more, be sure to wrap your text at 72 columns. Sending mail in HTML, or without decent line wrapping, is simply an invitation to have your email discarded unread.

This may seem harsh, but you need to consider to whom you're writing. Most email clients are simply not suited to handle thousands of messages a day, scattered across dozens of mailing lists and several dozen discussions, in a manner accessible to a human mind. Even the most popular Windows-based email clients, such as Microsoft Outlook, cannot perform such fundamental tasks as discussion threading. I receive thousands of email messages a day, and many OpenBSD developers are in even worse straits. We simply cannot cope without competent mail tools, and HTML is not a necessary part of a competent mail tool. Presentation of a large number of messages in a sensible order is necessary.

On a similar note, most attachments are unnecessary. You do not need to PGP sign your email, and those business-card attachments just demonstrate that you really shouldn't be running OpenBSD. On a similar note, be sure to not use a long signature line. The "standard" for email signatures allows for four lines of text, no more. Long ASCII art signatures, even really nifty ones featuring the official OpenBSD Blowfish, are Right Out.

Also, do not send your message to multiple mailing lists. At this point, your messages should almost certainly go to misc@OpenBSD.org. Most especially, do not cross-post between misc@OpenBSD.org and tech@OpenBSD.org!

Finally, use a good subject line. Many people who receive those thousands of email messages decide what messages to read based entirely on the subject line. Moderately advanced mail readers allow the reader to delete entire discussions based on subject line. Something like "Problem with OpenBSD" will be ignored by the vast majority of people. A subject line like "Internal modem not recognized at boot" will attract readers who are familiar with that sort of problem, and who are best able to help you. Some mail readers do even more sophisticated threading based upon the mail message headers; if you want to start a new discussion on a mailing list, it's best to compose the message from scratch rather than replying to an existing message.

---

[2] In fact, quite a few users of other free UNIX-like operating systems use this sort of mail reader as well. This advice applies equally well to most parts of the free software community. Personally, when I get an email that is unreadable in plain text, I assume that the person who sent it is either ignorant or rude. Ignorant people have nothing to tell me, and I don't have time for rude people. If you are using a graphic mail client such as Microsoft Outlook, send your mail in plain text. What's more, be sure to wrap your text at 72 columns. Sending mail in HTML, or without decent line wrapping, is simply an invitation to have your email discarded unread.

Sending Your Email

Finally, put all of your information together and send your question with relevant documentation to misc@OpenBSD.org. Yes, there are other mailing lists for discussing OpenBSD, but people who post questions or problems to them are almost overwhelmingly told to go ask on misc@ instead. You might be referred to another mailing list, but it's much better to post a message to a specific list if that message starts with "The people on misc@ recommended I ask this here."

It's easy to let frustration turn a simple request into a rampaging demand for immediate assistance. Remember to be polite; the people who are receiving your message may decide to help you out of the goodness of their hearts, but they are under no obligation to do so. If you want someone to be obliged to help you, get a support contract.

Also remember, the reason you're having a problem is because of something you do not understand. You're seeking enlightenment. If you ask someone to fix your problem for you, you're going to get a poor response.

Responding to Email

Your answer may be a brief note with a URL, or even just two words: "man such-and-such." If that's what you get, that's where you need to go. Don't go asking for more detail. If you have a question about the contents of the reference you're given, or if you're confused by the reference, treat that as another problem. Narrow down the source of your confusion and ask about it. Man pages and tutorials are not perfect, and it's possible that some parts seem to be mutually exclusive or contradictory if you don't fully comprehend them.

Finally, follow through. If you're asked for more information, provide it. If you don't know how to provide it, treat that as another problem. Go back to the beginning of this chapter and try to figure it out. The bottom line is, if you develop a reputation as someone who doesn't follow up on requests for more information, you won't even get a first reply.

Now that you know how to get more help on OpenBSD, let's proceed to the installation that's discussed in the next chapter.

2

INSTALLATION PREPARATIONS

I am script kiddie.
Windows is warm and tasty,
blowfish goes down hard.

A successful OpenBSD installation requires the OpenBSD software, supported hardware, and a bit of thought about how you want your installed machine to look and behave. A developer's multiboot laptop will have very different requirements than a dedicated firewall, which will look completely different than a Web server. Proper preparations will make your OpenBSD installation quick and easy.

We're going to spend a great deal of time on the requirements, considerations, and decisions you need to make before installing OpenBSD. Once you know what you have to do, the actual install process is quite simple. Many of the problems people have installing OpenBSD come from not understanding their many choices.

The instructions given in this chapter cover almost all situations, but the final word on installing OpenBSD is the install document included in the release. For example, before installing OpenBSD on an i386, you must read INSTALL.i386 for that release!

NOTE   *If you have trouble, be sure to check the other documentation discussed in Chapter 1 for people with similar problems.*

OpenBSD Hardware

OpenBSD supports a wide variety of hardware architectures: i386, Alpha, 32- and 64-bit Sparc, both the 68000 and PowerPC varieties of Macintosh, and a variety of less well-known platforms. Take a look at http://www.OpenBSD.org/plat.html for a full list of supported platforms. This page contains links to a page for each hardware platform, in which the state of hardware support is discussed in full detail. For example, the i386 page gives a full list of all i386-compatible hardware supported in the latest development version of OpenBSD, -current (see Chapter 14).

This chapter covers the i386 platform, (aka "80386-compatible" or "Standard PC"), which includes the 386, 486, and Pentium lines and their descendants. They're the most common machines, and you probably have one sitting around you could use to learn on. In fact, even old systems can run OpenBSD; you probably have something in a back closet that would do nicely. Many of the examples in this book were performed on a Pentium 166 with 48MB RAM and a stack of 2GB hard disks. (The extra hard disks weren't necessary, but I had them, and a computer can always use more disk space.) We're going to cover installing Open-BSD on both a dedicated machine and on a few varieties of dual-boot systems.

Although OpenBSD will work on ancient hardware, that hardware needs to be in good shape. If your old Pentium box kept crashing because it has bad RAM, it won't behave any better with OpenBSD than it does with its current OS. Also, OpenBSD will be most useful with certain minimum hardware configurations. Here are some basic recommendations, based on my own experiences. These are all i386-based; if you have some other hardware platform, you can draw on these and make your own comparisons.

Proprietary Hardware

Some hardware vendors over the last ten years thought that it was a good idea to keep their hardware interfaces secret, so that competitors wouldn't be able to copy their designs. This has generally proven to be a bad idea; a flood of commodity parts has largely trampled this sort of hardware in recent years.

Developing device drivers for a piece of hardware without the interface specifications is quite difficult. Some hardware can be supported well without full documentation, such as Intel's EtherExpress network cards, and is common enough to make struggling through the lack of documentation worthwhile. Other hardware simply cannot be supported without full and complete documentation, such as Sun's Ultra-SPARC III processor.

If an OpenBSD developer has specifications for a piece of hardware and interest in that same hardware, he'll probably implement support for it. If not, that hardware won't work. In most cases, unsupported proprietary hardware can be replaced with better and less expensive open versions.

Processor

Your brand of processor is really irrelevant. OpenBSD doesn't care if it's running on an Intel, AMD, or IBM, or even an old Cyrix or one of those nifty Transmeta processors. It simply probes the CPU on booting and uses whatever chip features it recognizes. I've run very effective firewalls on 486 machines, easily handling a T1 of traffic. Still, I would recommend that you get 100 MHz or faster CPU. Some of the demonstrations in this book take less than 15 minutes on modern AMD1800+ and days on a 25 MHz 486.

Although OpenBSD will run on a multiple-processor system, it will only use one processor. If you have a choice between an SMP system and one with a single processor, you may as well just use the single-CPU machine for OpenBSD.

Memory (RAM)

Memory is good, and the more memory you have the happier you will be. In fact, adding RAM will do more than anything else to accelerate your system. You should have at least 16MB of RAM at a bare minimum, and preferably at least 32. Mind you, if you can get a couple of gigs of RAM in your system, OpenBSD will take full advantage of it.

Most weird crashes and unexplainable problems can be traced back to bad memory, so be certain that the memory you are using is good. Memory is the most likely failure point in an old machine.

Hard Drives

Hard drives can be a big performance bottleneck. While IDE drives are cheaper than bricks, they can slow down your system roughly as well as bricks can. A SCSI disk system can transfer data to and from each and every drive on the SCSI bus at the full speed of the SCSI controller, while an IDE controller splits its available throughput between the drives on the bus. Also, a SCSI controller can have up to 15 drives, while an IDE controller can have no more than 2. In a throughput competition, I'll back 15 drives moving at full speed against 2 drives moving at an average of half-speed any day.

Still, if all you have are IDE drives, you can do some things to alleviate these problems. Most important, put your hard disks on separate controllers! Many systems now have a hard drive on one IDE controller and a CD-ROM on the other. When you add a second hard drive, put it on the same controller as the CD-ROM drive. You probably won't be using the CD-ROM nearly as often as you use the hard drive, after all, and this will reduce contention on each IDE channel.

You'll be happiest with at least 1GB of disk on your system, though I'm assuming in this book that you have at least 10GB of disk. If you have a smaller disk, you'll want to be careful to clean up after yourself. For example, at one point I recommend keeping old source code around for later use; if you don't have enough disk space, don't do that!

Getting OpenBSD

Before you proceed much further, let's talk about how you can get OpenBSD. OpenBSD is available on CD-ROM and over the Internet.

CD-ROMs

You can purchase OpenBSD CD-ROMs direct from the OpenBSD Project or from any number of online vendors. Just go to the OpenBSD website and look for the "Getting OpenBSD" link. The OpenBSD Project will be happy to sell you CD-ROMs and assorted other OpenBSD merchandise, such as T-shirts and posters.

The main OpenBSD distribution point is in Canada, which may be a problem for those of you in other countries. You can get OpenBSD from a variety of resellers, many of which are listed on the OpenBSD ordering page. Pick a vendor in your country and you can save on customs duties — or, at least, you can pick a vendor on your same continent and save on shipping charges!

CD-ROM Layout

Each of the CD-ROMs contain the software for a few hardware platforms. For example, in the OpenBSD 3.2 CD-ROM set, disk 1 contains the i386 and Alpha software, disk 2 contains the VAX and MacPPC software, and disk 3 contains the Sparc and Sparc64 software. You'll find some extra tidbits scattered throughout all the CD-ROMs, however, so you can't just get by with one disk. For example, the operating system source code is kept on disk 3 in this particular release. Here's a look at the contents of the first CD-ROM.

```
3.2/
HARDWARE
PACKAGES
PORTS
README
TRANS.TBL
song32.mp3
```

The 3.2 directory contains the actual software of OpenBSD 3.2. Almost anything you want to install your software is in this directory.

The HARDWARE file gives a brief overview of the hardware this release of OpenBSD supports. It makes an excellent quick reference if you're wondering about hardware support for your particular machine or architecture.

The PACKAGES file gives instructions for installing precompiled software packages on OpenBSD. We cover this information in more detail in Chapter 13.

The PORTS file gives instruction for compiling your own software from the ports collection, also discussed in Chapter 13.

The README file gives valuable pointers to information elsewhere on the CD-ROM. While I've made every effort to be complete in this book, if you have any trouble at all *always* refer to the documentation for the release of OpenBSD you're working with!

Finally, the song32.mp3 file contains a song written to celebrate this Open-BSD release. (It might not be technically necessary, but it's certainly fun.)

Finding OpenBSD on the Net

You can install OpenBSD directly from the Internet, over HTTP or FTP. Every bit of OpenBSD is available this way, from programs to source code to add-on packages. You can download the entirety of OpenBSD piecemeal or just grab the entire software distribution from the FTP site. Installing via FTP or HTTP is one of the most popular ways to get OpenBSD.

What you will *not* find on the Internet is a set of official OpenBSD ISO images of any release. The OpenBSD Project uses CD-ROM sales to fund Open-BSD development, and it would really prefer that if you want a CD-ROM, you purchase one. The disk images of the official install CD-ROMs is copyrighted by Theo de Raadt. The OpenBSD team adds some extras to the CD-ROM package, such as stickers and artwork, to make it more appealing.

With a bit of searching, you will find OpenBSD ISO images on various Internet sites. Some of these are duplicates of the official ISO images, and are distributed in violation of Theo's copyright. This is not only illegal in most parts of the world, it's also just plain rude. Other ISO images on the Net are releases built by third parties who are not OpenBSD team members. While the release process is well documented, it still isn't a very simple operation. You're welcome to grab one of these ISO images and try to use it, but you should be warned that they have not been through the usual OpenBSD quality assurance process. Also, any joker can put up an ISO image, but you have no way to really know that such an image doesn't contain a Trojan, backdoor, or other booby trap unless you thoroughly audit the image and compare it against an official OpenBSD install. If you're going to go to that amount of trouble, you might as well shell out a few dollars and purchase an official CD-ROM anyway, or just try a FTP install!

FTP Install Sites

The main OpenBSD FTP site is at the University of Alberta, in Calgary, Canada. You can expect that the students are using all the bandwidth they can get for educational purposes, without sparing a thought for your OpenBSD needs. This makes the main FTP site slower that you might like. Fortunately, OpenBSD is mirrored all over the world.

Go to the OpenBSD website and check the "FTP" link. This will bring up a whole list of mirror sites in a variety of formats — FTP, HTTP, AFS, and so on. The list includes mirrors on every continent, including places such as Peru, Thailand, and Lithuania. There's almost certainly one closer to you than the University of Alberta.

OpenBSD FTP/HTTP Layout

No matter how you get OpenBSD over the network, you'll find the distribution site laid out much like this.

```
❶3.0/
3.1/
3.2/
3.3/
❷OpenSSH/
❸README
❹distfiles/
❺ftplist
❻patches/
❼snapshots/
❽songs/
❾src/
tools/
```

The ❶numbered directories are for the various releases of OpenBSD. Above, we see that this FTP site contains versions 3.0, 3.1, 3.2, and 3.3. You'll only have one release directory on a CD-ROM, of course — the directory for the release you have.

The ❷OpenSSH directory contains the OpenBSD team's implementation of SSH, which has been adopted by many different software projects, both free and commercial (i.e., Solaris). OpenBSD includes OpenSSH, and so you really don't have to worry about getting it separately.

The ❸README file contains very basic information about obtaining Open-BSD and where to get more information on the software.

The ❹distfile directory contains the source code of a great deal of add-on OpenBSD software. Not all mirror sites carry this directory, as it's quite large.

The ❺ftplist file lists the official FTP and HTTP installation mirrors. When you install via FTP later, the install program will grab this file to allow you to choose a mirror site close to you.

The ❻patches directory contains directories for each previous release of OpenBSD, and various patches for that release. Security problems and critical bugs can be patched after a release, and they are made available here.

The ❼snapshots directory contains recent experimental versions of Open-BSD, generally from between releases. If you want to see what's coming in future versions of OpenBSD, you can install a snapshot. Because these are works-in-progress, support is minimal. The developers appreciate bug reports on snapshots, but don't support snapshots.

The ❽songs directory contains the "soundtracks" for each release of OpenBSD.

If all you want to do is browse the source code of the most recent release of OpenBSD, you can trawl through the ❾src directory. The source code is kept here in plain-text, human-readable format. There are easier ways to browse the source code, however: the OpenBSD website includes the source code on the Web, complete with revision history and developer comments.

Finally, the tools directory contains odds and ends that are useful for the OpenBSD Project's internal workings.

Whether you have a CD-ROM or FTP access to the software, what you're almost certainly most interested in is the release directory for the latest version of OpenBSD.

The OpenBSD Release

If you look within the release directory on either the FTP site or the CD-ROM, you'll see the following:

- A directory for each architecture OpenBSD supports. (On CD-ROM, this is scattered between different disks.)
- A "packages" directory containing precompiled software for this release (see Chapter 13.)
- A "ports.tar.gz" file containing the compressed ports tree (see Chapter 13.)
- A compressed file containing the source code of the X Window System for this release.
- A "tools" directory containing installation tools.

Take a look through your CD-ROM or FTP site, and make sure you can find the directory for your hardware architecture. I'll be using the i386 directory in the rest of this chapter; if you're on a different hardware platform, substitute the correct architecture directory everywhere.

Choosing Your Install Method

While OpenBSD is available via CD-ROM and on the Net, you have an even wider range of choices for installation. The fastest and easiest way to install is from an OpenBSD CD-ROM. This eliminates many network issues that can complicate what should be a simple install.

If you don't have an OpenBSD CD-ROM, but you do have an Ethernet connection to the Internet, FTP installs are an excellent choice. If you choose to install from a reasonably close mirror site, and you have sufficient bandwidth, FTP installs are quite fast and reliable.

You can also install over HTTP. You're stuck with the inherent limitations of the HTTP protocol when installing via the Web; HTTP does not include the error-correcting protocols found in FTP. You might use this if you're behind a Web-only proxy server or if your closest mirror only speaks HTTP.

You can also install from a local FAT or EXT2 file system, such as found on many Microsoft or Linux machines. Your system must be partitioned properly for this to work (see "Partitioning"). This would allow you to "upgrade" part of your system to OpenBSD, which is especially useful on multiple-boot systems. To do this, just download the parts you need from the release directory on a FTP server. If you're not sure which parts you need, you can safely download the entire release directory for your architecture — it'll take up a little more room, but will ensure you have everything you might need.

Finally, you can download the files you need and make your own local OpenBSD install server.

Local Installation Servers

One reason ISOs are popular is that you can reuse them to install many machines at the cost of a single download. If you want to install a few (or many!) OpenBSD machines without buying a CD-ROM, and yet without using up bandwidth for each install, just download the entire release directory for your architecture. If you copy these files to a local FTP or HTTP[1] server, you can install any number of machines from these files. All you need to know is how to connect to this server, and any user names and password required to access it.

You only need to download the directories for the architectures you need. If you know exactly what you want to install, you only need to download the installation sets you plan to install (see "Distribution Sets").

Distribution Sets

Each architecture directory contains a variety of documents and files containing instructions and programs applicable to that type of hardware. For example, in the 3.1/i386 directory you'll see several INSTALL documents and a tutorial on the i386 boot architecture.

You'll also see several compressed files with names like comp31.tgz, misc31.tgz, and so on. These files are distribution sets, or compressed chunks of OpenBSD. Each distribution set contains a subsection of OpenBSD. By choosing the distribution sets you install, you can choose how much functionality your OpenBSD system will have. For example, the documentation is kept in a separate distribution set. If you're short on space and have documentation elsewhere, you might choose to save a little space and not install them on this machine. If this is a secure machine, you probably don't want a compiler on it. And if this is your experimental "learning OpenBSD" machine, you probably want to install everything.

Each distribution set has a name and a version number. For example, one distribution set of OpenBSD in release 3.1 is base32.tgz. In the next release, these same tools will be called base33.tgz.

Here are the distribution sets for OpenBSD. You'll find these on all architectures, unless noted in the architecture's release notes. If this is your first OpenBSD install, take a moment to decide which distribution sets you need. If at all possible, install them all while you're learning the OS. You can always trim them down in future installs.

bsd

This small distribution set contains the kernel. The kernel is important. The installer will complain if you don't have it and issue all sorts of dire warnings. Worse, your new system will not boot without it.

---

[1] Some architectures also support installs over NFS, but not all of them, so we won't cover it here.

baseXX.tgz

This contains OpenBSD's core programs, all the things that make OpenBSD UNIXish. All the programs in /bin, /sbin, /usr/bin, and /usr/sbin, the system libraries, and the miscellaneous programs you expect to find on a UNIX system are in this distribution set. Without this distribution set, your OpenBSD system will not work at all.

etcXX.tgz

You might guess that this distribution set contains the /etc/ directory, but it also contains assorted other files and directories that are required by the system, such as /var/log, as well as root's home directory. You must install this distribution set if you want your OpenBSD system to actually run.

manXX.tgz

If you need the manual pages for the programs in the base and the etc set, install this distribution set. The manual pages for other sets are installed with the distribution set.

compXX.tgz

This distribution contains C, C++, and Fortran compilers, tools, and the associated toolchain for each. It also includes the manual pages and documentation for the compilers. You will want this set if you plan to develop or compile software on this system. You need this set to use the ports collection. While this distribution set isn't large, you might choose to not install in on a secure machine such as a firewall. (Intruders are generally delighted to find a properly configured compiler on a firewall; such tools make a hacker's life much easier.)

gameXX.tgz

This distribution set contains a variety of simple games and documentation for them, based on games originally distributed in the BSD 4.4-Lite software collection. Some of these, such as fortune(1), are considered UNIX classics, and old farts won't be happy unless they're installed. Others, such as rogue(6), have more advanced versions available as a port or a package. You don't really need this, unless you want to see what us old farts called "computer games" back in the day.

miscXX.tgz

This contains dictionary files and typesettable documentation. If this system is intended as a desktop, you probably want these. If it's a server, you probably don't need them.

xbaseXX.tgz

This contains the core of XFree86, such as programs, headers, libraries, and so on. If you want to use X, you need this. Although you might not have a console or monitor on this system, remember that X will allow programs on this server to display on a workstation. These functions will not work without this distribution set.

xbaseXX.tgz

This contains the fonts for XFree86. If you plan to use X on a local display, install this.

xservXX.tgz

This contains all of the XFree86 video card drivers. If you plan to use X on a local display, install this.

xshareXX.tgz

XFree86's documentation and text files are included in this distribution set. If you're one of those few people who know everything there is to know about XFree86, you can get by without this.

Partitioning

The most difficult part of installing OpenBSD is deciding how to partition your hard drive. When you don't know how partitions work, choosing a partition layout can be troublesome. Unlike many installers that have fancy menus or graphic tools, OpenBSD's installer expects you to know how to use low-level disk management tools.

Partitions are logical subsections of a hard drive. Different partitions can be handled in different ways and can even have different file systems or different operating systems on them. We're going to discuss partitioning for both single-OS and multiple-OS installs.

NOTE   *Get a piece of paper to make some notes about your partitioning. Start by writing down the size of your hard disk. This is the amount of space you have to divide between your partitions. Write down the size of every partition you want and the order in which you want those partitions to lie. This will make installing OpenBSD much easier!*

Why Partition?

Partitioning might seem like a pain; why should you bother? Many commercial operating systems allow you to simply have one large partition over your entire hard disk, giving you a single 80-gig partition. What are the advantages of partitioning?

Different operating systems have different partition types and different requirements for disk layout. A Microsoft operating system simply cannot recognize an OpenBSD disk format and will insist upon formatting it before using it.

Although OpenBSD can mount partitions designed for most other popular operating systems, do not put the main OpenBSD system programs on a foreign partition. Let each OS run on its own section of disk. If you want to have multiple operating systems on your machine, you must partition.

But when you're running a dedicated OpenBSD machine, why should you bother to split up your hard drive? On a physical level, different parts of the disk move at different speeds. By putting frequently accessed data on the fastest parts of the disk, you can improve system performance. The only way to arrange this is by using partitions. Also, the operating system handles each partition separately. This means that you can configure each partition differently or set it to use different rules. The root partition is the only partition that should have device nodes, for example, so you can tell other partitions to not recognize device nodes. Partitions that contain user data should not have setuid programs, and you might not even want to allow them to have programs at all. Separate partitions enforce that easily. You want the main system configuration directory to be unchangeable, so an intruder or a clumsy user cannot alter it? That's trivial with separate partitions. If one partition is damaged, chances are that damage will not extend to other partitions. You can boot the system using the intact partitions and attempt to recover the data on the damaged partition. Finally, correct use of partitioning can enhance security. Not only will hackers have a more difficult time if they do break into your machine, but your own users will find it more difficult to accidentally damage the system. Before partitioning a hard drive, decide what the system will be used for. Is this a mail server? A Web server? A desktop machine? We'll discuss the requirements for each partition for different types of servers.

Standalone OpenBSD Partitioning

If you're installing a dedicated OpenBSD machine, you don't have to worry about sharing the hard drive with another operating system. This simplifies the partitioning process — you only have to worry about OpenBSD's requirements.

The main partitions you'll need to consider are / (root), swap space, /tmp, /var, /usr, and /home. If you forget to create any of these partitions, the installer will put the files that should go in the partitions into your root partition. This will quickly fill up your root partition!

Root

The root partition holds the main system configuration files and the most essential UNIX utilities needed to get a computer into single-user mode. Your system should have fast access to its root file system, so put it first on the disk. Because it holds only these basic utilities and configuration files it doesn't need to be large; on a modern hard drive, I find a 500MB root partition comfortably roomy. I would recommend no smaller than 50MB for a root partition. (You could scrape by with a few megabytes smaller; the exact minimum size varies with the version of OpenBSD.)

If you're familiar with other some other UNIX-like operating systems, such as some distributions of Linux, you might be used to simply using a single large root partition and putting everything on it. This is a bad idea for a variety of reasons. With a partition safely constraining your log files, a process or user gone amok cannot fill your entire drive; while it could fill a partition, you would still be able to create and edit files on other partitions, giving you the flexibility you need to address the actual problem. Also, with a single partition, you cannot control where files are put on the disk. This hurts performance. Damage to the disk is probably spread across many different files in unrelated parts of the system, which means that your chances of recovering from a damaged disk or file system problems drop dramatically.

Root Limitations

Over the years, i386 systems have been expanded time and time again to surpass their own limits. They're based upon an architecture that could originally handle a maximum of 640KB of RAM, after all! The OpenBSD kernel — indeed, all modern operating system kernels — work around these limits in a manner mostly transparent to the user, but when the system is first booting you're trapped with the BIOS limitations.

Many old i386 systems have a 504MB limit on hard drives, on which the BIOS cannot get at anything beyond the first 504MB of data on a disk. If your BIOS cannot find your operating system kernel in that first 504MB, it cannot boot the system. Check your hardware manual; if it makes any references to a 504MB limit, this affects you. You absolutely *must* place your entire root partition within the first 504MB of disk.

Additionally, for some time i386 systems had a similar (not identical) 8GB limit. OpenBSD still obeys that 8GB limit. Even if your system is not susceptible to the 504MB limit, your entire root partition must be completely contained within the first 8GB of disk.

Of course, if you follow my advice and make your root partition 500MB you will never have to worry about either of these restrictions and the potential damage that they can inflict.

If you break these rules, your system will probably appear to work. The second you upgrade your system, or move the file /bsd, the computer will quite probably refuse to boot. Save yourself much pain; make the root partition 500MB, and the first partition on the disk, and this problem will never affect you.

Swap Space

The next partition on your drive should be swap space, the disk space used by virtual memory. When your computer fills its physical memory, it will start to move information that has been sitting idle in memory into swap. If things go well, your system will almost never need swap space, but if you do need it, it needs to be fast.

So, how much swap space do you need? This is a matter of long debates between sysadmins. The short answer is, "It depends on the system." General wisdom says that you should have at least twice as much swap as you have physical memory. This isn't a bad rule, so long as you understand that it's very general. More won't hurt. Less might, if your system runs out of RAM.

If you find that you need more swap space, you should probably buy more memory instead. If that's not an option, you can use a regular file as a swap file. Still, if you have a reasonable amount of disk space, simply assigning an amount of swap equal to twice the amount of RAM you have is sensible.

You should also consider possible future upgrades. If a computer has 500MB of RAM today, but you plan to upgrade it to 3GB of RAM in a couple of months, perhaps assigning 6GB of disk space to swap is a good idea. After all, if you can afford three gigs of RAM and you have the hardware to manage it, certainly that much disk is not an issue!

Swap Splitting

If you have multiple disks, you can vastly improve the efficiency of your swap space by splitting it among multiple drives. Put the first swap partition on the second-outermost ring of the drive with your root partition, and other swap space on the outermost edge of their drives. This splits reads and writes among multiple disk controllers.

For swap splitting to work best, however, the drives must be SCSI. If you have IDE drives, the drives need to be on different IDE controllers. Remember, each IDE controller splits its total data throughput among all the connected hard drives. If you have two hard drives on the same IDE controller and you're accessing both drives simultaneously, each disk will average half as fast as it would if you were running it alone. The major bottleneck in using swap space is data throughput speed, and you won't gain speed by creating contention on your IDE bus.

/tmp

The /tmp directory is system-wide temporary space. If you do not create a separate /tmp partition, it will be included on your root partition. This means that your system-wide temporary space will be subject to the same conditions as the rest of your root drive. This probably isn't what you want, especially if you plan to mount your root partition read-only!

Requirements for a /tmp directory are generally a matter of opinion — after all, you can always just use a chunk of space in your home directory as temporary space. On a modern hard drive, I like to have at least 500MB in a /tmp directory. Automated software installers frequently want to extract files in /tmp, and having to work around these installers when /tmp fills up is possible but tedious.

/var

The /var partition contains frequently changing logs, mail spools, temporary run files, the default website, and so on. If your server is a Web server, your website logs will go to this partition, and you may need to make it 1GB or more. On a small "generic Internet mail/Web server," I'll frequently give /var 20 percent of my remaining disk space. If the server handles only email or databases, I'll kick this up to 70 percent or more, or just assign a space to the remaining partitions and throw everything else I have on /var. If you're really cramped for space, you might assign as little as 30MB to /var. (Again, actual minimum requirements vary depending on your version of OpenBSD.)

/usr

The /usr partition holds the operating system programs, system source code, compilers and libraries, and other little details like that. Much of this changes only when you upgrade your system.

On a modern hard drive, I recommend using about 6GB on your /usr partition. This should be more than sufficient for all the contents of /usr and just about any add-on packages you might desire, and should also leave room for any OpenBSD source you might want to install. Without the X Window System, you could make /usr as small as 200MB. If you need X, you should assign /usr at least 350MB.

/home

The /home partition is where users keep their files. If you have more disk space than is good for you, assign it here. Your home directory will quickly fill up with all sorts of stuff that you'll be tripping across years from now.

The /home partition can easily be the last on your disk; it doesn't need to be fast. It also doesn't need to be large; the only files on the drive will be the ones that you need.

NOTE   *If you've been adding this up, you should notice that it's entirely possible to have a complete OpenBSD system (without the X Window System) in less than 300MB. Just for kicks, compare that to the amount of space a minimal install of Windows XP requires or the size of an minimal Solaris 9 box installation. Your complete install, with all your user programs, may be far larger than 300MB — but all that space is used up because of things you specifically want, not OS overhead.*

Multiple Hard Drives

If you have a second hard drive of comparable quality to your main drive, you can make excellent use of it with proper planning. First, use the outer edge of the drive for swap, as discussed earlier in the "Swap Splitting" section. Use the rest of the drive to segregate your data from your operating system. Do this by assigning the remainder of the drive to the partition that stores files for whatever your server does the most of. If it's a Web server, make the second drive /www or /home. If it's a mail server, use it for /var or /var/mail. If it's a network logging host, assign the second drive to /var/log.

In general, segregating your operating system from the data you're serving increases system efficiency. Like all rules of thumb, this is debatable. But no sysadmin will tell you that this is an actively bad idea, while one can argue endlessly about what the "absolute best" idea is.

If you have no idea what your system will be for, make your second drive /usr and split your first hard drive amongst /var, /tmp, /, and swap space.

If your second drive is much slower than your main system drive, don't bother using it. Not only will its performance be poor, chances are that it is much older than your main drive and far more likely to fail.

If you need to install more than one operating system on your computer, an extra hard drive is an excellent and easy way to do that.

Multiple OS Partitioning

Many people need to run multiple operating systems on one computer, and OpenBSD allows you to do that. By far, the easiest way to do this is to install a hard drive in your computer for each operating system. This allows you to use each OS's native disk tools without risking tramping on your other operating system. In this day of dirt-cheap hundred-gig hard drives, however, this is an added complication for many people who simply want to divide up their hard disk appropriately.

When you divide up a single hard disk between multiple operating systems, you fall into another level of partitioning, known as MBR (Master Boot Record) partitions. The boundaries of these partitions are stored in the Master Boot Record on a disk, and are managed by tools such as UNIX fdisk(8), DOS fdisk, or Microsoft's Disk Administrator. Any operating system can see MBR partitions; they may not recognize that one of these partitions is designated for OpenBSD, but they realize that this is a discrete section of disk. Within these large partitions, you create smaller OpenBSD-specific partitions for /home, /usr, and so on.

The fdisk tools allow you to, say, take your 80GB disk and designate the first 20GB for OpenBSD, the second 20GB for Microsoft Windows XP, the third 20GB for FreeBSD, and the last chunk for Linux, should you wish. You then use each OS's native tools to manage those chunks of disk space. You would then use a separate "boot manager" to choose between operating systems at boot time.

When you decide where to put disk space for any one OS, you need to allow for OpenBSD's boot limitations. Just because you have multiple operating systems on a hard drive doesn't mean that you can ignore the 504MB limit or the 8GB limit. If you have enough disk space to install more than one operating system, chances are your system does not suffer from the 504MB limit. Still, the OpenBSD root partition must be contained entirely within the first 8GB of disk, not the first 8GB of disk space assigned to OpenBSD. In most cases, this means that OpenBSD must be the first operating system on your disk. Also, OpenBSD on a hard disk must be a single contiguous section; you cannot dedicate the first 20GB of your hard drive to OpenBSD, have a 20GB Microsoft partition, and have a 40GB OpenBSD partition to round out your disk.

Put your OpenBSD partition first on the disk, and you won't have any problems. We discuss multiboot partitioning and installation at length in Chapter 4.

Disk Sectors

You need to be aware of disk sectors to use the installation tool. We'll discuss sectors in more detail in Chapter 18, but for now you just need to be aware that a sector is a tiny section of a disk. Each sector has a number. Sector 0 is at the beginning of the disk, and the sectors are numbered sequentially until the end of the disk.

Partitions can be defined by the sectors that they occupy. On most disks, the Master Boot Record takes up the first 62 sectors. The next partition would start at sector 63 and go on for a size you indicate.

Decisions Complete!

You now know where to get OpenBSD and which method you will use to install it. You should know which distribution sets you want to install on your first machine and how you want to divide your hard disk. These are the most difficult issues you will face in installing OpenBSD. Hopefully, you have a piece of paper with your decisions noted; if so, the only real thinking you will have to make during the installation is which key to press to get your desired result. We're going to cover that in the next chapter.

3

DEDICATED INSTALLATION

Bootable floppy,
CD-ROM or FTP,
hard drive comes to life

Armed with your OpenBSD software and a
computer with supported hardware, you are
now ready to face an actual installation. We will
cover a full installation on the i386 architecture
via CD-ROM and FTP/HTTP. (We'll cover installing
from a hard disk in Chapter 4, as you won't be using that
method unless you're using multiple operating systems.)
You may or may not need to use a floppy disk to boot your
system, so be sure you have one handy just in case.

If OpenBSD is one of several operating systems you plan to install on this
machine, you still need to read this chapter. While the next chapter covers the issues
involved with sharing a hard drive between OpenBSD and several other operating
systems, it does not discuss actually installing OpenBSD! You'll want to understand
OpenBSD's standalone installation process before beginning to install on a multiboot
system.

Before you install, be absolutely certain that any data you have on this machine is backed up elsewhere! When you install OpenBSD and use the entire hard drive, as we're doing in this chapter, you will reformat the hard disk; you'll lose any data on the hard drive.

The first thing you need to do is check your hardware and prepare your BIOS.

Hardware Setup

Before you even begin, be sure OpenBSD supports your hardware! You can find the supported hardware list for the most recent version of OpenBSD on i386 at http://www.OpenBSD.org/i386.html, or on the FTP site or CD-ROM in the release directory as i386/INSTALL.i386. These documents include lists of hardware that is supported at this time.

The devices on the hardware compatibility lists are frequently identified by chipset, not by the vendor. After all, when you buy a computer the network card is frequently just listed as a "10/100 Ethernet," not an "Intel i8255x-based PCI Ethernet card." To make matters worse, many vendors use identical hardware under a separate brand name or use different hardware under the same brand name. For example, Linksys is famous for having four very different cards all called the EtherLink. You might have to dig in the hardware manual for this information, or ask your vendor. If nothing else, you can just try to install and see if everything works. The boot-time messages will give you a great deal of information on what sort of hardware you have.

BIOS Setup

Before you try to install, confirm that your system's BIOS is properly configured. Because every BIOS is slightly different, I won't go over exact instructions on how to configure. Most computer systems tell you how to access the system BIOS when you first boot the computer and include a simple menu-driven system to make changes. Consult your motherboard manual if you have any problems.

First, set "Plug and Play OS" to NO. This tells your BIOS to do some basic hardware setup, rather than relying upon the OS to do everything. Modern versions of Microsoft Windows expect to handle hardware setup. OpenBSD takes advantage of the BIOS' ability to configure the hardware itself. Many PCI devices will work poorly if you do not set this option!

Also configure your boot device. If you are installing from CD-ROM, set your boot device to CD-ROM, then floppy disk, then hard drive. (If your CD-ROM boot gives you trouble, you can use a floppy disk as a fallback.) If you are installing from some other media, your first boot device should be the floppy disk and the hard disk second.

Making a Boot Floppy

If you do not have an OpenBSD CD-ROM, or if your hardware does not boot from CD-ROM, you need to start your install with a boot floppy. The OpenBSD boot floppy actually contains a very small subset of OpenBSD, including just the tools needed to recognize your hardware, format your disks, and download and extract the appropriate distribution sets in the correct locations.

You'll find a few boot floppy images in the architecture release directory. The purpose of these images may change over time, so confirm in the release install document if you have any trouble. Each name includes the release number — for example, the images for OpenBSD 3.4 will be named floppy34.fs, floppy34B.fs, and floppy34C.fs. Download the disk image that most closely describes your system; you only need one.

floppyXX.fs This image is for the most common i386 hardware. This will boot your average workstation or low-end server.

floppyXXB.fs This image is for high-end servers. It includes gigabit Ethernet cards, SCSI, and RAID drivers.

floppyXXC.fs This image is for laptops and other PCMCIA/Cardbus systems.

Once you have the appropriate image file, you'll need to copy it onto a floppy disk. You cannot use basic file system–level copying, such as Windows drag and drop. These are image files, meaning that they include the file system and not just the files on the file system.

Creating Floppies on UNIX

If you're already running a UNIX-like system, dd(1) is the only command you need. You also need to know your floppy drive's device name, which is probably /dev/fd0, /dev/floppy, or /dev/rfd0. Once you have that, you just tell dd(1) to copy the image to the disk in that device. If the device name was /dev/fd0c, you'd enter

```
dd if=floppy33B.fs of=/dev/fd0c
```

to write the floppy33B.fs image to floppy disk.

If dd(1) runs for a while and then gives an error, you may have a bad floppy disk. Floppies tend to go bad very easily, and you should try another one. If dd gives you an error immediately or exits silently without writing to the floppy disk, you probably need to specify a different floppy device driver.

Creating Floppies on Windows 9x

If you're running a Microsoft Windows 9x-based operating system, such as Windows Me, Windows 98, or Windows 95, you'll need a program to copy the disk images. Microsoft doesn't provide one, but OpenBSD does, which you'll find in the "tools" directory of the release directory. The program fdimage.exe is specifically designed for these older Microsoft operating systems and does not work on Windows NT–based operating systems.

Fdimage.exe is a free program that can copy disk images and is quite easy to use. For example, to copy the floppy image floppy33.fs to the floppy in your a: drive, enter the following at a DOS prompt:

```
C:> fdimage floppy33.fs a:
```

The floppy will churn for a while, and finally spit out an OpenBSD boot floppy.

Windows 9*x* has restrictions on filenames; each filename is restricted to eight characters, with a three-character extension after a period. While the GUI desktop displays long filenames, these are actually aliases for the names available in DOS mode. The names of floppyXXB.fs and floppyXXC.fs are nine characters long, with a two-character extension. This means that Windows will rename these files to something its innards can accept, retaining these names as aliases visible in the GUI. At a DOS prompt, however, you'll need to find out what DOS calls your floppy image before you can boot it. The file floppy33B.fs may well be called something like floppy~1.fs.

Again, if you have trouble, your floppy is probably bad.

Creating Boot Floppies on Modern Microsoft Systems

If your computer is running Windows NT or one of its descendants (such as Windows 2000, Windows XP, Windows 2003, and so on), fdimage.exe will not work. OpenBSD includes a program for this, ntrw.exe, in the tools directory of the release directory. Like fdimage.exe, ntrw.exe is designed to copy a disk image to a disk. Windows NT–based systems do not rewrite filenames, so you should be able to open a command prompt and just type:

```
C:> ntrw floppy33C.fs a:
```

If it doesn't work, you probably have a bad floppy disk.

Booting

Put your boot media in the drive and power up your system. You should see the usual BIOS messages go flashing past and then the OpenBSD boot prompt.

```
boot>
```

If you should need to interrupt the boot process for any reason, you can enter the appropriate commands here. We'll discuss various reasons to interrupt the boot in Chapter 6, as well as elsewhere in the book. If you wait for five seconds, the boot messages will follow.

```
booting fd0a:/bsd: +173028=0x43d3e4 start=0xd0100020
entry point at 0x100020

Copyright (c) 1982, 1986, 1989, 1991, 1993
Copyright (c) 1995-2002 OpenBSD. All rights reserved. http://www.OpenBSD.org
    The Regents of the University of California.  All rights reserved.
```

At this point, device driver messages will start to flow past, as OpenBSD probes your hardware and assigns drivers to all the system components that it recognizes.

The Install Program

The OpenBSD installer is just a shell script that calls programs to download files, format disks, and in general prepare your system for use. It might not be pretty, but it is extremely fast and in educated hands it is extremely powerful.

NOTE   *The installer changes very slightly between releases of OpenBSD. Some of the words may change, and some of the questions may be rearranged. The following was prepared with a prerelease version of OpenBSD 3.3. Do not blindly follow these directions; instead, use them as examples!*

Once the boot messages pass, you'll see the following text:

```
erase ^?, werase ^W, kill ^U, intr ^C, status ^T
(I)nstall, (U)pgrade or (S)hell? i
```

We'll examine the "Upgrade" option in Chapter 14. The "Shell" command will drop you into a command line, where you could work with the few commands available on the boot disk. We want the "Install" option now, however. Hit "i" and then ENTER. The installer will display a welcome message and a few basic instructions.

```
Welcome to the OpenBSD/i386 3.2 install program.

This program will help you install OpenBSD in a simple and rational way. At
any prompt except password prompts you can run a shell command by typing
'!foo', or escape to a shell by typing '!'. Default answers are shown in []'s
and are selected by pressing RETURN. At any time you can exit this program by
pressing Control-C and then RETURN, but quitting during an install can leave
your system in an inconsistent state.

Specify terminal type: [vt220]
```

If you're using a standard i386 keyboard and monitor, just press ENTER as the default. If you have an unusual terminal hooked up to your i386 system, you're probably one of those old hands and know exactly what terminal type you have. If you're a new user who hooked up some ancient unidentified dust-covered piece-of-crud terminal you found in a disused laboratory at the back of the abandoned fertilizer plant because you thought it would be nifty, stop now and get a standard monitor and keyboard. While that antediluvian console will probably work, your first install is *not* the time to try it!

```
Do you wish to select a keyboard encoding table? [n]
```

A keyboard-encoding table allows you to remap your keyboard from the standard U.S. QWERTY style to that used in some other language. Entering "y" will give you an option to choose one. Most readers of this book will be perfectly comfortable with the standard QWERTY keyboard, so just hit ENTER to take the default.

```
IS YOUR DATA BACKED UP? As with anything that modifies disk contents, this
program can cause SIGNIFICANT data loss.

It is often helpful to have the installation notes handy. For complex disk
configurations, relevant disk hardware manuals and a calculator are useful.

Proceed with install? [n] y
```

This is your last chance to save any data that might be on your hard drive. If you're not sure about the quality of your backup, just hit ENTER to take the default and abort the installation. If you're certain you do not need any data on your hard drive, enter "y" to continue.

Disk Setup

The first thing the installer actually does is allow you to partition your disks.

```
You will now initialize the disk(s) that OpenBSD will use. To enable all
available security features you should configure the disk(s) to allow the
creation of separate filesystems for /, /tmp, /var, /usr, and /home.

Available disks are: sd0 sd1 wd0. ❶
Which one is the root disk? (or done) [done] wd0
```

Note that the installer has identified the disks attached to this system. OpenBSD found three disks, ❶which it calls sd0, sd1, and wd0. Any drive beginning with "sd" is a SCSI disk, while any drive beginning with "wd" is an IDE drive. Count the drives that the installer found; is that the number of drives you have in this machine? If not, then OpenBSD did not find all of your hard drives. You probably have an unsupported hard drive controller.

In this example, we're going to use the IDE drive for the operating system and the SCSI drives for database files and home directories. Type "wd0" and press ENTER.

```
Do you want to use *all* of wd0 for OpenBSD? [no] yes
```

If you want to share a single hard drive between multiple operating systems, take a look at the next chapter. Right now, enter "yes" here.

Creating OpenBSD Partitions

The install program will now guide you through creating partitions on your disk. This is perhaps the most complicated part of installing OpenBSD. Get out your scratch sheet where you wrote down how you wanted to divide your disk. You will need it here.

```
You will now create an OpenBSD disklabel inside the OpenBSD MBR
partition. The disklabel defines how OpenBSD splits up the MBR partition
into OpenBSD partitions in which filesystems and swap space are created.

The offsets used in the disklabel are ABSOLUTE, i.e. relative to the
start of the disk, NOT the start of the OpenBSD MBR partition.
```

A *disklabel* defines OpenBSD partitions within an MBR partition. The entire disk is designated as a single MBR partition, as we dedicated the disk to OpenBSD. A small chunk of the disk will be allocated to the Master Boot Record, however, and the installer tells you how many sectors it occupies.

```
# using MBR partition 3: type A6 off 63 (0x3f) size 39179889 (0x255d671)

Treating sectors 63-39179952❶ as the OpenBSD portion of the disk.
You can use the 'b' command to change this.

Initial label editor (enter '?' for help at any prompt)
>
```

One important fact here is that the installer tells you how many ❶sectors are available on the MBR partition. Because we have dedicated this disk to OpenBSD, we know that there are 39179953 sectors on this disk — remember, computers start numbering at zero! We can use all but the first 62 sectors.

You're now at a command prompt within OpenBSD's disklabel(8) tool. This tool has its own command set, which you can view by entering a question mark at the disklabel prompt. We're going to examine some of the basic commands here.

Understanding a Disklabel

The "p" command prints the disklabel as it currently appears. A disklabel contains two basic sets of information: some physical information about the disk and information about the partitioning of the MBR partition. Let's look at the physical information first. While it doesn't usually have a direct impact upon the installation process, you may need to know how to read it if something goes wrong.

```
> p
device: /dev/rwd0c❶
type: ESDI❷
disk: ESDI/IDE disk❸
label: SAMSUNG SV2011H ❹
bytes/sector: 512❺
sectors/track: 63❻
tracks/cylinder: 16
sectors/cylinder: 1008
cylinders: 16383
total sectors: 39179952❼
free sectors: 39179889❽
rpm: 3600❾
```

Your first entry is the disk's ❶device name, shown as /dev/rwd0c in this example.
The middle of the name, wd0, is the disk name. The leading "r" means that we're
addressing the disk in raw mode, while the tailing "c" means that we're
examining the "c" partition. "c" is the OpenBSD partition name used for the
whole MBR disk.

The type ❷is a general label describing the interface used by the disk. Any
IDE disk will show up as ESDI (Enhanced Small Device Interface), while SCSI
disks are labeled SCSI.

The disk ❸field shows what sort of disk is attached to this interface. In this
case, it's an IDE disk, but we knew that from the device name already.

The label ❹displays the manufacturer's name and model number for the
drive.

The ❺bytes per sector line shows how many bytes are in a single sector.
Almost all drives put 512 bytes, or half a K, in a single sector.

The next few lines, where disklabel prints out ❻the sectors per track, the
tracks per cylinder, the sectors per cylinder, and the number of cylinders on the
drive, can be confusing. Hard drives have expanded dramatically over the years;
many different sorts of hardware perform some sort of "translation" to make the
hard drive work as you would expect. This means that by the time this information reaches the disklabel program, the hardware, the BIOS, or both may have
altered it repeatedly. You cannot trust that these values reflect the physical design
of the disk. (If you're interested in the workings of disk translation, take a look at
the INSTALL.chs document in the i386 directory of the distribution directory.)
Fortunately, you don't need to do anything with them.

The fields that tell you the ❼total sectors on the disk and the ❽number of
free sectors are accurate, however. The whole purpose of the translations that the
hardware performs is to give an accurate sector count, after all!

Finally the ❾rpm field tells you the rpm (revolutions per minute) of the
disk.

All of the above cannot be changed without changing the underlying hardware. The following section, which displays the actual OpenBSD partitioning of
the disk, can and must be altered.

```
16 partitions:❶
#        ❷size  ❸offset  ❹fstype  [❺fsize ❻bsize  ❼cpg]
  c: 39179952       0     unused      0    0

>
```

The first line shown here says that you can have up to ❶16 OpenBSD partitions on this hard drive.

The comment line ❷ shows what each of the six columns beneath it mean.

The first ❶ gives a partition letter. A unique letter identifies each partition on a disk. As we said earlier, the "c" partition represents the whole drive.

The ❷size is the number of sectors the partition takes up. In our example, the "c" partition takes up 39179952 sectors. This includes the sectors occupied by the Master Boot Record — remember, "c" is the whole disk.

The ❸offset column shows how far from the beginning of the disk this partition begins. As the "c" partition is the whole disk, it has an offset of zero.

The ❹fstype column shows the file system type the partition has.

The last three columns describe fragmentation behavior of the file system and are not meant to be changed by anyone. The OpenBSD file system is highly fragmentation resistant. If you're curious, start reading at newfs(8) and its related manual pages. If you're an advanced user, the installer does give you a chance to alter these — but you really shouldn't unless you know *exactly* what you're doing and why.

Under ❺fsize, you will see the fragment size for any file fragments on the disk, in bytes.

The ❻b size is the size of a block on disk, in bytes.

Finally, ❼cpg shows the number of cylinders per cylinder group.

Anytime you feel confused in the disk partitioning process, print your current disklabel and compare it to your notes on how you want the partitioning to look.

Now that you can see what the disk partitioning looks like, let's add a partition or four.

Adding Partitions

This IDE drive is 20GB, and I want to divide it as follows.

- 500MB root
- 500MB swap
- 10GB /usr
- 9GB /var

I don't have a /home partition on this drive; I plan to put it on one of the SCSI drives.

To add a partition, enter "a". This will drop you into an interactive dialog.

The important thing to remember here is that partitions are created on the disk in the order that you create them in the disklabel. You want your root partition to be first on the disk, so you need to create it first. (Remember, if you put your root partition further in the disk you might break the 8GB limit!)

```
> a
partition: [a]
```

Traditionally, the first partition on a disk is the "a" partition. Hit ENTER to take the default.

```
offset: [63]
```

The offset is the number of sectors from the beginning of the disk this partition begins. Remember, sectors 0–62 are used by the Master Boot Record. The installer is smart enough to know this, and presents a default that picks up where the last partition left off. Hit ENTER to accept it.

```
size: [39179889] 500M
```

By default, the installer presents you with the number of sectors remaining on the disk as your partition size. This is useful for the very last partition on the disk, but it's not what you want to use here.

The default unit here is in sectors. Rather than having to convert the partition size you want into sectors, however, the installer recognizes the following abbreviations for sizes:

- b for bytes
- c for cylinders
- k for kilobytes
- m for megabytes
- g for gigabytes

Here, we tell the system to create a 500MB partition. Partitions can only be created along cylinder boundaries, so the installer will round it off to the nearest cylinder unless you happen to enter a value that exactly matches a cylinder.

```
FS type: [4.2BSD]
```

You can either choose a 4.2BSD file system, or "swap." The installer knows that the "a" traditionally needs a file system, so it defaults.

```
mount point: [none] /
>
```

We want this first partition to be our root partition, so enter a slash. The partition is created, and you are dropped back to the disklabel prompt. Swap space is next on the list.

```
> a ❶
partition: [b] ❷
offset: [1024128] ❸
size: [38155824] 500M ❹
Rounding to nearest cylinder: 1024128 ❺
FS type: [swap] ❻
```

This looks almost exactly like our first example. We ❶ tell disklabel to add a partition. As it's our second partition, it defaults to ❷ partition b. It begins at an ❸ offset just after where your previous partition ends. We have to ❹ enter a size, which is the first non-default choice we enter. Disklabel automatically ❺ rounds this off to a suitable cylinder boundary. The "b" partition is traditionally swap space, so disklabel defaults to ❻ creating this as swap space. Swap space doesn't have a mount point, so we're done.

Our next mount point has a couple of minor surprises, however.

```
> a
partition: [d] ❶
offset: [2048256]
size: [37131696] 10G
Rounding to nearest cylinder: 20971440
FS type: [4.2BSD] ❷
mount point: [none] /usr ❸
>
```

Here, the automatic partition lettering has skipped "c" and gone to ❶ "d." What gives? Remember, the "c" partition represents the entire disk, so "d" is the next available letter. Because "b" is the traditional swap space, disklabel defaults to making this partition (and all subsequent partitions) ❷ a standard OpenBSD file system. Finally, we have to tell disklabel where we want this partition ❸ mounted.

Our last partition on this disk, /var, is the easiest to create of all.

```
> a
partition: [e]
offset: [23019696]
size: [16160256]   ❶
FS type: [4.2BSD]
mount point: [none] /var ❷
>
```

Disklabel knows which partition letter to assign, and the offset, and it even knows how many ❶ sectors are left on the hard drive! All we have to do is assign a ❷ mount point.

Now that you've completely filled the disk, use the "p" command to print your edited disklabel. The top of the disklabel is unchanged, but our partition table looks considerably different.

```
> p
...
16 partitions:
#        size    offset    fstype    [fsize bsize   cpg]
  a:  1024065        63    4.2BSD     1024  8192     16  # /
  b:  1024128   1024128      swap
  c: 39179952         0    unused        0     0
  d: 20971440   2048256    4.2BSD     1024  8192     16  # /usr
  e: 16160256  23019696    4.2BSD     1024  8192     16  # /var
>
```

All of our partitions are visible here, along with comments recording which partition we intended to assign them to. You can check your work here.

Writing a Label to the Disk

Once you are satisfied with your work, hit "q" to write your edited disklabel on the disk. If you don't like your work, you can hit "z" to quit disklabel without writing any changes.

```
> q
Write new label?: [y]
```

You'll get one last chance to change your mind. Once you write a new disklabel, recovering any data on the disk will become extremely difficult! You should have backed up any vital data on this disk before starting the install, but this is a good time to confirm you didn't, say, microwave the backup tape. Hit ENTER to continue.

```
The root filesystem will be mounted on wd0a.
wd0b will be used for swap space.
Mount point for wd0d (size=10485720k), none or done? [/usr]
```

You have a final chance to set the mount point for your partitions. The mount point you chose is in the default, but if you want to rearrange things, you can do it here. Hit ENTER to go on. The installer will cycle through all of the partitions on the disk, asking you to confirm their mount points.

```
Mount point for wd0e (size=8080128k), none or done? [/var]
Mount point for wd0d (size=10485720k), none or done? [/usr] done
```

When you have confirmed all of your mount points, the installer starts asking you where you want to mount your disks again at the beginning of the list! This might seem annoying, but think about it. If you realized on your last partition that you had made an error on the mount point, you might need to rearrange earlier partitions. Enter "done" to end the loop, and proceed to the next disk.

Subsequent Disks

If you have more than one hard drive, the installer dumps you back at the beginning of the hard drive dialog.

```
Available disks are: sd0 sd1.
Which one do you wish to initialize? (or done) [done] sd0
```

If your other hard drives will not be used for OpenBSD, you can enter "done" here to proceed. Otherwise, choose the hard disk you want to work on next. The disklabel process works exactly the same, with some slight modifications in the partitioning process. This hard drive is going to be one large partition, mounted on /database. While "a" is traditionally the root partition, you can only have one root partition per operating system! It's perfectly safe to assign the "a" partition to /database, and on the third drive you can assign it to /home without a problem.

Other Disklabel Operations

The disklabel editor is extraordinarily powerful and will let you do many things. Most of these functions should never be necessary, but are available if you need them. disklabel(8) also has many functions that are not intended for use when installing a system, but are useful when working with disks on a running system.

Expert Mode

Expert mode gives the advanced UNIX user access to some of the less-frequently tweaked options in the disklabel setup, such as the ability to change the block and fragment size. Most people do not need this, and would actually find the options simply clutter. (It's not as if disklabel isn't complicated enough already!)

Access expert mode by entering a capital X at a disklabel prompt. You won't see anything immediately, but it will make other commands produce more output and provide more options.

Changing Basic Drive Parameters

You remember all that stuff at the top of the disklabel that recorded basic physical characteristics of the drive? You can change all that. This is almost never necessary — in fact, if you think of doing it as a solution to a problem, you're probably on the completely wrong track.

If you enter "e", the disklabel program will walk you through each entry on the upper part of the disklabel. The existing values will be presented as defaults, allowing you to quickly walk through the variables until you reach the one you want to change.

```
> e
Changing device parameters for /dev/rwd0c:
disk type: [ESDI]
label name: [SAMSUNG SV2011H ]
...
```

Edit this information at your own risk! You can render your disk unbootable or your partitions unusable by changing this information. Certain parts of the disklabel describe physical characteristics of the hard drive, and by changing them you are lying to your computer. Computers do not like being lied to and will go utterly ballistic if they catch you lying about basic hardware.

Deleting Existing Partitions

If you find that you have made a mistake on a partition, you might just want to blow it away. Delete partitions with the "d" command.

```
> d
partition to delete: [] e
>
```

That's it! There are no warnings, no prompts, no "are you sure?" dialog boxes, so be sure before you enter the partition letter!

Modifying Existing Partitions

You can modify an existing partition with the "m" command. Disklabel will walk you through each of the values you entered when creating the disk, offering your original values as defaults and giving you an opportunity to change them. As usual, just hit ENTER to take the defaults.

In most cases, it's easier to just delete and recreate the partitions. In this example, though, we correct a very obvious mistake with the mount point of the partition.

```
> m
partition to modify: [] a
FS type: [4.2BSD]
offset: [63]
size: [1024065]
mount point: [/usr] /
>
```

Deleting Existing Disklabels

You might screw up the disklabel badly enough that you just want to erase it all and start over. Or, you might be recycling disks from another operating system, and want to clear away any old disklabels or partitioning information. That's very easy to do with the "z" command.

```
>z
>
```

Again, there is no chance to change your mind. Disklabel assumes that if you entered "z" you meant "z", and that's that. If you want an "Are You Sure?" prompt, get another operating system.

Online Help

You can enter a single question mark (?) to get a brief listing of disklabel commands.

If you want more detailed help, the "M" command will display the man page for disklabel(8).

Final Disk Configuration

Once you have labeled all of your disks, you'll see the following message:

```
Done - no available disks found.

You have configured the following partitions and mount points:

wd0a /
wd0d /usr
wd0e /var
sd0a /database
sd1d /home
```

Take one last look at your disks, and confirm that this is where you want your partitions. While the partitioning process made recovery of data difficult, the next step will make recovery darn near impossible.

```
The next step creates a filesystem on each partition, ERASING existing data.
Are you really sure that you're ready to proceed? [n] y
```

The default is to not proceed. Hit "y" here to go on, and you'll see messages much like this for each of your partitions.

```
/dev/rwd0a:     1024064 sectors in 1016 cylinders of 16 tracks, 63 sectors
        500.0MB in 64 cyl groups (16 c/g, 7.88MB/g, 1920 i/g)
```

Once all of your partitions have been formatted, you'll see the mount point and mount option information for each partition.

```
/dev/wd0a on /mnt type ffs (rw, asynchronous, local, ctime=Sun Oct 13 12:59:20
2002)
/dev/sd0a on /mnt/database type ffs (rw, asynchronous, local, nodev, nosuid,
ctime=Sun Oct 13 12:59:20 2002)
...
```

Note that OpenBSD 3.2 and later mounts everything but / nodev and nosuid. Thanks to the systrace mechanism (Chapter 10), setuid programs are not necessary on OpenBSD.

Network Setup

Now that you have disks to write information on, the installer will prompt you for networking information.

```
Enter system hostname (short form, e.g. 'foo'): openbsdtest
```

If you've been around networks for any length of time, you've probably seen host names that include a domain name, such as "laptop.BlackHelicopters.org." This is not the style of host name the installer wants to see here! Just enter the machine's name within the domain: For example, this system's full name is "openbsdtest.BlackHelicopters.org" so I enter "openbsdtest."

Even if your system is not on a network, it needs to have a local host name.

```
Configure the network? [y]
```

If you are installing from CD-ROM and don't want to bother with the network right now, you can hit "n." I recommend that you configure the network while you're in the install program; however, it's much simpler for a new user to do it here than to go back and configure it later.

```
If any interface will be configured by DHCP, you should not enter
information that will be supplied via DHCP, e.g. the DNS domain name.

Enter DNS domain name (e.g. 'bar.com'): [my.domain] BlackHelicopters.org
```

If your network has a DHCP server, just hit ENTER here.

```
Available interfaces are: fxp0 fxp1.
Which one do you wish to initialize? (or done) [fxp0]
```

If you only have one network card, just hit ENTER. Multiple network cards require a bit more thought.

If Your System Has Multiple Network Cards

While your driver names and device numbers will vary, if you have two identical network cards you may have difficulty determining which physical card has which interface name. My test computer has two identical network cards. These particular cards use the "fxp" driver and are numbered 0 and 1. There is no way to look at the hardware and identify which is which. If you are installing over the network, you must configure the card that is attached into the network! Trying to install any software over the network is extraordinarily frustrating when you aren't plugged in. It is very difficult to tell which card it is from the information presented within the installer or even on the command line.

This is one place where a shell escape comes in very handy. You can escape to a command shell with CONTROL-C, or run a single shell command by putting an exclamation point in front of it. The "ifconfig -a" command will tell you which network card is hooked up to the network. (We discuss ifconfig at some length in

Chapter 8 and Chapter 9, but for right now just run the command as a single shell command. Network interfaces that are not plugged in or that have failed for some other reason will have a "media" line that says "no carrier," while cards that have plugged in and are talking to the network will have a "media" line that says how they are connected.

```
!ifconfig -a
loo: flags=8008<LOOPBACK,MULTICAST> mtu 33224
fxp0: flags=8843<UP,BROADCAST,RUNNING,SIMPLEX,MULTICAST> mtu 1500
        address: 00:02:b3:63:e4:1d
        media: Ethernet autoselect (100baseTX full-duplex)
        status: active ❶
fxp1: flags=8802<BROADCAST,SIMPLEX,MULTICAST> mtu 1500
        address: 00:02:b3:63:e3:ec
        media: Ethernet autoselect (none)
        status: no carrier ❷
```

The ❶fxp0 card is connected to the network at 100 megabits full duplex and is active, while the ❷fxp1 card is not connected and hence has "no carrier." You want to configure the fxp0 card, so enter "fxp0."

```
IP address for fxp0 (or 'dhcp')? 192.168.1.250
```

We have an IP address for this system, but entering "dhcp" will make the system get IP address and domain information from the DHCP server.

```
Symbolic (host) name? [openbsdtest]
```

We want to use the same host name, so hit ENTER here.

```
Netmask? [255.255.255.0]
```

If you have a netmask other than 255.255.255.0, enter it here. Otherwise, hit ENTER.

```
The default media for fxp0 is
        media: Ethernet autoselect (100baseTX full-duplex)
Do you want to change the default media? [n]
```

Media options tell a network card how to connect to the network. In this case, the card seems to have picked up the network connection automatically. If you have an older network card, this may not work so seamlessly; you may need to tell your card to use the 10baseT connector instead of the BNC attachment, for example, or to use full-duplex instead of half-duplex. You'll have to look at the OpenBSD manual page for your card. You might think this would be difficult to do before you have OpenBSD installed, but don't forget that the manual pages are available on the OpenBSD website.

You can repeat the process for the other network card or just enter "done" to tell the installer you have finished configuring network cards. The installer will then ask you for the default route on your network and the IP address of your primary nameserver.

```
Enter IP address of default route: [none] 192.168.1.1
Enter IP address of primary nameserver: [none] 192.168.1.5
Would you like to use the nameserver now? [y]
```

The next question might seem curious — if you have your network configured, why would you need to do more configuration?

```
Do you want to do more, manual, network configuration? [n] y
```

If you're an experienced network administrator, you've probably seen networks where your could only connect to the Internet if you had a particular secondary route set, or where multiple DNS servers were required. This also gives anyone who wants to install over a network an opportunity to test their network configuration. If you have a problem with network installs, this will make your life simpler.

Testing Network Connectivity

If you take the option to do additional network configuration, you'll be dropped at a command prompt with a small selection of UNIX tools to work with. Even a simple test, such as "ping," will confirm your system is talking to the network. Try to ping the host you plan to install OpenBSD from or your default gateway. While not all the standard UNIX commands are available on the install disk, quite a few basic tools are.

```
Type 'exit' to return to install.
# ping 192.168.1.1
PING 192.168.1.1 (192.168.1.1): 56 data bytes
64 bytes from 192.168.1.1: icmp_seq=0 ttl=64 time=0.366 ms
64 bytes from 192.168.1.1: icmp_seq=1 ttl=64 time=0.171 ms
^C--- 192.168.1.1 ping statistics ---
2 packets transmitted, 2 packets received, 0% packet loss
round-trip min/avg/max/std-dev = 0.171/0.268/0.366/0.098 ms
```

This indicates that the system can ping the default gateway, 192.168.1.1. Hit CONTROL-C to interrupt the ping. If, on the other hand, you issue the command and see nothing for several seconds, you have a connectivity problem.

```
# ping 192.168.1.1
PING 192.168.1.1 (192.168.1.1): 56 data bytes
--- 192.168.1.1 ping statistics ---
3 packets transmitted, 0 packets received, 100% packet loss
#
```

Again, hit CONTROL-C to interrupt the test.

In this case, confirm your IP address and default gateway are correct. Do you have a link light? Do basic network troubleshooting to identify the problem, and perhaps carefully inspect the output of the ifconfig command to try to identify any problems.

Once you know you're on the network, return to the installer by typing "exit".

```
# exit
```

Root Password

The installer will now ask you for your root password. Your root password should be several characters long and include a mix of upper and lower case alphanumeric characters and symbols.

```
Password for root account (will not echo):
Password (again):
```

Be sure you remember the root password! While it can be recovered by booting into single-user mode, you don't really want to go through that hassle to cover your own mistakes.

Installation Media

Now that you have a network connection and a disk to put files on, you can tell the system where to install from.

```
You will now specify the location and names of the install sets you want to
load. You will be able to repeat this step until all of your sets have been
successfully loaded. If you are not sure what sets to install, refer to the
installation notes for details on the contents of each.

Sets can be located on a (m)ounted filesystem; a (c)drom, (d)isk or (t)ape
device; or a (f)tp, (n)fs or (h)ttp server.
Where are the install sets you want to use? (m, c, f, etc.) f
```

In this chapter, we will discuss installations over the network (FTP and HTTP), and installations from CD-ROM. The "mounted filesystem" and "disk" installs are more commonly used in a multiple-boot installation, so we'll cover them in the next chapter. (And if you know how to prepare an OpenBSD installation tape, you probably don't need this tutorial!)

CD-ROM Installs

If you're installing from CD-ROM, you probably booted off of it. If you had to boot off a floppy disk, be certain that your CD-ROM is in the computer before proceeding! If you enter "c" to choose CD-ROM media, you'll see the following message:

```
The following CD-ROM devices are installed on your system.
Please make sure the CD is in the CD-ROM drive and select
the device containing the CD with the installation sets:

cd0❶

Which CD-ROM contains the installation media? [cd0] ❷

Enter the directory relative to the mount point that contains
the file: [3.2/i386] ❸
```

You almost certainly have only ❶one CD-ROM drive installed. If you have multiple CD-ROM drives, they will be named cd0, cd1, cd2, and so on. You may have to look at the system's boot-time messages to determine which drive is which. Enter the name of your CD-ROM drive in the ❷appropriate space. The installer knows which on the CD-ROM the architecture's distribution directory can be found, but if this is a custom CD-ROM not created by the OpenBSD team you may need to ❸enter a custom path.

That's it! You're now ready to go.

Network Installs

On any sort of network install, from any source, the installer will ask you several basic questions:

- What server is the installation media found on?
- Where on this server is the installation media?
- What are my logon and password to access this resource?

You'll want to have these answers available before you start. The FTP and HTTP install processes are almost identical, so we're only going to cover FTP. In most cases the questions are exactly the same, except for the scripts saying "HTTP" instead of "FTP." If you have a choice, use FTP. (FTP is a more reliable protocol for transferring large amounts of data than HTTP.)

```
HTTP/FTP proxy URL? (e.g. 'http://proxy:8080', or 'none') [none]
```

If you are behind a FTP or HTTP proxy server, you can enter the URL here. If you aren't, just hit ENTER.

```
Do you want a list of potential ftp servers? [y]
```

The installer can fetch a list of mirror sites for the release you are installing. If you already know which OpenBSD mirror site you are going to use, you will have an opportunity later to enter it directly. Otherwise, you should probably take a look at the list of servers.

```
❶1  ❷ftp://ftp.openbsd.org/pub/OpenBSD        ❸Alberta, Canada
    2   ftp://ftp.openbsd.org.ar/pub/OpenBSD      Buenos Aires, Argentina
    3   ftp://mirror.aarnet.edu.au/pub/OpenBSD    Canberra, Australia
...
```

Each line is an official OpenBSD mirror for this release and includes an ❶index number, a ❷URL, and a ❸physical location. If you're not certain which mirror is closest on the network, choose a mirror that is physically close.[1] Remember the index number for your closest mirror. In my case, this looks best.

```
66  ftp://ftp3.usa.openbsd.org/pub/OpenBSD       Boulder, CO, USA
```

At the end of the server list, the installer asks you which mirror to use. If you had previously chosen a particular mirror or have a local FTP server you're using, you could enter that host name here. Otherwise, just enter the server number.

```
Server IP address, hostname, or list#? [] 66
Using   ftp://ftp3.usa.openbsd.org/pub/OpenBSD
Does the server support passive mode ftp? [y]
```

Passive mode FTP is a more modern version of the FTP protocol, designed to cooperate with packet-filtering firewalls. Some very old FTP servers do not support passive mode FTP properly, however. Almost all public OpenBSD mirrors support passive mode FTP; if you have problems getting the software from a particular server, however, you might try setting this to "no."

```
Server directory? [pub/OpenBSD/3.2/i386] pub/OpenBSD/3.2/i386
```

If you entered a number from the FTP server list, the installer remembers which directory of the FTP server the software can be found in. Otherwise, enter the full path to the architecture's release directory here.

```
Login? [anonymous]
```

OpenBSD mirrors generally allow anonymous access. If you are installing from a local mirror, you might need to enter a username and password here.

---

[1] In an ideal world, before starting you would have identified your closest mirror with ping(8) and traceroute(8). But I'm not about to walk you through these commands for every operating system that you might have!

Distribution Sets

Now that you know where you are installing from, you can choose what to install. The installer will present a list of all the distribution sets available in this version of OpenBSD.

```
The following sets are available. Enter a filename, 'all' to select
all the sets, or 'done'. You may de-select a set by prepending a '-'
to its name.

        [X] base32.tgz
        [X] etc32.tgz
        [X] misc32.tgz
        [X] comp32.tgz
        [X] man32.tgz
        [X] game32.tgz
        [ ] xbase32.tgz
        [ ] xshare32.tgz
        [ ] xfont32.tgz
        [ ] xserv32.tgz
        [X] bsd

File Name? (or 'done') [xbase32.tgz] all
```

The defaults shown are a reasonable choice for a server without the X Window System. If you're satisfied with these choices, you can just enter "done". To install a complete set of OpenBSD, including X, enter the name "all." If you want something in between, such as adding one distribution set to the list, type its name.

```
File Name? (or 'done') [xbase32.tgz] xshare32.tgz
```

To remove a distribution set, enter its name with a leading -.

```
File Name? (or 'done') [xbase32.tgz] -man32.tgz
```

After each modification, the installer will present you with an updated lists of distribution sets it will install. When you're happy with the list, type "done" and ENTER. You'll get a final chance to change your mind.

```
Ready to install sets? [y]
```

Hit ENTER, and the installer will begin writing OpenBSD from the installation media onto your hard drive. You'll see a message much like this for each distribution set you chose to install.

```
Getting etc32.tgz ...
54% |**************************               |   793 KB    00:04 ETA
```

This will go very quickly if you're installing from CD-ROM, and at network speeds otherwise.

Once the distribution sets you chose are installed, you'll have an opportunity to change your mind and add more distribution sets. This can be useful if a network site you installed from did not have all the sets you needed or if network issues prevented you from downloading them.

```
Extract more sets? [n]
```

Custom Installation Sets and Scripts

If you have downloaded the installation sets to a local FTP server or have built some other local installation media, the OpenBSD installer allows you to add your own custom files or scripts to the install process. This is very useful if you have a "standard build" for your network and want to replicate one set of changes to every freshly installed machine.

The installation script looks for a set called "siteXX.tgz" in the same directory as the other distribution sets. Replace the "XX" with the release name — for example, a custom site file for OpenBSD 3.3 would be called "site33.tgz." This file is a standard gzipped tar file rooted in /. This file is extracted last, using the standard xvpf options, allowing the administrator to add custom files or packages (see Chapter 13) to every system installed with that set.

As a final step in the install process, the installer will look for a shell script called /install.site. If such a script is found, it is run as the last stage of the install process. You can use this to remove unwanted programs, install other software or any other actions desired. The easiest way to get /install.site onto your new system is to include it in siteXX.tgz.

Final Installation Steps

Hang on, you're almost there! Now that you have the files on your disk, you just need to answer a few last questions.

```
Do you expect to run the X Window System? [y]
```

Answering "y" enables the kernel settings for running an X server locally. If you plan to have the GUI running on this system, answer "y." If you are using this machine without a GUI, answer "n". You can use X remotely on this system without a GUI, you simply cannot run the local XFree86 server.

```
Saving configuration files......done.
Generating initial host.random file ......done.
What timezone are you in? ('?' for list) [US/Pacific]
```

The installer will easily set your initial time zone for you. If you don't know your correct time zone, enter a question mark. The installer will list the time zones it knows of and allow you to choose one. OpenBSD expects the BIOS clock to be set in UCT.

After choosing your time zone, you will see a flurry of messages as the install rebuilds device nodes, installs bootblocks, and in general cleans up after itself. Finally, you will see the completion message.

```
CONGRATULATIONS! Your OpenBSD install has been successfully completed!
To boot the new system, enter halt at the command prompt. Once the
system has halted, reset the machine and boot from the disk.
# halt
```

Enter the word "halt," and the system will shut itself down. Do not just power off the computer! You want to shut the system down gracefully.

```
syncing disks... done

The operating system has halted.
Please press any key to reboot.
```

One press of the ANY key, and your system will reboot into OpenBSD!

4

MULTIBOOT INSTALLATION

*Blowfish and penguin
arguing over fridge space
roommates most vexing*

 As hard drives grow larger and larger, it's becoming more and more common to have multiple operating systems on a single disk. You can do this fairly simply with OpenBSD, if you follow a few basic guidelines. While you wouldn't do this on a network server, you might on your desktop or laptop, especially when migrating between operating systems. Sharing a disk between operating has two distinct problems. First, you have to divide the disk between the operating systems. Second, you must have a method to tell the computer which operating system to boot. We'll deal with both of these.

We're going to discuss the techniques, problems, and issues when sharing a hard drive between OpenBSD and any of four other popular operating systems: Windows XP Professional, Windows 98, Linux, and FreeBSD. The concepts are useful for other operating systems, however. If you want to multiboot, say, BeOS or NetBSD on your OpenBSD system, you can use the information given here as a guideline and probably do it without too much trouble.

Dual-Boot Install Overview

Careful planning is essential when installing two operating systems on a single hard drive. Each operating system has restrictions on where it may lie on the disk, and you must satisfy those restrictions for every OS you install. For example, Windows 98 expects to be the first operating system on the disk, but OpenBSD's root partition expects to be within the first 8GB. This can make life difficult. Consider the restrictions on each operating system, and figure out a method you can meet them while still getting both operating systems on one drive. Write down your partitioning needs before starting an install.

You then need to create MBR partitions for each operating system, using the appropriate tool for that OS. Once you know where these MBR partitions belong, you can start to install your operating systems. Operating systems should be installed in the order that they go on disk — if Windows XP is the first operating system on your disk, install that first. This allows you to use each operating system's native tools to create the MBR partition for that operating system. Not all operating systems work well within MBR partitions created by another operating system: For example, the Windows XP installer will see partitions created by OpenBSD, but may choke when attempting to put a file system on them.

Once you have all of your operating systems on the disk, install a boot manager to control the OS you want to start at boot time.

NOTE   *Each additional operating system adds complexity to the installation and disk partitioning process. Be prepared to reinstall the various operating systems a few times until you have everything set up as you like. Do not load any data on your computer until you have every operating system installed and every partition formatted the way you want!*

MBR Partitions

In Chapter 3 we discussed OpenBSD partitions and briefly mentioned MBR partitions. You didn't need to worry about MBR partitions unless you wanted to have multiple operating systems on one computer. The Master Boot Record includes some basic disk partitioning information, marking the locations of up to four partitions.

These partitions are used for different purposes in different operating systems. Windows-based operating systems use these as "logical drives." If you're old enough, you'll remember when a Windows 95 computer could only have a 2GB C: drive, and if you had a larger disk you needed to split it up into logical drives. At one point I had Windows C:, D:, E:, and F: drives on one 8GB hard drive!

OpenBSD, Linux, and FreeBSD all like to support more than four partitions on a drive. They have to have their own partitioning scheme within a single MBR partition. For example, when you have a dedicated OpenBSD machine with five partitions (/, swap, /tmp, /var, /usr, and home), these partitions are all subdivisions of a single MBR partition. That MBR partition just happens to fill the whole disk. OpenBSD partitions need to go within a single MBR partition.

Dedicate a single MBR partition to each operating system on a hard drive. (If you need more than four operating systems, you need to invest in a commercial product that will let you do so.)

A Dozen Different fdisks

Every operating system includes tools to manage MBR partitions. Unfortunately, every operating system handles MBR partitions in a slightly different manner. More unfortunately, most of these tools are named "fdisk." Each tool operates differently, and while some of them look similar or have a common heritage they are not guaranteed to be interoperable. The upshot of all this is that you should create the MBR partitions used by an operating system by the operating system's native tools. When you're installing a dual-boot OpenBSD/XP system, use OpenBSD's fdisk(8) to create the MBR partitions only for OpenBSD and use the Windows XP installer to create the partition for Windows XP. Do not use the OpenBSD fdisk tool to create Windows XP partitions, and do not try to create OpenBSD partitions with XP! This might look workable, but minor differences between fdisk implementations might make the partition unusable.

Because this is an OpenBSD book, we'll focus on OpenBSD's fdisk. Check the documentation for the other operating systems you're using for details on their fdisk implementations. The concepts are the same, but many of the details differ.

Dual-Boot Installation Restrictions

Various operating systems have restrictions on how they may be placed on the disk. Here is a brief overview of these restrictions for the operating systems discussed here. Note that this sort of information may change rapidly, especially for the open-source operating systems! Also, if you search the Internet, you will find suggestions for getting around all of these limitations. Most of these suggestions are very complicated and unsupportable, and if I recommended them my email would be flooded by people who couldn't make them work. Others cost money. Feel free to seek out these methods and try them yourself, but you're on your own.

OpenBSD

- The root partition must be completely contained within the first 8GB of disk.
- There can only be one OpenBSD MBR partition per hard disk.

Windows (Any Version)

- Must be the first operating system on the hard drive.

Linux, FreeBSD

- None.

Suggested Combinations

Windows operating systems, both 9x-based and NT-based, must go first on the hard drive. I suggest giving these operating systems a C: drive of 7GB or smaller. (Remember, early versions of Windows only support 2GB drives, so this won't be a problem.) If you put a 500MB OpenBSD root file system directly after your Windows partition, you can easily fit it within the 8GB limit. Subsequent OpenBSD file systems should follow immediately afterward. Because OpenBSD can only use a single MBR partition, you need put all your OpenBSD partitions immediately after that. If you have disk space left you can add a third MBR partition to the hard drive after your OpenBSD install and use this for a Windows D: drive or even install Linux or FreeBSD for a triple-boot system.

When installing OpenBSD with FreeBSD or Linux, I recommend putting OpenBSD first on the hard drive and installing the other operating systems further out on the disk.

Windows NT/2000/XP Installs

When you install Windows NT–based operating system, the installer will ask you how much disk space to use on your drive. (This question is the Windows fdisk and disklabel tool, all in one.) Tell it 7GB or less, and Windows will create an appropriate MBR partition for itself.

If you wish to access your Windows files when running OpenBSD, format this Windows file system as FAT32. OpenBSD cannot read NTFS partitions. As you find yourself growing more comfortable with OpenBSD, you will probably find yourself booting into Windows less and less frequently, and being able to access that disk space is nice. I know people who started off with dual-boot systems, but finally converted their Windows partitions into MP3 storage without having to reinstall.

Do not attempt to lay out your OpenBSD partition, or subsequent Windows partitions, with the Windows installer! You will quite possibly confuse OpenBSD, Windows, or both. Similarly, do not attempt to create Windows NT partitions (even FAT32 ones) with the OpenBSD installer. Once you have both Windows and OpenBSD installed, you can go in and create additional Windows logical drives.

Windows 9x installs

While early editions of Windows 95 only handled 2GB partitions, most later versions handle large hard drives just fine and automatically take over all the disk space they can get. Most versions do not ask you how much they should get, as it's obvious that anyone who is running Windows wants to dedicate their whole machine to it, right? You must use a tool such as fips.exe to resize your hard drive.

OpenBSD includes fips.exe in the "tools" directory under the release directory. The documentation included with fips.exe is fairly good, and Windows 9*x* is becoming increasingly rare among the people likely to be installing dual-boot systems, so we aren't going to go into any detail on how to make it work. Just read the instructions and follow them precicely.

Remember, make your Windows 9*x* partition no larger than 7.5GB; you want to have enough room to get an OpenBSD root partition on your system!

Linux/FreeBSD Installs

If you are sharing a hard drive between OpenBSD and Linux, install OpenBSD first. Both Linux and FreeBSD can recognize OpenBSD partitions and will easily work around them.

Linux can read OpenBSD file systems, if you have a Linux kernel that supports BSD disklabels. Similarly, OpenBSD can read EXT2FS file systems. OpenBSD also recognizes file systems from FreeBSD 4 or earlier, and FreeBSD recognizes OpenBSD file systems. If you want to dual-boot FreeBSD 5 or later with OpenBSD, you need to create your FreeBSD partitions as UFS1. OpenBSD does not support FreeBSD's UFS2. In any of these combinations, you may have to edit the OpenBSD, Linux, or FreeBSD disklabels to include the sector information for the other operating system partitions to actually be able to mount those partitions, however.

Hard Disk Geometry

"Rectangular, with rounded corners."

Sorry, that's not the geometry we mean. *Disk geometry* generally refers to the layout of the disks internally. If you open the case of a hard drive you'll find a stack of round disks, commonly called *platters*. They're covered with a layer of magnetic material that extends from the middle of the disk to the outer edge. When the disk drive is on, these disks spin at thousands of revolutions per minute (rpm). (This is the rpm count you'll see on the box and in advertising, and has a great deal to do with the performance of an individual disk.)

You will also see a *head* on each side of each platter. The head moves between the center of the disk and the edge so it can read data from the hard drive beneath it. A fairly typical new hard drive has 16 heads. That's enough for 8 platters, with a head on each side. So, we can read from 16 different locations on the platters simultaneously, so long as the data you want happens to be on different sides of different platters. Every head has a unique number, starting with 0.

Each platter has a number of circular tracks, or *tracks*, arranged much like the growth rings in a tree. These tracks hold data as a string of 0s and 1s. A head moves over a particular track at a certain distance from the center of the disk and reads this data as the platter spins by beneath it. When you request data from a different track, the head shifts its position and lets that track rotate past beneath it.

If you stack the particular tracks from all the platters on top of one another, you have a *cylinder*. For example, the innermost track of each platter forms one cylinder, numbered 0. The next-innermost forms cylinder 1. The 3,022nd track of each platter forms cylinder number 3021. Many operating systems expect to find that MBR partitions encompass complete cylinders and get quite upset if they don't.

Each track is broken up into segments, called *sectors*, which can each hold 512 bytes of data. Each sector within a track has a unique number, starting with 1. What's more, every sector on a hard drive has a unique number. If a particular hard drive has 39,179,952 sectors, you can expect to find each with a number 0 through 39,179,951. Many tools expect to address hard disks by sector numbers. When part of a disk goes bad, smart disks mark the affected sectors and don't use them.

So, sectors combine into tracks, which are arranged in rings on each platter. Tracks can be stacked into cylinders, and they all combine to make up the hard drive. This all seems simple enough, and it would be, if you could reliably use this information.

Over the years, various limitations have been hit in both hard disk and operating system design. We touched upon the 504MB and 8GB limits in Chapter 2. These limits could only be avoided by tricking the system BIOS and/or operating system. If the most popular operating system can only accept 63 sectors per track, but the hard drives your company manufactures have 126 sectors per track, you have a problem — unless, of course, you teach your hard drive to lie. If you claim you have half as many sectors per track, but you have twice as many platters, you can make the problem go away. Everything still adds up to the same number of sectors, after all, and all the tools can still find a unique sector-by-sector number. By the time hard drive information reaches the operating system, it has quite possibly been through one or more of these translations.

When you have only one operating system on a hard drive, this works fine. If your operating system receives or performs a slightly different translation on the disk, however, the translated geometry will not precisely match. The individual sector numbers will still match, but cylinder boundaries may not be the same within the translated geometry. Because many operating systems expect their MBR partitions to begin and end on a cylinder boundary, this is a problem. This is why we use only an operating system's native tools to create MBR partitions for that OS.

Now that you understand the hardware and the translations it undergoes, let's look at how to manage these partitions.

Using fdisk During an Install

For this example, I'm dividing a 20GB IDE hard drive between Windows XP and OpenBSD. The first 7GB of the hard drive hold a standard install of Windows XP, on a FAT32 file system. I want to put an 8GB OpenBSD install immediately after that. Prepare your hardware as you normally would, and boot off your OpenBSD installation disk. The install process is identical up until the point you see the disk usage menu.

```
Available disks are: sd0 sd1 wd0.
Which one is the root disk? (or done) [done] wd0
Do you want to use *all* of wd0 for OpenBSD? [no]
```

We don't want to use the whole hard drive for OpenBSD, so take the default. This brings up a whole new tool, OpenBSD's interactive fdisk(8).

Reading MBR Partitions

After a few instructions, the installer will fire up fdisk(8) and automatically print out your partitioning from the Master Boot Record. The top of fdisk's output contains some basic disk geometry information.

```
Disk: wd0    geometry: ❶2438/❷255/❸63 [❹39166470 Sectors]
```

This line describes what fdisk(8) believes is the disk geometry in the number of cylinders, heads, and sectors a disk has. According to fdisk(8), this disk has ❶2438 cylinders (numbered 0 through 2,437), ❷255 heads (numbered 0 through 254), and ❸63 sectors per cylinder. If you compare this information to what the physical label on the hard drive says, it almost certainly won't match. That's all right — it's just been translated. One interesting thing to note is that fdisk(8) reports that this hard drive has the same ❹total number of sectors as every other tool reports, however.

A little beneath that, you get a table describing the MBR partitions themselves.

```
       Starting     Ending    LBA Info:
#: id  C  H  S -  C  H  S [   start:   size  ]
-----------------------------------------------------------------------
*❶0: ❷0B ❸0 ❹1 ❺1 - ❻891❼254❽63 [    63:  14329917 ]❾Win95 FAT-32
  1: 00  0  0 0 -  0  0 0 [     0:        0 ] unused
  2: 00  0  0 0 -  0  0 0 [     0:        0 ] unused
  3: 00  0  0 0 -  0  0 0 [     0:        0 ] unused
```

This isn't nearly as confusing as it looks at first glance. The first column gives the ❶MBR partition number, between 0 and 3. We then see the ❷Partition ID. This is a unique hex number used to identify the type of file system on the partition. Partition ID 0x0B represents FAT32.

fdisk then prints the ❸cylinder, ❹head, and ❺sector where this partition begins. The first partition on this disk begins on cylinder 0, head 1, sector 1 — the beginning of the disk.[1]

The next three columns show the cylinder, head, and sector where this partition ends. Compare these numbers to the total number of cylinders, heads, and sectors in the drive. This disk has 2,438 cylinders, of which we are using ❻892. Within cylinder number 891, we are using up through ❼head 254 (all of the heads) and ❽sector 63 (all of the sectors). This Windows partition completely fills the first 2,438 cylinders. We say that such a partition ends on a cylinder boundary. All of your partitions should begin and end on a cylinder boundary.

At the end of the line, we have the ❾partition type in clear English. We could get this information by looking up partition ID 0x0B in a table, but it's certainly convenient to print it here.

---

[1] Cylinder 0, head 0, sector 1 is the Master Boot Record itself.

Finally, fdisk presents a command prompt.

```
fdisk: 1>
```

We want to create a new MBR partition, immediately following the existing FAT32 partition.

Creating MBR Partitions

Actually entering the values for a new MBR is easy enough, once you know which keys to press. And OpenBSD's online help (available by entering a question mark) is clear enough on telling you which keys to press. Figuring out which numbers you want to enter is the hard part! To create a new partition, we have to tell fdisk(8) where the partition starts, where it ends, and what sort of partition it is. Let's tackle the easy one first: the partition type.

OpenBSD Partition Type

All OpenBSD partitions have a partition ID of A6. You can install OpenBSD on partitions of other partition IDs, but you might have some problems with doing that and have to hack around some assumptions in the operating system. Don't do it.

Partition Beginning

We know that the previous partition ends at the end of cylinder number 891. Our new partition should begin at the beginning of cylinder 892. This would be head 0, sector 1, cylinder 892.

Partition Ending

Our new partition should end on a cylinder boundary. This means that it will end on some cylinder, head 254, sector 63. But which cylinder?

Here, you have to resort to some basic math. No, stop screaming; it isn't that bad: Just get out your calculator. This hard drive has 2,591 cylinders and can hold about 20GB, or 20,000MB. Each cylinder holds roughly the same amount of data. 20,000MB divided by 2591 cylinders equals a little over 7.719MB/cylinder. Dividing the desired partition size in megabytes by the actual MB/cylinder ratio shows that we need 1,036 cylinders for OpenBSD. The first partition goes through partition 891. 891 + 1036 = 1,927, so our OpenBSD partition will end on cylinder 1,927.

Editing a MBR Partition

Armed with this information, we can create a new OpenBSD partition. Enter "edit" and the number of the partition you want to edit.

```
fdisk: 1>e 1
Partition id ('0' to disable) [0 - FF]: [0] (? for help) A6❶
Do you wish to edit in CHS mode? [n] y❷
```

First enter the ❶partition type, A6 for OpenBSD. If you're curious, you can enter a question mark and see a list of the myriad of partition types OpenBSD's fdisk(8) recognizes. fdisk(8) will then ask you if you want to edit the MBR partition table in CHS (cylinder/head/sector) mode. If you don't want to use CHS, you'll have to figure out which sector your first cylinder starts on and your last cylinder ends on. You don't want to do that. Enter "y" ❷.

You'll then be prompted for the starting and ending cylinder information.

```
BIOS Starting cylinder [0 - 2437]: [0] 892
BIOS Starting head [0 - 254]: [0] 0
BIOS Starting sector [1 - 63]: [0] 1
BIOS Ending cylinder [0 - 2437]: [0] 1927
BIOS Ending head [0 - 254]: [0] 254
BIOS Ending sector [1 - 63]: [0] 63
fdisk:*1>
```

Note that the fdisk prompt has changed and now displays an asterisk. This means that you have changed the MBR partition and that your changes have not yet been saved to the disk. You could type "exit" now, and fdisk would quit without saving your changes. That wouldn't help us install OpenBSD, but you could do that if you made an error and didn't know how to recover.

Once you have created an OpenBSD partition, go back and view the MBR partition table with the "print" command.

```
fdisk:*1> print
Disk: wd0     geometry: 2438/255/63 [39166470 Sectors]
Offset: 0    Signature: 0xAA55
     Starting      Ending     LBA Info:
 #: id C  H  S -  C  H  S [    start:    size  ]
-------------------------------------------------------------------
*0: 0B 0  1  1 - 891 254 63 [      63:  14329917 ] Win95 FAT-32
 1: A6 892 0 1 - 1927 254 63 [ 14329980:  16643340 ] OpenBSD
 2: 00 0  0  0 -  0  0  0 [      0:        0 ] unused
 3: 00 0  0  0 -  0  0  0 [      0:        0 ] unused
fdisk:*1>
```

The new OpenBSD partition shows up! Double-check your work, and make sure this is what you want the system partitioning to look like.

Set Active Partition

One of your partitions needs to be marked "active," meaning that when the system boots the BIOS will hand control of the system over to the operating system on that partition. (We'll use boot loaders to get around this later, but for now you need to use it.) Set your OpenBSD partition to be active during the install, so you can boot into OpenBSD after the install and make sure you actually have a working system before proceeding. Use the fdisk command "flag" and a partition number to mark a partition as active.

```
fdisk: 1> flag 1
Partition 1 marked active.
fdisk: *1>
```

If your OpenBSD partition is not partition 1, enter the proper partition number.

Completing fdisk

Once you are satisfied with your fdisk configuration, enter "quit" to leave fdisk(8) and write your changes to the MBR.

```
> quit
Writing current MBR to disk.
...
```

fdisk will print out your MBR partition information one last time, and then the install program proceeds to the disklabel section.

Other fdisk Options

fdisk has many other options, some of which are not particularly useful while installing. Here are some of the fdisk options you might find useful at this time. For a complete list of possibilities, see fdisk(8).

Starting Over

If you find that you've completely ruined the MBR partition table and you just want to start over, the "reinit" command removes all the MBR partitions that currently exist. It then creates a single OpenBSD partition that spans the whole drive, as partition ID 3. This will, of course, obliterate any other operating system on your hard drive.

Disable a Partition

If you have an MBR partition configured and you don't want to use it, you need to either change it to a valid configuration or disable it. In many cases, disabling the partition is the easiest thing to do. You'll frequently encounter this when you're reinstalling every operating system on a computer. For example, when installing various combinations of OpenBSD and Windows late one night when the caffeine had just run out, I found myself with the following ludicrous MBR partition table.

```
#: id  C  H S -  C  H S [    start:    size ]
-------------------------------------------------------------------------
0: 0C ❶0  0 1 - 776 239 63 [     0:  11748240 ] Win95 FAT32L
1: A6 777  0 1 - 1813 239 63 [ 11748240:  15679440 ] OpenBSD
2: 0C 1814  0 1 -❸2590 239 63 [ 27427680:  11748240 ] Win95 FAT32L
*3: A6 ❷0  1 1 - ❹2590 239 63 [     63:  39175857 ] OpenBSD
```

Look closely at the ❶start cylinder for MBR partition 0, and compare that to the ❷start partition for MBR partition 3. They're identical. Similarly, the ❸ending cylinder for MBR partition ID 2 and ❹MBR partition ID 3 are identical. Partition 3 contains partitions 1 and 3 — and, if you look closely, partition 1 as well. In this case, there's no room for partition 3, and it would be best to just disable it so it doesn't interfere with anything. Edit the partition, and set the partition ID to 0 to disable it.

```
fdisk:*1> edit 3
     Starting     Ending     LBA Info:
 #: id  C  H S -  C   H  S [   start:    size  ]
--------------------------------------------------------------------------
*3: A6  0  1 1 - 2590 239 63 [     63: 39175857 ] OpenBSD
Partition id ('0' to disable) [0 - FF]: [A6] (? for help) 0
Partition 3 is disabled.
fdisk:*1>
```

If you go back and look at the partition table, all the entries within partition 3 are now set to 0.

Disklabel on Multiboot Systems

When you are only using part of a hard drive for OpenBSD, you need to handle your OpenBSD partitions a little differently. Before you start to divide up your new MBR partition, take a look at the disklabel you're starting with.

```
> p
...
total sectors: 39179952❶
free sectors: 16643340❷
rpm: 3600

16 partitions:
#     size offset fstype [fsize bsize  cpg]
❸ a: 16643340 14329980  unused    0   0
❹ c: 39179952       0   unused    0   0
❺ i: 14329917      63    MSDOS
```

Normally, on an empty disk, you'll see that the total number of sectors equals the free sectors. You haven't installed any OpenBSD partitions on this disk, but the ❶total sectors and ❷free sectors are most certainly not equal. disklabel(8) has found the FAT32 MBR partition and adjusted the free space appropriately. Later on, you'll also see the ❹"c" partition that represents the whole disk is just what you would expect in a dedicated OpenBSD system.

There's also an ❺"i" partition with a file system type of MSDOS. Although this appears at the bottom of the disklabel, it has an offset of 63, so it's at the beginning of the disk. This is your Windows installation. You might want to make a note of the disklabel partition letter, as it will come in useful when you want to access that disk from OpenBSD, or you can read the disklabel later with disklabel(8). (See Chapter 18 for details.)

You also automatically get an ❸"a" partition, of the same size as the free space available on the system. The "a" partition is normally the root partition, but it's assigned a size that fills the entire MBR partition you've set aside for Open-BSD! Remember, your root partition must fit entirely within the first 8GB of disk, so you're going to need to re-create this partition with a proper size.

NOTE   *A bit of addition will show that the existing partitions do not use up all the space available on this disk. We still don't have an MBR partition at the end of this disk for the second chunk of Windows space. After completing the OpenBSD install, we'll boot into Windows XP and use the Disk Manager MMC snap-in to partition and format the unpartitioned space.*

So, start by deleting the "a" partition created by fdisk, and then add a new "a" partition.

```
> d a
> a a
offset: [14329980] ❶
size: [16643340] ❷ 500M
Rounding to nearest cylinder: 1023876
FS type: [4.2BSD]
mount point: [none] /
>
```

Here, we see that disklabel understands the ❶offset from the Windows partition, and it knows how many ❷sectors are available in the OpenBSD partition. Other than the unusual offset, this looks exactly like creating a root partition in a dedicated OpenBSD system.

The rest of the install process is absolutely identical to the standard Open-BSD install. Once you're finished, however, you'll need to find a way to tell your computer which operating system to boot. That's the job of a boot manager, as we'll see shortly.

Installing from a Foreign File System Partition

OpenBSD can be installed from files on a partition dedicated to another operating system. You could install Windows XP in the first 7GB of your hard drive, download the distribution directory (or desired files thereof) into a directory on your Windows install, and use that as an installation source. Here, we're going to install OpenBSD from files downloaded on a Windows NT 4.0 install and stored in the directory c: obsd.

During the installation dialog, you will see the familiar installation set selection question:

```
Sets can be located on a (m)ounted filesystem; a (c)drom, ❶(d)isk or (t)ape
device; or a (f)tp, (n)fs or (h)ttp server.

Where are the install sets you want to use? (m, c, f, etc.) d
```

The ❶disk option allows you to install from an existing disk. Choose it, and you'll
see the following menu:

```
Available disks are: sd0 sd1 wd0.
Which one contains the install sets? (or done) [sd0]
```

That installer sure likes to assume drive sd0, doesn't it? My Windows install is on
drive wd0, so enter that. You'll be shown a complete list of the partitions on this
drive.

```
The following partitions have been found on wd0:

 a: 1024002 8193150   4.2BSD    1024 8192  16  # (Cyl. 8128*- 9143)
 b: 1208592 9217152      swap            # (Cyl. 9144 - 10342)
 c: 39179952      0 unused      0   0    # (Cyl.  0 - 38868)
 d: 12582864 10425744  4.2BSD   1024 8192  16  # (Cyl. 10343 - 22825)
 e: 2097648 23008608   4.2BSD   1024 8192  16  # (Cyl. 22826 - 24906)
 f: 14060214 25106256  4.2BSD   1024 8192  16  # (Cyl. 24907 - 38855*)
 i: 8193087      63     MSDOS ❶            # (Cyl.  0*- 8128*)

Partition? [a]
```

The only annoying thing here is that you have already created OpenBSD partitions by this point, and you'll have to sort through them all. Still, the ❶MSDOS
file system is easy to find amidst all this. It's on partition "i," so enter that.
    As OpenBSD cannot identify all sorts of file systems automatically, you will
have to choose the file system type on that partition. The "default" should work
for most cases, but you may have to explicitly enter "msdos" if you have a problem. You can easily install from MSDOS, Linux, and UFS partitions with the
installer.

```
The following filesystem types are supported:
default     (deduced from the disklabel)
ffs
msdos
Which filesystem type? [default]
```

The installer will then ask you which directory you placed the installation sets on.

```
Enter the pathname where the sets are stored (or '?') /obsd
```

At this point, the installer will pick up the installation sets, and you can proceed
normally.

Boot Managers

A *boot manager* is a program that controls which operating system boots on a computer. Previously, we used an active partition to tell the BIOS the partition to hand control to. A boot manager allows you to choose on the fly the partition you want to use. A computer with only one operating system on it does not need a boot manager, but if you've installed more than one OS you'll need one.

We're going to discuss GAG, the Graphical Boot Manager. GAG really is an acronym for Graphical Boot Manager — in Spanish, the author's native language. The program is astonishingly simple to manage and quite pretty to look at, and it works perfectly to boot any number of operating systems, including OpenBSD.

If you have a preferred boot manager that you are experienced with, use it! Linux and FreeBSD both include excellent boot managers, and the Windows NT boot manager can be used to handle OpenBSD partitions with a bit of research. I generally find that GAG is the simplest way to go for dual-boot OpenBSD/Windows systems, however.

Finding GAG

GAG has a home page, at http://www.rastersoft.com/gageng.htm. You can find documentation here, as well as a variety of links to booting resources. Just download the zip file and uncompress it. You'll find a copy of the GAG license (GPL), a directory containing the GAG source code, a disk image, and rawrite.exe, the Windows program to burn a disk image to floppy.

The GAG disk image, disk.dsk, is a boot floppy image, much like the OpenBSD install disk. You can copy this image to a disk with any of the tools you used to create the boot floppy in Chapter 2. You should have your OpenBSD system up and running, so here's how to do it in OpenBSD.

```
# dd if=disk.dsk of=/dev/fd0c
```

Once you have the bootable floppy, boot from it. It should very quickly present you with a text-based menu system. You can find extensive documentation in the instructions available through this menu. Check out the instructions, and then hit the "install GAG" option ("4" in GAG 4.1). You'll have a chance to choose your keyboard layout, and your language, then GAG will bring up a nice graphic menu with two options:

```
Boot from Floppy Disk
Key 1

Set up GAG
Key S
```

You want to tell GAG about your system, so hit "S." This will bring up another text-based menu, with the "command letter" being highlighted in red. Choose "Add an Operating System," and you'll see a list of options much like this.

```
A    Boot from floppy
B    0Bh  MS-Windows FAT32
C    A6h  OpenBSD
```

Hit "B" to tell GAG about your Windows system. It will ask you for a description to show on boot, and offer you a choice of graphic logos to choose from. You can repeat the process for to configure GAG to load OpenBSD as well, and even use the cute little blowfish logo.

When you're done, be certain to tell GAG to save the setup in the hard disk.

The next time you boot, you will get a graphic menu offering you both operating systems on your hard drive.

NOTE *I found that Windows XP complained the first time it booted after installing GAG. The problem goes away on subsequent reboots, so don't worry too much about it.*

You can also configure GAG to load a default operating system and to boot that default after a certain number of seconds, or just about anything you would like.

Congratulations! You now have a full dual-boot system.

5

POST-INSTALL SETUP

It fills the hard drive,
looking quite dumb and clunky.
Thought you were done? Ha!

So you have OpenBSD installed, you've ejected the install floppy, and you've hit a key to reboot the machine and bring up the operating system for the first time. A bare-bones UNIX system is actually pretty boring; while powerful, it doesn't actually *do* much of anything. Here are some of the basic steps you should take after an install to establish a firm platform for later work. Any experienced system administrator will want to jump right into things such as correct the system time zone, set a default gateway, install basic mail aliases, and so on. If you know what these basic things are and just want to get your system up and on your network in a hurry, this is for you.

OpenBSD has a general configuration file that controls which of its integrated programs run and how they function. We'll discuss this system, /etc/rc.conf, in some detail.

Basic Configuration

OpenBSD includes a very nice afterboot(8) manual page that gives much good advice for new systems administrators. Some of that advice gives an overview of material that we'll cover later in this book, while some of it only applies to particular situations or network environments. You should skim afterboot(8) on your version of OpenBSD, as it has lots of pointers to things you might want to set up. Here, we'll cover the steps that should be done on every OpenBSD system.

All of the steps here must be performed as root. We'll discuss creating additional users in Chapter 7 and how to avoid use of the root account whenever possible. That's not necessary yet, however.

Time Zone

All of the time zones OpenBSD supports are in the /usr/share/zoneinfo directory tree. You'll find quite a few time zone names in this directory. You'll also find several subdirectories for various countries or continents, each containing either city names or local time zones. Find the file for the time zone you like or for a city whose time zone you share.

To set the time zone, just create a new symbolic link to the file from /etc/localtime.

```
# ln -fs /usr/share/zoneinfo/America/Detroit /etc/localtime
```

OpenBSD also supports POSIX-style time zones, which have their own rules. Those time zone files are stored in /usr/share/zoneinfo/Etc. Do *not* use POSIX times unless you are absolutely certain you understand them.

Date

Now that you have a time zone, set the correct date. OpenBSD supports programs such as xntpd(8) and ntpdate(8), but does not include them by default. OpenBSD does include rdate(8), if you have a time server accessible from your network. (This may not be an option behind a firewall, of course.) You might have to set the date by hand.

Date(1) can be used to set the system date. Confirm that you know the current year, month, day of the month, and time (in 24-hour format). To give them to date(1), just run them all together in order. In the following example, we set the date to the year 2002, month of August, day 16 of the month, and 1:24 p.m. (13:24).

```
# date 200208161324
Fri Aug 16 13:24:00 EDT 2002
#
```

Fortunately, date(1) spits out the date as it understands it, so you can check your work easily.

If you have access to a NTP server, you can set the time with rdate(8). While rdate(8) is generally used for older time protocols, OpenBSD's rdate(8) will speak to a NTP server if you use the -n flag.

```
# rdate -n timeserver.company.com
```

Set Host Name

You can set the system's host name in /etc/myname. For example, my test system is called openbsdtest.AbsoluteOpenBSD.com.

```
# cat /etc/myname
openbsdtest.AbsoluteOpenBSD.com
#
```

Ethernet Interface Configuration

If you have installed OpenBSD over the network, your Ethernet network card is already set up and working. If you installed from CD-ROM, you probably want to configure any network cards in the system. (If you want to connect to a network via PPP, see Chapter 9.) For a complete list of cards recognized by your installed OpenBSD system, run ifconfig -a.

If you're not familiar with Ethernet, IP addresses, default routes, and so on, you probably want to wait to configure your network until you read Chapters 8 and 9. This section is meant for experienced systems administrators who already know what they want to do, and just need to know which files to touch to do it. For a complete description of the configuration options for your version of OpenBSD, check hostname.if(5).

Each Ethernet card has its own configuration file, named /etc/hostname. interfacename. For example, the network card fxp1 has a configuration file named /etc/hostname.fxp1. The format of the file is very simple when using IPv4 addresses:

```
inet ❶ipaddress ❷netmask ❸broadcastaddress ❹options
```

This string is used as an argument to ifconfig(8).

The IP address ❶ is standard dotted-quad notation, such as 10.8.3.250.

The ❷netmask can be given in dotted-quad format (255.255.255.0) or in hexadecimal (0xffffff00).

The ❸broadcast address gives you an option to hard-code the broadcast address on this network. If you put in the word NONE instead of an address, however, OpenBSD will compute the correct broadcast address from the IP address and the netmask you gave earlier.

Finally, the ❹options can be any valid arguments at the end of an ifconfig(8) statement. If you don't want any options, you can set this to the word NONE.

For example, if you wanted to give the fxp1 card an IP address of 192.168.1. 250, without any extra options and letting OpenBSD figure out its own netmask, you would use the following entry in /etc/hostname.fxp1.

```
192.168.1.250 255.255.255.0 NONE NONE
```

The next time you reboot, the system will get the network information from this file and configure your interfaces appropriately.

For more complicated uses of /etc/hostname.interfacename, take a look at Chapter 9.

DHCP

If this machine is a DHCP client, you can just put the string "dhcp" in /etc/hostname.interface.

Default Gateway

To set your default gateway on an Ethernet network, just place the IP address of the default gateway on a single line in /etc/mygate. This file should have no other entries. On your next reboot, the system will read this file and by default route packets to this IP.

Nameservice

If you want to contact other machines on the Internet from your OpenBSD machine, you probably want to configure your DNS client. Configure DNS resolution in /etc/resolv.conf.

The first line of /etc/resolv.conf tells the computer its local domain name. Label the domain name with the "domain" keyword.

Nameservers can appear on subsequent lines, each labeled with an IP address. Remember to use an IP address for a nameserver, not a host name. (It's very difficult to use a nameserver to look up a host name when you cannot find the nameserver!) When you're finished, /etc/resolv.conf should look something like this.

```
domain AbsoluteOpenBSD.com
nameserver 192.168.8.33
```

We discuss /etc/resolv.conf in greater detail in Chapter 14.

Mail Aliases

Every standard OpenBSD system sends status emails on a regular basis. If you're on a middle-sized network, you probably have central systems administration email accounts that go to the proper people. Edit the mail aliases file, /etc/mail/ aliases, to direct those emails to that central account.

In /etc/mail/aliases, you'll see a section that looks like this.

```
# Well-known aliases -- these should be filled in!
# root:
# manager:
# dumper:
```

Remove the leading pound sign from each of the "root," "manager," and "dumper" lines. Then put in your correct email address after the colon.

```
# Well-known aliases -- these should be filled in!
root: support@AbsoluteOpenBSD.com
manager: support@AbsoluteOpenBSD.com
dumper: support@AbsoluteOpenBSD.com
```

Once you have done this, run newaliases(8) without any arguments to update the aliases database. Emails will now start going to the appropriate accounts.

Testing your Work

Once you have everything set up, reboot your system. After the reboot, log in and confirm that everything worked correctly. Generally speaking, if you follow the steps above you should get sensible answers from date(1), uname(1) should return the correct host name, and you should be able to ping sites on the Internet by name.

Integrated Program Configuration

OpenBSD includes a wide variety of programs that have been hooked into the operating system, for ease of management. These are programs that both are widely useful and can be secured in a sensible manner. These programs are enabled, disabled, and (to some extent) configured via /etc/rc.conf.

When the OpenBSD kernel finishes its initial system setup and hands control of the system over to userland, init(8) runs the shell script /etc/rc. This script starts all the programs that are integrated with the system and performs general system configuration, such as configuring network interfaces and starting servers. It also has hooks to identify programs that you add commonly, but which are not part of the base system. When /etc/rc finishes, the system is considered "fully booted" and is ready for general use.

/etc/rc.conf contains shell script variable assignments. These assignments control what /etc/rc runs and the command-line options those programs receive. Each variable assignment has three legitimate values: a NO in all upper case, empty quote marks (""), or command-line flags in quote marks ("-D"). Each variable looks something like this:

```
ftpd_flags=NO     # for non-inetd use: "-D"
```

A NO means that this particular piece of functionality is not enabled. In our example above, the FTP server is not running in standalone mode.

If you just use empty quote marks, /etc/rc will try to start the program controlled by that variable without any command-line arguments. This may or may not be appropriate, depending on the program you're trying to run.

Anything within quote marks is used as command-line arguments to the program run by /etc/rc.conf. If the program has typical "default" flags, they're usually given in the comment after the variable assignment. In our example above, if we were to enable ftpd in standalone mode, "-D" would be a sensible value for this flag.

/etc/rc Daemon Configuration

The /etc/rc script only performs command-line configuration. It does not affect any configuration files used by the programs it starts. For example, OpenBSD includes the Apache web server. /etc/rc.conf contains command-line arguments used to start the httpd process, but it does not affect the httpd.conf file used by Apache. Edit a daemon's configuration files appropriately before enabling it!

Common /etc/rc.conf Assignments

The following are the /etc/rc.conf entries found in an OpenBSD 3.2 system. They may differ slightly from the flags found in your particular release of OpenBSD. If you come across an unfamiliar variable, check /etc/rc to see what it does.

This section deliberately does not list all possible options to each variable. Check the manual page for the program the variable starts for specific details. This section merely gives a few basic pointers on what is available and hints about things you might want to look at.

Routing Options

The following options configure OpenBSD's routing management, for both IPv4 and IPv6.

routed_flags

This enables the routing daemon, routed(8). Routed(8) handles RIP (version 1 and 2) and IRDP routing. If you need anything more complicated than routed(8), you probably want to install gated(8).

mrouted_flags

This controls the multicast routing daemon, turning your OpenBSD system into a multicast router. Under normal (non-multicast) environments, you do not want to enable this! For multicast routing to work properly, be sure to enable multicast_router later in this file.

multicast_host

This tells the system that it will support multicasting. Multicasting is a very tricky process, and if you're really interested in it read /etc/netstart for details on how this variable is used.

multicast_router

If you set this to YES, OpenBSD will look for a multicast router running on the local system. If this entry is set to an interface name, OpenBSD will look for a multicast router outside that interface.

gated

This manages the gated(8) routing program. Note that gated is not installed by default; you must install it before using it.

gated_flags

This gives any flags to gated(8), if you install and run it.

Packet Filtering

These variables control the behavior of the integrated packet filter, pf(4). We go into great detail about pf(4) in Chapters 17-19.

pf

If you are using packet filtering or NAT, set this to YES.

pf_rules

This points to the file containing all the packet filter rules, /etc/pf.conf by default.

pflogd_flags

This gives additional flags to be given to pflog(8). The pflog program starts automatically if pf(4) is enabled.

Diskless Clients

The following variables control OpenBSD's support for servers for various sorts of diskless clients.

bootparamd_flags

This enables and manages rpc.bootparamd(8). If you provide boot information to diskless clients from this machine, you want this.

rbootd_flags

This enables the remote booting protocol used by diskless HP workstations. Take a look at rbootd(8) for details.

mopd_flags

mopd services bootfile requests from MOP diskless clients (generally, older DEC workstations).

Time Management

OpenBSD supports two different styles of time server, timed(8) and ntpd(8). Timed is older, but is integrated with OpenBSD. Ntpd is newer and used more widely, but is an add-on; we install ntpd in our example in Chapter 13. Both must run very early in the startup process, so they have hooks in /etc/rc.

The two protocols are not interchangeable!

rdate_flags

You can run rdate(8) at boot, to set the system time from a central time server. If you want to use this, put the name or IP address of your rdate server in quotes here. Do not confuse this with ntpdate(8), however; it is a different program, and does not interoperate with Network Time Protocol!

timed_flags

The timed(8) program is used to synchronize time on a network. This is different than ntpd. However, do not confuse the two; they do not interoperate!

ntpdate_flags

This enables setting the system clock from a central time server via Network Time Protocol. If you want to use ntpdate, give this variable the value of the NTP server you want to update from.

ntpd

This starts and the ntpd continuous time synchronization client.

Daemons

The following variables control the assorted network daemons integrated with OpenBSD.

sshd_flags=""

This manages the ssh daemon, sshd(8). You will find the global configuration files in /etc/ssh (see Chapter 19).

named_flags

This enables and configures the nameserver, good old-fashioned ISC BIND. Setting this to two empty quotes starts the nameserver in the default configuration. Note that OpenBSD includes BIND version 8. This version of BIND supports the most commonly used functionality and has been independently audited by the OpenBSD team. You're welcome to install a newer version of BIND, if you need it.

named_user

named(8) should run as a regular user, not as root. The default user, called "named," is good for almost all circumstances.

named_chroot

This is the directory where named(8) should chroot after starting. The default, /var/named, is fine for just about any installation.

sendmail_flags

This enables and gives command-line options to sendmail(8). By default, OpenBSD's sendmail listens only on the localhost address.

httpd_flags

OpenBSD includes the Apache web server. Note that in normal use on OpenBSD, Apache is run in a chroot environment. To have Apache not chroot, use the "-u" flag. This is not recommended.

dhcpd_flags

This enables and starts the DHCP server daemon, dhcpd(8). It is configured via /etc/dhcpd.conf.

lpd_flags

This starts and configures the Line Printer Daemon.

ftpd_flags

If you only have a few FTP connections, you can choose to run ftpd(8) out of inetd. Set this variable to "-D" if you want ftpd(8) to run in standalone mode. This is suitable if your server is primarily a FTP server.

inetd

This starts and manages the inetd server. See Chapter 19 for some hints on running inetd.

identd_flags

This starts and configures the identification daemon identd(8). While it's most commonly used out of inetd(8), you can run it in standalone mode by giving this variable the proper flags.

rwhod

If you set this to YES, OpenBSD will start rwhod(8) upon boot.

syslogd_flags

This starts and configures the system logger, syslogd(8).

wsmoused_flags

When set to empty quotes, this turns on PS/2 or USB mice in console mode. You can highlight, cut, and paste in a text-mode console with console mice. See moused(8) for other possible options.

IPv6 features

/etc/rc.conf includes several variables for IPv6 and related features. Although we aren't covering IPv6 in this book, we'll mention these here just so you have some sort of clue what they mean when you stumble across them.

isakmpd_flags

This manages the other IPSec key management daemon, isakmpd(8).

rtadvd_flags

This enables and configures router advertisements for IPv6 routing.

route6d_flags

Route6d supports RIP over IPv6. If you need to route RIP over IPv6, you want this. Be sure to enable IPv6 packet forwarding if you want this!

rtsold_flags=NO

rtsold(8) helps a system find an IPv6 router. Set this to the name of your network interface if you want to use it. Be sure to set the sysctl net.inet6.ip6.aceept_rtadv to 1 if you enable this (see Chapter 11).

NFS

While you need to configure NFS in /etc/exports, /etc/rc.conf tells the system how to start a variety of programs and services that support NFS.

nfs_server

If you set this to YES, OpenBSD will start the NFS server.

lockd

If you set this to YES, OpenBSD will start rpc.lockd(8). You need to have the NFS server enabled to run this properly.

amd

This starts and configures the automounter daemon, amd(8).

amd_dir

This variable gives the location where amd(8)-mounted directories are mounted.

amd_master

This variable points to the file containing amd(8)'s master map.

portmap

Set this to YES to enable portmap(8). If you are using NFS in almost any way, you want this.

nfsd_flags

This gives any flags to the server-side NFS request services, nfsd(8). Nfsd starts automatically if the machine is configured as a NFS server.

AFS configuration

OpenBSD has considerable support for AFS. If you're not using AFS, you can leave all of these settings unchanged.

afs

This enables mounting and running AFS file systems. For this to work, you must also set afs_mount_point and afs_device.

afs_mount_point

This is the directory where AFS files are mounted.

afs_device

This is the device name used by afsd(8).

afsd_flags

These are extra flags handed to afsd(8). Afsd runs automatically if you set afs=YES.

Kerberos Setup

OpenBSD includes Kerberos version V.

krb5_master_kdc

This enables the Kerberos V ("Heidmal") domain controller server.

krb5_slave_kdc

This enables the Kerberos V slave domain controller server.

Miscellaneous Variables

The following is a catch-all of other variables that appear in /etc/rc.conf.

rarpd_flags

This enables and manages the rarpd(8) daemon, which provides a TCP wrappers–style service for MAC addresses.

apmd_flags

This starts and configures the Advanced Power Management daemon, apmd(8).

xdm_flags

This manages the xdm(1) X display manager.

check_quotas

When set to YES, OpenBSD will regularly limit users' disk usage as described in quota(1).

savecore_flags

This gives options to savecore(8), should the system find a kernel dump upon rebooting after a panic.

ypserv_flags

This gives any flags to the ypserv(8) information services daemon. Ypserv starts automatically if YP services are configured.

yppasswdd_flags

This allows you to hand any flags to the yppasswd daemon. Yppasswd starts automatically if YP services are configured.

shlib_dirs

Put extra directories to be included by ldconfig(8) during boot here.

Installing the Source Code

At various points, we'll refer to the OpenBSD system source code. I recommend installing it immediately, as it will save you minor annoyance later.

The source code is available on one of the CD-ROMs in the set. If you installed OpenBSD via FTP, you can also download the source code via FTP. You can find the source code on the same FTP server you installed OpenBSD from, in the release directory, as a file called "src.tar.gz." Just extract this directory under /usr/src.

```
# cd /usr/src
# tar -xzvpf srcsys.tar.gz
...
```

Installing the Ports Collection

You will almost certainly want the OpenBSD ports collection. For details why, see Chapter 13. You can grab the ports collection from the CD-ROM or from the FTP server you installed from as a file called "ports.tar.gz." Extract this under /usr.

```
# cd /usr
# tar -xzvpf ports.tar.gz
...
```

Further Setup

Now that you have the system basically configured, you'll probably have a few other tasks you want to accomplish. Refer to the rest of this book, the OpenBSD FAQ, and the manual pages to learn how to proceed.

6

STARTUP AND BOOTING

Single-user mode
unscheduled in the nighttime?
Something just went "boom!"

 Now that you have performed some basic configuration of your OpenBSD system, we're going to look at the startup process. To properly manage any computer platform, you must understand its booting system.

In general, when a computer boots it fires up the built-in operating system, or BIOS. The BIOS figures out little things like what hard drives are attached, what sort of CPU is installed, how much memory is available, and so on, then loads a minimal boot handling program from one of the hard drives. On i386 systems, this is where the Master Boot Record comes in; other hardware platforms have their own method of bootstrapping the operating system. This boot loader finds and starts the kernel, and the kernel starts the operating system, attaches device drivers to hardware, and performs other operating system setup. Finally, the kernel starts init(8), which starts various processes and enables the user programs, network interfaces, daemons, and so on. Large chunks of this cannot be managed — nobody actually configures init(8)! However, many parts of the process can be managed.

First we'll discuss OpenBSD's cross-platform booting process. At the end of that section you'll understand how single-user mode works and why it's there, plus the most useful of the things you can do at the boot loader. Then we'll learn how to set up and use a serial console, a vital task for remote system administration. While some hardware integrates serial console support into the hardware, the i386 platform doesn't. Setting up a serial console is fairly straightforward, as is accessing the serial console from another computer.

Much of what people consider "system configuration" is actually handled by the shell script /etc/rc, which is started by init(8). All sorts of system features, file systems, and daemons are configured during this process. While we discussed the various options available in /etc/rc.conf in the previous chapter, we didn't touch on how those options are actually used. We'll explain how the configuration process works, and the OpenBSD configuration options that are available out-of-the-box.

Lastly, we'll discuss how to automatically start or stop programs when the system boots and shuts down.

Boot Configuration

When your hardware's BIOS finishes counting onboard memory and finding all the system hard drives, it will pass control of the system to the boot loader. The boot loader is a small program that handles initial system configuration and booting the kernel. OpenBSD provides the ability to interrupt the booting process, configure the system before it boots, and adjust your kernel settings, or even boot an alternate kernel. This program is documented in boot(8), but we'll cover some of the basic functions here.

Boot Prompt

When your hardware hands control of the boot process over to the OpenBSD partition, you'll see a prompt much like this.

```
boot>
```

The boot loader runs from the BIOS bootstrap loader, and provides very rudimentary configuration abilities. The boot program's main purpose is to load the kernel into memory and start it. The boot loader loads the kernel, waits for five seconds, and starts the kernel. Because this runs before the kernel starts, the boot program gives you the opportunity to issue pre-booting instructions to the kernel.

Delaying the Boot

Once this prompt has been idle for five seconds, the system will boot! If you're not exactly sure what you're doing, you might want to tell it to delay the boot for a little longer. You can do this by increasing the timeout value.

```
boot> set timeout 60
boot>
```

This tells OpenBSD to boot after being idle for 60 seconds, which is not an unreasonable delay when you're poking around the boot loader trying to figure out what you want to do! Now, let's look at some more useful functions than slowing your system down.

Booting Single-User

Single-user mode is the earliest point where your OpenBSD system can give you a command prompt. At this point the kernel has probed all the hardware, attached drivers to hardware it's going to acknowledge, and started init(8). No file systems are mounted, except for a read-only root partition. The network is not started, no daemons are running, security is not implemented, and file system permissions are ignored. You get a bare-naked command prompt on a minimally running system.

To boot into single-user mode, use the -s flag on the boot command.

```
boot> boot -s
```

Why would you want to use single-user mode? Suppose you've upgraded a program on your system, and it now crashes your computer on every boot, before you can log in. A computer can easily get caught in a panic loop where it crashes and restarts until someone manually intervenes and shuts down the offending program. You might have a disk go bad, and crash the system before the boot can finish. Perhaps you made some stupid mistake in configuring your system, and now it just won't finish booting at all, or perhaps you need to clear some file flags (see Chapter 10). Any of these require intervention before the boot finishes.

Generally speaking, you want a fully functional file system before doing much of anything in single-user mode. If your system crashed, you'll have to check the file system consistency before mounting any file systems. The following commands will clean and mount all of your file systems. (fsck(8) and mount(8) have many more options; check out Chapter 18 for the most common ones or the man page for the full gory details.)

```
# fsck -p
# mount -a
```

Once you're in single-user mode and have your file systems mounted, all of the usual command-line functions should be available. You can edit configuration files, start and stop programs, and generally do whatever you like. What exactly you want to do depends on exactly what your problem is.

Starting the Network in Single-User Mode

The shell script /etc/netstart can start the network while in single-user mode. You could go and run all the appropriate commands by hand, but /etc/netstart will read the appropriate /etc/ files and do all the grunt work for you. You need to explicitly run this script through sh(1).

```
# /bin/sh /etc/netstart
```

Of course, if network configuration problems are *why* you're running in single-user mode, this script will only re-create your problem!

Booting in Kernel Configuration Mode

The -c flag to boot makes the system come up in kernel configuration mode. This allows you to change some of a kernel's built-in constants. We'll discuss this at great length in Chapter 11. For now, you just need to know that the mode exists so that other examples here make some sort of sense.

Booting Alternate Kernels

You can choose to boot a kernel other than /bsd. You might need this if you're building your own kernel, as discussed in Chapter 11. Just give the boot command the full path to the kernel you want to boot. For example, if your kernel in /bsd is faulty and you need to boot off your known-good /bsd. GENERIC kernel, do the following:

```
boot> boot /bsd.GENERIC
```

This should get your system up and running and let you install a proper kernel in /bsd.

You can use any other boot flags with this. For example, boot -s /bsd. GENERIC will boot the GENERIC kernel in single-user mode.

Booting from an Alternate Hard Disk

You might have multiple OpenBSD installs on different hard disks on one computer, for either testing or redundancy purposes. By default, OpenBSD boots from the first disk it finds. If you have four IDE disks, for example, it boots from the first disk on the first IDE controller. You could have a separate root partition installed on another disk, with a separate /etc/fstab pointing to emergency /usr and /var partitions.

To tell the boot loader to use a root partition on another drive give the full path to the kernel you want to boot, including the device name of the drive the root partition is on. This is much like booting an alternate kernel, just adding the hard drive device name as part of the path. Here, we boot the kernel /bsd.old on the "a" partition (traditionally root) on the third IDE hard disk, also known as "wd2a." (If you have four IDE disks, this is the master drive on the second controller.)

```
boot> boot wd2a:/bsd.old
```

The OpenBSD installer will do its very best to put the root partition on the "a" partition, but if you managed to put it elsewhere you will have to enter the proper partition here.

Other Useful Boot Commands

If you forget which kernels you have on a system, the "ls" command lists all the files in the root directory. You can list other directories on the root partition by giving a full path, i.e., "ls /etc."

The "boot" command by itself will boot the system immediately, without waiting for the five-second timeout. Similarly, the "reboot" command tells the system to do a warm boot.

The "help" command lists all available boot loader commands, including the less frequently used ones that we don't discuss here. If you want truly detailed help with the boot loader, however, you should go read the boot(8) man page.

Finally, you can combine the boot flags to achieve exactly the effects you want. To boot an old kernel in single-user mode, you would do this:

```
boot> boot -s /bsd.old
```

/etc/boot.conf

The /etc/boot.conf file allows you to permanently reconfigure the system's booting process. Entries in this file are parsed before you get the boot prompt, so you have the opportunity to override anything you enter in this file. Commands here are parsed and processed automatically.

You can tell your OpenBSD system to boot a different kernel every time giving the command here. If /etc/boot.conf contains the following, your system will automatically boot using the kernel file /bsd.CUSTOM:

```
boot /bsd.CUSTOM
```

You can change the boot prompt timeout by setting it here as well. For example, if a five-second delay is just too long and you want barely enough time to hit the spacebar and start typing before the system boots, you might set your timeout to two seconds.

```
set timeout 2
```

By far, however, the most popular use of /etc/boot.conf is to configure a serial console.

Serial Consoles

All these nifty boot functions let you do some pretty useful things in trouble situations, but how are you supposed to use them if your server isn't right in front of you? If your computer is on the other side of the country or wedged uncomfortably behind the last ten years of payroll records in the basement storeroom, and you want to perform some low-level hardware maintenance, a serial console will make your life far more pleasant.

A true serial console allows you to run a serial cable between two computers and have complete access to the hardware BIOS, the early operating system boot messages, and startup processes. One computer (the client) will be able to see all the messages that appear on the console of the booting machine (the server). This makes remote system management much easier. Serial consoles are invaluable when you're trying to debug a system crash — the debugging messages come over the serial port where they can be captured easily, rather than displayed on a glass screen to be copied by hand.

Real UNIX hardware (such as HP and Sparc) has a serial console capability. Most i386 hardware does not support this functionality. A very few Intel motherboards, such as the L440GX, do support serial consoles, but it's a feature you must specifically shop around for.

Because i386 hardware is the most common these days, that lack is something of a problem. Fortunately, it's possible to work around this and build a highly functional serial console anyway. While OpenBSD's i386 serial console doesn't give you access to the hardware BIOS, it does let you interface with the OpenBSD boot process. You could also choose to install an actual hardware serial console.

Hardware Serial Console

Nothing any operating system can do will give you access to the i386 BIOS messages across a serial port. This stuff happens before the operating system starts and before the hard drive even starts to spin up.

Some hardware solutions can work around this by pretending to be a video board and directing the console out to a serial port. The best I've seen is the PC Weasel (http://www.realweasel.com/). By putting the Weasel in your computer and running a null modem cable between the Weasel and another computer's serial port you can manipulate the BIOS remotely, interrupt the boot to come up in single-user mode, and generally muck around with the hardware just as if you were at the actual keyboard and monitor attached to the system. Other companies do manufacture similar devices, but they either require proprietary client software or are far more expensive.

Software Serial Console

OpenBSD includes a software serial console. As OpenBSD boots, it decides where to put its console. This defaults to the monitor and keyboard, but with a few tweaks you can have the console come up on a serial port. The only hardware requirement is that your system has a serial port. Some systems are increasingly arriving "legacy-free," meaning that they lack an ISA bus, serial ports, and even PS/2 ports. My latest laptop had a nasty surprise in lacking an actual serial port. You might need to buy a PCI serial card for your server if this is the case.

This serial console does not kick in until the OpenBSD boot loader starts, so you will not see the BIOS messages. You do get a chance to interact with the OpenBSD boot process, which is good enough for most cases — after all, you presumably made sure that the BIOS was correct before shipping the computer across the country!

Non-i386 Serial Consoles

Every different hardware platform has its own standards for serial consoles. If you're running on one of these platforms, check your hardware documentation. In general, if your hardware supports serial consoles, you need to set it up at the hardware level. Your Sparc hardware will support OpenBSD's console just as well as it supports Solaris's console.

Serial Console Physical Setup

You must have a null modem cable to use a serial console. A regular modem cable will not work! Get the best cable you can find; if you have an emergency and need the serial console, you're probably not in the mood to deal with line noise.

Plug one end of the null modem cable into the first serial port on your OpenBSD server. Traditionally, this is the first COM port. You can use any serial port that is convenient, so long as you remember which port it is.[1] You can choose to use any serial port as your serial console. Plug the other end of your null modem cable into an open serial port on another system. I recommend that you use either another OpenBSD or UNIX system, or a terminal server if you have a lot of servers that include serial consoles. You can use a Windows system as your serial console terminal, but that won't give you any remote-control functionality. (Yes, you could use VNC or Windows Terminal Services on the Windows system, but you're starting to look at a complicated and error-prone setup when a simple 486 running OpenBSD would do.) In a pinch, on a local system that didn't have a monitor or keyboard, I've used a vt100 emulator running on my PalmPilot — the screen was cramped, but it worked.

If you have two OpenBSD machines at a remote location and want to use serial consoles on both of them, simply attach the console cable to the second serial port on the other server. If you have three machines, you can daisy-chain them into a loop. By combining twos and threes, you should be able to get a serial console on every one of your systems. I've worked in areas with dozens of UNIX servers tightly packed together, and serial consoles saved a huge amount of space that monitors and keyboards would have taken up.

---

[1] A surprising number of people go to a lot of trouble to set up a serial port, then either forget which port it is on or forget which physical port is actually COM1.

Serial Console Client

Before you can test your serial console, you need to configure your client to access the serial console. The key to setting up your client is to remember the following:

- 9600 baud
- 8 bits
- no parity
- 1 stop bit

If you can configure your client program to use these settings, the serial console will "just work." Conveniently enough, these are the default settings on Microsoft's HyperTerm program.[2] If you don't like HyperTerm, you can find any number of vt100 terminal programs for Microsoft platforms. Even Macintosh and Palm platforms have any number of free vt100 terminal programs kicking around. If your second computer also runs OpenBSD or, for that matter, almost any version of open-source UNIX, you can use the OpenBSD terminal program. Because this is an OpenBSD book, we'll discuss exactly how to do this.

OpenBSD accesses serial lines with tip(1), a program that allows you to connect to a remote system in a manner similar to telnet. To run tip and have it connect to a remote machine's serial port over a serial cable connected to the local machine's first serial port, do this:

```
# tip tty00
```

A port name is shorthand for specifying the settings and speed to be used when accessing a serial port. The file /etc/remote contains a list of port names for a variety of platforms.

Configuring the Serial Console

You can tell OpenBSD to boot either off the serial console or off the physical console, by an entry in /etc/boot.conf or a command at the boot prompt. The "set tty" command tells OpenBSD where to put the console. The common choices are com0 (for classic i386 COM1), com1 (for classic i386 COM2), or pc0 (for the physical hardware).

Plug in your serial console and access it from a client machine. Now reboot your test OpenBSD system. At the initial boot loader prompt, type:

```
boot> set tty com0
```

All of a sudden, your physical keyboard won't seem to be doing anything, and nothing else comes across your screen. On the other hand, your serial console client will abruptly show the boot loader prompt.

---

[2] I'm refraining from making any comments about how this one of those rare times that Microsoft has done anything conveniently. That would be too cheap a shot even for me.

```
boot>
```

Anything you type in your serial console client is passed to the OpenBSD boot loader, just as we discussed in "Boot Configuration" earlier. It's just as if you were at the console. You can load alternate kernels, perform preboot configuration (as discussed in Chapter 11), boot in single-user mode, and do any of the other booting tricks we discuss in this chapter.

To switch back to the PC's physical console, use the pc0 device.

```
boot> set tty pc0
```

The keyboard and monitor will work again.

If you want to use the serial console permanently, you can place a "set tty" entry in /etc/boot.conf.

```
set tty com0
```

Multiuser Startup

We examined /etc/rc.conf in some detail in Chapter 5. Now let's see how those variables are processed by the system.

Whenever your system boots to the point where it can execute userland commands, it runs the shell script /etc/rc. This script mounts all file systems, brings up the network interfaces, configures device nodes, sets up shared libraries, and does all the other tasks required to bring a system up to multiuser mode. These are an awful lot of tasks, and some of them aren't necessary on all systems. The purpose of /etc/rc.conf is to tell /etc/rc what to run, what values to run with, and what to not bother with. Everything you set in /etc/rc.conf is used in /etc/rc in one way or another. The /etc/rc system actually has six associated files: /etc/rc, /etc/rc.conf, /etc/rc.local, /etc/rc.securelevel, /etc/netstart, and /etc/rc.shutdown.

/etc/rc

Every configuration step on an OpenBSD box, from setting the host name to starting server programs, can be performed by a simple shell command. As such, /etc/rc is a basic shell script. This script reads in variable assignments from /etc/rc.conf as well as files such as /etc/myname and /etc/hostname.*, and acts as those variables tell it to. The /etc/rc script also starts every other /etc/rc script at the appropriate time. When /etc/rc exits, the system fires up getty(8) and presents login prompts on all the appropriate terminals.

Generally speaking, you should not need to edit /etc/rc unless you are a very experienced systems administrator with truly unique needs. Editing the other /etc/rc.* files, especially /etc/rc.conf, should do everything you need.

/etc/rc.conf

This file contains nothing but variables used by other /etc/rc scripts. We covered it in extreme detail in Chapter 5. Various other /etc/rc.* scripts use /etc/rc.conf to get their configuration information.

/etc/netstart

While the name doesn't look like the others, /etc/netstart is definitely a system startup script. This script reads /etc/hostname.if*, /etc/mygate, and /etc/myname, and uses that information to configure all network functionality: interfaces, bridges, routing, and so forth. You can run this script in single-user mode to bring up the network without starting any of the other software that normally starts in multi-user mode.

/etc/rc.securelevel

This shell script runs just before the system raises its securelevel (see more about this in Chapter 10), but after the network is started. Many programs, particularly those that affect the kernel or file systems in some way, will not run once the securelevel is raised. The examples in the file relate to ntpd(8) and related programs, but you can edit /etc/rc.securelevel to include any programs that must be run before securelevel is raised. If at all possible, however, you're better off starting local programs from /etc/rc.local. We'll look at adding proper shell commands to these files in "Editing /etc/rc Scripts," later in this chapter.

One important detail in /etc/rc.securelevel is the securelevel setting itself. We discuss securelevel in Chapter 10. For now, just don't touch the line that sets the securelevel unless you're already familiar with BSD and know exactly what you're getting with securelevels!

/etc/rc.local

The /etc/rc.local shell script runs at the very end of system initialization. Once every other system process has been started, /etc/rc.local runs. This is the usual place to put startup commands for systems such as databases, small servers, and any other programs you want to run at boot time. You can place your add-on shell commands here, as discussed in "Editing /etc/rc Scripts," later in this chapter.

/etc/rc.conf.local

In various circumstances, you might not want to edit /etc/rc.conf for each machine. Perhaps you share one rc.conf amongst several machines, but have a few machines that require particular tweaks. If you're a developer and upgrade frequently, handling /etc/rc.conf can be tedious. That's where /etc/rc.conf.local comes in.

/etc/rc.conf.local starts off as an empty file. You can put any rc.conf variable assignments you like into this file. Entries in /etc/rc.conf.local override any values in /etc/rc.conf. For example, /etc/rc.conf contains this line.

```
identd_flags=NO
```

Let's suppose you want to change this value without editing the /etc/rc.conf line. You could create a line like the following in /etc/rc.conf.local.

```
identd_flags="-b -u nobody -elo"
```

When /etc/rc runs, it will use the values from /etc/rc.conf.local instead of /etc/rc.conf. This minimizes the number of changes necessary to /etc/rc.conf and makes upgrading easier.

/etc/rc.shutdown

The /etc/rc.shutdown script runs whenever you use reboot(8), halt(8), or a keyboard shutdown (i.e., CTRL-ALT-DELETE on i386). The commands here are shut down commands that require specialized shutdown sequences. Database programs use this feature frequently, which you need to shut down correctly to prevent data loss.

Editing /etc/rc Scripts

Well, now that you know how the files fit together, what are you supposed to do with them? While OpenBSD's integrated software is started by /etc/rc, add-on software needs to be started separately. The ports and packages system tells you how to create these script commands and where to put them. If you install your own software, however, you need to create a script that handles its startup and shutdown process. Plus, to change an existing add-on package's startup process, you must understand how the script works.

Port-Based Software Startup

A port (or package) is a piece of add-on software that has been configured for OpenBSD. We discuss ports and packages at great length in Chapter 13. If your port needs to have a startup sequence added to an /etc/rc script to work, the installation process will tell you exactly what to add to which /etc/rc file. It should tell you to add some lines of shell script to either /etc/rc.local or /etc/rc.securelevel. For example, if you install the SNMP port, ucd-snmp, you'll see the following message at the end of the install process:

```
 ...
| To have snmpd start at boot time, you must have an entry similiar to the
| following in /etc/rc.local.
|
|        ❶if [ -x /usr/local/sbin/snmpd ]; then
|               ❷/usr/local/sbin/snmpd ❸-c /etc/snmpd.conf && ❹echo -n ' snmpd'
|        ❺fi
|
| This will start snmpd and use /etc/snmpd.conf for the configuration.
| (see snmpd(1) and snmpd.conf(5) for more options)
```

You can literally just copy the text you're given and add it to /etc/rc.local, and it
will work. But understanding what you're looking at here, and why it works, will
make you a better sysadmin. If you want to start your program in a slightly different manner, you'll have to edit this.

The first line ❶ checks for the existence of the /usr/local/bin/snmpd file.
If that file exists, the script executes the next lines, up until the ❺fi (or "finish")
entry. If there is no such program, then the rest of this little script is skipped
entirely. The next line has the real meat of the script. The startup system will run
❷/usr/local/bin/snmpd, with the arguments ❸-c /etc/snmpd.conf, and it will
print to the console ❹"snmpd" so you'll know it started.

It would be simple enough to have a port automatically add its startup information to /etc/rc.local or /etc/rc.securelevel and save you a step. This could
potentially be a security hole, however! For example, I frequently install the net-
snmp package just to get the cool SNMP client tools it includes. I don't want the
SNMP server daemon to be running. More than once, on other UNIX-like operating systems, I've installed this package and completely forgotten about its daemon portion. My system is running a daemon I don't want it to be running, until
I either remember or notice and manually shut it off. OpenBSD absolutely
requires you to enable every daemon that runs on the system, even once you've
installed the binaries for it.

Uninstalls

When you uninstall this piece of software, remove the corresponding startup
entry from the /etc/rc script. The script will not cause even minor problems by
being there, but it is rather sloppy to not clean up after yourself.

Custom Software Startup

Suppose you install a piece of software by hand, not using a port or package, and
need to have it start automatically? That's simple enough to deal with. Just write a
bit of shell code much like the entry a port gives. Your startup command doesn't
have to bother checking to see if the piece of software is installed, mind you. You
could just add the line to start the program to /etc/rc.local.

```
/usr/local/sbin/snmpd -c /etc/snmpd.conf
```

It's not that much harder to add a notification that the program started to your console messages.

```
/usr/local/sbin/snmpd -c /etc/snmpd.conf && echo -n ' snmpd'
```

If you stop here, your program will run just fine.

Uninstalls

When you uninstall the program, be sure to remove the matching /etc/rc.local entry.

If you uninstall the program without removing the /etc/rc.local entry, you'll start to see errors on boot complaining that "/usr/local/sbin/snmpd" does not exist. In my opinion, this is actually desirable behavior — all that the fancy check to see if a program exists really does is silence warnings when the program is gone, but the /etc/rc.local entry remains. I'm not sure how anyone could actually exploit such a script check without already having fairly deep access to the system, but it's sloppy in any event. And sloppiness is the biggest cause of system break-ins.

7

MANAGING USERS

*This one can log in,
this other can get email;
never give out root.*

 While computer attacks over the Internet
are the sort of network intrusions that are
publicized widely, the greatest security threats
often come from a system's own users. More
companies lose vital data thanks to disaffected or
incompetent employees than outside intruders — and
incompetence is by far the most common of the two.
Giving all users unrestricted access to the system is not
only a bad idea for security reasons, but it will quickly
result in an unstable environment as each user makes
conflicting changes and diverts resources toward their
own ends.

One of the most common tasks for a systems administrator is adding, removing, and modifying user accounts. Despite what you might have learned from the Bastard Operator From Hell, the system exists for the users. Proper creation and management of user accounts is absolutely necessary. In this chapter we will discuss creating, adding, and editing user accounts, how to give groups of users access to different parts of the system, proper use of the root password, and how to entirely avoid using the root password.

Single-User Systems

Even if you are the only person using your OpenBSD system, you still need to create a user account for day-to-day use instead of using the root account. Read your email, surf the Web, and develop your software with your regular account, not with root. Using root for casual tasks increases your risks from user error and security issues. A careless keystroke by root can render an entire system unusable, while that same careless keystroke by a regular user will only generate a "permission denied" error.

If an intruder compromises an account, he can only inflict damage allowed by that user's permissions. If the compromised account handles your email and your web bookmarks, you may suffer some personal embarrassment. If that account is root, the intruder can inflict unlimited damage and you will need the install media and backup tapes. Using a regular account for day-to-day tasks means that you can take extra steps to lock down the root account. If you plan properly you can even entirely eliminate the need to become root and add another layer of security to your system.

In short, each operation should be performed with the minimum level of permission necessary. If you don't need root access to perform a task, don't use it! This is why OpenBSD's web server runs as a separate user, rather than root; not only does it protect the system from intruders, it protects the system from program errors.

Operating systems that treat every user as the equivalent of root have more problems as a result: the effectiveness of viruses, unexpected misconfigurations, and even most crashes can be traced back to this behavior. OpenBSD might be the most secure operating system in the world, but all those fancy security features cannot protect you from poor sysadmin practices.

Using root for routine tasks also creates bad habits. Under pressure, people do things the way they're used to. If you habitually use root on your desktop for routine work, when the time comes you need to work on a production system you'll have to fight with yourself to perform routine tasks properly. This sort of sloppiness is one of the biggest causes of security breaches. Even on my OpenBSD desktop, where I'm the only person who will ever use it, I do everything as a regular user specifically to develop and maintain good sysadmin habits.

Keeping all this in mind, it should be clear why you should use a regular account for day-to-day work.

Adding Users

OpenBSD uses many of the standard UNIX password-management programs, such as passwd(8) and vipw(8). OpenBSD also includes a friendly interactive user-adding program, adduser(8). We'll cover that program first and then go on to some of the other tools for more advanced uses.

Adding Users Interactively

If you start adduser(8) at the command line, without specifying any options, it drops you into an interactive shell. The first time you run it, it will ask you a series of questions to determine its default settings. It will save these settings, but don't worry too much; we'll look at how to change your defaults later. You must have root privileges to run adduser(8).

```
# adduser
Use option ``-silent'' if you don't want to see all warnings and questions.
Reading /etc/shells❶
Check /etc/master.passwd❷
Check /etc/group❸
Ok, let's go.
Don't worry about mistakes. I will give you the chance later to correct any input.
```

Whenever adduser starts, it checks the user configuration files. Vital information is kept in ❶/etc/shells, ❷/etc/master.passwd, and ❸/etc/group. Once adduser is convinced that your user configuration files are not corrupted, it will give you a chance to enter the username you want to create. You'll see in brackets the legal characters for usernames in OpenBSD — specifically, any letter or number, plus the underscore and the dash.

```
Enter username [a-z0-9_-]: phil
```

Once you have that, you'll get a chance to enter a real name for the user.

```
Enter full name []: Philip C.
```

Next, adduser gives you a chance to choose the users' shell. The list of shells is taken from /etc/shells, with the addition of the "nologin" option. The default shell is shown in brackets.

```
Enter shell csh ksh nologin sh [csh]: csh
```

Now you can choose a uid (user id number). By default, OpenBSD starts numbering uids at 1,000 and takes the first available uid. You can change this if you wish, but it's generally not necessary.

```
Uid [1000]:
Login group phil [phil]:
```

By default, each new user is assigned to a group with the same name as his username. You can assign the user account to a different group if you wish. If you have other system groups defined and you want this user to be part of one of these groups, you can enter it here. If you want this user to be able to use the root password, add them to the wheel group.

```
Login group is ``phil''. Invite phil into other groups: guest no
[no]: wheel
```

Adduser(8) will prompt you for an initial password and then show you your new user so you can double-check your work. Each field you entered previously is displayed for your approval.

```
Enter password []:
Enter password again []:
Name:    phil
Password: ****
Fullname: Philip C.
Uid:     1001
Gid:     1001 (phil)
Groups:  phil
HOME:    /home/phil
Shell:   /bin/csh
OK? (y/n) [y]:
```

At this point, you can cancel the whole thing by hitting "n." If the account looks correct, however, you can hit "y" and let adduser create the user.

```
Added user ``phil''
Copy files from /etc/skel to /home/phil
```

Finally, adduser will ask you if you want to create a second user. You can do that if you wish, or not.

```
Add another user? (y/n) [y]: n
Goodbye!
#
```

Congratulations! You have added a user to your system. Now that you know how the process works, let's take a look at customizing and configuring adduser(8) to give it the defaults you want.

/etc/adduser.conf

The first time you run adduser(8), it uses your answers to build its configuration file, /etc/adduser.conf. Value assignments in this file control adduser(8)'s behavior. If the variable has multiple legitimate values, those values are surrounded by parentheses. Without further ado, here are the standard things you may set in /etc/adduser.conf. To get a complete list of things that may be set in adduser.conf, you'll need to read the adduser script.

verbose = 1

The verbose flag tells adduser how much detail to give. If you have a verbose of 0, adduser(8) will only present a minimum of information when run. It will assume that you know it is checking the user files in /etc/, for example, and hence not bother to tell you about them. The standard is 1. If you want to debug the adduser program itself, you can set this to 2 for maximum debugging output. I habitually turn this to 0 without a second thought.

encryptionmethod = "blowfish"

OpenBSD supports a variety of encryption schemes for encoding passwords. Blowfish is the OpenBSD standard. If you want to share your password file with other UNIX-like operating systems, though, set this to "old" to get DES hashes.

dotdir = "/etc/skel"

All new user accounts get a set of default shell dotfiles. You can use the ones that OpenBSD provides in /etc/skel, or you can create your own customized for your environment. Any files in this directory will be copied to the user's home directory, so you can also use this to distribute any other files you like. Be sure that regular users cannot put "extras" in a directory you specify!

send_message = "no"

On many operating systems, new users automatically receive a welcome or instructional email message. By default, OpenBSD does not do this. If you put the full path to a file in this variable, however, the contents of that file will be emailed to each new user. If you set this to no, a message will not be sent. OpenBSD does have a default new user message in /etc/adduser.message, but you should feel free to create your own.

The adduser message accepts the variables $username and $fullname; this allows you to customize your welcome message somewhat. (If you're familiar with Perl, you can add your own variables by editing /usr/sbin/adduser.) If you wish, go ahead and create your own message instead of using the brief and generic default. I generally use an /etc/adduser.message.local somewhat like this:

```
$fullname,

Welcome to The Company.

Help is available at 800-555-1212, or online at
http://helpdesk.companyname.com.
```

Use of this account is governed by our acceptable use policy,
available at http://www.companyname.com/aup.html or on this system in
/usr/local/share/company/aup.

Thank you for your business. We look forward to serving you.

The Company Support Staff.

---

logfile = "/var/log/adduser"

Adduser will record the history of its actions in the file specified here.

home = "/home"

This variable controls the directory where users' home directories are located. This is one of the first things I take care of on any OpenBSD system. If you do not specifically create a /home partition, the default will place users' home directories on the root partition. This is bad, for a variety of reasons. The biggest problem in that your root partition is limited to 8GB in size, which greatly restricts the amount of user data your system can hold.

  If you expect to have a lot of user accounts on your system (i.e., for a web server), you almost certainly want a /home partition so you can mount it with the appropriate permissions. If you only have systems administrators accounts on this system, you might want to place user accounts under /usr/home and create a symlink from /home. Both work, but you should know about your choices.

path = ('/bin', '/usr/bin', '/usr/local/bin')

This contains the list of directories that can contain legitimate shells. This covers most standard situations, but if you find that you're installing shells in some unusual location, you'll want to edit this appropriately.

shellpref = ('csh', 'sh', 'ksh', 'nologin')

This is a list of legitimate shells. Adduser will let you choose from any of these when creating a new user.

defaultshell = "csh"

This is the default user shell. It can be any of the shells listed in "shellpref."

defaultgroup = USER

This is the primary group that the user is a member of. Traditional BSD systems assign each user to a group of the same name as the username. For example, our "phil" user is automatically a member of the group "phil," which was created just for him. You might want all users to be part of a separate group, such as "students" or "customers." If that's the case, you can set that on this line. You can add this user to other groups manually, but this will be the primary group.

```
uid_start = 1000
uid_end = 2147483647
```

These give the range of acceptable user ID numbers, or uids. The default is fine for most cases, but you might want to use different numbers to interoperate with your other UNIX-like systems.

Adding Users Non-Interactively

You might need or want to add users in a single, longer command. This is common if you have scripts or cron jobs that add users at regular intervals, for example, or if you're comfortable with remembering long commands with many options. Adduser's -batch flag enables this. When you use this mode, adduser takes four additional arguments: the username, the group name, the full name, and the password in encrypted format, much like this:

```
# adduser -batch chris wheel 'Chris B.' loser1
```

Here we create a user account for Chris, put him in the wheel group, and give him a password that encrypts to the string "loser1".

Passwords and Batch Mode

If you actually follow the previous example, you'll create the account without a known password! Remember, no modern UNIX stores its passwords in readable format; instead, it stores a "hash" of the password. If you take the password and perform some horrible computations on it, you'll create a hash. When you create or change a password, the system creates this hash and stores it in /etc/master.passwd. When you attempt to log in, the login process takes your password, generates a hash, and compares the hash of the offered password with the hash in the password file. If the hashes match, exactly, the login is permitted.

The example above creates an account with a password *hash* of loser1, not a password of loser1! This isn't even a legitimate hash, and no entered password will match it. Most of us cannot calculate Blowfish hashes from known text in our heads; we either need pre-generated encrypted passwords, or we need to enter unencrypted passwords on the command line and have adduser do the calculation for us, or we must create an account with no password at all.

Creating an account without a password is perhaps the simplest option. The account is disabled until you go back and enter a password, but this may be acceptable for accounts used to run daemons and services. Simply run adduser in batch mode, omitting the password.

```
# adduser -batch chris wheel 'Chris B.'
```

If you want to enter an unencrypted password on the command line, you can do this with the -unencrypted option. Be sure you put this option before the -batch option! For example, if I wanted Chris's account to really have a password of "loser1," I could enter this:

```
# adduser -unencrypted -batch chris wheel 'Chris B.' loser1
```

The user now actually has a password of loser1.[1] You might use this inside a
script, or at some time when nobody is around to look over your shoulder.

Generating Pre-hashed Passwords

If you're using this within a script, you probably want to pre-generate hashed
passwords. Encrypt(1) does this. By default, encrypt just gives you a blank line.
When you enter a word, it returns the Blowfish-hashed password. You can enter
any number of words, and each will be hashed separately. Hit CONTROL-C to
exit encrypt.

```
# encrypt
loser1
$2a$06$RdxEtBODNJ6MY67j77m/Bu.JYydNnErTo2cAVOInHg5gkCK1JrbBC
^C
#
```

If you're just doing one password or using this interactively, you probably want to
use encrypt's -p option. This gives you a non-echoing prompt for a word to be
hashed.

```
# encrypt -p
Enter string:
$2a$06$RHWwSGRFSat8byeBcm6W6.H9LKC7Cxi8A2pjqCOhUi8LfHtV6OeQK
#
```

Between these three choices, you should be able to handle passwords in
adduser's batch mode in any way you desire.

Other Adduser Batch Mode Options

When running adduser(8) in batch mode, you have several other options to
override the default configuration. I will frequently set up administrator accounts
in one way and user accounts in another, and use different tools to create each.
Frequently, sysadmin accounts are created in adduser's interactive mode — I
don't have many systems administrators on any given system. Someone else
running a script that I've written creates user accounts on a routine basis. You
can get a complete list of adduser options by reading adduser(8). These are
simply the options I find most useful.

NOTE   *All of these options must appear on the command line before the -batch command. The*
-batch command tells adduser that what follows is the actual account information.

---

[1] Mind you, this is an absolutely hideous password, for an extraordinarily wide variety of reasons.
But if you're interested at all in security, you know that already.

The -noconfig option tells adduser to not read the default /etc/adduser.conf. Using this in a script is an excellent way to make sure administrator-friendly settings in /etc/adduser.conf do not leak into regular user accounts.

The -dotdir option specifies a nonstandard directory where user dotfiles are stored. All files in this directory will be copied to the user's home directory.

-home tells adduser which directory to create a new users' home directory in. This is not the actual home directory, but rather the directory where the home directory will be placed. For example, if all of your web server customers have home directories on the /www partition, you might use -home /www on the batch adduser command line.

Account Limitations

A user account is subject to the following restrictions.

- Usernames can contain only lowercase letters, digits, dashes, or underscores.[2]
- The full name cannot contain a colon (:).
- The user's shell must be listed in /etc/shells.

Removing User Accounts

Part of any security policy is the timely removal of user accounts. You can do this with rmuser(8). It will ask me to confirm both the account name and that I want to delete the user's home directory. Rmuser will also delete any cron jobs belonging to the user, as well as that user's mail spool. For example, if Chris no longer has access to the system, I can delete him like this:

```
# rmuser chris
Matching password entry:

chris:*:1002:1002::0:0:Chris S.:/customers/chris:/usr/local/bin/tcsh

Is this the entry you wish to remove? y
Remove user's home directory (/customers/chris)? y
Updating password file, updating databases, done.
Updating group file:Removing group chris -- personal group is empty
 done.
Removing user's home directory (/customers/chris): done.
#
```

---

[2] Technically, you could create a username that contained any character you liked or even multiple identical usernames — but then you run into all sorts of potential problems. Stick with the defaults unless you know exactly what you're doing and are prepared to deal with the consequences.

Editing Users

OpenBSD supports the classic vipw(8) tool that allows an administrator to directly edit /etc/master.passwd, but for most cases chpass(1) will do everything you need in a much more friendly way. The only real need for vipw(8) is if you have damaged the password file somehow.

Any shell user can use chpass(1) to edit their own account information. You might not want to allow users to do this, however, as one piece of information that chpass(1) allows them to alter is their *hashed* password. Many regular users are not equipped to recognize a hashed password; I've seen people whom I believed Should Have Known Better try to change their password by entering it in the hashed password field. This locks them out until a sysadmin resets their password to a known value. While you might expect that an ignorant user would be intimidated by that long string of garbage, and hence decide to not touch it, that doesn't seem to be the case. I have yet to see anyone who is not intimidated by it a second time, however! As chpass(1) also allows them to change things such as their phone number and office location, however, you frequently cannot get away with disallowing use by regular users.

As root, you can edit any user's account information by running "chpass username." This brings up a text editor that displays the account information from /etc/master.passwd. For example, if I run "chpass chris" as root, here's what I get:

```
Changing user database information for chris.
Login: chris
Encrypted password:$2a$06$3M22I/s4FC8Mv80QOosPRed9KhzIUUrBD17pOW66TK.BInzP
Uid [#]: 1002
Gid [# or name]: 1002
Change [month day year]:
Expire [month day year]:
Class:
Home directory: /home/chris
Shell: /usr/local/bin/tcsh
Full Name: Chris B.
Office Location:
Office Phone:
Home Phone:
```

You can make any changes you need here, and they will be reflected appropriately in /etc/master.passwd and /etc/passwd. Chpass(1) doesn't change anything except those files. This means that if you move an account's home directory in chpass(1), you'll need to manually move the actual home directory. Otherwise, the user will get an unpleasant surprise when they try to log in!

User Editing Caveats

On OpenBSD systems, /etc/passwd is automatically generated from /etc/master.passwd via pwd_mkdb(8). Tools such as chpass(1) and vipw(8) do this automatically. If you're familiar with UNIX versions that allow you to directly edit

/etc/passwd, you need to retrain yourself when working on OpenBSD. Not only is your chance of making a mistake high, but your changes will be overwritten the next time someone uses a standard tool to change user information.

Groups of Users

UNIX classifies users into *groups*, each group consisting of people who perform similar administrative functions. A sysadmin can define a group called "www," add the people who edit web pages to that group, and give that group permission to read and write to web-related files. He could also create a group called "email," add the email administrators to that file, and set permissions on mail-related files so that users in that group can edit those files. Using groups in this manner is a powerful and oft-neglected tool for systems management.

What Groups Are You In?

Any user can identify the groups he has been assigned to with id(1). This command tells you which user you are logged in as and which groups you belong to. It also prints the numerical identifiers for your user ID (uid) and any groups you are assigned to (gid).

```
# id
uid=1000(mwlucas) gid=1000(mwlucas) groups=1000(mwlucas), 0(wheel)
#
```

If you are one of those lucky users who may use the root password to become the superuser, id(1) will tell you if you have done so and are in a root shell. (If you're running several X terminals on a UNIX desktop, it's quite easy to forget which window has your root shell in it.)

```
# id
uid=0(root) gid=0(wheel) groups=0(wheel), 2(kmem), 3(sys), 4(tty), 5(operator),
20(staff), 31(guest)
#
```

As you can see, root is a member of several groups by default. id(1) has several options, but they trim the output rather than provide additional information. If you want to only know the names of the groups you've been assigned to, for example, you could use "id -Gn". While this is useful for scripts, id's output is small enough that most people find it easier to skim the output for desired information than remember the options.

The id(1) command pulls this information from /etc/group.

/etc/group

The file /etc/group defines most group information. While the syntax of this file is fairly easy to understand, OpenBSD also provides some command-line tools to edit it. I generally find the /etc/group syntax simple enough to handle that I skip the command-line tools. If you're interested, the command-line tools are groupadd(8), groupdel(8), groupinfo(8), and groupmod(8). In most cases, it's just as easy to edit /etc/group directly. Each line in /etc/group contains four colon-delimited fields: the group name, the group password, the group ID, and a list of members. Here's a sample entry:

```
❶wheel:❷*:❸0:❹root,mwlucas,chris
```

The ❶group name is a user-friendly name for the group. In our example, the group is named "wheel." Group names are fairly arbitrary: You could call a certain group of users "bucksnort" if you wished. It's a good idea to choose group names that give you some idea of what they're for; while you might remember that the group "bucksnort" is intended for email system managers, will your coworkers understand that? Choose group names that mean something.

The ❷second field contains the group's encrypted password. Group passwords encouraged poor security practices, so most modern UNIXes don't support them. OpenBSD certainly doesn't do anything with group passwords. Some old software expects to find a password field in /etc/groups, however. Rather than leave this field blank or remove it entirely, we use an asterisk (*) as a placeholder, as in our example.

The ❸third field holds the group's unique numeric ID (gid). Many programs use the GID, rather than names, to identify groups. The "wheel" group has a gid of 0.

Last is a ❹comma-delimited list of all the users in that group. The users root, mwlucas, and chris are members of the group wheel.

Primary Group

When you create a new user the system creates a group that contains just that user, and it has the same name as the user. This is the user's "primary group." A user is automatically a member of his or her primary group, as listed in /etc/passwd. Some programs can be configured to treat users differently based on their primary group, rather than just general group membership.

Changing Group Memberships

If you want to add a user to a group, all you need to do is add their username to the end of the line for that group. For example, if I wanted to add "phil" to the "wheel" group, I would add ",phil" to the wheel group description.[3]

```
wheel:*:0:root,mwlucas,chris,phil
```

---

[3] Mind you, Phil would have to drug me into complete insensibility before I would add him to wheel. But that's an administrative decision, not a technical one.

Creating Groups

To create a new group, all you need is a name for the group and a group ID number. Technically, you don't even need a member for the group; some programs run as a member of a group, and the system uses the group permissions to control those programs just as users are controlled.

Traditionally, their group ID lists groups in order. The gid is an arbitrary number between 0 and 32,767. Generally speaking, group IDs below 1,000 are reserved for system administrator use. Programs that need a dedicated group ID usually use one in this range. User accounts have group IDs starting at 1,000 and going up. Some special groups start numbering at 32,767 and go down.

You can use any gid you want, but adhering to the standards will make life easier on your coworkers and successors.

So, let's add a group. This sample group is for a database program, so I'm going to call it "db." I'm arbitrarily adding this custom group with a gid of 5,000, and will start numbering these custom groups from there. I'll add our database administrator, phil, to this group.

```
db:*:5000:phil
```

That's it!

User Classes

Each OpenBSD user has a login class that defines limits on that user's access to system resources, how their environment behaves, and how users in that class authenticate. When you change the characteristics of a class, those limits affect all users in the class. All login classes are defined in /etc/login.conf.

You can change a user's class by running "chpass username" as root. Just put the class name in the "class" space provided, as shown in "Editing Users."

The Default Login Class

Whenever you create an account with adduser(8), that user is automatically assigned to the "default" class. The simplest way to manage login classes is to have the default class be the most commonly used class on your system. If your computer is an email server with a handful of administrators and several hundred mail users, set up the default class appropriately for the common case — the mail users. You can manually change the administrator's classes to a more appropriate one more easily than you can edit all those hundreds of users.

Class Definitions

Each class definition consists of a series of variable assignments. When a user logs in, login(1) uses these variables to establish the user's resource limits and environment setup. Each entry in the class definition begins and ends with a colon, although technically, each entry is all one line. The backslash character is a continuation marker, indicating that the computer should ignore the line break. Humans don't like 500 character lines of text, after all!

The standard /etc/login.conf starts with the "default" class. This gives the average user fairly broad access to the system. If you're running a modern system with gigabytes of RAM, you might find them too restrictive. If your OpenBSD box is a Pentium 166, however, these settings will basically give every user unlimited access to all system resources. If users consuming resources is a serious concern, you might well want to edit these settings. Here's a sample of the beginning of a login class.

```
default:\
        :path=/usr/bin /bin /usr/sbin /sbin /usr/X11R6/bin /usr/local/bin:\
        :umask=022:\
        :datasize-max=256M:\
...
```

There are many more variables in a login class, but this should be enough to give you the idea. You can completely change a user's experience by assigning him to the class that configures his login environment as you desire.

Some login.conf variables don't have a value; they change account behavior just by their presence. For example, the "requirehome" variable just needs to be in the class definition to have effect.

```
        :requirehome:\
```

Legal Values for /etc/login.conf Variables

You can give any of the following values to a login.conf variable assignment.

- Afull path to a text file.
- A comma-separated list of values.
- A number.
- A space-separated list of path names. If a ~ is the first character in a path name, the ~ is replaced by that particular user's home directory.
- A full path to a program.
- A size, either in bytes (default), kilobytes (k), or megabytes (m).
- A time, in seconds (default), minutes (m), hours (h), days (d), weeks (w), or years (y).

Some variables, of course, require particular sorts of values. A path to the home directory must be a full path, while the amount of memory the user may use cannot be a full path. In most cases, the legitimate answers are fairly obvious.

NOTE   *On many BSD systems, you must use cap_mkdb(8) to build a database file containing the values in /etc/login.conf for the changes to take effect. This is not necessary in OpenBSD; programs can parse /etc/login.conf directly. If you run cap_mkdb(8) on /etc/login.conf once, however, you must either continue to use it thereafter or remove the database file.*

OpenBSD's default /etc/login.conf contains a few different classes of users. If you want an idea of what sort of restrictions to put on users for various situations, check that file. Here, we're just going to discuss some of the commonly changed items.

Resource Limits

Resource limits allow you to control how much of the system any one user can tie up at one time. If you have several hundred users logged in to one machine, and one of those users decides to compile 30MB of source code, that person can consume far more than his fair share of processor time and memory. By limiting the resources that one user can monopolize at one time, you can make the system more responsive for less needy users. You can also give different login classes different resource limits.

Resource limits are frequently tied to each process. If you allow each process to use up to 20MB of RAM, and you allow each user to start 20 processes, one user could theoretically consume up to 400MB of memory. Here are several popular resource-limiting login.conf variables.

coredumpsize	The maximum size of any core dump
cputime	The maximum CPU time any process may use
datasize	The maximum memory size of data that can be consumed by one process
filesize	The maximum size of any file
stacksize	The maximum amount of memory on the stack usable by a process
memoryuse	The maximum amount of memory a process can lock
maxproc	The maximum number of processes the user can have running
openfiles	The maximum number of open files per process

Current and Maximum Resource Limits

The login.conf mechanism supports both advisory (or *current*) and maximum resource limits. Current limits (-cur) are generally advisory, and the user can override them at will. This works well on a cooperative system, where multiple users willingly share resources. Maximum limits (-max) are absolutes, and the user cannot exceed them.

To specify a current limit, add -cur to the limit name. To make a hard limit, add -max. For example, to limit the number of processes a user can have to 60, but give them a warning when they've used up half the maximum, you could do this:

```
:maxproc-cur=30:\
:maxproc-max=60:\
```

If you don't specify either -cur or -max, limits are hard limits and cannot be exceeded by the user.

Default Environment Setting

You can also specify default environment settings in /etc/login.conf. This can be better than setting them in a user's default .cshrc or .profile, as these settings affect all user accounts immediately upon each user's next login. Here are some common environment settings.

hushlogin	If present, no system information is given out during the initial login
ignorenologin	If present, the user can log in even when /etc/nologin exists
nologin	If present, the user cannot login
path	The default search path for programs
priority	The default process priority, or niceness
requirehome	If present, the user must have a valid home directory to log in
setenv	A list of default environment variables
shell	The shell given to the user; overrides the one in /etc/passwd
term	The default terminal type, if nothing else tries to set a terminal type
umask	The default umask
welcome	The file containing a message displayed to the user upon login

FTP Options

You can "chroot" FTP users to their home directory via the text file /etc/ftpchroot, but if you have a lot of FTP-only users you'll be better off using a login class to contain them. It is far more maintainable in the long run. Here are the FTP-affecting login.conf variables:

ftpchroot	If present, a FTP user is automatically chrooted into their login directory (by default, their home directory)
ftp-dir	The full path to a login directory for FTP users, to give several FTP users a common directory

If you chroot FTP users it's a good idea to tell them so with a "welcome" message (as described under "Default Environment Settings").

Controlling Password and Login Options

You can control various password operations in /etc/login.conf. Unlike the environment setup, many of these can only be set in this file. OpenBSD also includes some very extensive methods to control how authentication works: see Authentication. Here are some common options for boring password authentication.

localcipher

This controls the password encryption method. This defaults to blowfish hashing, but you could set this to "old" for compatibility with the 56-bit DES hashes used in many older versions of UNIX.

login-backoff

This controls how quickly a user can try to log in. After this many login attempts, the login program starts to slow down how often it offers a login prompt.

passwordcheck

This gives the full path to an external program that will validate new passwords for quality. OpenBSD expects to pass the password to the program on standard input. The program is expected to return a 0 if the password is adequate or a 1 if the password is inadequate.

passwordtime

This is the lifetime of a password and can be used to enforce regular password changes.

minpasswordlen

This is the minimum length of a password.

Authentication Methods

You can also choose valid authentication methods in /etc/login.conf. OpenBSD uses "BSD Authentication," which works in a different manner than the popular Pluggable Authentication Modules used in quite a few open-source operating systems. You just identify the authentication method you want in /etc/login.conf, and OpenBSD will attempt to authenticate users by that method. It couldn't be easier than that!

Merely setting an authentication mechanism does not configure the authentication method — it merely tells the system to use that authentication method. For example, telling OpenBSD to authenticate a certain class of users via Kerberos V doesn't magically set up a Kerberos domain. Accounts who use a particular authentication method will be locked out if that authentication mechanism is unavailable.

Some authentication methods are simply not compatible with some protocols, so not all authentication methods work with all programs that provide logins. For example, while SSH works with cryptocards, it doesn't work with the password-changing "lchpass" authentication method. You need to check the man page for each authentication method for bugs and test unusual combinations.

Some of these authentication methods require additional login.conf variables, which are described in the manual page for that authentication method. For example, if you want to use Radius authentication, you need to tell login.conf where to find your Radius server. The manual page that describes the necessary configuration is given in the following table of common authentication methods. Here are the actual authentication methods supported by OpenBSD's BSD Authentication.

krb4-or-pwd	Try Kerberos IV, then the local password file (see kerberos(1))
krb5-or-pwd	Try Kerberos V, then the local password file (see kerberos(1))
passwd	Use the local password file

krb4	Use Kerberos IV (see kerberos(1))
krb5	Use Kerberos V (see kerberos(1))
chpass	Do not log the user in, but instead change their Kerberos password or their local password if Kerberos is unavailable (see login_chpass(8))
lchpass	Do not log the user in, but instead change their local password (see login_lchpass(8))
radius	Use Radius authentication (see login_radius(8))
skey	Use S/Key (see skey(1))
activ	Use ActivCard X9.9 token-based authentication (see login_activ(8))
snk	Use Digital Pathways SecureNet Key authentication (see login_snk(8))
token	Use a generic X9.9 token authentication (see login_token(8)

Using Authentication Methods

Authentication methods are set by login.conf's auth variable, with a comma-separated list.

```
:auth=skey,passwd:\
```

One interesting thing is the ability to specify different authentication methods based on the service the user is connecting to. You can specify a "service name" after the "auth" keyword, to state that a set of authentication methods only applies to that particular service. For example, to allow only password authentication for FTP, you could use this:

```
:auth-ftp=passwd:\
```

Here are a few of the commonly used authentication services:

auth	Default used for all login requests that have no specific service attached
auth-ftp	FTP
auth-ssh	SSH
auth-su	su(1) authentication

For example, you could allow a user to log in with either their local password or S/Key, but if they want to use su(1) to become root, they must authenticate with S/Key. Here's a snippet from login.conf implementing that:

```
:auth=passwd,skey:\
:auth-su=skey:\
```

The default /etc/login.conf uses termcap(5) format. Termcap is powerful and flexible, and it can be confusing to the beginner — entire books have been written about it. The authentication entries in the default login classes use termcap expansions, but you can easily replace those with explicit declarations as we use in this section. Investing time in learning termcap(5) will enhance your sysadmin skills, but is beyond our scope here.

The Root Password

UNIX has an all-or-nothing concept of security. While the root user may do absolutely *anything*, other users may only do things root permits them to. This one fact has been responsible for a wide number of system intrusions. What's more, this coarse-grained approach causes any number of problems for system administrators. While you can create groups and use them to handle permissions for a variety of files, groups don't work well for sysadmin tasks. Only root can add users; only root can configure the network; only root can install system-wide software. Different people might handle these tasks separately. But they all need root privileges to do their work, so either you need to trust these people to stay out of each other's way or you need to configure an add-on access control tool. Only give the root password to those users you trust. All other users should be given access to particular tasks via sudo(8).

Using the Root Password

The su(1) command allows one user to become another user, if you have that user's password. I could use Chris's password to access Chris's account, just as if I was him. I could use Phil's password to effectively become Phil. Or, I could use the root password to become root.

Using su is very straightforward: Just type su, and the system will prompt you for a password. Enter the root password, and you will have a root shell!

```
# su
Password:
#
```

One thing to remember is that su gives you the shell of the user you're switching to. You might not want to do that — if you're on a system with multiple administrators, someone will not like the shell assigned to root. Do not change OpenBSD's root shell unless you know all the implications of doing so. Instead, use su's -m flag to keep your current shell and environment variables. For example, while my preferred shell is tcsh, OpenBSD's root shell is old-fashioned csh. If I use "su", I will get a csh shell. If I use "su -m", I will get my preferred tcsh shell. If you use "su -m", make sure that your shell doesn't contain any garbage that can confuse programs run as root. A nonstandard $PATH or $LD_LIBRARY_PATH environment variable combined with "su -m" can really interfere with your uptime.

Who May Use the Root Password?

Only users who are in the "wheel" group may use the root password. A user who is not in the wheel group cannot use the root password, even if he has the password. For example, suppose I get very lazy and write the root password on a sticky note and put it on my monitor. Phil wanders by, sees the password, and decides to give it a try from his account even though he isn't in the wheel group.

```
# su
Password:
you are not in group wheel
Sorry
#
```

What's more, his attempt will be logged in /var/log/authlog.

```
Jul  1 16:10:15 openbsd su: BAD SU phil to root on /dev/ttyp1
```

As a responsible security administrator, I should be checking my authorization log daily looking for these things. These errors are mailed to root each day as part of the daily security check, so there really is no excuse for not reading them.

Mind you, anyone who has this root password could walk up to the console and log in directly as root. He could then add himself to the wheel group if he wanted. This is bad. You could disallow root logins on the console, but you might need them sometime. The existence of the wheel group does not mean that you can skip hiding your root password!

If you have no users in the wheel group, then only the root account can get root access (without exploiting some sort of security hole, of course). If you forget to add your first account to the wheel group, you will need to log in to the console as root and make the necessary changes to /etc/group. If you've disabled root logins on the console, boot into single-user mode and make the changes.

Using Groups to Avoid Using Root

In addition to being a security concern, the root password distribution policy can cause contention in any organization. Many sysadmins hate giving out the root password, even to people who are responsible for maintaining part of the system. If this sort of sysadmin doesn't know how to properly manage the computer, this reluctance can prevent people from doing their jobs. Many other sysadmins hand out root to dang near anyone who wants it and then complain when the system becomes unstable. Both attitudes are untenable in the long run, especially when UNIX has powerful facilities for removing the need to use the root password.

One common situation is where a junior administrator is responsible for a particular portion of the system. I've had many DNS administrators work under me; these people don't ever install software, recompile the kernel, or do other low-level system tasks. They just answer emails, update zone files, and reload named. New junior admins frequently seem to think that they need root access to do this sort of work. By establishing your own groups, consisting of users who perform similar administrative functions, you can let people do their jobs without the root password. In this section, we'll implement group-level access control over nameserver files. The same principles apply to any files you should choose to protect. (Mail and web configuration files are other popular choices for this sort of delegation.)

OpenBSD has reserved user accounts for use by programs integrated with the system. For example, the nameserver runs under the user account called "named" and the group "named." As we covered earlier, if an intruder compromised the nameserver, she could only access the system with the privileges of the nameserver user. You can create a group called "dns" that includes the people who manage your nameserver. Do not use the program user for this sort of work! While you want programs run by the user named to be able to read files owned by the group "dns," you do not want the nameserver program to be able to write to files owned by the dns group. This further minimizes the damage a nameserver daemon compromise could inflict.

The simplest way to create a group to own files is to create a user to own them, and use that user's primary group as the group of the files. Adduser(8) will let you create a user to own these files. Because we already have a user "named," we'll call this administrative user "dns." The name isn't that important, but you should choose a name that you'll be able to remember easily.

```
# adduser -silent
Enter username [a-z0-9_-]: dns
Enter full name []: DNS Administration User
Enter shell csh ksh nologin sh [csh]: nologin
```

Give your administrative user a shell of "nologin," which gives the user the shell of /sbin/nologin. Nobody can log in with this account.

```
Uid [1001]:
```

If you want, you could specify a particular uid for these sorts of users. I've been known to choose uid numbers close to those used by the users for their related programs. For example, named has a uid of 70. I could decide to give dns a uid of 1,070 to keep some sort of relationship between my private system users and those used by OpenBSD. Remember, user IDs below 1,000 are reserved for OpenBSD's internal use.

```
Login group dns [dns]:
Login group is ``dns''. Invite dns into other groups: guest no
[no]:
```

The whole point of this sort of user is that they have their own group. Under no circumstances should you add such an administrative user to another group!

```
Enter password []:
Set the password so that user cannot logon? (y/n) [n]: y
```

Just hit return when you're asked for a password for this user, and adduser will give you a chance to set up the password so the user cannot log on. This is what you want; this administrative user should never need to log on for any reason.

Now that you have an administrative owner and a group for it, you can assign ownership of files to that user. A user and a group own every file. You can see existing file ownership and permissions with "ls -l".[4] Many new sysadmins pay close attention to the owner, and to the world permissions, but only skim the group permissions.

```
# ls -l
total 29
-rw-rw-r--  1 root   wheel    27136 Sep 14 09:36 file1
-rwxrwxr--  1 root   wheel     1188 Sep 14 09:35 file2
#
```

Here, file1 can only be read or written to by root or members of the group wheel, but can be read by anyone. Root or any member of the group wheel can read file2. If you're in the wheel group, you don't need to become root to edit or read file2 file; you can just open your text editor and go!

To change the owner of a file, use chown(1). To change a group owner on a file, use chgrp(1). Both take the same syntax; the name of the new owner and the filename.

```
# chown dns file1
# chgrp dns file1
# ls -l file1
-rw-rw-r--  1 dns dns   27136 Sep 14 09:36 file1
#
```

This file is owned by the user dns and in the group dns. Anyone who is in the dns group can read and write to this file, without using the root password. Finally, this file can be read by the nameserver. Add your junior administrators to the dns group in /etc/group, and abruptly they can edit files owned by the dns group without the root password.

The only thing the DNS administrators might need the root password for now is to restart the nameserver. This is easily dealt with by setting up a cron job to reload the nameserver on a regular basis. These admins still might want to reload the nameserver manually on special occasion, however. That's where sudo comes in.

---

[4] If you forget how UNIX permissions work, take a look at ls(1).

Hiding Root with Sudo

While proper use of groups can almost eliminate the need to give out the root password to edit files, that won't help with certain commands that can only be run by root. You could set up a cron job to, say, reload the nameserver each day at midnight, but on occasion your DNS administrator might need to restart the nameserver by hand. The ndc(8) command that's used for nameserver administration can only be run by root. Because root is an all-or-nothing affair, traditionally people who have had one minor task to perform have needed the root password.

OpenBSD includes the sudo(8) program and its associated tools, which implement fine-grained access control for commands that can only be run as particular users. With proper setup, the systems administrator can allow others to run any command as any other user. Sudo(8) is a very powerful tool, and can be configured to allow or restrict almost anything in any combination. This makes the documentation quite thick, with the result that the documentation tends to scare off new users. We're going to do a basic sudo setup that will cover almost all uses, but you should be aware that many more combinations are possible, and are documented in sudo(8) and sudoers(5).

Why Use Sudo?

Other than the obvious fine-grained access control sudo provides, there are a few other benefits to using sudo. One of the biggest advantages is the command logging. Every sudo(8) command is logged, making it very easy to track who has done what. Also, once you have sudo(8) configured correctly, the senior sysadmin can change the root password and not give it out. Nobody should need the root password if they have the correct sudo permissions, after all! Reducing the number of people who have the root password can help reduce security risk.

Also, sudo(8) can be run on almost all UNIX and UNIX-like operating systems. What's more, a single configuration file can be used on all of these systems, vastly easing administrator overhead.

Disadvantages to Sudo

By far, the most common disadvantage to sudo(8) is that junior administrators don't like it. If people have traditionally had root access on a system, they will perceive that they're losing something when the senior administrator implements sudo(8). The key to overcoming this is to make sure that people have the access that they have to actually perform the tasks that they're responsible for. If a junior administrator complains that he cannot perform a task, it means that he has either overreached his responsibilities or he needs more privileges.

The permissions syntax can be confusing until you understand it. Getting everything correct can be difficult the first time. Once you understand how sudo(8) manages its permissions, however, it's very quick and easy.

Finally, a faulty sudo(8) setup can create security holes. A thoughtless configuration will create holes in the system that a clever junior administrator can use to actually become root. This problem is best dealt with by a combination of careful configuration and administrative policy.[5]

Overview of Sudo

In short, sudo(8) is a setuid root wrapper that can run other commands as any user. It takes the command you want to run and compares it to its internal list of permissions and privileges. If sudo's permissions allow that particular user to run that command as the specified user, sudo runs that command. As root can run commands as any user, sudo can also run commands as any arbitrary system user. You can use this to give any user the ability to run particular commands as root, as any other user, or any combination desired.

The sudo system has three pieces. The first is the actual sudo(8) command, the setuid root wrapper. There's also a configuration file, /etc/sudoers. This file describes who may run what commands as which user and is fully documented in sudoers(5). Finally, the visudo(8) command allows administrators to edit the sudoers file without risking corruption of the sudo system. We'll consider each component in turn.

visudo

If the syntax in your sudoers file is incorrect, sudo will not run. If you're relying on sudo to provide access to the sudoers file and you corrupt the sudoers file, you can simultaneously lock yourself out of root-level activities on the system and be unable to correct your error. This is bad. Visudo(8) provides some protection against this sort of error.

Much like vipw(8), visudo(8) locks the file so only one person can edit the configuration file at a time. It then opens the sudo configuration file in an editor (vi(1) by default, but it respects the $EDITOR environment variable). When you exit the editor, visudo parses the file and confirms that there are no sudo syntax errors. This is not a guarantee that the configuration will do what you want, merely a confirmation that the file is actually valid. Visudo(8) will accept a configuration file that says "nobody may do anything via sudo" if the rules are properly formatted.

If visudo finds an error when you exit the editor, it will print out the line number and ask you what you want to do.

```
# visudo
>>> sudoers file: syntax error, line 44 <<<
What now?
```

---

[5] Despite the hopes of managers around the world, technical solutions only work so well at solving administrative problems. If people refuse to behave, eventually you need to break out the Big Stick and smack them until they get the idea.

Here, we've made an error on line 44. You have three choices: edit the file again, quit without saving any of the changes you made, or force visudo to write the sudoers file you created.

If you press "e", visudo will send you back to the editor. You can go to the line it complained about, and try to find your error.

If you enter "x", visudo will quit and revert the configuration file to what it was before you started editing. Your changes will be lost, but that may be all right. It's better to have the old, working configuration than to have a new, non-functional configuration.

Entering "Q" forces visudo to accept the file, syntax error and all. If your configuration file has incorrect syntax, sudo(8) will not run. Essentially, you're telling visudo(8) to break sudo(8) until such time as you log in as root to fix the problem. This is almost certainly not what you want to do!

/etc/sudoers

The sudoers file tells sudo who may run which commands as which users. OpenBSD stores the sudoers file as /etc/sudoers. (If you're using this section as a reference for the sudo system on another operating system, finding the sudoers file is your problem.) Never edit this file directly, even if you think you know exactly what change you want to make; always use visudo(8).

The various sample sudoers files you'll find on the Internet frequently look horrid and complicated, as they demonstrate all the nifty things sudo can do. At this stage you don't want to do nifty things — just boring, simple things like give particular users access to run certain commands. The bare syntax is very simple, however. Each rule entry in sudoers has the following format:

---
❶username   ❷host=❸command

The ❶username is the username of the user who may execute the command or an alias for the username.

The ❷host is the host name of the system where this rule applies. Sudo is designed so you can use one sudoers file on all of your systems. This allows you to set per-host rules.

The ❸command space lists the commands this rule applies to. You must have a full path to each command name, or sudo will not recognize it! (You wouldn't want people to be able to adjust their $PATH variable to access renamed versions of commands, now would you?)

You can use ALL keyword in any of these fields to match all possible options.

For example, suppose I trust user "chris" to run absolutely any command as root, on any system.

---
chris   ALL = ALL

Giving a single junior sysadmin total control of one of my systems isn't very likely. As Chris works for me, I know what duties I have assigned him and exactly what commands I want him to be able to run. Suppose Chris is in charge of the nameserver portion of this system. We control actual editing of the zone files with group permissions, but that won't help when the nameserver must be started, reloaded, or stopped. Here, I'll give him permission to run just the name daemon controller program, ndc(8), on any machine.

```
chris    ALL = /usr/sbin/ndc
```

If I'm sharing this file across several machines, it's quite probable that many of those machines are not even running a nameserver program. Here, I'll restrict which machine Chris may run this program on to the server called "dns1."

```
chris    dns1 = /usr/sbin/ndc
```

On the other hand, Chris is the administrator of the email server "mail1." This server is his responsibility, and he can run any commands on it whatsoever. I can set entirely different permissions for him on the mail server and yet use the same sudoers file on all the systems.

```
chris    dns1 = /usr/sbin/ndc
chris    mail = ALL
```

Multiple Entries in a Field

You can specify multiple entries in a single field by separating them with commas. Here, I'd like Chris to be able to mount floppy disks with mount(8), as well as control the nameserver.

```
chris    dns1 = /usr/sbin/ndc, /bin/mount
```

Running Commands as Non-root Users

You can specify a username in parentheses before a command to say that the user can use sudo to run those commands as that particular user. For example, suppose we have our nameserver set to run as the user "named," and all commands to control the server must be run as that user.

```
chris    dns1 = (named) /usr/sbin/ndc
```

/etc/sudoer Aliases

As you can imagine, once you have several different machines with multiple administrators with different levels of privilege, this gets complicated very quickly. When you have a few users with identical privileges, and large lists of commands that you'd like them to be able to use, maintenance becomes a challenge, as you have to wade through long lists of users, commands, and machines. Aliases can simplify these tasks and greatly clean up your sudo(8) configuration.

Basically, an alias is a group of users, hosts, or commands. When a user's duties change, you can just add them to the appropriate user alias to give them correct privileges. If you want your system operators to be able to back up the system but not restore data, you can remove restore(8) from their command alias. When you install a new server, adding the server name to the proper server alias will allow you to instantly give sysadmins the proper permissions to do their jobs.

An alias must be defined before it can appear in the sudoers file. For that reason, aliases generally appear at the top of the file. Each alias entry has a label saying what sort of alias it is, a label for the alias, and a list of the members of that alias.

User Aliases

User aliases are groups of users and are labeled with the string User_Alias. They contain a list of users that are in that alias.

```
User_Alias    DNSADMINS = chris,mwlucas
```

The user alias DNSADMINS contains two users, mwlucas and chris.

Run as Aliases

A *"run as" alias* is a special type of user alias. This lists users that other users can run commands as. We earlier mentioned that the nameserver could be run as the user "named." The DNS administrator would need to be able to run commands as that user, and you might have a run as alias for that. Many database applications require their own user, and run as that user. In many cases, a system administrator responsible for an application would also want to be able to run system backups as the user "operator". A run as alias allows you to do exactly that; one user can execute commands as another user, as specified by the sudo rules. These usernames could be listed in parentheses in front of the command, as described in "Running Commands as Non-root Users." Or, you could just create a single run as alias to group these commands. Run as aliases are labeled with Runas_Alias.

```
Runas_Alias    APPADMIN = dbuser,operator
```

Host Aliases

A *host alias* is just a list of hosts. It's labeled with the string Host_Alias. A host alias can be defined in terms of host names, IP addresses, or network blocks. Remember, if you're using host names your sudo configuration could be vulnerable to DNS problems! Here are examples of all three:

```
Host_Alias    DNSSERVERS = dns1,dns2,dns3
Host_Alias    SECURITYSERVERS = 192.168.1.254,192.168.113.254
Host_Alias    COMPANYNETWORK = 192.168.1.0/16
```

Command Aliases

A *command alias* is a list of commands. They're labeled with the string Cmnd_Alias. Here, we have an alias that includes all the commands necessary to back up or restore the system to or from tape.

```
Cmnd_AliasBACKUPS = /bin/mt,/sbin/restore,/sbin/dump
```

You might have a command alias that includes all the commands in a particular directory. Suppose we have a custom application that runs as a particular user and places all of its commands in the app user's home directory. Rather than list all the commands, you can just list a directory and use a wildcard to include everything in the directory.

```
Cmnd_AliasDBCOMMANDS = /usr/home/dbuser/bin/*
```

Long Lines

Every entry in /etc/sudoers must be on a single line. This can make the lines very long. If you have a long list of alias members or rules, you can skip to another line by using the \ character at the end of each incomplete line.

```
Cmnd_Alias    SHELLS = /bin/sh, /bin/csh, /usr/local/bin/ksh, \
          /usr/local/bin/tcsh, /usr/local/bin/bash
```

Using Aliases in /etc/sudoers

To use an alias, just put the alias name in the rule where you would normally list the user, command, or host name. Here, we've previously defined a user alias DNSADMINS. The users listed in the DNSADMINS alias get to run any commands at all on all of our servers.

```
DNSADMINS    ALL = ALL
```

Let's suppose that our user Phil has to manage an application that runs as a particular user. He can run any command on the system as this application user. We defined a run as alias in the last section for the user alias, APPADMIN, and an alias for commands needed to run the application, DBCOMMANDS.

```
phil ALL = (APPADMIN)DBCOMMANDS
```

As the application administrator, Phil might also have to run backups. We have already given the APPOWNER run as alias operator privileges, and we have a separate command alias for backup commands. We can combine them all like this:

```
phil ALL =  (APPOWNER) DBCOMMANDS, (APPOWNER)BACKUPS
```

This is much simpler to read than what this rule expands to.

```
phil ALL = (dbuser,operator)/usr/home/dbuser/bin/*,\
    (dbuser,operator)/bin/mt, (dbuser,operator)/sbin/restore,\
    (dbuser,operator)/sbin/dump
```

Some of the permissions granted by sudo in this case are unnecessary — having the database user run as alias is not necessary for running backups. Still, it's far tighter than just giving Phil the root password! You can also redefine rules to restrict your users as tightly as you desire.

Nesting Aliases

You can include aliases in aliases. For example, could group the DBCOMMANDS alias and the BACKUPS commands into a single group of commands.

```
Cmnd_Alias DBADMINS = BACKUPS,DBCOMMANDS
```

Using System Groups as User Aliases

Sudo(8) can pull group information from the system and incorporate it into sudoers as a user alias. Rather than explicitly define a user alias, you can give the OpenBSD group name preceded by a percent sign (%) to indicate it's a group name.

```
%wheel    ALL = ALL
```

Anyone in the system's wheel group can issue any command as root, on any server.

Duplicating Alias Names

You can reuse alias names. The user alias DBADMINS is not the same as the command alias DBADMINS. It's quite possible to have entries like this.

```
Cmnd_Alias    DBAPP = /usr/home/dbuser/bin/*
Host_Alias    DBAPP = server8,server12,server15
RunasAlias    DBAPP = dbuser,operator
User_Alias    DBAPP = chris,mwlucas
DBAPP    DBAPP = (DBAPP) DBAPP
```

If you do this, anyone who has to debug with your sudo(8) configuration will curse your name at great length. Even if you consider being cursed as a job perk, things like this tend to result in phone calls during the middle of whatever scant hours the senior sysadmin is permitted to sleep in.

Using Sudo

Now that you understand how sudo permissions are set, let's look at how to actually use sudo. Tell sudo that your account has privileges to run any command. (Because any readers of this book should already have root on at least one system — preferably their OpenBSD test box — this won't be a security issue.)

Sudo and Passwords

The first time you run sudo(8), it will prompt you for a password. Enter the password for your own account, not the root password. If you give an incorrect password, sudo will insult your typing abilities, mental facilities, or ancestry, and let you try again. After three incorrect passwords, sudo gives up on you. You'll have to re-enter the command you want to run.

Once you enter a correct password, sudo(8) records the time. If you run sudo(8) again within five minutes, it won't ask you for a password. After you don't use sudo for five minutes, however, you must re-authenticate. This makes work easier when you're issuing a series of commands under sudo, but times out reasonably quickly in case you walk away from the computer.

Checking Sudo Permissions

When you're a user on a system with sudo, one thing you'll probably want to know is what commands the systems administrator has permitted you to run. Sudo's -l flag will tell you this:

```
# sudo -l
Password:
User mwlucas may run the following commands on this host:
    (root) ALL
#
```

If you had tighter restrictions, they would be displayed.

Running Commands Under Sudo

To run commands via sudo, just put the word "sudo" before the command you actually want to run. For example, here's how you would become a root by using su via sudo:

```
# sudo su
Password:
#
```

Using sudo(8) to become root simply allows the senior sysadmin keep the root password a closely held secret. This isn't entirely useful, as with unrestricted sudo access junior administrators can change the root password. Still, it's a start toward keeping the system more secure.

You can run more complicated commands under sudo(8), with all of their regular arguments. For example, "tail -f" is excellent to view the end of a log file, and to have new log entries appear on the end of the screen. Some log files are only visible to root — for example, the log that contains sudo access information. You might want to view these logs without bothering to become root.

```
# sudo tail -f /var/log/authlog
openbsd/usr/src/usr.bin/sudo;sudo tail -f /var/log/secure
Jul 29 13:24:19 openbsd sudo:  mwlucas : TTY=ttyp0 ; PWD=/home/mwlucas ; USER=root
; COMMAND=list
Jul 29 13:30:03 openbsd sudo:  mwlucas : TTY=ttyp0 ; PWD=/home/mwlucas ; USER=root
; COMMAND=/usr/bin/tail -f /var/log/authlog
...
```

Running Commands as Other Users

You can choose to run commands as a user other than root, if you have the appropriate permissions. For example, suppose we have our database application where commands must be run as the database user. We saw in /etc/sudoers how to set up permission to do this. You tell sudo to run as a particular user by using the "-u" flag and a username. For example, the operator user has the privileges necessary to run dump(8) and back up the system.

```
# sudo -u operator dump /dev/sd0s1
```

Excluding Commands from ALL

Now that you know the basics of sudo, let's look at a common situation that trips up even experienced systems administrators. Sometimes you want to disallow users from executing certain commands, but give them access to every other command. You can try to do this with the "!" operator, but it's not entirely effective. Because it's a popular setup, however, we'll discuss how this works and then what's wrong with it.

First, define command aliases that contain the forbidden commands. Popular commands to exclude are shells (if you execute a shell as a user, you become that user) and su(1). Then give your user a command rule that excludes those aliases with the "!" operator.

```
Cmnd_Alias     SHELLS = /bin/sh,/bin/csh,/usr/local/bin/tcsh
Cmnd_Alias     SU = /usr/bin/su
mwlucas  ALL = ALL,!SHELLS,!SU
```

Looks great, doesn't it? And it seems to work.

```
openbsd~;sudo sh
Password:
Sorry, user mwlucas is not allowed to execute '/bin/sh' as root on openbsd.
openbsd~;
```

Remember, sudo uses full paths for all the commands. You're allowing the user to run any command they want, except for a few that are specified by their full path. All that user needs to do is change their path to one of these commands to run it! The easiest way to do this is by copying the command to another location.

```
# id
uid=1000(mwlucas) gid=1000(mwlucas) groups=1000(mwlucas), 0(wheel)
# cp /bin/sh /tmp/sh
# sudo /tmp/sh
# id
uid=0(root) gid=0(wheel) groups=0(wheel), 2(kmem), 3(sys), 4(tty), 5(operator),
20(staff), 31(guest)
#
```

Hello, root!

This sort of restriction can be bypassed trivially by anyone who understands even the basics of how sudo works. This problem is well documented in the sudo manual and the other literature. And people *still* insist upon using it to protect production systems!

The lesson is: if you have users that you do not trust with unrestricted access to the system, do not exclude commands from their sudo permissions. Instead, explicitly list the commands that they may use, and leave it at that. If these users want more access, they will have to ask you for particular commands — and if you don't trust them, you'll want to know what they're running!

Sudo Logs

All this tracking and accountability is nice, but where does it account to? Sudo messages are logged to /var/log/secure. Each log message contains a time stamp, the name of the user, the directory where sudo was run, and the command that was run.

```
Jul 29 11:21:02 openbsd sudo:    chris : TTY=ttyp0 ; PWD=/home/chris ; USER=root ;
COMMAND=/sbin/mount /dev/fd0 /mnt
```

In the worst case, you can backtrack exactly what happened when something breaks. For example, if one of my systems doesn't reboot correctly because /etc/rc.conf is missing or corrupt, I can check the sudo logs to see who touched it.

```
Jul 29 11:34:56 openbsd sudo:    chris : TTY=ttyp0 ; PWD=/home/chris ; USER=root ;
COMMAND=/bin/rm /etc/rc.conf
```

If everyone had been using su(1) or even using "sudo su" instead of sudo(8) to run each individual command, I would have had no clue about why the system broke. With sudo(8) logs, once I get this computer up and running again I know who to blame. In this case, my ability to justifiably scream at Chris until I feel better in and of itself makes sudo(8) worth implementing.

8

NETWORKING

TCP/IP:
Learn how it fits together,
You cannot escape.

BSD is famous for its network performance.
In fact, the TCP/IP network protocol itself was
first developed in the days when BSD lived in
Berkeley, and BSD was the first major deployment
of TCP/IP. Many other operating systems have chosen to
use the BSD network stack because of its high performance and liberal licensing. While other protocols were
considered more exciting during the 1980s, the wide
availability of the BSD stack made it the de facto standard.

Many systems administrators today have a vague familiarity with some of the
basics of networking, but don't really understand how it all hangs together. Good
sysadmins come from all walks of life, but they all have one thing in common: They

understand the network. Knowing what an IP address really is, how a netmask really works, and what a port number means is part of what transforms a novice into a professional. We'll cover some of these issues here.

NOTE *TCP/IP is a very dense topic, with many details, "gotchas," and caveats. While this section gives a good overview, we cannot possibly cover everything. If you want to know more about TCP/IP, pick up one of the big thick books on the subject. My favorite is Stevens's* TCP/IP Illustrated, *volumes 1 through 3.*

Network Layers

Every piece of the network is divided into layers. Each layer handles a specific part of the networking process and interacts only with the layers above and below it to provide a solid connection. New users often have trouble understanding this and laugh when it's said that layers "simplify" the networking process. We'll go over it in some detail, but the important thing to remember right now is that each layer only communicates with the layer directly above it and the layer directly beneath it.

The classic OSI network layer diagram has seven pieces, is exhaustively complete, and covers any situation in any network protocol. The Internet isn't "every situation" however, and this isn't a book about networking. We're limiting our discussion to the Internet and other networks that use the same protocols, so we can simplify this somewhat and divide the network into four layers: the application, the logical protocol, the physical protocol, and the physical layer.

The Physical Layer

At the very bottom we have the physical layer, which includes the network card and the wire, fiber, or radio waves running out of it. This layer includes the physical box that is a switch, hub, or base station, wires running from that device to the router, and the fiber that runs from your office to the telephone company. The telephone company switch is part of the physical layer, as are the transcontinental fibers. If someone can smash, drop, or cut it and inconvenience you, it's part of the physical layer. From this point on we're going to refer to the physical layer as a "wire," although it can be just about any sort of hardware.

A piece of wire, or some other physical media for signals to travel over — it's really that simple. If your wire is intact and meets the requirements of the physical protocol, you're in business. If not, you're hosed. Without a physical layer, the rest of the network will not function, period, end. One of the functions of Internet routers is to connect one sort of physical layer to another. The physical layer has no decision-making abilities and no intelligence; everything it does is dictated by the physical protocol.

The Physical Protocol Layer

The physical protocol layer is where things get interesting. The physical protocol talks over the wire. It encodes transmissions in the actual ones and zeros that are sent over the physical layer in the appropriate method for that sort of physical layer. For example, Ethernet uses Media Access Control (MAC) addresses and the Address Resolution Protocol (ARP); dial-up and wide area networks use the Point-to-Point Protocol (PPP). The physical protocol has to know how to speak to the physical layer.

While Ethernet and PPP are the most popular physical protocols, you will find many other protocols such as Asynchronous Transfer Mode (ATM), High Level Data Link Control (HDLC), and Internetwork Packet Exchange (IPX), as well as combinations such as the PPP over Ethernet used by some home-broadband vendors. While OpenBSD supports many different physical protocols, it doesn't support them all. If you have some unusual networking requirements, you will want to investigate whether OpenBSD can support them.

Some physical protocols have been implemented over many different physical layers; for example, Ethernet has been transmitted over twoax[1], coax, cat3, cat5, cat7, optical fiber, and radio waves. With minor changes in the device drivers, the physical protocol can address any sort of physical layer. This is one of the ways in which layers simplify the network. We will discuss Ethernet and PPP in some detail. Once you understand those, you should be able to figure out how to use other protocols without too much difficulty.

The physical protocol passes information to and from the physical layer to and from the logical protocol layer.

The Logical Protocol Layer

A computer program intended to run over any sort of network, over any sort of physical layer and physical protocol, cannot worry about the inner working of the physical protocol or physical layer. The logical protocol provides a consistent interface to programs that need to access the network, no matter which sort of physical layer it is running over. The most popular logical protocols are Internet Protocol (IP) and Transmission Control Protocol (TCP). These protocols provide things such as IP addresses and port operations. When a packet is transmitted, it includes a flag that identifies which protocol it uses. Logical protocols can work side by side and can even depend upon one another.

There are many logical protocols. See the file /etc/protocols for a mostly complete list. The ones we're most concerned with are IP and TCP (already mentioned), Internet Control Message Protocol (ICMP), and User Datagram Protocol (UDP).

The logical protocol talks to the physical protocol layer and to applications.

Applications

You can call applications another layer of the network. This is anything that the end user sees or any server program. Web browsers are applications, as are web servers, as are shell prompts and email clients, or compilers, or anything else. Applications only have to worry about the logical protocol and the application user.

---

[1] "Twoax" required two thick pieces of cable for each network connection. I saw this on an IBM System 38 in the fall of 1999, on a system that didn't speak TCP/IP. The moral of the story is: Be careful with what you implement today, because you may have to live with it for a *very* long time.

The Life and Times of a Network Request

Now that you understand something about the function of each layer, let's look at how this works in the real world. Some of this touches on stuff that we'll cover later in this chapter, but if you're reading this book you're probably conversant enough with networks that you'll be able to follow it. If you have trouble, you may want to read this section once again after finishing the chapter.

Suppose a user on a computer connected to the Internet via your company's Ethernet wants to look at the Yahoo web page. The user interfaces with the application and types in the URL. The web browser needs to know how to make requests of the next layer down, so it translates the host name into an IP address and sends a request for a connection to TCP port 80 on that IP address down to the logical protocol layer.

The logical protocol layer examines the request it has received from the application. Because the application has requested a TCP/IP connection, the logical protocol allocates the appropriate system resources for that sort of connection. The request is broken up into chunks, or *packets*, to be sent over Internet Protocol.

From here on, the logical protocol doesn't care about the application's actual request; instead, it wants to deliver these packets to the address required. The Internet Protocol subsystem checks its internal tables to see how to reach the requested IP address from this computer. It then bundles up the packets, adds on the IP routing information, and hands the packets to the physical protocol layer.

The physical protocol layer examines the request from the logical protocol layer. The logical protocol doesn't know anything about the packets it is given; it doesn't know that this is a web request or its final destination. All it knows about is getting each packet to its destination. The physical protocol just knows that it needs to add its own information to the packet. This packet-plus-physical-protocol chunk of data is called a *frame*. Finally, it hands the frame off to the physical layer for broadcast on the local Ethernet.

The physical layer simply transmits a bunch of zeros and ones over the local network. It has no idea what sort of protocol is being spoken, or how these numbers may be echoed through a switch, hub, or repeater, but one of the hosts on this network is presumably the router out of the network.

The physical layer of your router accepts these zeros and ones and hands them up to the physical protocol. The physical protocol will strip off the Ethernet information and hand the resulting packet up to the logical protocol handler within the router. The router's logical protocol layer examines the packet, specifically checking the destination address. Once it knows where the packet is supposed to go, it can consult its internal routing tables and decide how to get the packet to that destination. It then hands the packet down to a physical protocol layer. This might be another Ethernet interface, or (more likely) a PPP interface out over a T1.

Your wire can go through various physical changes as your data travels. For example, your T1 line can be aggregated into a DS3 over fiber, which could then be transformed into an OC192 cross-country link. Thanks to the wonders of layering and abstraction, you don't need to know about any of these.[2]

When your request finally reaches its destination, the computer at the other end of the transaction, it starts a return trip all the way back up the protocol stack. The physical layer gives each frame to the physical protocol, which does some basic sanity checking on the frame to be sure it hasn't been corrupted in transit. Once the physical protocol layer is satisfied that the frame is correct, it removes the physical protocol encapsulation and hands a naked packet up to the logical protocol.

The logical protocol, in turn, performs its own sanity checking. Remember how the logical protocol broke up the request into packets for easy handling? Now it assembles the packets into a stream of data. It then hands this stream of data to the application — in this case, a web server.

The application can process the request and return an answer. This answer descends the protocol stack again and travels across the network, bouncing up and down various protocol stacks along the way as necessary.

And if this doesn't all happen very, very quickly, your user will call the help desk and complain.

This seems like an awful lot of work, but it's an excellent example of why layering is important. Each layer knows only what it absolutely must about the layers above and below it, making it possible to swap out the innards of layers if desired. When a new physical protocol is created, the other layers don't have to care; the logical protocol just hands the request off to the physical protocol layer and lets that layer do its thing. When you have a new type of network card, all you need to do is write a driver that interfaces with the physical protocol; the application and logical protocol layers don't care.

Networking Basics

This section introduces the basics of networking in OpenBSD and some tools you need to be able to work well with it. Some parts are common to all sorts of TCP/IP networks, such as IP addresses. Others are specific to BSD-based operating systems, such as mbufs. The power offered by OpenBSD requires more understanding than that needed to run a point-and-click operating system.

Mbufs

OpenBSD optimizes networking by using mbufs. An *mbuf* is a discrete chunk of kernel memory set aside for networking. A packet starts off life as a mbuf. Rather than copying the contents of a packet to the next network layer, each layer passes around a pointer to the mbuf. Copying the data consumes far more time and resources than simply handing off responsibility for the data while leaving the data itself in the same spot.

---

[2] Unless, of course, some of it breaks, in which case your managers will want to know exactly what sort of equipment it is, how long it will take to repair, and why you need it anyway.

Mbufs are carefully designed to not require dramatic changes. When the logical protocol creates an mbuf, it leaves space at the front and back for physical protocol headers, which further minimizes the amount of copying required. A packet becomes a frame within the same mbuf.

Those of you who are C programmers should recognize a pointer here. The pointer to the mbuf is handed around, while the mbuf itself remains constant. The rest of us just need to have a basic idea of what an mbuf is. You'll keep tripping across mentions of mbufs throughout documentation on the OpenBSD network stack, so it's important to at least have a vague awareness of them.

How Many Mbufs?

Each kernel allocates a certain number of mbufs. When you run out of mbufs, you can't push more data. This raises the obvious questions: How many mbufs do you have, and how can you get more?

The netstat(1) command is a general interface into the network stack. It has many functions that are wildly different. While this is definitely a deviation from the UNIX philosophy of "small tools that each do one thing well," netstat has been this way for so long that nobody's really inclined to change it. The "-m" flag to netstat gives some basic mbuf information.

```
# netstat -m
❶18 mbufs in use:
      ❷   1 mbuf allocated to packet headers
          17 mbufs allocated to socket names and addresses
0/12 mapped pages in use
36 Kbytes allocated to network ❸(12% in use)
0 requests for memory denied
0 requests for memory delayed
0 calls to protocol drain routines
#
```

Here, we see ❶how many mbufs have been used and ❷what part of the network they're being used for. We also can see ❸how much of the kernel memory reserved for network operations is in use. This particular system has lots of kernel memory left and is using very few mbufs.

The number of mbufs a system has is controlled by the NMBCLUSTERS kernel option. Changing this requires patching your kernel. Take a look at Chapter 11 for some discussion of what this implies. Generally speaking, your system will complain if it starts running out of mbufs; you will see "mclpool limit reached" messages on the console and in /var/log/messages.

Bits

As a systems administrator, you're going to start seeing terms like 32-bit and 48-bit more and more frequently. Too many sysadmins just nod and smile when they see these terms, but don't really understand what they mean. If you're running OpenBSD, that means you have an interest in security, and there is *no* security without understanding, so we're going to briefly discuss bits here.

You probably already know that a computer treats all data as zeros and ones, and that a single one or zero is a bit. When a protocol specifies a number of bits, it's talking about the number as soon by the computer. A 32-bit number has 32 digits, all of which are either one or zero. You were probably introduced to binary math, or *base 2*, back in elementary school and remembered it just long enough to pass the test. Binary math is simply a different way to work with the same numbers we see every day.

In decimal math (or *base 10*), the math we typically use every day to balance our checkbook or figure out how much over the speed limit we're driving, digits run from 0 to 9. When you want to go above the highest digit you have, you add a digit on the left and set your current digit to 0. (This is the whole "carry the one" thing you learned many years ago, and now probably do without conscious thought.) Binary math is exactly the same, except that digits run from 0 to 1. When you want to go above the highest digit you have, you add a digit on the left and set your current digit to 0. It's the same thing, just with fewer digits.

Here are the first few decimal numbers converted into binary as an example.

Decimal	Binary
0	0
1	1
2	10
3	11
4	100
5	101
6	110
7	111
8	1000

When you have a 32-bit number, such as an IP address, you have a string of 32 ones and zeros. Ethernet MAC addresses are 48-bit numbers. Got that? Good.

Just to make things difficult, UNIX also uses hexadecimal numbers in some cases (such as MAC addresses and netmasks). Hexadecimal numbers are 4 bits long; each digit goes up to 16. This is accomplished by using the numbers 0 through 9, plus the letters A through F. When you reach the last digit, you reset the current digit to zero and add a digit to the left of the number. For example, to count to sixteen in hexadecimal you go "1, 2, 3, 4, 5, 6, 7, 8, 9, A, B, C, D, E, F, 10."

Numbers in hexadecimal are usually marked with a leading "0x." The number 0x11 is a hexadecimal number equal to the decimal number 17, while the number 11 is plain old decimal 11. (If a hex number is not marked by a leading 0x, it's usually in a place where the output is always in hex numbers.)

When you're working with hexadecimal, decimal, and binary numbers, the simplest thing to do is to break out a scientific calculator. All modern medium-end or better calculators have functions to convert between the three systems. Even the Microsoft Windows calculator has that function. If you want to stick with OpenBSD, you can install /usr/ports/math/hexcalc (see Chapter 13).

IP Addresses and Netmasks

An IP address is a unique 32-bit number assigned to a particular network node. Some IP addresses are more or less permanent, such as those assigned to servers. Others change as required by the network, such as those used by dial-up clients. Individual machines on a shared network get adjoining IP addresses; we'll explore what this means a little later.

Rather than expressing that 32-bit number as a single number, IP addresses are broken up into four 8-bit numbers. (We'll see why in a little bit.) These numbers are expressed as decimal numbers. While 192.168.1.1 is the same as the four binary numbers 11000000.10101000.00000001.00000001, or 11000000101010000000000100000001, or even the hexadecimal c0.a8.1.1 or 0x30052000401, the four decimal numbers are easiest to work with.[3]

If your company is hooking up to the Internet, your ISP will issue you a block of IP addresses. Frequently this is a small block, say, 16 or 32 IP addresses. If your system is colocated on a server farm, you might only get a few IP addresses. It all depends upon your needs. The size of your IP block determines your netmask — or, the size of your netmask determines how many IP addresses you have.

If you've done networking for any length of time, you've seen the netmask 255.255.255.0. You might even know that the wrong netmask will keep your system from working. In today's world, that simple netmask is becoming less and less common. To understand why this is, you need to understand something about the history of IP addressing.

Many years ago, IP addresses were issued in blocks of three sizes: class A, class B, and class C. (There were also a few chunks of class D and class E space, but those really aren't relevant to the discussion.) This terminology has been obsolete for quite some time, but we'll use it as a starting point.

Class A was very simple: The first of the four numbers in an IP address were fixed. The InterNIC might issue you a class A like "10.0.0.0." You could assign any of the last three numbers in any manner you liked, but all your IP addresses began with 10. For example, you could delegate 10.1.0.0 through 10.1.1.255 to your data center, 10.1.2.0 through 10.1.7.255 to your Detroit office, and so on. Only very large companies, such as Ford and Xerox, as well as influential academic computing institutions such as MIT, received class A blocks.

In a class B block, the first two of the four numbers in the IP address were fixed. Your class B block would look something like 192.168.0.0. Every IP address you used internally began with the first two numbers 192.168, but you could assign the last two numbers as you wanted. Many midsized companies got class B blocks.

Similarly, a class C block had the first three numbers fixed. This was the standard for small companies. The ISP would issue a block like 209.69.178.0 and let you assign the last number as you wanted.

---

[3] Yes, you could say that the decimal numbers are easiest to work with in all cases. But that would just show that you aren't a *real* computer person and possibly get you burned at the stake.

This scheme wasted a lot of IP numbers. Many small companies don't need 256 IP addresses. Many medium-sized companies need more than 256, but fewer than the 65,000 in a class B block. And almost nobody needs the full 16 million addresses in a class A block. Still, those were the choices. Before the Internet boomed, they were good enough. Remember, back in the 1980s the thought that private individuals would hook up to the Net from home, for entertainment, was laughable.

Today, IP addresses are issued by prefix length, commonly called a *slash*. You will see IP blocks such as 192.168.1.128/25. While this looks confusing, it's merely a way of using classes with much greater granularity. You know that each number in an IP address is 8 bits long. By using a class, what you're saying is that a certain number of bits are "fixed" — you cannot change them on your network. A class A address has 8 fixed bits, a class B has 16, and a class C has 24.

This isn't a class in binary math, so I won't make you draw it out and do the conversion. But think about an IP address as a string of binary numbers. On your network you can change the bits on the far right, but not the ones on the far left.

There's no reason that the boundary between the two must be on one of those convenient 8-bit lines that separate the decimal versions of the numbers. A prefix length is simply the number of fixed bits you are stuck with. A /25 means that you have 25 fixed bits, or one more fixed bit than what used to be called a class C. You can play with 7 bits. In the following sample, your fixed bits are all ones, and the bits you can change are zeros.

```
11111111.11111111.11111111.10000000
```

It's very simple — if you think in binary. You won't have to work with this every day, but if you don't understand the underlying binary concepts, the decimal conversion looks like total gibberish. With practice, you'll learn to recognize some bits of decimal gibberish as legitimate binary conversions.

So, that's the theory. What does this mean in practice?

First of all, blocks of IP addresses are issued in multiples of 2. If you have 4 bits to play with, you have 16 IP addresses ($2*2*2*2=16$). If you have 8 bits to play with, you have (2^8) 256 IP addresses. If someone says you have 13 IP addresses, you're either sharing an Ethernet with other people or they're wrong.

A netmask is simply another way of specifying how many bits are fixed. In the computing world, an 8-bit number runs from 0 to 255. If you have 24 fixed bits, also known as a /24, and formerly known as a class C, your netmask is 24 ones followed by eight zeros: 11111111.11111111.11111111.00000000, or 255.255.255.0. If you've been around a few networks, that should look familiar. If you have a /25, however, you have 25 fixed bits. This comes to 11111111.11111111.11111111.10000000, or 255.255.255.128.

It's not uncommon to see a host's IP address with its netmask attached, e.g. 192.168.3.4/26. This gives you everything you need to know to get the host on the network. (Finding the default gateway would be another issue, mind you!)

Computing Netmasks in Decimal

You probably don't want to repeatedly convert from decimal to binary and back. Here's a trick to calculate your netmask while staying in decimal land.

First, learn how many actual IP addresses you have. This will be a multiple of 2. You'll almost certainly be issued a network smaller than a /24. Subtract the number of IP addresses you have from 256. This is the last number of your netmask.

For example, if you have a /26, or 64 IP addresses, the last part of your netmask is (256–64=)192. Your netmask would be 255.255.255.192.

You still need to use a bit of logic to avoid binary conversions. Figuring out legitimate addresses on your network can be a bit of a pain. If your IP address is 192.168.1.100/26, you'll need to know that a /26 is 26 fixed bits, or 64 IP addresses. Look at the last number of your IP address, 100. It certainly isn't between 0 and 63, but it is between 64 and 127. The other hosts on your IP block have IP addresses ranging from 192.168.1.64 to 192.168.1.127.

At this point, I should mention that netmasks are frequently shown in hex numbers. You might feel like throwing up your hands and giving up the whole thing. To simplify your life, I'm including a table of netmasks, IP information, and general goodness for /24 and smaller networks.

Table 8-1: Netmasks and IP address conversions

Prefix	Binary Mask	Decimal Mask	Hex Mask	Available IPs
/24	00000000	0	0x00	256
/25	10000000	128	0x80	128
/26	11000000	192	0xc0	64
/27	11100000	224	0xe0	32
/28	11110000	240	0xf0	16
/29	11111000	248	0xf8	8
/30	11111100	252	0xfc	4
/31	11111110	254	0xfe	2
/32	11111111	255	0xff	1

Unusable IP Addresses

You now understand how slashes, netmasks, and IP address assignments work together and how, for example, a /28 has 16 IP addresses. Unfortunately, you cannot use all of the IP addresses in a block. The first IP address in any block is the network number. It's used for internal bookkeeping.

Similarly, the last number in any block of IP addresses is the broadcast address. According to the IP specifications, every machine on a network is supposed to respond to a request to this address. This allows you to ping the broadcast address and quickly determine which IP addresses are in use. For example, on a typical /24 network, the broadcast address is x.y.z.255. In the late 1990s, however, this feature was turned into an attack technique. It's now disabled by default on most operating systems, including OpenBSD.

In any case, the point is that you cannot assign either the first or last IP address in a network to an interface without causing some problems on the network. Some systems will fail gracefully; others will not. Go ahead, try it sometime — preferably after hours, when the network is not in use.[4]

Basic TCP/IP

TCP/IP is the general label applies to a whole bunch of different protocols that hold the Internet together. Each protocol has its own rules and methods. We're going to discuss four protocols here: Internet Protocol, Internet Control Message Protocol, Transmission Control Protocol, and User Datagram Protocol. You can get a partial list of protocols in /etc/protocols.

IP

IP provides two basic services: the formation of packets that can be transmitted over TCP/IP networks and the addressing scheme. We've already discussed both of those in as much detail as we're going to, so I'll leave it here. IP is protocol number 0.

ICMP

Internet Control Message Protocol is a standard for transmitting routing and availability messages across the Internet. Tools such as ping(8) and traceroute(8) use ICMP to gather their results. ICMP packets are vital to normal network behavior, but can be used to gather information about your network. We'll examine how this can be avoided without breaking basic functions in Chapter 17.

UDP

The User Datagram Protocol is arguably the most bare-bones data transfer protocol possible that can run over IP. It has no error handling, no content verification, and no defense whatsoever against data loss. Despite these drawbacks UDP can be a good choice for particular sorts of data transfer, and many vital Internet services use it.

When a host transmits data via UDP, it doesn't know if the data ever reaches its destination. Programs that receive UDP data simply listen to the network and receives what comes that way. When that program receives data via UDP, it has no way to verify the source of that data. While UDP packets include a source address, this is very easily faked. This is why UDP is called *connectionless*.

An application using UDP most often has its own error-correction requirements that don't jibe with those provided by protocols such as TCP. For example, client DNS queries need to time out within just a few seconds. TCP times connections out after several minutes. Because a system wants to reject a failed DNS request well before that, UDP is used.

---

[4] Or during peak usage hours, if you want a good story to tell at your next job.

TCP

Transmission Control Protocol includes such nifty things as error correction and packet recovery. The receiver must acknowledge every packet sent, or it will be retransmitted. Applications that use TCP can expect reliable data transmission (unless, of course, something goes wrong at the physical layer).

Unlike UDP, TCP is a connected protocol. For data to be transmitted, the two hosts must set up a channel for data to flow across. One host requests a connection, the other host responds to the request, and then the first host starts transmitting. This setup process is known as the *three-way handshake*. The exact specifics are not important right now, but you should know that this process happens. It will become quite important when we start talking about packet filtering in Chapter 17. Similarly, once a data transmission is complete the system must do a certain amount of work to tear down the connection.

How Protocols Fit Together

You can compare IP, ICMP, TCP, and UDP to sitting with your family at a holiday dinner. IP gives every person at the table a unique chair. ICMP lets you see the other people at the table, and understanding that to hand the peas to your doddering Uncle Chris you must pass it by Cousin Phil. TCP is where you hand someone a dish and the other person must say "thank you" before you will let go. Finally, UDP is like tossing a muffin at Aunt Betty: She might catch it, it might bounce off her forehead, or it could be snatched out of midair by the dog.

Network Ports

Have you ever noticed that computers have too many ports? Well, we're going to add TCP and UDP ports into the mix. Protocol ports permit one server to provide many different network services over a single protocol, multiplexing connections between machines.

When a TCP or UDP packet arrives at a system, it requests delivery to a certain port. Server programs attach, or *bind* to ports on a system. For example, Internet mail servers generally bind to TCP port 25. Connections intended for the mail server will try to connect to port 25. This means that other programs could connect to the same machine on other ports.

The /etc/services file contains a list of port numbers and the services that they're commonly associated with. It's possible to run almost any service on any port, but by doing so you'll confuse other Internet hosts that try to connect to your system. If someone tries to send you email, their mail program will automatically connect to port 25 on your machine. If your server runs email on port 77, and you have a web server on port 25, that mail will never arrive. What's more, people will never see the web page on that system.

/etc/services has a very simple format, with five columns: the official service name, the port number, the protocol, any aliases for that service, and comments. For example, one service that could be found on many UNIX hosts was Quote of the Day, also known as qotd. If you check /etc/services, you'll find the following entry:

```
qotd 17/tcp    quote
```

The Quote of the Day service runs on TCP and can normally be found on port 17. Many services have both the TCP and UDP ports of a certain number assigned to them, while others have only one of the protocols. For example, the "echo" service runs on port 7 of both TCP and UDP.

Many programs read /etc/services to learn which port to bind to. Depending on the program, you may have to edit /etc/services to assign that protocol to the port. The software instructions will generally tell you if this is the case.

Like all standards, the lists in /etc/services can be violated. The SSH daemon, sshd, normally listens on port 22, but I've run it on port 80 to escape firewalls in some unusual circumstances. This all depends on the program you're using to provide a service.

Low-Numbered Ports

The ports 1024 and below are called *low-numbered* ports. These are the ports reserved for core Internet infrastructure protocols and important services such as DNS, SSH, HTTP, and so on. Their standard port assignment is basically carved in stone. Only programs that start with root-level privileges can bind to low-numbered ports.

What Ports Are Open?

So, programs bind to ports. The two obvious questions here are, "which ports are open" and "what programs are listening to each?" You can identify this with netstat(1), the same program we used to check mbuf counts.

General Netstat Hints

Any time you use netstat(1) to look at network information you might want to use the "-n" flag. -n tells netstat to not perform DNS lookups on the IP addresses it sees. If most of your network connections are to IP addresses with names cached by your nameserver, then your output will be fairly fast even with DNS lookups. If the system must perform a DNS lookup for every IP address your command will run very slowly, especially if the network between you and your DNS server is performing badly.

The "-f" flag allows you to select a protocol family to examine with netstat(1). If you're only interested in IPv4 connections, use "-f inet". Other valid values for -f include inet6 (for IPv6 connections), ipx (Novell IPX), atalk (AppleTalk), and UNIX (pipes). See netstat(1) for a full list of protocols you can select.

Open Ports and Netstat

Netstat's "-a" flag shows open ports and existing TCP/IP connections. If this machine is an active server, you'll almost certainly want to use the "-n" flag to avoid the DNS lookups, and you'll want to use the "-f inet" option to specify IP connections only. (Try it some time without using either -n or -f, just for your own education.) You'll get a long list back, with six columns.

The first column, PROTO, gives the protocol that this particular connection or listening port is using. We have several TCP ports open, as well as a few UDP ports.

The Recv-Q and Send-Q columns show how many bits are waiting to be handled on this connection. If you see that your system has Recv-Q numbers continually, you know that it cannot process incoming data quickly enough. Similarly, if the Send-Q column keeps having entries, you know that either the network or the other system in the connection cannot accept data as quickly as you can send it. While occasional bursts of either Send-Q or Recv-Q entries are normal, individual entries in these columns should disappear quickly. You need to watch your own system to learn what is normal and what isn't.

The Local Address column is, as you might guess, an open IP address and port number on the local system. The first four numbers are the IP address, and the port number is appended with a period. For example, 192.168.1.250.22 is port 22 on the IP address 192.168.1.250. If this entry is an asterisk, a period, and a port number, it means the system is listening on all available IP addresses for an incoming connection on that port. That particular line does not show any active connections, but the system is ready to accept one.

The Foreign Address column shows the address and port number on the remote end of any connection.

Finally, the (state) column shows the status of the TCP handshake. You don't need to know all of the possible TCP connection states right now; just become familiar with what's normal. ESTABLISHED means that a connection is complete, and data is quite probably flowing over that connection. LAST_ACK, FIN_WAIT_1, and FIN_WAIT_2 mean that the connection is closing. SYN_RCVD, ACK, and SYN+ACK are all parts of the normal connection creation process.

Here we look at the netstat output on a brand-new, out-of-the-box OpenBSD install. I'm using SSH to connect to it, but it has no custom services running.

```
# netstat -na -f inet
Active Internet connections (including servers)
Proto Recv-Q Send-Q  Local Address          Foreign Address        (state)
❶tcp      0      0  192.168.1.250.22       192.168.1.200.49182    ESTABLISHED
 tcp      0      0  192.168.1.250.22       192.168.1.200.49181    ❷TIME_WAIT
 tcp      0      0  ❸127.0.0.1.587          *.*                    LISTEN
 tcp      0      0  127.0.0.1.25           *.*                    LISTEN
 tcp      0      0  *.22❹                   *.*                    LISTEN
 tcp      0      0  *.37                   *.*                    LISTEN
 tcp      0      0  *.13                   *.*                    LISTEN
 tcp      0      0  *.113                  *.*                    LISTEN
 tcp      0      0  127.0.0.1.111          *.*                    LISTEN
 tcp      0      0  *.111                  *.*                    LISTEN
Active Internet connections (including servers)
Proto Recv-Q Send-Q  Local Address          Foreign Address        (state)
 udp      0      0  *.700❺                  *.*
 udp      0      0  *.798                  *.*
 udp      0      0  *.512                  *.*
```

```
udp        0     0  127.0.0.1.111       *.*
udp        0     0  *.514               *.*
udp        0     0  *.111               *.*
#
```

The first entry ❶ shows us an existing TCP connection. The local address is 192.168.1.250.22, meaning that the remote side of my connection is talking to this machine on port 22 of the IP address 192.168.1.250. The remote machine is 192.168.1.200, and the connection is coming from port 49182. Finally, we see that this connection is ESTABLISHED; data is quite possibly flowing over this right now.

We also see a TCP connection that has terminated ❷ and is in the final stages of teardown.

The next line ❸ shows a port that's listening on the local host, but on no other IP addresses. Only systems that can connect to 127.0.0.1 can actually connect to this machine. Because the only machine that can do that is the local host, this port is only available to the local machine.

Shortly thereafter, we ❹ see that the machine is listening to TCP port 22 on all available IP addresses. Because there is no remote host and no state, this is a daemon listening for incoming connections.

Near the bottom, we ❺ see a series of available connections on UDP ports. You should rarely, if ever, see a remote host running over a UDP connection. They tend to appear *very* briefly.

What's Listening on Ports?

Now that you know which TCP and UDP ports are open, how can you tell which programs are listening on them? OpenBSD, like many UNIX-like operating systems, supports the lsof(8) program that helps track down which files are open. (Although lsof is not integrated with OpenBSD, it's available in /usr/ports/sysutils/lsof.) Although many people like lsof, it isn't the only way to get this information out of OpenBSD.

You can look in /etc/services and try to identify the program by the port number. This works well if you're certain that nobody has been tampering with your system. One fun trick an intruder can try is to run a program on a port that should be used by another program. You might not think anything about port 80 being open on a web server, as that's traditionally the port used by web servers. If one IP address has an SSH daemon listening on port 80, you'd never even notice. The only way to be absolutely sure what daemons are running on which ports is to check it yourself.

OpenBSD includes the fstat(1) program, which lists every open file, pipe, or port on the system and various information about its state. I highly recommend perusing fstat(1), as it is a terribly useful program in many different troubleshooting situations. The important thing for us at this moment, however, is that it displays which program is bound to a port. Let's examine TCP port 25, as shown in our example. According to /etc/services this should be "smtp," or email. It probably is, but it's definitely a good example to track down. Run fstat(1) and search its output for port 25. Network ports always appear with a colon before their names, so it's a good idea to include the colon. (Searching for the number 25 in the list of all open files and their states will generate an awful lot of false positives. Go ahead, try it sometime.)

```
# fstat | grep ':25'
root        ❷sendmail  29452  4* internet  stream tcp 0xe0b40d70 ❶127.0.0.1:25
root          sendmail  29452  5* internet6 stream tcp 0xe0b59004 [::1]:25
#
```

At the end of the line we see the IP addresses and port numbers that this connection is listening on, and near the beginning we see the name of the program that is listening on this port. What do you know; this really is the mail server program! My nasty paranoid suspicions were unfounded — this time.

If you're not sure what a program listening on a port does, be sure to check its man page.

Configuring Interfaces

Almost all network interface operations are performed with ifconfig(8). This program is a general interface configuration tool that can be used to examine every network interface on your system. To start with, the "-a" flag will list every interface on your system and its configuration. An OpenBSD system starts with quite a few interfaces, so don't be surprised at the length of the output! A typical entry for an Ethernet card looks like this:

```
fxp1❶: flags=8843<UP,BROADCAST,RUNNING,SIMPLEX,MULTICAST>❷ mtu 1500❸
        media: Ethernet autoselect (10baseT)❹
        status: active❺
        inet6 fe80::202:b3ff:fe63:e3ec%fxp1 prefixlen 64 scopeid 0x2❻
        inet 66.43.114.127 netmask 0xfffff800 broadcast 68.43.111.255❼
```

Not all interfaces have all the fields, but these are a good sample.

The first thing in any entry is the ❶interface name. The interface name is generally the same as the associated driver with a number added. In PCI cards, interfaces start numbering at zero and go up. (Some drivers, particularly ISA drivers, have hard-coded interface numbers depending on the IRQ or memory address of the card, and so may not start at 0.) This example, fxp1, means that this is the second card that uses the fxp driver. For a listing of device drivers, see Appendix A or the kernel configuration file and man pages on your release of OpenBSD.

A base install of OpenBSD includes quite a few network interfaces that you have probably never heard of. Most of these are software interfaces, created by the kernel for various special purposes. Here's a list of their names, and what they're for. While we won't cover all of them in this book, it's nice to know exactly what they're for.

loX	Loopback interface, for connections to the local machine via the network
pflogX	Interface for packet filter logging (see Chapter 19)
slX	SLIP network interface (see sl(8))
pppX	Kernel PPP network interface (see pppd(8))
tunX	User PPP network interface
encX	Encapsulation interface, to filter IPSec traffic via PF (see enc(4))
bridgeX	Ethernet bridging interface (see brconfig(8))
vlanX	Virtual LAN interface (see vlan(4))
greX	Encapsulation with Cisco GRE (see gre(4))
gifX	Generic traffic encapsulation interface (see gif(4))

Any interface name that appears in your ifconfig output, but is not listed here, is almost certainly an Ethernet card.

The ❷flags field gives driver-specific information, such as if the interface is working (the "UP" keyword and if the interface supports various physical protocol features.

The ❸MTU field, or maximum transmission unit, gives the maximum size of any piece of data that can be sent over this interface.1500 is a very common MTU.

The ❹media gives the sort of physical connection that is made to an Ethernet card. The sample here shows that the connection is 10baseT, or common 10-megabit Category 5 Ethernet. You can get a full list of valid media types in by running "ifconfig -m interfacename," and you can see what those media types mean in the network card's man page. For example, fxp(4) contains full descriptions of the six different valid connection types the card supports.

The ❺status line indicates if the network card is receiving and sending Ethernet data.

By ❻inet6, you will see the interface's IPv6 address. Similarly, the ❼inet line shows the interface's IPv4 address.

Ifconfig(8) has many other flags and functions, and we'll discuss the most common of them throughout this chapter.

IP Routing

When administering most UNIX-like operating systems, you don't need to understand routing. The network administrator gives you the IP address of the default route, you put it in the appropriate configuration file, and everything works like magic.[5] OpenBSD systems frequently tend to be part of the network infrastructure, however, or in demilitarized zones where the system must make routing decisions. You really must understand the basics of routing to administer OpenBSD.

Routing is simply making a decision on where to send a packet. If a computer is directly attached to a network, it doesn't need to make any decisions. Your OpenBSD system on the Ethernet network 192.168.1.0/24 already knows how to reach any IP address beginning with 192.168.1; it sends it out that Ethernet. What about an IP address of 209.69.69.12, however? Where should it send those packets?

Many computers use a default route, where they send all packets bound for IP addresses that they don't know about. This is very common in small office networks, where you have one router or firewall that provides network access for everyone in the office. Small companies frequently have only one network, and don't need complicated routing. The company router itself might have a default route pointing to the Internet service provider, who makes all the actual routing decisions for you.

Routed Internal Network Example

In a more complicated setting, your system will have to make routing decisions. Suppose your network has multiple routers attached to it, each going to a different network. Machines on your network will have to decide where to send packets. Here's an example of a fairly common double-firewall situation.

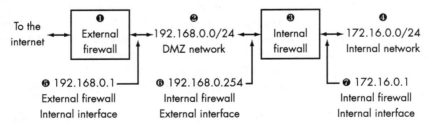

This sort of firewall setup is used whenever servers need different stages of protection. The ❶external firewall provides the outermost layer of protection. Any traffic coming in through the Internet hits this firewall first, and any traffic leaving the network goes through this firewall last. This firewall probably has fairly liberal traffic-management rules.

---

[5] Ignore any rumors about your network administrator occasionally being found in the network room with a knife, a black cockerel, and a bottle of rum. The truth is far stranger than mere magic.

The ❷demilitarized zone network is for machines that must be somewhat exposed to the Internet. Perhaps you have intrusion-detection systems here. In many web-farm situations, this is where the actual web servers live. In our example, the DMZ network uses the IP addresses 192.168.0.0/24.

The ❸internal firewall is very tightly secured device. Only the bare minimum permitted traffic may pass through it. This firewall is responsible for securing the most vital information on the network.

The ❹internal network holds the most vital, protected information on the network: financial information, customer databases, or your MP3 collection. In our example, the internal network has the IP addresses 172.16.0.0/24.

Many of the hosts in this network have very simple routing decisions. Anything in the internal network has only one route to reach anything. If the packet is going to an IP address not in the 192.168.1.1/24 network, it must be sent to the ❼default gateway on the internal network.

Similarly, the internal firewall has two networks directly attached. If it wants to send a packet to an IP within 172.16.0.0/24, it sends the packet out the ❼interface directly attached to that network. If it wants to send a packet to an address within the 192.168.0.0/24 range, it sends it to the ❻interface directly attached to that network. If it wants to reach an IP that isn't in those two ranges, it uses the default gateway of ❺192.168.0.1.

The external firewall is directly attached to the 192.168.0.0/24 network, so it can send packets there. It's directly attached to the Internet and can send any packets it doesn't know how to reach otherwise out there. That leaves out the 172.16.0.0/24 network, however. Packets bound for 172.16.0.0/24 should be sent to the ❻internal firewall's external interface. If you don't tell the external firewall this, however, it's not going to happen. As the external firewall is responsible for the internal network's Internet connectivity, the internal firewall not being able to find the internal network would mean that the internal network would be off the Internet; it could send data, but not receive any. The external firewall needs routing.

Similarly, hosts on the DMZ network need to know how to reach the 172.16.0.0/24 network. In theory they could just use the default route of the internal interface of the external firewall, and the external firewall would use ICMP redirects to tell them where to go. This is messy, increases traffic and lag, and is almost impossible to debug without a packet sniffer. It also assumes that all the network equipment and servers accept ICMP redirects and the firewall will pass ICMP redirects. You should use proper routing.

Let's set up routing for the external firewall in our example. Once you can do that, routing on the DMZ network hosts will be almost exactly the same.

Routing Commands

All routing is managed by route(8). Route(8) has several sub-functions that allow you to view, edit, and monitor the system routing table. While route(8) has full details, the ability to view, add, and delete routes should be enough to get you started.

Viewing Routes

Let's start by viewing the table with "route show." As OpenBSD supports both IP version 4 and IP version 6, the routes for both protocols are displayed. While the IPv6 route table is very similar, we're just going to examine the IPv4 table, and only enough of that to give you a good idea how all this works.

```
# route show
Routing tables

Internet:
❶Destination    ❷Gateway          ❸Flags
❹default        ❺isp-router.Absolut ❻UG
❼192.168.0.0    link#2               U
❽isp-router.Abso 0:2:16:bf:a1:8c    UH
...
```

Every route table entry has a destination, a gateway, and flags. ❶Destinations can be hosts or networks. The ❷gateway is the place where the system should send the packet to get to that gateway. A gateway can be a host name, a network interface number, or a hardware protocol address. The flags field contains markers that indicate what sort of route this is and how the route behaves. We'll discuss these in the next section, "Route Flags."

The first routing table entry is usually the ❹default route. By default, this system sends all packets to the machine whose host name begins with ❺"isp-router.Absolut." If this is your network and your external firewall, you should know what machine this is! In this case, this is the router where our Internet circuit hooks in, and our default route out of the entire network. This route has the ❻flags "U" and "G."

The ❼second route is for the directly attached network 192.168.0.0. You can tell that it is directly attached by the gateway entry of "link#2". If you look at the "ifconfig -a" output on this system, you'll see that the second real network card is the network with 192.168.0.1/24 assigned to it. The system knows to send requests for those IP addresses out that card.

Our ❽last shown route is for the machine whose name begins with "isp-router.Abso". Here, the routing table shows the physical protocol address for the gateway address. The system knows that the default gateway is this machine, and that the machine has the physical address. "0:2:16:bf:a1:8c". Given this information, it can route packets as it needs to.

Route Flags

The Flags column indicates how the routes in a system were generated or used. You can find a full listing of all route flags in route(4) and related manual pages, but some of the common ones are listed in Table 8-2. You don't need to understand what each of these flags means at this point. Just be familiar with the flags for each route that normally appears on your system, and if something different appears, start digging for more information.

Table 8-2: Common route flags

Flag	Description
U	The route is usable
G	This route is a gateway
S	This route is static (e.g., not added dynamically by a routing protocol)
L	This route is a protocol-to-link-address translation (i.e., the MAC address used to reach an IP address)
H	This route is for a particular host
C	This route is used when you dynamically create new routes (e.g., a gateway)
c	This route is used for protocol-specific new routes (e.g., how to reach the gateway)
W	This route was cloned from another route

Adding Routes

Adding routes is very simple with the "route add" command. All you need to know is the network block you want to route, the netmask for that block, and the IP address you want them routed to.

```
# route add 172.16.1.0 -netmask 255.255.255.0 192.168.1.254
add net 172.16.1.0: gateway 192.168.1.254
#
```

If you go back and look at your routing table, you'll see that route. Packets will start to flow back to your internal network. Congratulations!

To have this happen automatically at boot, just add the route command to /etc/rc.local.

Deleting Routes

Take a good close look at the route we added in the last example. Our internal network is 172.16.*0*.0/24, not 172.16.*1*.0/24. Oops! To delete a route table entry, you just need the network block and the netmask for that block.

```
# route delete 172.16.1.0 -netmask 255.255.255.0
delete net 172.16.1.0
#
```

Route(8) has many more useful functions; check the man page for full details.

Now that you understand the bare bones of the theory of networking, in the next chapter we'll see how this works out in practice.

9

INTERNET CONNECTIONS

You have a cable.
If you can connect through it,
victory is yours.

In this chapter, we'll discuss the basics of hooking up to the Internet through two very common methods: dial-up and Ethernet. OpenBSD supports other methods of network connections, such as PPP over Ethernet, but these two are by far the most common and the other connection methods use concepts and ideas common to dial-up and Ethernet. If you understand these tools, other connection methods will not be hard.

Dial-up Internet Connections

Many people, and quite a few small businesses, access the Internet via dial-up connections. This is still an easy and inexpensive way to get Internet access. OpenBSD's dial-up network support can handle a wide variety of situations, including dial-on-command, dial-on-demand, and dedicated lines, over a wide variety of protocols.

OpenBSD supports the dial-up methods Serial Line Internet Protocol (SLIP) and Point-to-Point Protocol. PPP is the standard used to connect to the Internet via dial-up almost everywhere, so we'll cover that. It's a fairly simple protocol; the connection has two ends, and anything you push into one end of the connection is sent to the other end. If you need SLIP support, take a look at sliplogin(8). Before you even start trying to configure PPP, be certain that you have all of the necessary information at hand. Your ISP can provide you with each of the following.

- Dial-up username
- Password
- ISP's modem bank phone number

I always recommend checking the phone line before trying to configure PPP. Pick up the phone and, if you don't have a dial tone, get one. If you have a dial tone, dial your ISP's modem pool. You should hear the modem bank answer with a high-pitched squeal. Just confirming that the phone number actually reaches the modem bank can save you some headaches later if your connection doesn't work. More than once I've learned that I needed to add the area code to a dial-up phone number to actually connect, or put a 1 in front of the number, or something.

If you're in an office setting, you should also confirm that you have an analog phone line. Some offices have digital phone systems that are simply not compatible with modems, under any operating system.

Modems

You also need a modem. Many internal modems are actually *software modems,* also known as Winmodems. These modems do much of the work required for dial-up in proprietary software that is only widely available for the Windows platform. Most internal modems are software modems. Winmodems generally show up in dmesg somewhat like this.

```
"Intel 82801CA/CAM Modem" rev 0x01 at pci0 dev 31 function 6 not configured
```

Note the "not configured" statement. If it's a Winmodem, it will not work with OpenBSD.

OpenBSD only supports hardware modems, which have actual communications chips to handle communications instead of relying on software. All external modems are hardware modems. If your internal modem is a hardware modem, you'll see an entry in /var/run/dmesg.boot identifying it as a modem but without the "not configured" statement. If it's a hardware modem,

OpenBSD will almost certainly recognize and configure it automatically at boot. If you have a burning desire for an internal hardware modem, many online vendors sell them, and you can pick them up used at various auction sites.

Configuring PPP

OpenBSD supports two different sorts of Point-to-Point Protocol: user PPP and kernel PPP. Kernel PPP has very low overhead, but not many features. User PPP is much easier to work with, and it has more features but more overhead in the system. We will discuss user PPP.

The user PPP program is extremely configurable. You can set your system up to allow multiple users to dial particular service providers, or to allow incoming calls to access your system, or to provide address translation services. If you're interested in any of that, you want to check ppp(8) for the full details. Most people who are using OpenBSD over a dial-up line either are using it as a workstation or as an Internet access device for a corporate network, so that is where we're going to concentrate our attention. The configuration is identical in both cases.

The /etc/ppp/ppp.conf file is the heart of PPP configuration. While it is possible to explicitly include other files, by default everything is in here. OpenBSD does not include ppp.conf by default, but it does include an /etc/ppp/ppp.conf.sample. This file makes a good place to start. You can create your own ppp.conf from scratch, but it's much easier to use the sample and trim out everything you don't want. Copy it to /etc/ppp/ppp.conf and open it in your favorite text editor.

ppp.conf is divided into sections, by labels. A *label* is a single word followed by a colon, and it marks the beginning of a section. Sections continue until the next label. As you might guess, any line beginning with a pound sign is a comment.

Default Entry

The *"default" entry* is a special label that is used to set up basic characteristics of your modem. Every other connection uses the default entry, unless told specifically not to. This allows you to configure your modem's base characteristics once, and use the same configuration to set up dial-up connections from multiple ISPs.

```
default:
 set log Phase Chat LCP IPCP CCP tun command❶
 set device /dev/cua01❷
 set speed 115200❸
 set dial "ABORT BUSY ABORT NO\\sCARRIER TIMEOUT 5 \"\" AT OK-AT-OK ATE1Q0 OK \\
dATDT\\T TIMEOUT 40 CONNECT"❹
```

At the beginning, ❶we tell PPP to log events in the listed categories. You can read ppp(8) if you're interested in what all of these mean. For the most part these are generally sensible things to log and will provide most of the debugging information you might need.

Then we tell PPP ❷which serial port is attached to the modem. This is the *only* line you might realistically have to change to dial up to a modern ISP. Modems always run on a serial port. In this example, the modem is attached to serial port number 2. If your modem is attached to serial 1, you will want to change this line to read:

```
set device /dev/cua00
```

As you should be able to guess, COM3 is /dev/cua02, and so on.

Then we tell PPP what ❸speed the serial port is running at. 115,200 bits per second, or 144 Kbps, is the maximum speed a standard serial port will run at. Your modem might run at only 56 Kbps, but you don't want to slow down your internal system for the modem. Let the modem and phone line throttle your bandwidth, if it's going to. This setting gives you enough speed in PPP to support an external ISDN terminal adapter, if you have one.

The last bit ❹is the connect string. This tells PPP how to handle the modem, what characters to expect when it connects, and various modem commands to connect your modem to a standard Internet dial-up account. Because the default will cover almost any circumstance where you're connecting to the Internet, we're not going to cut it to pieces. Again, you can find pretty full documentation of connect strings in ppp(8).

Connection Configuration

/etc/ppp/ppp.conf.sample includes several sample connections that cover almost any sort of connection, such as UNIX-style logins over PPP (much like a serial terminal), PPP connections with a static IP addresses, and so on. We care about the boring, dynamic IP dial-up shown in the "PAPorCHAPpmdemand" label, which is a good model for an average Internet dial-up.

```
PAPorCHAPpmdemand:
 set phone 1234567❶
 set login❷
 set authname MyName❸
 set authkey MyKey❹
 set timeout 120❺
 set ifaddr 10.0.0.1/0 10.0.0.2/0 255.255.255.0 0.0.0.0❻
 add default HISADDR❼
 enable dns❽
```

This configuration uses the settings from the default configuration, such as the modem port, the logging settings, and the connect string. All we have to set here is some basic information specific to this particular connection.

First, we ❶set the phone number you want to call with the "set phone" option. Do not use parenthesis, dashes, or other separators. You can use commas, but they will cause a delay between dialing numbers. (This may be what you want, of course.)

The ❷"set login" statement tells PPP to log in to the system on the other end.

Next, tell the system your ❸ dial-up username. In place of the string "MyName," put your username.

Your dial-up password goes in the ❹ "set authkey" line. This entry is why /etc/ppp/ppp.conf is readable only by root.

The ❺ timeout line tells PPP how many seconds the line should remain idle before disconnecting the connection. If you don't ever want the connection to go down, set the timeout to 0 or invoke PPP as a dedicated line (see "Using PPP").

The long, complicated-looking ❻ "set ifaddr" line tells PPP which range of IP addresses you will accept for your connection. (You could use this to specify a static IP address, which we'll look at later). The example given will work with almost any situation where you have a dynamic IP address.

The ❼ "add default" entry tells PPP to add a default route pointing to the host on the other end of the PPP connection. You don't need to edit this; it doesn't really matter what IP address lies on the other end of that tunnel, you just want to send your packets there.

Finally, the ❽ "enable dns" line tells PPP to update /etc/resolv.conf with the nameservers provided by your ISP's dial-up servers. If you have preferred nameservers listed in /etc/resolv.conf, you don't want to set this!

Example ISP Configuration

So, I'm going to use the example above as a basis for my own dial-up configuration. My ISP is AbsoluteOpenBSD. The modem number is 555-831-9944. My username is "mwlucas" and my password is "5k$l*!trB." My configuration will look like this:

```
AbsoluteOpenBSD: ❶
 set phone 5558319944 ❷
 set login
 set authname mwlucas ❸
 set authkey 5k$l*!trB ❹
 set timeout 120
 set ifaddr 10.0.0.1/0 10.0.0.2/0 255.255.255.0 0.0.0.0
 add default HISADDR
 enable dns
```

This looks almost exactly like the example PAPorCHAPpmdemand entry we dissected! Only the ❶ label, the ❷ phone number, the ❸ username, and the ❹ password have been changed.

NOTE *PPP has many more functions, including Network Address Translation, packet filtering, alternate phone numbers, and so on. You can find many examples in /etc/ppp/ ppp.conf.sample and ppp(8). We use PF for packet filtering functionality, as discussed in Chapters 17-19.*

Running PPP

You need root privileges to use ppp(8). (Regular users can be set up to allow them to use ppp(8), as we'll see later.) Just give the "ppp" command and the name of the connection you want to use.

```
# ppp AbsoluteOpenBSD
Working in interactive mode
Using interface: tun0
ppp ON openbsdtest>
```

At this point, you're speaking directly to the PPP daemon. You can issue commands, set instructions, and generally boss it around. To tell it to connect to the ISP, enter "dial."

```
ppp ON openbsdtest> dial
ppp ON openbsdtest>
```

Although you shouldn't see anything back from the PPP daemon, you should be able to go to another console or terminal window and ping the outside world. You can also use ifconfig(8) to examine your Internet connection interface. tun0 is the first user PPP network interface. If the link is down, it will look like this.

```
# ifconfig tun0
tun0: flags=8011<POINTOPOINT,MULTICAST> mtu 1500
#
```

Once the link comes up, the tun0 interface will show the new IP address of your system, the IP address of the remote side of the connection, and a status of "UP".

```
# ifconfig tun0
tun0: flags=8011<UP,POINTOPOINT,MULTICAST> mtu 1500
        inet ❶192.168.1.108 --> ❷192.168.1.250 netmask 0xffffff00
#
```

The ❶first IP given is your local IP address, and the ❷second is the remote side. You should be able to ping the other side of the network connection: in this case (192.168.1.250).

To disconnect the PPP session, just give the "quit" command.

```
PPP ON openbsdtest> quit
#
```

This interactive mode supports many different commands, and allows you to perform all sort of connection customization and debugging, as documented in ppp(8).

Connection Types

While interactive mode provides all sorts of detailed functionality, most people never need any of it. It's nice to have the ability in case something goes wrong, but most people just want to configure a dial-up connection to their ISP and have it Just Work. You can do this by specifying the connection type. We'll discuss the most common types of connection and how they work. (You can find more in ppp(8), but these are overwhelmingly the most commonly used.)

Background Connections

A *background* connection dials up the Net when you run the "ppp" command, but becomes a background process as soon as the connection is established. This may take a moment; you won't get a command prompt back until your modem has finished dialing the ISP, all protocol details have been negotiated, and your interface and routing are configured. Choose a background connection with the "-background" flag.

```
# ppp -background AbsoluteOpenBSD
Working in background mode
Using interface: tun0
PPP enabled
#
```

This connection will remain open until the other side disconnects or you tell the PPP daemon to disconnect. Unfortunately, there is no simple command to terminate a backgrounded PPP(8) daemon cleanly. You have to send it a HUP (hang up) signal.

```
# ps -ax | grep ppp
10137 ??  Is      0:00.01 ppp -background AbsoluteOpenBSD
# kill 10137
#
```

While the "kill" command will return immediately, PPP will need to take a few seconds to actually bid farewell to your ISP and hang up. In a moment or two, however, you should notice the PPP process disappearing.

```
# ps -ax | grep ppp
#
```

On-Demand Connections

An *on-demand* connection waits until you requires network access, then dials your ISP and hooks you up to the Internet. It remains connected until the line has been idle for a certain length of time. You tell ppp(8) to run in on-demand mode with the "-auto" flag.

```
# ppp -auto AbsoluteOpenBSD
Working in auto mode
Using interface: tun0
#
```

The PPP daemon will wait in the background, idle, until you try to access the Internet. You will notice a delay in accessing the Net while your modem connects and PPP(8) negotiates with the ISP, but it will work. The connection will terminate once no data has been transmitted for a number of seconds equal to the timeout value in the connection description.

When you want to terminate the connection, you need to kill the ppp process as for background connections.

NOTE *Any outbound packets will cause an on-demand connection to dial out! If you pay for Internet access by the minute, or if you have a per-dial charge, you want to be careful what programs you run. Some will try to connect to the Internet regularly. The /etc/ppp/ ppp.conf.sample file contains examples of some filters you can use to prevent dialing out on common "garbage" connection requests.*

Permanent Connections

A *permanent* connection is always on. Because we're talking about connecting over phone lines, we'll assume you want to reconnect if something disconnects the line. This is commonly used for small company Internet access via ISDN, or even via standard dial-up (as is still common in some parts of the world). You can tell ppp to keep the connection up if at all possible with the "-ddial" flag.

```
# ppp -ddial AbsoluteOpenBSD
Working in ddial mode
Using interface: tun0
#
```

Again, to shut down dedicated-dial PPP you must kill the process.

Ethernet

Ethernet is a more complicated and more interesting protocol than PPP and is extremely popular in corporate and home networks. If you're already familiar with Ethernet, you probably learned everything you needed to know about configuring your system to talk to your local network in Chapter 5. If not, read on.

Ethernet is a shared network; many different machines can connect to the same Ethernet and can communicate directly with each other. This gives Ethernet a great advantage over PPP. Ethernet has physical distance limitations that make it practical only for offices, colocation facilities, and other comparatively short-range networks.

Many different physical networks have been used to run Ethernet over the years. Once upon a time, most Ethernet cables were thick chunks of coaxial cable. Today, most are comparatively thin cat5 cables with eight strands of very think wire inside them. You may also encounter Ethernet over optical fiber or radio. For purposes of our discussion we'll assume that you're working with category 5 cable, which is the most popular choice today. No matter what physical media you're using, the theory of Ethernet doesn't change. (Remember, the physical layer is abstracted away!)

Prerequisites

Before you try to configure your system to access an Ethernet, you need to have some basic IP address information. If your network runs DHCP, that's all you need to know. If your machine will have a static IP address, you need the following information:

- Your machine's IP address
- The netmask for that IP address
- The default gateway

While it would be nice to be able to check for a dial tone on your Ethernet cable, that requires specialized (but reasonably inexpensive) equipment.

Ethernet Physical Protocol

Ethernet is a broadcast protocol, which means that every packet you send on the network is sent to every workstation on that network. (Today this isn't necessarily true, as we'll discuss later.) Your network card's device driver sorts out the data intended for your computer from the data meant for other computers. One side effect of Ethernet's broadcast nature is that you can "sniff" other computers' connections, capturing everything sent and received by those systems. While this can be very useful when diagnosing problems, it's also a major security issue. Capturing clear-text passwords is trivial on an old-fashioned Ethernet.

Ethernet started out supporting only a couple of megabits per second, but has grown beyond its original design to handle gigabit speeds. Most people use 10/100 megabits per second (Mbps) speeds, and gigabit Ethernet cards have just recently dropped below $100 each.

MAC Addresses

Every Ethernet network card has a unique identifier, its MAC address. A MAC address is a 48-bit number, and is sometimes called an *Ethernet address*. When a system wants to transmit data to another host on the Ethernet, it sends out an Ethernet request that basically says "Which MAC address is responsible for this IP address?" If a host responds, further data is addressed to that MAC address. This process is known as the Address Resolution Protocol, or ARP.

You can view your OpenBSD machine's current MAC and ARP knowledge with arp(8). The most common form is the "arp -a" command, which shows the MAC addresses and host names of all hosts that the system has previously communicated with on the local network.

```
# arp -a
petulance.blackhelicopters.org (192.168.1.2) at 00:30:65:31:dc:4d
pedicular.blackhelicopters.org (192.168.1.200) at 00:02:2d:0c:9a:40
#
```

Here we see that the host petulance.blackhelicopters.org has an IP address of
192.168.1.2, and a MAC address of 00:30:65:31:dc:4d. If a MAC address shows up
as "incomplete," the host cannot be contacted. In such a case, check your
physical layer (the wire), the remote system, and your system configuration.

Hubs, Switches, and Bridges

An Ethernet *hub* is a central piece of hardware to physical connections to many
other Ethernet devices. They simply forward all Ethernet frames received to
every other device hooked to them. Hubs broadcast all Ethernet traffic that they
receive to every attached host and other attached hubs. Each host is responsible
for filtering out the traffic they don't want. This is the classic way Ethernet works.

A *switch* is like a hub, but filters for the hosts by tracking the MAC and IP
addresses of attached devices and, for the most part, only forwarding packets to
the device that they are meant for. Because each Ethernet host has a finite
amount of bandwidth (for example, a 100 Mbps card can handle 100 megabits
per second), switching reduces the load on individual systems by limiting the
amount of data transferred to each device. Switches are more expensive than
hubs, however.

A bridge is any device that joins two different Ethernet segments. The more
flexible switches largely supplant them. You might have two small Ethernet hubs
joined by a bridge. Hardware bridges are no longer common, but OpenBSD
includes extensive bridging functionality. Bridging is discussed in brconfig(8).

Configuring Your Ethernet Card

You can assign an IP address to your Ethernet card with ifconfig(8). The basic
syntax is very simple:

```
ifconfig interface-name IP-address netmask
```

For example, if your network card is fxp0, your IP address is 192.168.1.250, and
your netmask is 255.255.255.0, you would type:

```
# ifconfig fxp0 192.168.1.250 255.255.255.0
```

You can also set an interface's media options with ifconfig(8). Some combinations of cards and switches cannot successfully autonegotiate a connection
speed, so you'll need to manually force the media to be what you want. For
example, suppose your network card thinks that you have a full-duplex connection to the switch, while the switch thinks you have a half-duplex connection.
In case of doubt, the switch is usually right. Get the name of the valid media types
from the driver's man page.

```
# ifconfig fxp0 media  100baseTX
```

You can, of course, combine these.

```
ifconfig fxp0 192.168.1.250 255.255.255.0 media 100baseTX mediaopt full-duplex
```

Multiple IP Addresses on One Ethernet Card

One network card can respond to requests for multiple IP addresses. One server
might have to support hundreds or thousands of domains and need an IP
address for each. You can add extra IP addresses to a single card quite easily with
IP aliases. With IP aliasing, you tell a network card that "although your real IP
address is such-and-such, answer to requests for this IP address as well." You can
add extra IP addresses with ifconfig(8).

```
# ifconfig fxp0 alias 192.168.1.5 netmask 255.255.255.255
```

The alias should have the keyword "alias" immediately after the interface name
and a netmask of 255.255.255.255. (You can use other netmasks to assign a range
of IP addresses, as we'll see in "Blocks of Aliases IPs.")
      You can see any aliases assigned to a card by using ifconfig.

```
# ifconfig fxp0
fxp0: flags=8843<UP,BROADCAST,RUNNING,SIMPLEX,MULTICAST> mtu 1500
        address: 00:02:b3:63:e4:1d
        media: Ethernet autoselect (100baseTX full-duplex)
        status: active
      ❶inet 192.168.1.250 netmask 0xffffff00 broadcast 192.168.1.255
        inet6 fe80::202:b3ff:fe63:e41d%fxp0 prefixlen 64 scopeid 0x1
      ❷inet 192.168.1.5 netmask 0xffffff00 broadcast 192.168.1.255
#
```

Here we see the ❶primary IP address on this card and the ❷alias IP. The primary
IP address appears first.
      You can configure the additional IP addresses at boot by using additional
ifconfig statements in /etc/hostname.if, much like this:

```
alias 192.168.1.5 netmask 255.255.255.255
```

The only real difference between this entry and the standard hostname.if
ifconfig statement is the "alias" keyword.
      All outgoing connections use the system's real IP address. You might have
2,000 IP addresses bound to one network card, but when you ssh outward, the
connection comes from the primary IP address. Keep this in mind when writing
firewall rules and other access-control filters.

IP Aliases on a Loopback Interface

OpenBSD allows you to bind IP addresses to a loopback interface. This means that the machine will respond to those IP addresses, no matter which interface the packet arrives on, allowing you to change network cards with impunity.

A standard OpenBSD system has two loopback interfaces, lo0 and lo1. lo0 is reserved for the standard "localhost" address, 127.0.0.1, and for connections to the local system. Adding extra IP addresses to this interface can cause confusion. The lo1 interface is provided specifically for hosting additional IP addresses. You configure IP aliases on lo1 in exactly the same way you configure them on any other network interface, either in /etc/hostname.lo1 or on the command line.

```
# ifconfig lo1 alias 192.168.1.5 netmask 255.255.255.255
```

Blocks of Alias IPs

One special feature of OpenBSD's ifconfig(8) is that it supports adding blocks of IP aliases by netmask. For example, suppose you need to assign the entire 192.168.9.0/24 address block (also known as a class C, for those network engineers stuck in the 1980s) to be aliases on a particular machine. Rather than using a whole slew of "ifconfig lo1 alias" commands, you can tie the whole block to the interface by giving a netmask.

```
ifconfig lo1 alias 192.168.9.0 netmask 255.255.255.0
```

Of course, you can use this in /etc/hostname.lo1 as well.

This is quick, easy, and creates a routing issue. For the system to respond to a packet, that packet must arrive at the system. Route that block of addresses to this machine, as discussed in Chapter 8, and everything will work properly.

Congratulations, you're hooked up to the Internet! Before you get too comfortable out there, let's look at some of OpenBSD's advanced security features in the next chapter.

10

ADDITIONAL SECURITY FEATURES

Hackers at the gates?
Puffy the Barbarian
defends against friends.

Securing a computer means ensuring that only authorized people use the system's resources for authorized purposes, because even if you have no important data on your system you still have valuable CPU time, memory, disk space, and bandwidth. Many folks who thought that their systems were too unimportant to bother securing found themselves an unknowing relay for an attack that disabled a major company.

An intruder can combine several hundred insecure systems into a powerful distributed network assault vehicle that can bring down major sites such as eBay or CNN. (Admittedly, websites such as Slashdot can have identical effects without intruder involvement.) You don't want to wake up one morning to learn that your ISP has suspended your account for hacking or, worse, hold an unscheduled midnight conversation with serious men in dark suits who repeatedly remind you that the death penalty can be sought for certain types of computer crime. Computer security is a serious business.

Sadly, over the last few years, it has become more and more simple to take over insecure computers. Precompiled point-and-click programs for getting unauthorized system access can now be downloaded from any number of places on the Internet and can be found through security websites such as Packet Storm. It takes just one skilled attacker to write an exploit and several thousand bored teenagers with nothing better to do can download it and make life difficult for the rest of us. Even if you don't care about your particular computer, you must secure it.

Generally speaking, operating systems are not broken into; the programs running on the operating system are. Even OpenBSD's rigorous security auditing cannot protect badly written programs from themselves, although OpenBSD does include tools to mitigate the damage such programs can cause.

This chapter focuses on securing your systems, people who may attack your systems, and special security features included in OpenBSD. Auditing a network is a topic that fills thick books, and really isn't on topic for this book. OpenBSD gives you many tools to secure it against hackers, to protect programs running on it, and to minimize the damage an intruder can cause.

Who Is the Enemy?

I'm going to arbitrarily lump potential attackers into three groups: script kiddies, disaffected users, and skilled attackers. You will find more fine-grained profiles in books dedicated to network security, but these categories are easily explained, are easily understood, and encompass 99 percent of all the attackers you're likely to encounter.

Script Kiddies

The most numerous attackers are *script kiddies* (often called "script kitties" in the OpenBSD community). Script kiddies are not sysadmins: They are not skilled and most have absolutely no idea what the heck they are doing. They download small attack programs that work on a point-and-click basis and go looking for systems that the program works on. They're the equivalent of drive-by shooters looking for easy targets. Fortunately, script kiddies are particularly easy to attack against; keeping your programs securely up-to-date will deter most of them.

The other two groups can use any attack that can be used by script kiddies.

Disaffected Users

The second group causes the majority of security problems I've dealt with — a system's legitimate users. Disaffected employees and users know where a system's problems are, and are frequently able to use those problems to their own advantage. If your support people use a password-free modem in a back closet to access the computers, and you have to fire one of them, you may well have unexpected calls at that modem! The ex-employee wouldn't even have to call it himself; he could just post the phone number somewhere on the Internet and let the script kiddies go wild. Or perhaps some company administrator gives the phone number to their child so they can get Internet access, and that child shares the phone number with friends. While an unsecured modem might be an extreme example, almost every network has some "fix" that was hurriedly and thoughtlessly implemented and that can be exploited by a motivated person who knows about it.

The best way to stop these people is to not be sloppy. Keep your systems up-to-date. When someone leaves the company change all administrative passwords, disable any accounts that person had, and tell all employees that the person has left and not to share information with him. And get rid of the unsecured modem, or the decrepit SunOS server with a telnet port open to the world, or whatever hurried hack you put into place thinking that nobody would ever find it.

A skilled attacker can probably use any attack available to a disaffected user.

Skilled Attackers

The last group is actually fairly dangerous: skilled attackers. These are competent systems administrators, security researchers, and penetration specialists who want access to your systems in particular. If one of these people wants into your network, they stand a very good chance of finding any holes that exist and getting in.

Still, the security measures that will stop the first two groups cold can change the tactics that skilled attackers must use. If you secure your network well, the intruder will have to show up at the door dressed as a telephone company repairman lugging a packet sniffer or dumpster-dive for old sticky notes with passwords scribbled on them, rather than break in via the network. This dramatically raises his exposure and can even make a break-in more trouble than it's worth.

Hackers

You'll frequently hear the word "hacker" used to describe people who break into computers. This word has different meanings, depending on the speaker. In the technical world, a hacker is someone who is interested in the inner workings of things. Some hackers are interested in everything; some have a narrow field of interest. In the open source community, "hacker" is generally a title of respect. In the popular media, a hacker breaks into computers. I recommend entirely avoiding the word so as to avoid confusion. In this book, I call people who break into computers "intruders." (In person I call them a variety of names that No Starch Press has yet to print in *any* of their books.)

OpenBSD Security Announcements

Your first and best line of defense against intruders is to keep your computer software up-to-date. That means that you need to know when to update your system and what to update. An outdated system is a script kiddie's best friend.

OpenBSD project members are continually auditing the system source code, trying to find new ways to break it. Also, because of OpenBSD's reputation as the most secure operating system in the world, people who are not part of the project scour the code looking for errors. (There's nothing like saying "We're the best!" to cause people to try to kick you in the kneecaps.) Occasionally, someone finds an error that can be exploited. The OpenBSD security team maintains a low-traffic mailing list, security-announce@OpenBSD.org, and subscribing to it is a very good idea. In the event that a security issue is found it will be posted on this list, along with corrective actions that you need to take to keep the script kiddies out.

It's also a good idea to subscribe to other mailing lists, such as BugTraq, for general announcements about software that can run on OpenBSD.

Checksums

You'll see heavy use of checksums throughout OpenBSD — indeed, throughout the entire UNIX world. Elsewhere in this book, I will assume that you can use checksums. If you're completely comfortable with checksums you can skip this section, but if you're the least bit foggy read on.

A *checksum* is the result of taking a chunk of data, such as a file, and performing complicated mathematical computations on it to produce a short string of characters. ("Short" is a relative term, but even an 80-character result is far shorter than the thousands of lines of source code it might encompass.) The resulting number is called a *fingerprint*. If the original file changes in any way, even by something as trivial as adding a space or a period, the fingerprint changes.

Checksums give a systems administrator a chance to verify data integrity. Many software distribution sites, including OpenBSD and its mirrors, include checksums for the files that they provide. For example, every OpenBSD architecture release directory includes a file called MD5, which includes MD5 checksums for each of the OpenBSD distribution sets.

Using Checksums

OpenBSD includes tools to calculate MD5, SHA-1, and RMD-160 checksums. The most popular type is MD5, but the others are perfectly valid. Each algorithm is very different and generates a different result. You must use the appropriate tool for the type of checksum you are trying to verify! When you're given a MD5 checksum for a file, for example, computing the RMD-160 checksum for that file really doesn't help much.

If you want to verify the checksum on a file you have downloaded, just run either md5(1), sha1(1), or rmd160(1), giving the filename as an argument. Here, we compute the MD5 checksum for the OpenBSD 3.2 i386 misc32.tgz distribution set:

```
# md5 misc32.tgz
MD5 (misc32.tgz) = ba112a10afb86c78a19712705a5f476a
#
```

If you check the MD5 file in the 3.2/i386 directory, you will see that the correct MD5 checksum is, indeed, "ba112a10afb86c78a19712705a5f476a." This file is identical to the one that was used to calculate the checksum.

Non-Matching Checksums

What if the checksum doesn't match? You have a few choices, depending on whether you suspect malice or laziness.

If someone has tampered with the file since the vendor made it available, the checksum will be different. This file may contain a Trojan, backdoor, or some other intruder-friendly poison. Look around for a copy of the file from another mirror site. If all of the distribution files you find have the same non-matching checksum, you may be facing a simple case of distributor sloppiness.

In the free software world, it's not uncommon for a software author to change the software he's distributing without making either a version bump or a checksum update. While the OpenBSD project uses checksums rigorously, and updates them at any excuse, this isn't necessarily the case for other projects. If the checksums don't match, but are consistent across the board, contact the software author or distributor and ask if they forgot to update the checksum file. You may have actually found a trojaned distribution file, however.

If nothing else, you can always closely examine the file for differences from a known-good version of the file, and see what changes have been made. This sort of careful scrutiny found the OpenSSH trojan in 2002.

NOTE   *If someone has compromised a server and replaced a piece of software with a trojaned version, the may well have replaced the checksum file on that server as well. In those places where OpenBSD relies upon checksums from third parties, it includes a known-good checksum. When in doubt, download the file from one server and the checksum from another!*

File Flags

UNIX file system permissions are standard across various versions of UNIX, but OpenBSD extends the permissions scheme with file flags. These flags work with permissions to enhance your systems' or users' security by changing the way the file can be accessed. File flags can make a file unchangeable or make it so that existing data cannot be removed and the file can only be added to. File flags work only in combination with securelevels; however, the two systems are interrelated, and you must understand both parts before implementing them.

Viewing a File's Flags

You can see any flags set on a file with "ls -lo:"

```
# ls -lo test
-rw-r--r--  1 mwlucas  mwlucas  ❶uchg 0 Dec  3 13:42 test
#
```

This file has the ❶"uchg," or user-immutable, flag set. In comparison, if a file has no flags set, ls -lo will only show a dash in the space where the flag is displayed.

```
# ls -lo test
-rw-r--r--  1 mwlucas  mwlucas  -  0 Dec  3 13:42 test
#
```

An out-of-the-box OpenBSD system doesn't have any files marked by flags. You can certainly mark anything that you want, however.

Flag Types

Here are the most commonly used file flags and brief descriptions of how you might use them. There are a few other flags, but their use is rare; see chflags(1) for a complete list.

sappnd

The system-level append-only flag can only be set or removed by root. Files with this flag can be added to but cannot be removed or otherwise edited, a particularly useful feature for log files. Setting sappnd on a .history file can be interesting in the event of a system compromise. A popular script kiddie trick is to remove .history or to link it to /dev/null so that the sysadmin cannot see what was done, but sappnd prevents this tactic from working without changing any UNIX file system permissions on the .history file itself. It's almost funny to watch the record of someone trying to remove a sappnd file — you can almost see the intruder's frustration grow as he tries more and more outrageous things to make the file disappear. (Admittedly, no amount of entertainment is sufficient compensation for having your system broken into!) This flag cannot be removed when the system is running at securelevel 1 or higher.

schg

The system-level immutable flag can only be set or removed by root. Files with this flag set cannot be changed in any way: not edited, not moved, and not replaced. Basically, the kernel will prevent all attempts to touch this file in any way. This flag cannot be removed when the system is running at securelevel 1 or greater.

uappnd

Only the file owner or root can set the user append-only flag. Like the system append-only flag, sappnd, a file with this flag set can be added to but not otherwise edited or removed. This is most useful for logs from personal programs and the like and is primarily a means users can employ to preserve vital files from accidental removal. The user or root may remove this flag at any time.

uchg

Only the owner or root can set the user immutable flag. Like the schg flag, the user immutable flag prevents a user from changing the file. Again, root can override this, and the user at any securelevel can remove it.

Setting and Removing File Flags

Set file flags with chflags(1), giving the desired flag and the filename as arguments. For example, to be sure that your kernel isn't tampered with, you could do this as root:

```
# chflags schg /bsd
```

This would prevent both an intruder and a legitimate administrator from removing the kernel file.

You can also recursively change the flags on a directory tree with the "-R" argument. For example, to make /bin immutable use this command:

```
# chflags -R schg /bin
```

And boom! Your basic binaries cannot be changed. Upgrades, maintenance, and the placing of trojans just got a lot more difficult.

To remove a flag, use chflags(1) and a "no" in front of the flag name. For example, to unset the schg flag we just set on the kernel, enter this command:

```
# chflags noschg /bsd
```

Remember, you must be running at securelevel 0 or below to unset schg and sappnd flags. So, without further ado, we'll discuss securelevels and what they mean.

Securelevels

Securelevels are kernel settings that change basic system behavior to disallow certain actions. The kernel will behave slightly differently as you raise the securelevel. For example, at low securelevels the file flags we discussed can be removed. A file might be marked "do not change," but you can remove the marker and then delete or edit the file. When you increase the securelevel, the flag cannot be removed. Similar changes will take place in other parts of the system. Taken as a whole, the behavior changes that result from increased securelevels will either frustrate or stop an intruder. You can set the system securelevel at boot in /etc/rc.securelevel. Securelevel ranges from -1 to 2.

Securelevels make system maintenance difficult. After all, many actions that you might take during normal upgrades and administration are also things that intruders might do to cover their tracks or further compromise a system. You will need to adjust your use of securelevel features to fit your environment.

Despite the name, a securelevel is not an all-purpose general security dial. Turning up securelevel arbitrarily will do nothing but annoy users and administrators. Additionally, securelevels cannot be reduced without rebooting the system, so don't experiment blindly.

Setting Securelevels

Securelevels come in four levels: -1, 0, 1, and 2, with -1 being the least secure; 2 is the most secure. OpenBSD's default securelevel is 1. This value is set at boot time in /etc/rc.securelevel. Look in this file, and you will see a line like this:

```
securelevel=1
```

Change the 1 to your desired securelevel. The next time you reboot, the system will come back up at this securelevel. If you want to raise the securelevel without rebooting, you can adjust the kern.securelevel sysctl to your desired value.

```
# sudo sysctl -w kern.securelevel=1
kern.securelevel: -1 -> 1
#
```

Securelevel may not be lowered while the system is running; it can only be raised. After all, if the administrator could lower the securelevel, so could an intruder.

Securelevel -1

Securelevel -1 provides no additional kernel security whatsoever. If you're learning OpenBSD and are frequently experimenting with system features and configuration, you may want to run the system at this securelevel. The standard UNIX security features, such as permissions, are fully functional.

Securelevel 0

The only time securelevel 0 is used is when the system is first booting, and it offers no special features. When the system reaches multi-user mode, however, the securelevel is automatically raised to 1. Setting securelevel=0 in /etc/rc.securelevel is functionally equivalent to setting securelevel=1. At securelevel 0, no special security features are in place.

Securelevel 1

At securelevel 1, OpenBSD's default, things become interesting.

- Nobody may write to the /dev/mem and /dev/kmem devices. Many old security exploits relied upon being able to write to these devices.
- The raw disk devices of all mounted file systems are read-only — all disk access must be done via standard devices. Programs should only access mounted file systems through the standard devices, anyway, so this doesn't change day-to-day operations.
- The schg and sappnd flags cannot be removed. You will need to reboot into single-user mode to remove these flags.
- Kernel modules cannot be loaded or unloaded. Why OpenBSD does support kernel modules, by default the kernel is monolithic, so this has very little effect on a legitimate systems administrator.

Securelevel 2

This is the highest securelevel OpenBSD offers, and it disables a variety of features that may be required during normal maintenance. These are also features that an intruder would be greatly interested in, so you may find them worthwhile. Using a high securelevel makes your system less flexible, but prevents many unauthorized changes. Securelevel 2 includes all the effects of securelevel 1, but causes the following additional changes.

- Raw disk devices are always read-only.
- The system clock can be set neither backward nor close to the overflow point.
- pfctl(8) cannot alter PF or NAT rules.
- The DDB kernel debugger sysctl values cannot be changed (see ddb(4)).

Securelevel 2 can seem irrelevant or tedious to a new systems administrator, but the features it provides can be very important. For example, intruders have used direct access to raw disks to make changes to the file system without paying attention to permissions flags on files, but setting the raw devices read-only prevents this sort of trickery. Intruders have been able to do all sorts of nifty tricks with the kernel debugger, but by making it unavailable except under the conditions the systems administrator desires these techniques are also made less useful. And once your packet filtering rules are in place and properly tuned, you should not need to change them.

Which Securelevel Do You Need?

The securelevel appropriate to your environment will depend on your situation. If you've just put an OpenBSD machine into your test environment to see what you can make it do, you might want to run at securelevel -1. I frequently run "crashboxes" at securelevel -1 just so I can make any desired change. These machines are not in production use, however.

If your system has been newly placed into production use, securelevel 1 is probably what you want. This eliminates many popular intruder techniques, but leaves the system mostly flexible.

If your system is highly secure and well tuned, use securelevel 2. Be well aware of the administrative details of this decision, however. If you're using OpenBSD as your corporate firewall, your management might not take it well if you must reboot the entire system just to make a minor rule change.

Living with Securelevels

If you've been liberal with the schg flag, you will find that you cannot upgrade or even patch your system without incurring downtime. (In many enterprise environments, network managers would rather you brought your troupe of plague-carrying rats into the office than incur downtime.) The same conditions that make an intruder's life difficult will make your job a living hell, if you don't know how to work around them.

If you've protected /etc/rc.conf and /etc/rc.securelevel with schg, you'll first have to lower the securelevel to edit your configuration. Of course, the securelevel is set in /etc/rc.securelevel, so you'll need to take control of the system before /etc/rc runs in order to edit that file. Boot into single-user mode, mount the file systems you need, and use "chflags noschg" to gain the ability to edit the files in multi-user mode. Once you finish your maintenance, you can reset the flags.

Systrace

One of the more exciting features in OpenBSD is systrace(1), a system call access manager. With systrace, a system administrator can say which system calls can be made by which programs, and how those calls can be made. Proper use of systrace can greatly reduce the risks inherent in running poorly written or exploitable programs. Systrace policies can confine users in a manner completely independent of UNIX permissions. You can even define the errors that the system calls return when access is denied, to allow programs to fail in the desired manner. Using systrace requires a practical understanding of system calls, what programs must have to work properly, and how these things interact with security. While these are often considered advanced system administration skills, even junior administrators can learn them.

Systrace has several important pieces: policies, the policy-generation tools, the runtime access management tool, and the sysadmin real-time interface.

System Calls

Sysadmins fling the term "system calls" around a lot, but many of them don't know exactly what it means. A *system call* is a function that lets you talk to the operating system kernel. If you want to allocate memory, open a TCP/IP port, or perform input/output on the disk, that's a system call. System calls are documented in section 2 of the online manual.

UNIX also supports a wide variety of C library calls, which are often confused with system calls but are actually just standardized routines for things that could be written within a program. You could easily write a function to compute square roots within a program, for example, but you could not write a function to allocate memory without using a system call. If you're in doubt whether a particular function is a system call or a C library function, check the online manual.

Some standards define "functions" that must be provided by the operating system. These functions might be system calls, or library calls. How a function is provided is considered an implementation detail, and an operating system can move a function between the system calls and the C library as appropriate.

You may find an occasional system call that is not documented in the online manual, such as break(). You'll need to dig into other resources to identify these calls. (Break() in particular is a very old system call that is used within libc, but not by programmers, so it seems to have escaped being documented in the man pages.)

Systrace Policies

A *policy* is just a description of system calls that a particular program may execute and how those calls can be made. While this sounds simple, as with many other things, the details can cause sleepless nights and caffeine overdoses.

Systrace(1) describes the complete systrace language. System calls have been used for many different things, and their usage has been expanded over the last 30 years, until it would seem impossible to write a permissions file to describe all the permutations that systems calls can appear in. It turns out to be very possible, but admittedly difficult. Fortunately, almost all of the system calls ever needed can be described by a small subset of the complete syntax.

A policy rule describes a permitted system call and the manner it can be made in. It has the general format shown here:

```
❶abi-❷sycall: ❸term1 ❹comparison-operator ❺term2 then ❻permit
```

OpenBSD can run binaries from a variety of operating systems, as discussed in Chapter 13, and systrace can theoretically support all of them. At the time of this writing, only the native and Linux ABIs are supported. Each ABI has its own list of system calls, and you must tell systrace ❶which ABI this system call applies to.

The ❷syscall is the name of the system call.

While you could simple "permit" or "deny" this system call, it's frequently more useful to allow execution conditionally. You could allow Apache to open a TCP/IP socket, but only if it's trying to open port 80. That's where the comparison comes in. If the ❸first term ❹matches the ❺second term in a particular way, you can decide ❻to permit or deny the system call request. Systrace supports the following commonly used comparison operators:

- The "match" operator matches if the two terms are the same as per regular filename globbing. This allows use of the asterisk (*) wildcard in terms.

- The "eq" operator matches if the two terms are exactly identical.

- The "sub" operator matches if the second term is a substring of the first.

- The "re" argument lets you specify a grep(1)-style regular expression as your second term. The rule matches if the first term matches the regex.

Systrace also supports "neq" (not equal to), "nsub" (not a substring), and "ipath" (argument in this path), but these terms are only rarely used.

The simplest way to see how systrace policies work is to look at some sample policy statements. Many of the following samples are taken from the default policy for named(8), kept in /etc/systrace/usr_sbin_named.

Sample Systrace Policy Rules

Before reviewing the named policy, let's review some commonly known about the nameserver daemon's system access requirements. Zone transfers occur on TCP port 53, while basic lookup services are provided on UDP port 53. OpenBSD chroots named into /var/named by default and logs everything to /var/log/messages. We might expect system calls to allow this access.

Now, let's see how the reality of system calls compares to our expectations.

Permitting System Calls

---

❶native-❷accept:: ❸permit

When named(8) tries to use the ❷accept() system call, under the ❶native ABI, it is ❸allowed. What is accept()? Run "man 2 accept," and you'll see that this accepts connections on an existing socket. A nameserver will obviously have to accept connections on a network socket!

Using Match Comparisons

Here's a rule for bind(), the system call that lets a program listen on a TCP/IP port.

---

native-bind: ❶sockaddr match "inet-*:53" then permit

What the heck is a ❶"sockaddr"? Check bind(2), and you'll see that this is a variable used as an argument to the bind() system call. This is where things start to get scary; how do you know what the argument should look like? If you're not a programmer, your best bet is to read existing systrace policies to see how other people use this. In this particular case, the program may bind to port 53, over both TCP and UDP protocols. If an attacker had an exploit to make named(8) attach a command prompt on a high-numbered port, this systrace policy would prevent that exploit from working — without changing a single line of named(8) code!

Using eq Comparisons

Here, we compare the argument used by a system call to a path on the system. If they match, the system call is permitted.

---

native-chdir: filename eq "/" then permit

At first glance, this would seem insensible. If the program tries to go to the root directory or to the directory "/namedb", systrace will allow it. Why would you possibly want to allow named to access to the root directory, however? Well, on OpenBSD, named(8) runs in a chroot jail. The program can certainly access the root directory of the chroot! This is one example of how system calls can be very confusing.

Using sub Comparisons

The named policy doesn't have any sub comparisons, so here's one taken from the lpd(8) policy.

```
native-connect: sockaddr sub ":515" then permit
```

All this is looking for is a string that contains the characters ":515". We could use a wildcard and a "match" comparison, but the sub comparison takes fewer system resources than the match comparison.

Using re Comparisons

If at all possible, avoid "re" comparisons. They use a lot of system time, especially when "match" or "substring" would do almost as well. Here's a policy that lets a command call execve(2), if the filename begins with the string "make".

```
native-execve: filename re ❶"/make$" then permit
```

If you don't recognize the ❶regular expression, go read grep(1).

Syscall Aliases

Systrace groups certain system calls with very similar functions into aliases. You can disable this functionality with a command-line switch and only use the exact system calls you specify, but in most cases these aliases are quite useful and shrink your policies considerably. The two aliases are "fsread" and "fswrite."

Fsread is an alias for stat(), lstat(), readlink(), and access(), under the native and Linux ABIs. fswrite is an alias for unlink(), mkdir(), and rmdir(), in both the native and Linux ABIs. As open() can be used to either read or write a file, it is aliased by both fsread and fswrite, depending on how it is called.

Optional Arguments

Systrace can log successful system calls, and can also give different errors as you decide.

If you put an error code name in square brackets after the "deny" keyword, that error code will be returned to the program when it tries to access that system call. Programs will behave differently depending on the error that they receive; named will react differently to a "permission denied" error than it will to an "out of memory" error. You can get a complete list of error codes from errno(2). Use the error name, not the error number. For example, here we return an error for nonexistent files:

```
filename sub "<non-existent filename>" then deny[enoent]
```

If you put the word "log" at the end of your rule, successful system calls will be logged. For example, if we wanted to log each time named(8) attached to port 53, we could edit the policy statement for the bind() call to read:

```
native-bind: sockaddr match "inet-*:53" then permit log
```

Filtering by User and Group

You can also choose to filter rules based on user ID and group ID, using the "uid" and "gid" keywords. You must use the numbers, as given in /etc/group and /etc/passwd. Here, we allow a program to use the setgid() system call, if it's trying to change to the group ID 70.

```
native-setgid: gid eq "70" then permit
```

Privilege Elevation

Finally, systrace allows a program running as a regular user to perform certain behaviors as another user, using the "as userid" keywords. We could run named(8) entirely as a regular user if we changed the bind() call to something like this:

```
native-bind: sockaddr match "inet-*:53" then permit as root
```

While I expect to see this being used more and more in OpenBSD installations in the future, systrace is new enough that it has not yet been made the default. Also, systrace does impose a minor amount of overhead, and policies can vary widely from environment to environment, so it may never be the default.

Making a Systrace Policy File

Each systrace policy file is in a file named after the full path of the program, replacing slashes with underscores. For example, our policy for /usr/sbin/named is called usr_sbin_named. The policy file starts with a policy and an ABI statement.

```
❶Policy: /usr/sbin/named, ❷Emulation: native
```

The ❶"Policy" statement gives the full path to the program this policy is for. You can't fool systrace(1) by giving the same name to a program elsewhere on the system. ❷The "Emulation" entry shows which ABI this policy is for.

Syscalls Without Rules

If a program running under systrace(1) tries to make a system call that is not listed in the policy, the system call will be denied. Systrace denies all actions that are not explicitly permitted and logs the rejection to syslog. If a program running under systrace has a problem, check /var/log/messages to discover what system call the program wants and decide whether you want to add it to your policy, reconfigure the program, or live with the error.

Creating Systrace Policies

In a true paranoid's ideal world, sysadmins would read the source code for every application on their system and be able to build system call access policies by hand relying only on their intimate understanding of every feature of the application. Most system administrators don't have that sort of time and would have better things to do with that sort of time if they had it. You have a couple of choices for building system call policies in the real world: using an available policy or using a tool to build your policy for you.

Public Systrace Policies

The Hairy Eyeball project, at http://blafasel.org/~floh/he/, contains systrace policies for hundreds of programs. Even if you only want to use systrace for one or two programs, I recommend that you download the entire Hairy Eyeball distribution, for use as examples if nothing else. Using a predefined policy can save you a lot of annoyance, but you still need to be able to edit these to fit your particular circumstances. Also, you'll have to generate policies from scratch for programs that are not in the repository.

Policy Generation with systrace(1)

Systrace(1) includes a policy-generation tool that will generate a policy that lists every system call the application wants to run. You can then use that policy as a starting point to narrow down the access you will give the application. We'll use this method to generate a policy for inetd(8). Use the "-A" flag to systrace and the full path to the program you want to run.

```
# systrace -A /usr/sbin/inetd
```

If you had any flags to add to inetd, you would add them at the end of the command line.

Now exercise the program you're developing a policy for. This system has ident, daytime, and time services running out of inetd(8), so run programs that require those services. Fire up an IRC client to trigger ident requests, and telnet to port 13 and 37 to get time services.

Once you have put inetd through its paces, shut it down. Inetd has no control program, so you need to kill it by process ID. Checking the process list for inetd will show two processes:

```
# ps -ax | grep inetd
24421 ??  Ixs     0:00.00 /usr/sbin/inetd
12929 ??  Is      0:00.01 systrace -A /usr/sbin/inetd
#
```

Do not kill the systrace process, pid 12929 in this example! That process has all the records of the system calls that inetd(8) has made. Just kill the inetd process, and the systrace process will exit normally.

Now check your home directory for a ".systrace" directory, which will contain systrace(1)'s first stab at an inetd(8) policy. Remember, policies are placed in files named after the full path to the program, replacing slashes with underscores.

```
# ls .systrace
usr_libexec_identd    usr_sbin_inetd
#
```

Systrace created two policies, not one! In addition to the expected policy for /usr/sbin/inetd, there's one for /usr/libexec/identd. If you're familiar with inetd(8), you've probably already guessed why this happened. Those new to inetd should go off to the /etc/inetd.conf discussion in Chapter 14, where they would learn that the time services are implemented internally within inetd, while ident requires a separate program that inetd calls to service requests. As inetd(8) spawned identd(8), systrace(1) captured the identd system calls as well.

By reading the policy, you can improve your understanding of what the program actually does. Look up each system call the program uses, and see if you can restrict access further. An experienced systems administrator can probably find ways to tighten access, but junior sysadmins can just use the autogenerated policy. If you just run the autogenerated policy, you're already improving your system's security. For example, the autogenerated policy contains rules that only allow it to listen on particular TCP/IP ports and only read certain files on the system.

Using Systrace Policies

Applying a policy to a program is much like creating the systrace policy itself; just run the program as an argument to systrace, using the "-a" option.

```
# systrace -a /usr/sbin/inetd
```

If the program tries to perform any system calls that are not listed in the policy, the system call will fail. This may cause the program to behave unpredictably. Systrace will log failed entries in /var/log/messages. For example, after running inetd under this particular systrace policy I found messages like this throughout /var/log/messages:

```
Dec  2 01:31:11 openbsdtest systrace: deny user: _identd, prog: ❶/usr/libexec/
identd, pid: 27046(1)[12989], policy: /usr/libexec/identd, filters: 24, syscall:
native-fsread(5), filename: ❷/etc/spwd.db
Dec  2 01:31:11 openbsdtest identd[27046]: /etc/pwd.db: Operation not permitted
Dec  2 01:31:11 openbsdtest identd[27046]: getpwuid() could not map uid (25) to
name
```

We can trace this back and see what exactly happened. In the first log entry, ❶identd tried to read ❷/etc/spwd.db. This is the secure hash of the password file. Identd(8) should certainly be able to look up system users – that's the service it provides, after all! I'm not certain why identd(8) wants the secure version of this hash, however. This needs to be researched. On the other hand, if nothing seems to be breaking, you might just want to live with it.

Editing a policy is very simple: Just add the desired statement to the end of the rule list, and it will be picked up.

Real-Time Systrace Monitoring

You could edit your policies by hand, of course, but that's the hard way. Systrace includes a tool to let you edit policies in real time, as the system call is made. This is excellent for use in a network operations center environment, where the person responsible for watching the network monitor can also be assigned to watch for system calls and bring them to the attention of the appropriate sysadmin.

You can specify which program you wish to monitor by using systrace's "-p" flag. This is called "attaching" to the program. For example, earlier we saw two processes containing "inetd". One was the actual inetd process, the other was the systrace process managing inetd. Attach to the systrace process, not the actual program — in this case, process 12929. Also give the full path to the managed program as an argument.

```
# systrace -p 12929 /usr/sbin/inetd
```

At first, nothing will happen. When the program attempts to make an unauthorized system call, however, a GUI will pop up. You will have the options to allow the system call, deny the system call, always permit the call, or always deny it. The program will hang until you make a decision, however, so decide quickly!

Note that these changes will only take effect so long as the current process is running! If you restart the program, you must also restart the attached systrace monitor, and any changes you set in the monitor are gone. You must add those rules to the policy if you want them to be permanent, so be sure to take notes.

This requires that the people monitoring the system are willing to respond in real time. A program running under systrace without monitoring will just refuse unrecognized system calls and get on with life. If you use the GUI, however, the program will hang until you respond! Running interactive systrace monitoring on your high-throughput Web server may not be a good idea until you think you have all the bugs worked out.

While systrace has a vast number of functions and abilities, this should be enough to get you started. Experiment with the tool, look at some existing policies, and be sure to read section 2 of the man pages when you're in doubt!

Software Security Features

OpenBSD handles its internal memory in a slightly different way than most other UNIX-like operating systems, and also builds software slightly differently, all to enhance security. Generally speaking, most free software developers are satisfied if their software compiles and runs most of the time, and are not so careful about the internal security of their software. In the past several years, however, we've seen root-level exploits in everything from web servers to MP3 players. As the OpenBSD team cannot audit all software that any admin might install, they've taken the step of securing third-party software during the building and running process. These features may or may not work on all hardware platforms, but is certainly a step in the right direction. OpenBSD's five standard security features are the non-executable stack, PROT_ purity, WorX, separate read-only segments, and propolice.

Non-Executable Stack

The stack is a section of memory used to keep track of mathematical operations or system internal operations. On OpenBSD, memory on the stack cannot be executed, which eliminates many possible attack techniques.

Executing code on the stack is generally considered poor programming practice, but some developers did it anyway. When OpenBSD implemented this change, it caused quite a few programmers to receive numerous bug reports about their software, and forced them to change this behavior to something more secure. This is good not just for the security of OpenBSD users, but all people who use that software.

PROT_ purity

According to the POSIX specification, each page of memory has three possible permissions: read (PROT_READ), write (PROT_WRITE), and execute (PROT_EXEC). In theory, if you set a piece of memory to be read and write only, information in that chunk of memory cannot be executed as a program. In practice, most implementations of UNIX assume that if you have read permissions on a page of memory, the contents of that page can be executed. In many cases, this is because of limitations in the hardware, but the most common cause is poor kernel programming. An attacker can possibly exploit this.

As of release 3.3, the OpenBSD kernel carefully tracks memory permissions and enforces them on hardware that allows it. The Sparc, Sparc 64, Alpha, and HP hardware architectures support this out-of-the-box. Older hardware, such as VAX and 68K Macs, cannot support this at all. The popular i386 architecture divides memory into two regions, *executable* and *not-executable*. As of release 3.3, the stack is stored in the non-executable area. While PowerPC is slightly more flexible than i386, it's not good either.

For the forthcoming OpenBSD 3.4 release, the i386 platform will get per-page memory execution protection by widely separating the text and data memory segments. Similarly, the PowerPC platform will divide executables and data between different areas of memory to create the same effect. This requires careful tweaking within the kernel and the ld(1) linker.

Many of the other software security features are based upon PROT_ purity.

WorX

WorX stands for "Write or Execute" and may be written as W^X or "PROT_WRITE XOR PROT_EXEC." In an OpenBSD system, pages of memory are either writable or executable — but not both. This is heavily dependent upon PROT_ purity, of course.

A common exploit technique is to trick a program to write information to memory, and then execute the contents of that piece of memory. An attacker may convince a program to write to a chunk of memory, but the kernel will not allow that memory to be executed. Attackers who rely upon this will be quite frustrated trying to break into an OpenBSD machine!

NOTE   *On ELF-based systems, shared-library programs have two segments called GOT and PLT that on some architectures need to be both writable and executable. These have been isolated in their own segments, hence protected from such attacks.*

Read-Only Segments

A segment of memory containing program code traditionally had two parts: actual code and read-only data. This was the standard in the day of a.out binaries, but the practice continued when the world moved on to ELF binaries. The read-only data has been split out into its own segment. While this would be difficult to actually exploit, it's not impossible. It also enhances performance and caching, however, so it's worth implementing.

Propolice

Propolice checks function return addresses upon completion of a function, to guarantee that they have not moved. A *canary,* or random value constant per run, is used to make the check un-fakeable by an attacker. A common exploit technique is to overwrite or overflow variables. If a return address moves, the program is immediately shut down, and an error is logged to syslogd. Additionally, propolice rearranges the placement of objects in internal memory so that the objects most likely to overflow (i.e., buffers) are more easily detected. While having a program crash under attack is unpleasant, a logged crash is much better than a rooted machine!

With these security features in place, software running on OpenBSD is largely protected even from itself.

With the ability to control how software executes, where it can be executed, what system calls a program can use, and what the kernel itself permits, Open-BSD can prevent any number of attacks.

Now that you understand the basics of OpenBSD's advanced security features, let's look at how to configure the kernel itself.

11

BASIC KERNEL CONFIGURATION

Kernel, not colonel!
This is blowfish, not chicken.
Less grease, more function.

Depending on your experience level, the "kernel" is either the subject of great mystery, something you reconfigure whenever the whim strikes you, or something you know to leave well enough alone. In a commercial operating system, such as Microsoft Windows or Sun Microsystems' Solaris, the systems administrator doesn't touch the kernel.

In some open-source operating systems, such as Linux or FreeBSD, rebuilding the kernel is recommended on any number of occasions. OpenBSD falls somewhere in the middle: The standard kernel is meant to be perfectly usable without modification, but you have tools to perform any tweaks or renovations desired. Additionally, you get the complete set of source code and kernel-building tools in case you need to perform wholesale kernel surgery.

The OpenBSD kernel can be dynamically modified, in most cases even while the system is fully functioning, via sysctl(8). We cover that in detail. Some hardware requires special tweaks in the kernel to run correctly on OpenBSD. We'll describe how those adjustments can be made with config(8) and how this same technique can be used to alter general kernel parameters.

What Is the Kernel?

The easy answer is, "the kernel is the file /bsd."

That's probably not what you *really* wanted to know! You'll hear many different definitions of *kernel*. While everybody knows it's important, many people don't really know what the kernel actually does. The following definition isn't complete, but it's good enough for our purposes, and it's simple to understand:

The kernel is the interface between the hardware and user software.

The kernel allows you to write data to disk drives and to the network. The kernel gives instructions to the CPU and shuffles bits into memory chips. When you open a web page, your web browser asks the kernel to fetch data for it. The kernel provides a reasonably simple interface to the hardware through system calls. (If you're truly interested in the interfaces that the kernel provides, the man pages in section 2 describe all the system calls, the kernel interface provided for user-level software.)

For what might seem to be a simple task, the kernel's responsibilities are actually quite difficult. To start with, different pieces of hardware will provide their resources in varying ways. Even hardware with similar functions (e.g., network cards) can have very different hardware interfaces. The kernel has to cope with this through a variety of device drivers. Without this device driver, the kernel simply won't know how to transfer information to or from the card. The way your kernel investigates some hardware during the boot sequence defines how the hardware behaves, so you have to control that. Some network cards will identify themselves in a friendly manner, while others will lock up hard if sent the wrong sort of query. Also, different programs expect to access the system hardware in a variety of ways. For example, your kernel controls memory usage. If you have a program that demands that memory be allocated in a way your kernel doesn't support, you will have problems with that program.

The kernel is the first program to run when the system is booted. When you watch your system boot, those messages you see before init(8) starts are all from the kernel and are displayed in a different color than those displayed by init(8). The kernel manages all other processes, starting with init(8) and going from there.

Startup Messages

One common question is, "What hardware did your kernel find when it booted?" If the kernel handles all device drivers and other hardware support, the list of devices it found should include all the hardware in the system. Kernel messages are temporarily stored in the system message buffer. You can view the contents of this system message buffer with dmesg(8). This buffer is "circular," however; as it fills up, the oldest messages are deleted to make room for new messages. This means that the boot messages are the first to go!

Fortunately, OpenBSD saves the boot-time system messages in the file /var/run/dmesg.boot. Let's take a look at the dmesg from our test system. It starts with a kernel notification:

```
OpenBSD 3.1 (GENERIC) #59: Sat Apr 13 15:28:52 MDT 2002
    deraadt@i386.openbsd.org:/usr/src/sys/arch/i386/compile/GENERIC
```

This identifies the version of OpenBSD we are running, the name of the kernel, the kernel version, the date the kernel was compiled, and the machine and directory where the kernel was built.

```
cpu0: F00F bug workaround installed
cpu0: Intel Pentium/MMX ("GenuineIntel" 586-class) 166 MHz
cpu0: FPU,V86,DE,PSE,TSC,MSR,MCE,CX8,MMX
```

The first item on almost every line describes the device driver or hardware component. In this case, the hardware component is the CPU. Each piece of hardware of a type is numbered, starting with zero.

Further detail on each line tells us something about the hardware. Some of this might mean nothing to you, but it's good to have the information available. If you've been kicking around the computer world for a while, you might remember the "Pentium F00F" bug. OpenBSD has a workaround for this, which it activated on this machine. Similarly, OpenBSD identifies the exact sort of CPU this is, and which model and speed it is. Finally, it identifies instruction sets available on the CPU.

Other messages don't describe particular pieces of hardware, but instead aggregate other information.

```
real mem = 83472384 (81516K)
avail mem = 71708672 (70028K)
```

This computer has 81,516KB of physical memory. Of that, 70,028KB are available to programs other than the kernel.

Device Attachments

One of the more interesting things about the boot-time message buffer is that you can see where each piece of hardware is attached.

```
pci0 at mainbus0 bus 0: configuration mode 1 (bios)
pchb0 at pci0 dev 0 function 0 "Intel 82439HX" rev 0x03
pcib0 at pci0 dev 7 function 0 "Intel 82371SB PCI-ISA" rev 0x01
```

Here, OpenBSD found a PCI bus. The kernel then found a device it identifies as pchb0, attached to the PCI bus, and it gives a part model number. If you wanted to know exactly what this device driver did, you could check section 4 of the manual, which would tell you that pchb is a "PCI-Host Bridge." Similarly, a bit of digging would tell you that pcib means a PCI-ISA bridge.

The information in quotes is chosen by the device driver developer as a name for the device and may not always be completely accurate. While it's rare for this information to be completely wrong, it might only describe one aspect of a chipset and not others.

If you keep reading the dmesg on an OpenBSD system, you start to see that every piece of hardware plugs into some other piece of hardware. On this test system, the ISA bus is attached to the PCI-ISA bridge:

```
isa0 at pcib0
```

If you keep looking, you'll see various pieces of equipment plugged into the ISA bus.

```
pckbc0 at isa0 port 0x60/5
```

Here's our keyboard controller, plugged into the ISA bus. Later, we find the actual keyboard.

```
pckbd0 at pckbc0 (kbd slot)
```

So, the keyboard is plugged into the keyboard controller, which resides on the ISA bus, which is plugged into the PCI-ISA bridge, which is plugged into the PCI bus, which is plugged into the main bus.

Dmassage

I find the dmassage script useful to identify exactly what's attached to what interfaces on a computer. (Dmassage is an add-on available at http://www.sentia. org/projects/dmassage/, not part of OpenBSD itself.) We'll look at some other functions of dmassage in a little bit, but the one we care about here is "-t." This shows a "tree" of system devices and where they are attached.

```
# ./dmassage -t
root
 \-mainbus0
    |-bios0
    |   \-pcibios0
    \-pci0
       |-dc0
       |   \-dcphy0
...
```

While this isn't directly useful, it can help you get a better idea of how devices are interconnected in your particular system.

Device Numbering

If you have multiple devices of a single type in your system, each is numbered. Because we're in the computer world, the first unit is number zero, the second number one, and so on. For example, our test system has two hard drives. Early in dmesg.boot we'll see:

```
wd0 at pciide0 channel 0 drive 0: <QUANTUM BIGFOOT_CY2160A>
wd0: 32-sector PIO, LBA, 2014MB, 4092 cyl, 16 head, 63 sec, 4124736 sectors
wd0(pciide0:0:0): using PIO mode 4, DMA mode 2
```

The wd device driver is for IDE hard disks. Here we see the disk size, and a whole bunch of characteristics about this drive. A little later on, we'll see the second hard drive.

```
wd1 at pciide0 channel 1 drive 1: <WDC AC38400L>
wd1: 16-sector PIO, LBA, 8063MB, 16383 cyl, 16 head, 63 sec, 16514064 sectors
```

As the second IDE hard drive, this is called wd1. Subsequent IDE hard drives would be numbered wd2, wd3, and so on.

Each piece of hardware that uses a particular device driver is separately numbered. For example, SCSI hard drives use the "sd" drive. If the SCSI drive is the third hard drive, it is numbered sd0.

The important thing to remember is that every piece of hardware has a unique instance of the device driver. If you have 31 SCSI hard drives in your web server, they will be labeled sd0 through sd30.

NOTE *At times, you'll need to know the device name to use a piece of hardware correctly. Take a moment to review /var/run/dmesg.boot on your OpenBSD system. Start to get a feel for how your hardware shows up. Most device drivers have a man page in section 4 and are worth reviewing for a thorough education.*

Sysctl(8)

The OpenBSD kernel, like every BSD-based kernel, includes a variety of tunable parameters. These parameters are known as system controls, or *sysctls*. Some sysctls are static and can be viewed but not changed. Others can be changed by the sysadmin. Sysctls are a powerful feature; they will allow a systems administrator to solve problems or change system behavior without reconfiguring applications or recompiling the kernel. Developers like sysctls, as they allow programs to easily grab current information out of a running kernel. Changing the way a system behaves can impair programs or annoy users, however, so you need to know what you're doing before changing sysctls.

You can view sysctl values, and change those values that can be changed, with the sysctl(8) program. Throughout this book, I'll be mentioning sysctl values and how they affect system behavior. You should have a good general understanding of what sysctls are before changing them, however.

Sysctl Values

Sysctls are arranged in a Management Information Base, or MIB, tree. An MIB tree organizes information into categories and then divides each category into sub-categories. For example, the main categories in the OpenBSD sysctl MIB tree include categories such as kern (kernel), vm (virtual memory), net (networking), and so on. The net category includes sub-categories such as inet (IPv4 networking) and inet6 (IPv6 networking). The inet category includes sub-branches for TCP and UDP, and so on. Each "last" category includes a variety of individual values that can be read or, possibly, tweaked. So, a typical single MIB might be something like this.

```
net.inet.tcp.rfc1323
```

This MIB is part of the network stack. It represents the IPv4 section of the network stack and specifically the TCP section. It represents support for RFC1323, or a certain type of TCP extensions. How do I know this? Well, understanding these off the top of your head requires a certain amount of UNIX and/or networking experience. OpenBSD expects that you'll be able to figure out the meaning of some sysctl values, such as this one, by reading them. Others are much more obtuse, but are well documented in man pages.

So, if you want to explore sysctls, the next step is to get a list of them from your computer.

Viewing Available Sysctls

Before trying to change any sysctl options, take a look at the sysctls available on your system. The sysctls in a kernel depend on that kernel's configuration. We're going to assume here that you're using the GENERIC kernel shipped with your release of OpenBSD. You don't need to be root to view sysctls.

Some sysctls contain information that's coded in a particular format that isn't particularly easy to view. For the moment, we'll set those sysctls aside and only consider the ones that are most easily read. The following command will print all the readable sysctls available in your kernel and save the output to the file sysctl.out for easy viewing later:

```
# sysctl -a > sysctl.out
```

Take a look at the resulting sysctl.out file. Some sysctl values at the top of the list have pretty obvious meanings. Here are the first four from an OpenBSD 3.1 system:

```
kern.ostype = OpenBSD
kern.osrelease = 3.1
kern.osrevision = 200206
kern.version = OpenBSD 3.1 (GENERIC) #59: Sat Apr 13 15:28:52 MDT 2002
    deraadt@i386.openbsd.org:/usr/src/sys/arch/i386/compile/GENERIC
```

kern.* sysctls concern the kernel itself. Here we see some basic information about the kernel. The kern.ostype and kern.osrelease sysctls are fairly obvious. Why would an OpenBSD system have a sysctl to report the operating system, though? Shouldn't you know that already? Well, the sysctl interface can be found on any BSD-based operating system, and checking the value of this sysctl is a good way for programs to identify the operating system that they're running on. Kern.osrevision might make you wonder for a moment, but it's actually just the date when this particular version was released — June of 2002. Finally, the kern.version sysctl gives the exact version of the booted kernel and its compile date and location. Pretty darn easy, no? So, let's look at the next few.

```
kern.maxvnodes = 1310
kern.maxproc = 532
kern.maxfiles = 1772
kern.argmax = 262144
kern.securelevel = 1
```

Yuck! What the heck is all this? If you're an experienced sysadmin, you could make a real good guess about what something like "maxvnodes" means. New users probably have no clue. If you run "apropos vnode" you'll get a whole list of possible matches, however, and vnode(9) will look like a good place to start. Similarly, a bit of web and manual page searching as discussed in Chapter 1 will lead you to the definitions of the others.

When you know the name of a sysctl and you simply want to view the current value of that sysctl, give the sysctl name as an argument to sysctl(8). For example, to view the system's current securelevel (see Chapter 10), check the value of the kern.securelevel sysctl.

```
# sysctl kern.securelevel
kern.securelevel = 1
#
```

The current value of kern.securelevel is 1.

You can go somewhere in between the two and view all the portions of the sysctl tree under a certain category. For example, the net category covers all network-related sysctls, net.inet covers all IPv4 networking sysctls, and net.inet.udp covers the sysctls specific to UDP networking. To view everything in that section of the sysctl tree, just give the category name as an argument to sysctl.

```
# sysctl net.inet.udp
net.inet.udp.checksum = 1
net.inet.udp.baddynamic = 587,749
net.inet.udp.recvspace = 41600
net.inet.udp.sendspace = 9216
#
```

OpenBSD provides four sysctls for UDP networking. You can view any portion of the sysctl tree in this way, going as many categories deep as you like.

Changing Sysctl Values

Some sysctls are read-only. For example, the hw.ncpu sysctl shows how many processors are in the computer.

```
# sysctl hw.ncpu
hw.ncpu = 1
#
```

This system has one CPU. (Because OpenBSD currently only addresses one processor on multi-processor systems, this isn't such a great surprise.) Programs can use these sysctls to get operational information to make decisions on how they should run.

On the other hand, a system kernel can decide whether or not to forward packets. Packet forwarding is when a computer receives network packets on one network card and sends them out on another. Firewalls (Chapter 17) and routers typically forward packets. The net.inet.ip.forwarding sysctl controls this feature in OpenBSD. If this sysctl is set to 0, packets are not forwarded. If you set this to 1, packets can be routed through the system.

```
# sysctl net.inet.ip.forwarding
net.inet.ip.forwarding = 0
#
```

To change this, use sysctl's "-w" flag and the desired value.

```
# sysctl -w net.inet.ip.forwarding=1
net.inet.ip.forwarding: 0 -> 1
#
```

If you wanted to perform some network maintenance and stop forwarding packets temporarily, you could turn this back to 0 to turn off packet forwarding. This will annoy your users to no end, but if you're running the firewall I hope you know that already.

NOTE *In simple on-off (or boolean) sysctls, 0 means "off" and 1 means "on." Many sysctls are not of the on/off variety, instead having a range of valid numeric values, so you cannot assume that a sysctl with a value of 1 or 0 is boolean!*

Setting Sysctls at Boot

Sysctl changes revert to their defaults when you reboot your computer. This probably isn't desired, in most cases. You can set sysctls at boot in two different ways: in /etc/sysctl.conf and /etc/rc.local.

Changes specified in /etc/sysctl.conf take place early in the booting process. This is when most kernel customizations should occur. If you customize your network stack, for example, you want changes to take place before the system opens any network connections! You can list any sysctls you want to change, an equal sign, and their desired value, in /etc/sysctl.conf.

By default, the /etc/sysctl.conf file contains a variety of commonly used sysctls. Each is commented out with a pound sign and is set to the most common non-default setting. If you want to change the particular behavior, all you do is uncomment the particular entry. Let's look at some of the particular entries in /etc/sysctl.conf. (You may well have different entries in your system, depending on the version of OpenBSD you are running.)

net.inet.ip.forwarding

This controls forwarding of IPv4 packets through the system. If this is set to 1, packets will be forwarded according to the internal routing table (see more about this in Chapter 8). If it is set to 0, packets will not be forwarded.

net.inet6.ip6.forwarding

This controls forwarding of IPv6 packets, much as net.inet.ip.forwarding does for IPv4 packets. While we won't go into IPv6 in this book, you should be aware that it's available and that it's managed separately.

net.inet.tcp.rfc1323

This controls use of RFC1323 TCP congestion control. It's enabled by default, as almost everything on the Internet uses RFC1323 congestion control today. RFC1323-compliant network devices can have slow network connections to non-RFC1323 devices. You might want to set this to 0 if you're having trouble communicating with older TCP/IP devices.

ddb.panic

OpenBSD uses the ddb kernel debugger. On those rare occasions when an OpenBSD system panics, it automatically drops the console into the debugger. If you just want the system to reboot upon a panic, set this to 0.

ddb.console

If set to 1, this sysctl allows you to enter the kernel debugger while at the console by hitting CTRL-ALT-ESCAPE. This option is mostly only of interest to developers and others actively debugging the kernel.

vm.swapencrypt.enable

This tells OpenBSD to encrypt all data written to the swap file. It's possible for malicious users or intruders to pull data out of a swap file. While this data is usually scrambled well by normal system activity, a persistent user might eventually learn something from it. If your system tends to swap, and if you have shell users who you don't trust, you might want to set this. Note that you'll need to unmount and remount your various swap partitions for this to take effect. The simplest way to do this is to reboot.

machdep.allowaperture

This allows programs to access the video driver. If you're running XFree86 version 3, the X server needs access to the standard VGA framebuffer and BIOS. You can get that by setting mach.allowaperture to 1. If you're running XFree86 version 4, you'll need access to the whole first megabyte of physical memory, which may cause a few security problems. You can get that access by setting machdep.allowaperture to 2.

machdep.kbdreset

When it is set, you can shut down the computer correctly by pressing CTRL-ALT-DELETE. If you leave this unset (the default), pressing CTRL-ALT-DELETE will have no effect on the system.

Table Sysctls

So far, all of the sysctl values we've looked at have been fairly normal alphanumeric values. Not all sysctls have such friendly values, however. Many are *tables*, meaning that they can only be viewed with a special tool. (OpenBSD includes these tools, of course.) The sysctl program will allow you to view all sysctls, including the tabular ones, by using the "-A" flag. (There is no flag to specify just the tabular sysctls, but that would not be useful anywhere except for this example right now.)

```
# sysctl -A > sysctl-A.out
```

Look through this file, and you'll see an occasional line with additional information or instructions. For example, in the section of hardware sysctls we see the following snippet.

```
sysctl: use vmstat to view hw.diskstats information
```

There's a sysctl hw.diskstats, containing information only visible via vmstat(8). Each tabular sysctl in the output will give similar instructions, telling you how to access the information.

As you can probably guess, tabular sysctls are read-only (at least via sysctl(8)).

Kernel Alteration with config(8)

While sysctl will let you perform minor tweaks on the kernel, it won't let you change certain values hard-coded into the kernel binary. Some of these values are used to create initial data structures within the kernel and cannot be changed once the kernel is up and running. Others relate to device drivers. The sysctl interface simply cannot handle these sorts of changes; you need to edit the existing kernel file and reboot, allowing the system to start over from scratch and set things up as you want them. That's where config(8) comes in.

What Is Config(8)?

The config(8) program has two completely separate functions. The first builds a kernel compilation directory from a text configuration file, which we'll look at in Chapter 12. The function we're interested in now is to edit an existing kernel binary, allowing the sysadmin to tweak the kernel in any number of ways even after it's built.

Preparation

Before you make any changes to your working kernel, no matter how minor, be utterly sure you make a backup copy! In the worst case, you want to be absolutely certain that you have a kernel that will boot. The kernel is just a file, /bsd by default. Copy that to another file. I recommend naming backup kernels after the kernel configuration they were built from. The default OpenBSD kernel configuration is named GENERIC, as you see when the system boots.

```
# cp /bsd /bsd.GENERIC
```

Always keep a known-good kernel on your system. A bad kernel can prevent a computer from booting, and if you don't have a reliable one on hand your computer will need to be partially or completely reinstalled. (A bad kernel can also damage your data, your file system, or anything else on your computer, which means you'll be reinstalling anyway, but that's fairly rare.) You can boot off this backup kernel by following the instructions back in Chapter 6. Kernel bugs can take weeks or months to show up, so keep a default GENERIC kernel on hand forever.

Also, the OpenBSD boot loader will look for /bsd.old if it has problems loading /bsd. You can keep backup kernels here. On those occasions when I must customize my kernel I often use /bsd as my test kernel, /bsd.old as a proven custom kernel, and /bsd.GENERIC as the provided GENERIC kernel. That way, the system has a better chance of actually booting should I make a mistake with the kernel.

Device Drivers and Config

Most of the hard-coded information in the kernel relates to device drivers, especially device drivers for older ISA cards. If you've been using a computer for a long time you probably remember manually setting IRQs and memory port addresses on your first network card. The kernel uses these bits of information to identify each card. Essentially, the kernel consults an internal list of IRQs and port numbers, compares it to what it found on its hardware probe, and assigns the drivers appropriately. "This card answers at IRQ 10 and memory port 0x300? Well, it must be a NE2000-compatible network card then! Let me assign that driver to it." (It's more complicated than this, of course, but this probe and table is a vital part of the process.) If you want OpenBSD to recognize such a card, you need to tell the kernel which driver to assign to the IRQ and memory port.

NOTE   *In the appendix, I discuss the various device drivers available in OpenBSD and how to find documentation about them. For now, when I say that a particular device driver works on a particular piece of hardware, just nod and smile and go along with it.*

Editing the Kernel with config

When editing kernels with config, there are three command-line options you need to worry about. The "-e" flag tells config that you're editing a kernel binary; none of the examples in this section will use if you omit that flag. Then you need one of either "-f" or "-o". The "-f" flag tells config(8) to edit the kernel file in place — that is, if you're editing the kernel file /bsd, when you're finished the edited copy will still be /bsd. As a rule, I do not recommend doing this. The "-o" flag lets you specify another location to write your edited kernel. The last argument config(8) requires is the name of the kernel binary to be edited. In the following example, we're editing the file /bsd and writing our edited copy to the file /bsd.test.

```
# config -e -o /bsd.test /bsd
OpenBSD 3.1 (GENERIC) #59: Sat Apr 13 15:28:52 MDT 2002
    deraadt@i386.openbsd.org:/usr/src/sys/arch/i386/compile/GENERIC
Enter 'help' for information
ukc>
```

The first two config(8) commands you should become familiar with are "help" and "list." The help command lists all the commands available inside the config kernel editor. We will walk through all of these later in the section, but it's good to have a reminder close at hand.

The list command gives a complete list of all the devices configured inside the kernel, one screen at a time.

```
ukc> list
  0 audio* at sb0|sb*|gus0|pas0|sp0|ess*|wss0|wss*|ym*|eap*|eso*|sv*|neo*|cmpci*|
clcs*|clct*|auich*|autri*|auvia*|fms*|uaudio*|maestro*|esa*|yds*|emu* flags 0x0
  1 midi* at sb0|sb*|opl*|opl*|opl*|opl*|ym*|mpu*|autri* flags 0x0
  2 nsphy* at aue*|xe*|ef*|gx*|stge*|bge*|nge*|sk*|ste*|sis*|sf*|wb*|tx*|tl*|vr*|
neo|ne1|ne2|ne*|ne*|ne*|dc*|dc*|rl*|fxp*|fxp*|xl*|xl*|ep0|ep0|ep0|ep*|ep*|ep*|
ep* phy -1 flags 0x0
  ...
```

Hit ENTER to see the next screen. On an OpenBSD 3.1 system, the standard kernel has 278 entries. Most entries are for hardware that isn't on any one particular system but that OpenBSD supports out of the box.

What Entries Mean

Let's consider a few lines from the kernel configuration editor.

```
0  ❶audio* at ❷sb0|sb*|gus0|pas0|sp0|ess*|wss0|wss*|ym*|eap*|eso*|sv*|neo*|
cmpci*|clcs*|clct*|auich*|autri*|auvia*|fms*|uaudio*|maestro*|esa*|yds*|❸emu*
❹flags 0x0
```

Line 0 shows the kernel's support for the ❶audio(4) device driver. OpenBSD's audio driver attaches to any of a variety of cards, shown here separated by pipe symbols. The list ranges from ❷sb0 (SoundBlaster device zero) to ❸emu* (any Creative Labs SBLive! card, at any device number). At the end of the line, we have ❹flags that are given to the driver. Flags tweak a driver's behavior. We'll see examples of how flags work later in this chapter. While this line is quite long, all it really means is that the audio driver is installed, it will attach to any of a wide variety of sound cards, and it has the default flag settings.

```
141 ❶ne0 at ❷isa0 ❸port 0x240 size 0 iomem -1 iosiz 0 ❹irq 9 drq -1 drq2 -1
flags 0x0
```

Line 141 is the driver for an old-fashioned ❶NE2000 ISA network card. This driver will check ❷ISA bus number zero driver for a card at ❸memory address 0x240 and ❹irq 9. It runs with the default flags. (Other characteristics shown are very, very unlikely to change, and these days most people won't even remember what they are.)

```
255 ❶pf ❷count 1 (❸pseudo device)
```

This is a device driver for a ❸pseudo-device. Pseudo-device drivers give the system some device-like functionality, but there is no actual hardware. This example, ❶pf, is the kernel's public interface for its packet-filtering engine, PF (see Chapter 17). The kernel can support one instance of PF at any given time.

Finally, you'll see several lines like this:

```
248 free slot (for add)
```

This is an empty space for the system administrator to add additional devices to the kernel. We'll see how to take advantage of these in "Adding Devices," later in this chapter.

Configuring Existing Device Drivers

Suppose you have an old-fashioned ISA NE2000 network card. Many NE2000 cards were quite durable and are still lying around support supply rooms even today. If you're using an older system to learn OpenBSD on, it's not unlikely that you'll have to deal with one of these unruly beasts. (On the other hand, it's also quite possible that some component of this system is cooked from years of abuse, and you'll find yourself suffering from unexplained crashes and errors.) The card is hard-configured to use IRQ 11 and memory port 0x280. As many of these cards could only be configured via a proprietary driver from a DOS boot disk, it's probably easier to edit your OpenBSD kernel configuration than to reconfigure the card.

The first step is to identify which NE2000 drivers are in our existing kernel. We do that with the "find" command, giving the name of the device driver. You can find a list of device drivers for various sorts of hardware in Appendix A, or on the OpenBSD web page for your architecture (i.e., http://www.OpenBSD.org/i386.html). The "ne" driver, per both of these resources, supports NE2000 cards.

```
ukc> find ne
 91 ❶ne* at ❷pci* dev -1 function -1 flags 0x0
 92 ne* at ❸pcmcia* function -1 irq -1 flags 0x0
141 ne0 at ❹isa0 ❺port 0x240 size 0 iomem -1 iosiz 0 ❻irq 9 drq -1 drq2 -1 flags
0x0
142 ne1 at isa0 port 0x300 size 0 iomem -1 iosiz 0 irq 10 drq -1 drq2 -1 flags 0x0
143 ❼ne2 at isa0 port 0x280 size 0 iomem -1 iosiz 0 irq 9 drq -1 drq2 -1 flags 0x0
204 ne* at ❽isapnp0 port -1 size 0 iomem -1 iosiz 0 irq -1 drq -1 flags 0x0
ukc>
```

Line 91 is a ❶NE2000 card, but is attached to the ❷PCI bus. ISA cards don't attach to the PCI bus without using a hammer and a saw, so this probably isn't what we want. The asterisk indicates that the kernel will change the device number as needed, to the first available number. We'll see later that ne0, ne1, and ne2 are hard-coded into the kernel, so the first PCI NE2000 card the kernel finds will be called ne3.

Line 92 is a ❸PCMCIA card for a laptop. This also isn't what we want.

Line 141 is attached to the ❹ISA bus and has a memory address of ❺0x240 and an ❻IRQ of 9. These are fairly standard values. If our card were set to these values, it would "just work." (We could probably rewire our card to use these values, but then we wouldn't learn how to use the kernel configuration tool, now would we?)

Lines 142 and 143 are other ISA NE2000 cards, but neither has the correct IRQ and memory port. Remember, on these old cards, both the IRQ and the memory port must be set correctly for the card to be recognized. Line 143 is close, with the correct memory port but an incorrect IRQ.

Line 204 is an ❽ISA plug-and-play card, with no IRQ or memory port configured. If your card is hard-coded to a particular IRQ or memory port, this entry won't work. If your card were a plug-and-play ISA NE2000, well, you wouldn't have to worry about this process. (Instead, you would be worrying about plug-and-play, and gaining a deeper appreciation for PCI's autoconfiguration features.)

Of all the existing NE2000 drivers in the kernel, ❼line 143 is the closest to what we need. Let's modify it to match our card. We do this with the "change" command, and either the device driver name or the line number. Because many devices can use the same device driver, it's simplest to use the exact line number. If you give a device driver name, the change command will walk you through every line with that device name until you find the one you want.

```
ukc> change 143
143 ne2 at isa0 port 0x280 size 0 iomem -1 iosiz 0 irq 9 drq -1 drq2 -1 flags 0x0
change [n]
```

Yes, this is the one we want to change. Enter "y" at the prompt.

```
port [0x280] ?
```

The port is correct. Hit ENTER to leave the value unchanged. Similarly, hit ENTER for the size, iomem, and iosiz questions. Stop when you reach the IRQ.

```
size [0] ?
iomem [-1] ?
iosiz [0] ?
irq [9] 11
```

We want IRQ 11, so enter "11" and hit ENTER. You'll have a chance to change the device driver flags, which you want to ignore. Finally, you'll see the whole line for the card.

```
flags [0] ?
143 ne2 changed
143 ne2 at isa0 port 0x280 size 0 iomem -1 iosiz 0 irq 11 drq -1 drq2 -1 flags 0x0
ukc>
```

The kernel now will attach the ne2 driver to an ISA card at memory port 0x280 and IRQ 11. The next time we reboot, the kernel should do the right thing with this card.

NOTE   *This might seem like a lot of work just to change an IRQ. Why not use sysctls for port and IRQ addresses? By the time the system is running enough to read /etc/sysctl.conf, the kernel has already finished probing the hardware and has attached every device it found to what it thinks is an appropriate device driver. You need to catch this early, very early — perhaps even before the system has found all of its hard drives. There are ISA SCSI cards, after all!*

Adding Devices

Suppose you have a system with four of these ISA NE2000 cards in it. Such a system would be more than adequate for a T1 firewall with several different security zones behind it. Our kernel only has three entries for ISA NE2000 cards, however. You want to use the "add" command to create a new device driver instance.

```
ukc> add ne3
Clone Device (DevNo, 'q' or '?') ?
```

The "add" command might be more appropriately called the "copy" command. You cannot add an instance of a device that is not compiled into the kernel; you can only copy an existing driver. If you enter "q", you'll cancel the add command and go back to the ukc prompt. If you enter a line number, the configuration tool will copy that line into one of the blank slots reserved for adding device drivers. If you, like me, cannot remember which line number you wanted to copy, entering a question mark will make the add command list every device that's related to the device you want to add.

```
Clone Device (DevNo, 'q' or '?') ? ?
 91 ne* at pci* dev -1 function -1 flags 0x0
 92 ne* at pcmcia* function -1 irq -1 flags 0x0
❶141 ne0 at isa0 port 0x240 size 0 iomem -1 iosiz 0 irq 9 drq -1 drq2 -1 flags 0x0
❷142 ne1 at isa0 port 0x300 size 0 iomem -1 iosiz 0 irq 10 drq -1 drq2 -1 flags
0x0
❸143 ne2 at isa0 port 0x280 size 0 iomem -1 iosiz 0 irq 11 drq -1 drq2 -1 flags
0x0
205 ne* at isapnp0 port -1 size 0 iomem -1 iosiz 0 irq -1 drq -1 flags 0x0
Clone Device (DevNo, 'q' or '?') ?
```

We can choose to copy any of the lines for ISA network cards: ❶line 141, ❷line 142, or ❸line 143. I'm choosing 143. It doesn't matter which line we copy, as by the time we have four of these cards in the system we're almost certainly madly shuffling memory ports and IRQs to try to fit everything in.

```
Insert before Device (DevNo, 'q' or '?') ? 144
```

You can decide where in the kernel's device driver list you want your copied device to appear. I'd like this card to appear next to the other NE2000 drivers. If I insert this device driver before line 144, everything after line 144 will be shifted down by one.

At this point you should be back at the ukc prompt. To be sure that your copy worked correctly, view all the "ne" devices.

```
ukc> find ne
 91 ne* at pci* dev -1 function -1 flags 0x0
 92 ne* at pcmcia* function -1 irq -1 flags 0x0
141 ne0 at isa0 port 0x240 size 0 iomem -1 iosiz 0 irq 9 drq -1 drq2 -1 flags 0x0
142 ne1 at isa0 port 0x300 size 0 iomem -1 iosiz 0 irq 10 drq -1 drq2 -1 flags 0x0
❶143 ne2 at isa0 port 0x280 size 0 iomem -1 iosiz 0 irq 11 drq -1 drq2 -1 flags
0x0
❷144 ne3 at isa0 port 0x280 size 0 iomem -1 iosiz 0 irq 11 drq -1 drq2 -1 flags
0x0
206 ne* at isapnp0 port -1 size 0 iomem -1 iosiz 0 irq -1 drq -1 flags 0x0
ukc>
```

Our new line ❷144 is a copy of line ❶143, except for the device number. We must change the IRQ and memory port to make this card work, but we now have the appropriate number of instances of device drivers for this card in the kernel.

Finding Conflicts

So, some old device doesn't work? It might be the classic IRQ/port conflict. Many old devices can only be identified by their memory port and IRQ. If OpenBSD thinks that something is running on IRQ 10 and tries to attach the wrong driver to it, you will have trouble. You might want to pull conflicting devices from your kernel.

For example, suppose your network card has IRQ 10, but isn't being detected on boot or doesn't work properly. See what your kernel thinks is running on IRQ 10 with the "show" command.

```
ukc> show irq 10
142 ne1 at isa0 port 0x300 size 0 iomem -1 iosiz 0 irq 10 drq -1 drq2 -1 flags 0x0
❶146 we1 at isa0 port 0x300 size 0 iomem 0xcc000 iosiz 0 irq 10 drq -1 drq2 -1
flags 0x0
❸161 sp0 at pss0 port 0x530 size 0 iomem -1 iosiz 0 irq 10 drq 0 flags 0x0
❹162 wss0 at isa0 port 0x530 size 0 iomem -1 iosiz 0 irq 10 drq 0 drq2 -1 flags
0x0
ukc>
```

Line 142 shows your ne200 card. Line ❶146 is a "we0." Running "man 4 we" tells us that this is a SMC EtherEZ. Line ❸162 is wss0, or the Windows Sound System driver according to the man pages. Line ❹161 is difficult, as there's no man page for "sp"! The sp device is attached to the pss0 device, however, and "man 4 pss" tells us that sp0 is the sound port attached to the Personal Sound System driver.

At this point, you need to rely upon your own knowledge of your hardware. What is actually installed in your computer? My first suspect in this case would be the other network card driver, but any of these drivers could conceivably interfere with your system. You might need to change the IRQ your card is using to make it work with your other hardware; if two pieces of hardware both try to claim IRQ 10, no amount of kernel configuration will help!

In this case I know that none of these other pieces of hardware exist on this computer. I can safely disable everything else that thinks it should attach to IRQ 10, using the "disable" command.

```
ukc> disable we1
146 we1 disabled
ukc> disable sp0
161 sp0 disabled
ukc> disable wss0
162 wss0 disabled
ukc>
```

Show everything attached to IRQ 10 in your kernel now.

```
ukc> show irq 10
142 ne1 at isa0 port 0x300 size 0 iomem -1 iosiz 0 irq 10 drq -1 drq2 -1 flags 0x0
146 we1 at isa0 ❶disable port 0x300 size 0 iomem 0xcc000 iosiz 0 irq 10 drq -1
drq2 -1 flags 0x0
```

```
161 sp0 at pss0 ❶disable port 0x530 size 0 iomem -1 iosiz 0 irq 10 drq 0 flags 0x0
162 wss0 at isa0 ❶disable port 0x530 size 0 iomem -1 iosiz 0 irq 10 drq 0 drq2 -1
flags 0x0
ukc>
```

Note the keyword ❶ "disable" in each of the entries we turned off.

You can also search and display kernel device driver entries by memory port numbers, DRQ values, iomem, iosiz, and any other hardware characteristic.

Changing Non-Device Driver Information

In addition to all the nifty things you can do with device drivers, the config program allows you to change several of the most important kernel configuration options. These are the things that sysadmins most commonly need to change in a kernel, so the OpenBSD folks have made it as easy as possible to alter them.

Each of these kernel options has a simple numerical value. You can view the value by just entering the term in the ukc editor. For example, the number of NMBCLUSTERS that is available in the kernel is shown under the nmbclust command.

```
ukc> nmbclust
nmbclusters = 2048
ukc>
```

This kernel has 2,048 nmbclusters. To change the number allocated, just give the new value after the option name. Here, we change NMBCLUSTERS to be 4,096.

```
ukc> nmbclust 4096
nmbclusters = 4096
ukc> nmbclust
nmbclusters = 4096
ukc>
```

Without further ado, here are the kernel options that can be modified with config(8) in OpenBSD 3.3. These may be slightly different in your version of OpenBSD.

timezone

This is the time zone of the kernel, in minutes west. For example, Eastern Standard Time is five hours ahead of Greenwich Mean Time. That's 600 minutes. Mind you, there are easier ways to correct your system time than mucking about in the kernel, such as using any of the time-keeping programs.

nmbclust

nmbclust controls the number of NMBCLUSTERS in the kernel. This is the amount of memory reserved for networking operations. Increase this if you start to see errors on the console or in /var/log/messages like "mclpool limit reached."

cachepct

This adjusts the BUFCACHEPERCENT kernel option. BUFCACHEPERCENT is the percentage of physical memory dedicated to the buffer cache.

nkmempg

This controls the value of NKMEMPAGES in the kernel. NKMEMPAGES is the number of pages of memory dedicated to the kernel. If you start getting panics with an error message of "out of space in kmem_map," increase this value.

shmseg

This is equivalent to the SHMSEG kernel option. SHMSEG controls the number of segments of System V–style shared memory segments available to each process. Many programs, databases in particular, require large amounts of shared memory. If your programs start having difficulty allocating shared memory in large programs, you may need to increase this.

shmmaxpgs

This manages the SHMMAXPGS kernel option. SHMMAXPGS gives the total number of shared memory segments available on the system. If your programs complain that they cannot allocate shared memory, you may need to increase this.

Completing Config

When you've made all your changes, be certain you finish running config(8) in the correct manner. The "exit" command discards all the changes you made and leaves the editor, making it easy to start over. The "quit" command saves your changes and writes them to a kernel file. Do not confuse these commands! There's nothing quite as mortifying as finally getting everything configured exactly the way you want it and then discarding all your work by typing four wrong letters.

Installing Your Edited Kernel

Your edited kernel is just a file. If you used "config -e -f" to edit your kernel, your edited kernel has overwritten your original kernel file[1], and you don't need to do anything to install your new kernel. If you used "config -e -o," your edited kernel is a file with the name you specified. To most easily boot off of this, you want to move your original kernel /bsd to somewhere else and rename your new kernel /bsd. As always, be absolutely sure you have a known good kernel before renaming or deleting anything!

The next time you boot, your computer will use whatever kernel is in /bsd.

---

[1] You're also a braver person than I am.

Boot-Time Kernel Configuration

You may find that you don't know exactly what configuration your system should have. Suppose you have one of our famous NE2000 network cards, but you don't know the IRQ or port address. You could keep reconfiguring the kernel and rebooting, but that's a lot of work. You can configure the kernel at boot, boot to single-user mode to see to see if the card is recognized, and either reboot to try again or write your changes to your kernel. This is much faster than booting to full multi-user to check each hardware change. Sadly you cannot alter the kernel constants here, such as NMBCLUSTERS.

Interrupt the boot as described in Chapter 6 and then tell the system to boot to configure mode with the "-c" flag and to single-user mode with the "-s" flag.

```
boot> boot -cs
```

You'll get a couple lines of boot output, and then be presented with a prompt.

```
UKC>
```

This looks an awful lot like our "config -e" prompt, doesn't it? Well, it should; it's almost exactly the same. You can edit the kernel to your heart's content at this prompt and then boot off of this modified kernel. This will allow you to change IRQ or memory port addresses so you can get your computer on the network, tweak the settings on other cards, and so on. When you exit the configuration tool, the system will continue the boot into single-user mode.

This is extremely useful for testing. If you're not sure if a change will help your problem, you can edit the kernel at boot and see what effect the changes have upon your system's behavior. These changes are not permanently written to the kernel, however; the next time you reboot, they vanish.

Making Boot-Time Kernel Changes Permanent

If you tweak your kernel at boot and like the results, you probably want to make the changes permanent. You can use config(8) to write the changes you made to a kernel file, which is a lot like editing a kernel binary by adding the "-u" flag to the mix. This applies any changes you made during the boot process to the kernel file.

For example, suppose you disabled all the "ahc" devices during a boot. Perhaps you removed your last ahc SCSI card, relying instead on some other card in the system. Here, we write an updated kernel to /bsd.new by running the following. We looked at "-e" and "-o" earlier in this chapter; only the "-u" flag is new.

```
# config -e -u -o /bsd.new /bsd
OpenBSD 3.1 (GENERIC) #59: Sat Apr 13 15:28:52 MDT 2002
    deraadt@i386.openbsd.org:/usr/src/sys/arch/i386/compile/GENERIC
Processing history...
 34 ahc* disabled
189 ahc0 disabled
```

```
192 ahc* disabled
Enter 'help' for information
ukc> quit
Saving modified kernel.
#
```

Here, you see that the system remembered the changes you made. All you have to do is run the command, and the program handles the changes you requested. Config(8)'s memory isn't perfect, and it might not always remember your changes. In this case, you'd need to run a standard "config -e" and add your changes by hand.

We've now taken simple kernel changes with config and sysctl about as far as they can go. To make more complex or drastic changes, you'll need to compile a custom kernel. We'll look at that in the next chapter.

12

BUILDING CUSTOM KERNELS

Rewiring the brain?
Knowing where the parts plug in
makes it possible.

The OpenBSD team strives to produce a good-quality kernel that requires no tweaking beyond setting the occasional IRQ or memory address, or possibly adding another instance of a device driver. The provided kernel works perfectly in almost all circumstances. On extremely rare occasions, you might need to actually build a custom kernel from source. In any event, knowing how the kernel is built can improve your understanding of the system.

The Culture of Kernel Compilation

The open-source world seems to have an ingrained love of recompiling and rebuilding kernels. If you run one of the other free UNIX-like operating systems such as FreeBSD, NetBSD, or Linux, you've almost certainly recompiled kernels. Mailing lists for these operating systems are full of suggestions on rebuilding, tweaking, and modifying the kernel. Kernel reconstruction is a recommended solution to many problems. This is perfectly understandable; you have the source, so use it! In these groups, recompiling the kernel is considered a rite of passage. If you cannot build a custom kernel for one of these operating systems, other users of that OS may even look down on you or tell you it's simple and walk you through it.

If you've come from this sort of background, OpenBSD may be something of a shock. Rebuilding the kernel isn't forbidden, but it's strongly discouraged. The OpenBSD community does not consider building a kernel necessary to prove your adulthood, and rebuilding the kernel is not an appropriate solution to most problems. You will only rarely see an OpenBSD developer suggest that anyone customize the kernel to address an issue, unless there is a serious security issue in the kernel itself. Those who build custom kernels are either masters of the platform, or ignorant newbies. Many people who think they're masters of OpenBSD learn otherwise when they attempt to use a custom kernel.

You've never built a custom kernel for a commercial UNIX such as HP/UX or Solaris, have you? Those kernels are delivered ready to run; while you can tweak them, you shouldn't have to outright replace them. And you might not have even realized that Microsoft operating systems *have* a kernel, but they do, and no Windows administrator would dream of tweaking it. OpenBSD kernel design leans strongly toward the commercial OS style; the kernel shipped with the product should be good enough for production use.

Suppose you contacted Microsoft about a problem with its latest Windows server operating system and explained that you were having trouble since you recompiled the XP kernel from source, stripping out a few options you simply didn't need and adding in support for experimental features. They would ask you to hold, mute their microphone, and laugh at your request for assistance. You would quite probably be put on speakerphone, just so everyone in the support team could hear what you were saying. You would get no solution to your problem, except perhaps, "Reinstall your system using the kernel provided." On the other hand, you would become a legend; those support people would reminisce about your call for weeks, and eventually you'd wind up as a story told to new tech support people to convince them just how nutty customers really were.[1]

---

[1] They would also probably ask you where you got the necessary information and source code to rebuild the kernel, but that's a separate issue.

Similarly, the OpenBSD project members feel no particular obligation to help users with customized kernels. You're an explorer in dangerous territory and on your own. If your custom kernel crashes, most of them simply won't care. Some developers get very cranky when people demand help with their customized kernels, or when people submit a problem report and don't mention that they're running a modified kernel. Just changing one kernel option might seem trivial, but that one kernel option could represent 20,000 lines of source code that you've just trivially gutted from the kernel. You wouldn't go to your doctor and say, "I'm having trouble when I eat; do you think it's because I ripped out my spleen to run my digestion a little faster?"

The OpenBSD Project is *much* more friendly than the closed-source vendors, in that they provide the source code for the kernel and give you the tools and instructions necessary to build that kernel. The territory might be dangerous, with rattlesnakes and outlaw hideouts, but they give you a map and a flashlight. If you can carve out some new territory for yourself, good for you!

On the other hand, those same developers are *extremely* interested in problems with the kernel they ship with the system. If you can demonstrate that a problem exists in the GENERIC kernel, and you can file a complete bug report, they will be all over it. The OpenBSD team cares very deeply about their product. They don't particularly care about what happens when you take their product and rearrange it, which is what you're doing when you customize the kernel.

Why Build a Custom Kernel?

If you're a kernel developer, you might need to build a custom kernel at any time to test new features. In that case, however, you're well aware of what you're doing and thoroughly acquainted with the risks you're taking.

Some people are interested in experimental features within the OpenBSD kernel. Some of these features are available in patchsets, or in OpenBSD-current, or within the existing code as unsupported kernel options. For example the RAIDFrame software RAID feature is not in GENERIC, but is of great interest to some people. Using RAIDFrame requires running a custom kernel – that's why it's not covered in this book. If you're running experimental features, you need to know that "experimental" is a Siamese twin with "unstable."

On occasion, repairing a security flaw requires a kernel patch. These situations are fairly rare, but when they occur you need to be able to rebuild the GENERIC kernel with the patch.

Finally, you might have a machine with a very low amount of memory. Because the OpenBSD kernel (since version 3.1) takes almost 5MB of RAM, you would save memory by reducing the size of the kernel. In most cases this isn't a problem, but if you're running on an old system you might wish to build a stripped-down kernel. This doesn't mean that this usage is approved – while people will certainly understand *why* you did it, this custom kernel will get no additional support from the community.

Problems Building Custom Kernels

The interdependencies between kernel modules are quite complex and not that well documented. The developers mostly assume that you are willing to read kernel source code and quite a few man pages. It can certainly be done without reading the source code, but you need to be prepared to dig through mailing list archives and websites looking for information on errors you suffer while trying to build your own customized kernel.

OpenBSD's cross-platform design means that the kernel configuration process can be difficult. Different cards run on some busses, don't run on others, and behave oddly on still others. Including the wrong card in your configuration or telling the kernel a card is attached to the wrong bus is a great way to build a non-functional kernel. If you have trouble building a custom kernel due to these complex interdependencies, you need to understand more about how your hardware fits together.

You might have problems building your custom kernel because of a corrupt source tree. Perhaps you applied a patch incorrectly, or you scrambled a file somehow, or you edited the source code in some file. You might try to see if you can compile the GENERIC kernel; if not, you either have a bad source tree or some deeper problem with your system.

If you have trouble building a kernel, feel free to ask for help on misc@openbsd.org. State up front that you are trying to build a custom kernel and include your kernel configuration, your version of OpenBSD, the hardware platform you're building it on, and a full description of your problem. Some mailing list reader may be willing to help you out, but they certainly aren't obliged to. (You will probably also get people asking you *why* you're doing this, much as people might ask, "Why are you cleaning your ears with a power drill?")

Problems Running Custom Kernels

Custom kernels can have all sorts of problems: programs might not run as expected, the system might not boot, or it might not find all of the hardware installed. Most disturbingly, the system might crash, frequently or not, either randomly or reproducibly.

Once you build a custom kernel, the amount of support you can expect from the OpenBSD developers is minimal. The OpenBSD developers spend most of their time on the GENERIC kernel and really aren't interested in errors that happen with customized kernels. If your custom kernel does not work on your system, but the GENERIC kernel does, that means that your custom kernel is broken. Resolving the issue is your problem, not theirs.

If you discover a problem while running a custom kernel, but you can reproduce that problem when your system boots with the GENERIC kernel, the OpenBSD developers will generally be interested. They're interested in just about any way the GENERIC kernel can be tortured beyond endurance. We discuss asking for help and reporting problems in Chapter 1. Be certain to report your problem as occurring on the GENERIC kernel, and include debugging output only from running on the GENERIC kernel. Do not include any information or troubleshooting from when you're running on your custom kernel. It's not only irrelevant, but you may make people think that you're trying to sneak custom kernel debugging past them. (Believe it or not, this sort of thing happens!)

For example, one of my OpenBSD machines is a Pentium 166 with 80MB of RAM. I have a custom kernel in this machine, which enables me to save a couple of megabytes of memory. It hasn't crashed yet, but it could. One day, I might figure out a way to panic the kernel. If I can reproduce this crash on the GENERIC kernel, the OpenBSD team will happily accept a bug report. If I can't reproduce the problem on their kernel, I'm not going to report it. If I debug the problem in depth, and create a patch that fixes the issue, then and only then will I report the problem — and the solution.

Preparations

Before you even contemplate customizing the kernel, make a backup of the generic kernel your system shipped with! Much like preparing to edit the existing binary with config(8), simply copying /bsd to /bsd.GENERIC will suffice. If you render your system unbootable with a bad custom kernel and don't have a good kernel to work with, you can look forward to repairing your system. This can be quite a pain, depending on the availability of the installation media.

Before you can build a custom kernel, you need the kernel source code. You can grab the source code from the root directory of an OpenBSD CD-ROM. It can also be found on any FTP mirror, in the directory for the release you're using. The tarred, compressed source code is in the file srcsys.tar.gz. Expand this file in the /usr/src directory.

```
# cd /usr/src
# tar -xzvpf srcsys.tar.gz
...
```

Depending on your disk speed, this may take quite some time.

Now that you have the source code, let's look at the kernel configuration.

Configuration File Format

Kernel configuration is done via text files. There is no fancy graphical utility to configure the kernel, no menu-driven system; it's still much the same as found in 4.4BSD. (If you're not comfortable with text configuration files, you have absolutely no business building your own kernel.)

Each kernel configuration entry is on a single line. There is a label to indicate what sort of entry this is and then a description of the entry. Many entries also have comments, set off with a pound sign, much like this:

```
option          FFS            # UFS
```

The various configuration choices available for OpenBSD 3.3 are discussed in some detail in Appendix A. Later and earlier releases are slightly different, as the kernel evolves between releases. There are four different types of labels for kernel configuration entries: options, device drivers, pseudo-devices, and miscellaneous instructions.

Options are kernel functions that are not tied to or dependent on particular hardware. Options handle things like file systems, networking protocols, and compatibility layers. The boot-time kernel configuration tool is a kernel option. All options are labeled with "option."

Device drivers give the kernel the necessary information to support particular pieces of hardware. If you want OpenBSD to support a particular piece of hardware, the kernel must include the appropriate device driver. Device drivers kernel configuration entries are frequently quite long and include flags and settings that tell the kernel where to find the device and how it should be handled. Device drivers have no common label, but their entry starts with the name of the device.

```
ec0    at isa? port 0x250 iomem 0xd8000 irq 9  # 3C503 ethernet
```

Pseudo-devices are kernel entries that behave much like devices, but they have no real hardware attached to them. Pseudo-devices are frequently abstractions that sit on top of other hardware. They can be open, read to, written to, and closed, just like real hardware. For example, the packet filter sits on top of the network stack and captures network traffic. The loopback device is used for network connections to the local machine and has no actual hardware associated to it. The kernel will attach this pseudo-device to whatever appropriate hardware it finds. Pseudo-devices are labeled with "pseudo-device," much like this.

```
pseudo-device   loop    2       # network loopback
```

Finally, you have instructions directly to the kernel configuration process. You can have instructions to make(1), marked by the "makeoptions" label, or instructions to the config program itself. Here's an example of an instruction to config(8).

```
config          bsd     swap generic
```

With that information, you're ready to look at an actual kernel configuration.

Configuration Files

OpenBSD divides the configuration process into machine-dependent and machine-independent sections.

Machine-Independent Configuration

The machine-independent configuration files can be found in the directory /usr/src/sys/conf. If you are interested in reading kernel source code, this is a decent place to start. If all you want to do is build a kernel, you're mostly interested in the GENERIC file. This file contains the kernel configuration information that is identical on each of the hardware platforms OpenBSD runs on. Every kernel built on OpenBSD, by default, contains this file. Any change made to the machine-independent section of the system occurs in every OpenBSD kernel.

The machine-independent configuration file won't contain device drivers; devices are tied to particular hardware. It also won't contain any special building instructions, because they vary from hardware to hardware. It won't contain hard-coded system limits, data structure sizes, and so on; those vary from hardware to hardware. As you can imagine, an OpenBSD system running on a 15-year-old VAX has considerably fewer system resources than a modern Pentium IV–based i386 system! So, what's left? Options and pseudo-devices. For example, every OpenBSD kernel must support a file system or it won't be able to write anything to disk.

```
option          FFS             # UFS
```

The kernel doesn't know, yet, what sort of hardware this file system will be on, but it knows how to make a file system. Similarly, every OpenBSD system supports the integrated packet filter (see Chapter 15), networking (Chapter 9), and so on.

Machine-Dependent Configuration

Machine-dependent kernel source lies somewhere under the directory /usr/src/sys/arch. This directory contains a directory for each hardware platform OpenBSD supports. It also contains some "work in progress" architectures, which are not yet fully supported. While this book focuses on the i386 platform, or the "standard PC," the process of kernel building is the same across all hardware platforms. The kernel configuration directory is in the conf subdirectory of the platform directory; in our case, we want to look at /usr/src/sys/arch/i386/conf.

Traditionally, a kernel configuration file is in all capital letters. Here you'll see the GENERIC kernel, as well as a few special-purpose configuration files. The RAMDISK, RAMDISKB, and RAMDISKC files are the kernel configurations for the installation floppy disk images A, B, and C, respectively. The DISKLESS file is a sample configuration for diskless OpenBSD workstations. For the moment, let's look at the GENERIC kernel config file.

The very first entry in this file identifies the type of hardware you're using.

```
machine         i386
```

The configuration program uses this check your configuration, so it can notify you of any mistakes. It won't allow you to include Sun-specific hardware on an i386, for example. Different hardware also has a variety of different low-level characteristics, such as the number of bits in different types of C data structures, and the kernel needs to know about them.

Another early entry in this file is a special configuration instruction.

```
include "../../../conf/GENERIC"
```

When you configure the kernel, the configuration tool will automatically grab the machine-independent configuration. This means that you don't have to worry about all of the very basic stuff, such as file systems and network stacks; the building process will automatically include them.

These configuration files contain the information specific to the hardware, such as device drivers and hardware-dependent options.

Take a moment and skim the hardware-dependent configuration file. There are a few hundred lines here! How can you possibly wade through all of this? Like so many other things in UNIX, it's not hard once you know what you're doing.

Your Kernel Configuration File

To build your own kernel, you need a configuration file. Do not just edit the GENERIC kernel file; that's a system file, and it will be overwritten when you upgrade or reinstall. Once you've spent some time tweaking your kernel, the last thing you want to do is destroy the record of how you assembled it! Traditionally, custom kernels are named after the machine they're built for, and the filenames are all in capital letters. For example, my computer named "openbsdtest" has a kernel configuration of OPENBSDTEST.

You also need to decide whether you want to have a single configuration file or maintain the split between machine-dependent and machine-independent files. When you build your first kernel, I recommend keeping the split. You will have enough trouble trying to build a usable kernel without messing with the required items in the machine-independent section. Most of what is in the machine-independent configuration is absolutely required to build a normally working OpenBSD system. In either case, it's simplest to start with the GENERIC configuration.

If you want to keep the split, just copy the machine-dependent GENERIC configuration to a file of the name you want in the same directory.

```
# cp GENERIC OPENBSDTEST
```

If you want to have one configuration file containing both machine-independent and machine-dependent information, just combine the files in the machine-dependent configuration directory. (This file will be machine-dependent, after all!) Then edit this file to remove the line that includes the machine-independent configuration file.

You might be tempted to use the material in Appendix A to create your own kernel configuration. You're certainly free to do that, if you are either a Kernel Lord or an irremediable "doofus." Anyone who has been there before would highly recommend you start with the GENERIC configuration and edit that. The interdependencies are complicated enough that building a configuration from scratch is almost certainly doomed to fail.

Now that you have a kernel configuration of your own, let's see what we can do with it.

Busses and Attachments

Every device in the system is attached to some other device. We saw an example of this in Chapter 11, with the dmassage program that generated a simple drawing of what hardware was attached to which bus. Not all systems have all busses; while OpenBSD supports PCI devices, for example, it runs just fine on ISA-only systems.

mainbus0

On i386 hardware everything sits on top of the main bus, called "mainbus0." This is the foundation of your kernel. Your SCSI hard disk might be on top of the SCSI bus, which sits on top of a SCSI card, which is plugged into the PCI bus, but that PCI bus will be attached to the main bus.

Connection Configuration

The kernel must know how these busses and cards hook together. You'll see quite a few entries in your copied kernel configuration that look like this.

```
isa0      ❶at mainbus0
isa0      ❷at pcib?
```

Older computers just have an ISA bus that is ❶directly attached to the main system bus, and we must tell the kernel how to recognize that configuration. On PCI-based computers, the ISA bus is frequently ❷plugged into the PCI-ISA bridge instead of directly to the main bus. (This is a matter of hardware design, not kernel design.) With the above configuration, if the ISA bus is in either of these locations the kernel will find it. If you have some special hardware with the ISA bus attached elsewhere, this kernel will *not* find it.

Also, note the device numbers. This configuration is for ISA bus number zero. As systems only have one ISA bus, this is perfectly acceptable. A system can have multiple PCI buses, however. That's why the second configuration line has a question mark by the device number for the PCI bus; this entry will match any PCI bus. Some device drivers must have a hard-coded number, while others will accept a question mark instead. Generally, non–Plug-and-Play ISA cards must have a hard-coded device number.

You can follow the hardware connections through the kernel configuration. We previously mentioned how a simple SCSI disk can live at the end of a long chain of hardware. Let's see how. A SCSI disk uses the "sd" driver.

```
sd*❶      at ❷scsibus? target ? lun ?      # SCSI disk drives
```

Here, we have ❶any number of SCSI disks. They can be attached to ❷any SCSI bus.

If you have an AdvanSys 1200B UltraSCSI controller, it'll use the adv driver. If you search your kernel configuration for this driver, you'll find it easily.

```
❶adv*     at pci?❸ dev ? function ?    # AdvanSys 1200A/B and ULTRA SCSI
❷scsibus* at adv?
```

The ❶first entry tells the kernel to recognize AdvanSys card. The kernel will also attach a ❷SCSI bus to this card, when found. A check of the GENERIC kernel configuration shows that the kernel is configured to attach a SCSI bus to any SCSI card. The adv card expects to be plugged into a ❸PCI bus. Where does our PCI bus come from? Well, GENERIC has the following entries for the PCI bus.

```
pci*     at mainbus0 bus ?
pci*     at ppb? bus ?
pci*     at pchb? bus ?
```

Depending on which sort of PCI bus you have and how it is attached to the system, you might be done. You could continue tracking these devices back, and see how everything hooks together, but you should have the idea by now.

For our SCSI disk to work, every step of the attachment chain must be in the kernel configuration. You can have the drivers for the SCSI disk and SCSI card in your kernel, but if you don't have the entry for the SCSI bus to connect the two, the disk won't work. Every device must be able to find the devices beneath it. After all, if your kernel can't find the PCI bus, it won't find the devices attached to it!

Stripping Down the Kernel

Every device driver and option in the kernel uses memory. One reason for rebuilding a kernel is to reduce its memory footprint, leaving more memory for other applications. In most cases, purchasing more memory is a better move than recompiling the kernel, but this may not be an option. This will have the added side effect of decreasing the amount of time your system takes to boot by a few seconds. To do this, simply find every line in the kernel configuration that doesn't have matching hardware in your system and comment it out with a pound sign (#).

For example, we saw in "Connection Configuration" that the kernel can recognize two sorts of ISA bus connections: one to the main bus and one to the PCI-ISA bridge.

```
isa0     at mainbus0
isa0     at pcib?
```

Your computer will only have one ISA bus in it, however! One of these configuration entries is useless. You can find out which is correct by looking at your computer's boot-time messages, in /var/run/dmesg.boot. My test system has the following entry for its ISA bus.

```
isa0 at pcib0
```

The ISA bus in this system is attached to the PCI-ISA bridge. I could remove the entry for the ISA bus attached to the main bus.

Each line in /var/run/dmesg.boot matches a line in the kernel configuration. The simplest way to trim out unnecessary device drivers is to remove device driver entries that don't match anything in your system. For example, I see 37 SCSI card drivers in the 3.1 GENERIC kernel. Even if I have a SCSI card, chances are that 36 of those drivers are completely useless. I can comment them out, along with the SCSI bus drivers that depend upon them.

Dmassage and Kernel Configuration

Matching lines in /var/run/dmesg.boot to kernel configuration statements is a very tedious task and a perfect candidate for automation. The dmassage program we looked at in Chapter 11 can do this for us. Dmassage's "-s" flag will compare an existing kernel configuration and /var/run/dmesg.boot and comment out any entries in the kernel configuration that do not appear in the dmesg.boot. Dmassage will dump the output to standard out, so be sure to redirect to a file. Here we'll use dmassage to strip down a GENERIC kernel and create a new minimalist version of the kernel configuration.

```
# dmassage -s GENERIC > OPENBSDTEST
```

One problem with using dmassage in this manner is that dmassage doesn't consider removable devices. If you are using USB hardware, for example, you'll want to go through your stripped kernel configuration and put the appropriate device drivers back in. Laptop PCMCIA cards have similar problems. To add these devices back to your kernel configuration, just remove the leading pound signs.

Alternately, you could boot with every device you own plugged in. This would make them show up in /var/run/dmesg.boot, and hence dmassage would keep them in the kernel configuration.

Enhancing the Kernel

So, you know how to remove options from the kernel. But how do you add them? And, more importantly, how do you know what to add? You have two major sources of information on what to add: options(4) and the GENERIC kernel configuration itself.

The options(4) man page lists every kernel option available for general use. Many of these options are already included in the GENERIC kernel, but some are not. You might want to add some of them, depending on your needs. In most cases, though, additional options aren't necessary.

The GENERIC kernel configuration includes quite a few commented-out device drivers. Some of these are commented out because they conflict with other device drivers, and some of these conflicts are quite annoying to work around otherwise. For example, the Mitsumi CD-ROM drive (quite famously) conflicts with other hardware and consequently prevents a successful installation. The driver for non–Plug-and-Play joysticks can cause problems during the boottime hardware probe. Most of this hardware is not only rare, but also obscure. It's commented out in GENERIC because supporting it by default causes more trouble than it's worth. You might want to uncomment one of these, if you have the appropriate hardware to use them. Just remove the comment, and it's ready to go.

Changing the Kernel

You might find that you need to change the options on a device driver, much as you can do with config(8) (see Chapter 11). Device drivers that have IRQs, port addresses, and driver flags hard-coded all have that specified in the kernel's device entry. To change any of these settings, simply edit the configuration file. For example, the default configuration for our ISA NE2000 card looks like this:

```
ne0     at isa? port 0x240 irq 9                # NE[12]000 ethernet
```

The IRQ and memory port number are specified right on the line. Change them to any sensible values to accommodate your hardware. Changing hardware information isn't enough reason in and of itself to recompile your kernel, but if you're recompiling anyway you might as well correct them.

config(8)

Now that you have a configuration file, you can prepare to actually compile your kernel. You use config(8) for this. The config program will read your configuration file and prepare a kernel compilation area that contains all the necessary source code and other information to build your custom kernel. The syntax is extremely simple: Just enter "config" and the name of your kernel configuration file. For example, to config the OPENBSDTEST kernel file, just type this.

```
# config OPENBSDTEST
Don't forget to run "make depend"
#
```

If you see this, everything went correctly.

At times, config(8) will give you additional instructions. In particular, it may tell you that you must run make clean before trying to compile the kernel. Obey config(8); it doesn't issue those messages just to amuse itself![2]

---

[2] It waits until you reboot on the new kernel to be amused.

Config Errors

If, on the other hand, you made a mistake, you'll see something like this.

```
# config OPENBSDTEST
OPENBSDTEST:491: syntax error
*** Stop.
#
```

The number is the line number where the error lies. I see this most often when I don't have a carriage return at the end of the last line of my configuration. The simplest way to avoid this problem is to put a single blank line at the end of the configuration file. If you have an error on some other line, then you've made a different error.

One common problem is misspelling the name of an option or device driver.

```
# config OPENBSDTEST
OPENBSDTEST:148: susbeep0: unknown device `susbeep'
*** Stop.
#
```

In this case, you not only get the line number but the name of the unknown device or option. There is no "susbeep" device, but there certainly is a "sysbeep" device. Oops.

You might neglect to include some vital part of the system in your configuration. For example, if you have devices attached to a certain bus, but that bus is not in your kernel configuration, config(8) will complain. Loudly.

```
# config OPENBSDTEST
OPENBSDTEST:41: bios0 at mainbus0 is orphaned
 (no mainbus0 declared)
OPENBSDTEST:48: pci* at mainbus0 is orphaned
 (no mainbus0 declared)
*** Stop.
#
```

Here, the key to solving the problem is very straightforward: Read the error message. Most often, config will tell you outright when you have neglected to include something that another device depends on. In this example, I overenthusiastically commented out the mainbus declaration. Every device that claims to be plugged into the main bus is "orphaned," or unattached to anything.

The internal error checking performed by config(8) does not guarantee that your kernel will work as expected, or even compile. The only errors it catches are ones where the configuration is either internally inconsistent or just flat-out invalid. The first real test comes when you try to actually build your configured kernel.

Building a Kernel

If config(8) runs successfully, it will build a compilation directory including a Makefile and a whole slew of header files. The traditional place for this compile directory is under the appropriate platform directory, /usr/src/sys/arch/i386 in our case. There you'll find a directory named "compile." This directory contains a subdirectory for each kernel configuration that you have run config(8) on, each named after the kernel config file. For example, the OPENBSDTEST kernel configuration is in /usr/src/sys/arch/i386/compile/OPENBSDTEST.

If config(8) gave you any special instructions, obey them first. Then issue the following commands to build your kernel:

```
# make depend❶
# make❷
#
```

Each of these will take quite some time, and generate quite a lot of output. The ❶make depend command builds dependencies between the various objects that comprise the kernel. The ❷make command actually builds the binary that will become your kernel.

Build Errors

If your kernel fails to build, don't immediately despair. Chances are, you have a perfectly explicable error. First, read the message that the compile gives. Almost all the time, the error message you get explains what you need to do to get a successful kernel compile. Generally you need to change your kernel configuration in some way, because of an error that config(8) could not catch. Only rarely is the actual OpenBSD kernel code "uncompilable."

If you still cannot build the kernel, follow the support process discussed in Chapter 1. Remember, kernel compilation is not a standard practice in OpenBSD, and the support you will get is pretty minimal unless your error is obvious to someone else.

Installing Your Kernel

Once compiled, your custom kernel can be found as a file called "bsd" in the compile directory. Confirm that you have your current, well-running kernel backed up, and copy this file to /bsd. That's it! The next time you reboot, you will be running on your new kernel.

Some people do not like to copy their custom kernel to /bsd until they are absolutely certain that the kernel will boot. You can copy this custom kernel to any file in the root partition and use the alternate kernel booting process to boot your custom kernel. You can assume that your new kernel will work and install it immediately, but be prepared to fall back to a good kernel, or you can assume your new kernel will fail and test it before installing it. Because the kernel install process is so simple, once you've mastered booting alternate kernels (see Chapter 6) you really don't have much to worry about.

Identifying Your Booted Kernel

If you have been running on a custom kernel for some time, you might even forget what configuration you're actually running on. The uname(1) command will tell you the name of the kernel configuration file used to build the kernel you booted on. (This is not necessarily /bsd; remember, you can boot an alternate kernel, as discussed in Chapter 6.) While uname(1) has many flags, the "-v" flag will give you the name of your kernel configuration and the number of times you have compiled that particular kernel.

```
# uname -v
OPENBSDTEST#0
#
```

Congratulations! You're running on your new kernel. At this point, you should have your base system functioning as desired. Let's see how to actually make it useful.

13

ADD-ON SOFTWARE

Software repair steps:
retry, reboot, reinstall?
No need for that here!

Most people don't use an operating system —
they use software, which needs an underlying
operating system. No matter how robust
OpenBSD is, it's completely useless if applications
can't run on it. OpenBSD supports a wide range of
software and has several tools to make software
management quick and effective. One difference that is
surprising between OpenBSD and other operating
systems is how much software is *not* included in the
system, but is instead available for adding on if necessary.

Many commercial operating systems include hundreds or thousands of small programs: from games, desktop toys, and fancy-looking clocks to disk scrubbers and Web browsers. Most users never touch most of the programs on their system, but they're there taking up disk space and possibly memory just the same. This makes it easy for the user, so long as everything works properly. Each program lugs along its own infrastructure, however, and this can cause problems. There's a reason that Windows became famous for "DLL Hell."

OpenBSD includes almost nothing. You get exactly what you need to provide the infrastructure for software and nothing more. While a traditional UNIX system includes compilers, games, and manual pages, you don't even have to install those when you install OpenBSD! Even if you install the full OpenBSD software, it will include far less than a Windows, Macintosh, or commercial Linux operating install. That's because almost everything is considered an add-on package. OpenBSD makes it very easy to install additional software through the ports and packages system.

The advantage to this sparseness is that you know exactly what is on your system. This makes debugging problems simpler and helps to ensure that some shared library or other chunk of code that you've never heard of won't break your programs. The downside is that you may need to do a bit of thinking to decide exactly what you do need, and you'll have to install those programs. OpenBSD makes installing software as easy as possible.

Making Software

Building software is complicated because source code must be treated in a very specific manner to create a usable binary program — let alone an optimized one. Programmers have developed tools for building software, specifically to hide this complexity. The main software-building tool is called make(1). Make looks in the current directory for a file called Makefile, which contains instructions for the computer to follow. Makefiles can be long and complicated creatures, and you don't really have to know their internals, so we're not going to dissect one here.

Each Makefile includes various targets, or types of instructions, to carry out. For example, "make install" tells make(1) to check the Makefile for a process called "install." If make(1) finds such a procedure, it will execute it. Each target contains one basic step in building, installing, or configuring a piece of software. Make(1) can also perform a huge variety of functions, some of which far outstrip the original intentions of its creators. But it seems that's the fate of all good UNIX programs.

Source Code

Source code is the human-readable instructions for the actual machine code that makes up a program. You might have already been exposed to source code in some form. If you've never seen source code before, take a look at the various files under /usr/src. Here's a snippet of source code from an indispensable OpenBSD program, fortune(6):

```
if (All_forts && offensive != NULL) {
  path = offensive;
  if (was_malloc)
    free(path);
  offensive = NULL;
  was_malloc = TRUE;
  DPRINTF(1, (stderr, "\ttrying \"%s\"\n", path));
  file = off_name(file);
  goto over;
}
```

Once you have the source code for a program, installing it is pretty straight-forward. You build (or *compile*) the program on the operating system and architecture you want it to run on. (If you're extremely skilled, you can *cross-compile* a program on a different architecture, or even a different operating system. Of course, if you're that skilled, you've probably skipped this section of this book. In any event, the OpenBSD team discourages cross-compiling in the strongest possible terms.) If the program was written for an operating system and architecture that is sufficiently similar to where you're building it, it should work. Once you've built the software successfully on your platform, you can copy the resulting program (or *binary*) to other identical platforms, and it should run.

Some programs are written well enough that they can be compiled on many different platforms. A few programs specifically include support for widely divergent platforms; for example, the Apache Web server can be compiled and installed on both UNIX-like and properly configured Windows systems just by typing "make install." This is quite uncommon, however, and represents a truly heroic effort by the software developers.

If your software is not written so it can compile on your operating system and architecture, your compilation will spew all sorts of horrible errors and fail. In some cases, your compilation will give you all sorts of warnings and seem to complete, but the resulting binary will not function properly or at all.

Crossing Platforms

When you have the source code to a program, a sufficiently skilled sysadmin or programmer can learn why a program won't build or run on a particular system. In many cases, the problem is very simple and can be fixed with minimal effort. This is one reason why access to source code is important.

In the days when every UNIX administrator was a programmer, this debugging absorbed a major portion of the administrator's time. Every UNIX was slightly different, so all systems administrators had to understand the platform a program had been written for, and its differences from their platform, before they could hope to get a chunk of code to run. The duplication of effort was truly obscene.

Slowly, tools such as autoconf and configure were created to help address these cross-platform issues. Still, not every program used these tools, and the tools themselves created their own problems. Systems administrators still had to be able to edit source code and Makefiles just to have a chance of making programs run.

The Ports and Packages System

The OpenBSD ports and packages system is a software-building system designed to simplify the configuration and installation of software. Originally developed by the FreeBSD Project, ports were quickly picked up on and expanded upon by the OpenBSD team.

Ports are instructions for compiling software on that particular version of OpenBSD, and packages are simply precompiled ports. Packages install more quickly, and can save a lot of time when installing software that doesn't need customization. Ports install more slowly, but can be easily customized or optimized for your environment.

The basic idea behind the ports and packages system is very simple: If software must be modified to run on OpenBSD, then the modifications should be automated. Because you're automating the installation process, you should record what files the software installs so you can most easily uninstall it. And because you have a software-building process that creates the exact same result every time, and you've recorded everything that the program-building process creates, you can use these as instructions to install your compiled program on any other OpenBSD system.

The whole system, including the build process, the package-building process, and the install/uninstall process, is called the *ports collection*, the *ports tree*, or even just *ports*.

The Ports Tree

A *port* is a set of instructions on how to apply fixes to, or patch, a set of source code files. By combining patches with installation instructions, OpenBSD can maintain a complete record of everything the software-install process has done. This frees you from struggling to install a program and allows you to concentrate instead on making the program work properly.

If you followed the post-installation hints in Chapter 5, you installed the ports tree, and should have something like the following under /usr/ports.

```
# ls /usr/ports
❶CVS          chinese       games          mbone    russian
❷INDEX        comms         graphics       misc     security
❸Makefile     converters    ❹infrastructure net      shells
❺README       databases     japanese       news     sysutils
archivers     devel         java           packages textproc
astro         ❻distfiles     korean         palm     www
audio         editors       lang           plan9    x11
benchmarks    education     mail           print
```

```
cad           emulators   math       productivity
#
```

NOTE *If you don't see something like this in /usr/ports, you need to install the ports tree to continue. See "Installing the Ports Collection" in Chapter 5.*

The directory ❶CVS contains information for the revision control system used by OpenBSD, Concurrent Versions System. (See Chapter 16.) This has no impact on the day-to-day operations of your ports tree.

The ❷INDEX file contains a list of all the ports. See "Finding Software" for instructions on how to use this effectively.

The ❸Makefile contains instructions for building or managing the entire ports collection. This is mostly useful when building packages for an OpenBSD release, but we'll discuss occasional bits of functionality useful to sysadmins.

The ❹infrastructure directory contains related tools for building the ports tree. Global ports settings appear here, as well as machine instructions for everything else we'll look at.

The file ❺README contains a brief introduction to the ports collection and pointers to various man pages that describe its functionality.

Finally, the ❻distfiles directory contains source code for the various ports. It starts off empty; when you install a port, OpenBSD will populate this directory.

The remainders of these directories are software categories. Each category contains a further layer of directories, and each directory under a category is a port of a piece of software. OpenBSD has over 2,000 ports, so this directory tree is vital to keeping them in any sort of manageable order!

The following directory listing shows the contents of the "benchmarks" folder, where benchmarking software that is known to run on OpenBSD is kept. This is one of the smaller categories; some categories, such as "x11," have hundreds of entries!

```
# ls /usr/ports/benchmarks/

CVS       bonnie     iozone    netperf   tcpblast
Makefile  bytebench  lmbench   netpipe   xengine
#
```

Just like the CVS directory in the main ports tree, the category's CVS directory contains CVS information that doesn't matter in day-to-day operations.

The Makefile contains a list of valid ports within the category. You could build all of the ports in this category at once using this Makefile. This function is mostly only useful when building packages for redistribution, as the OpenBSD project does during a release.

Ports Subcategories

Some ports have subcategories, where many different but related pieces of software are included in one port directory. For example, here are the contents of the directory for /usr/ports/www/netscape, the port for the Netscape Web browser.

```
# ls /usr/ports/www/netscape
CVS              ❶communicator        ❷navigator
Makefile         ❸communicator-linux  ❹navigator-linux
Makefile.inc     ❺communicator-old    ❻navigator-old
#
```

This contains six subcategories. They contain the latest ❶Netscape Communicator and ❷Netscape Navigator releases for BSD/OS, the latest ❸Netscape Communicator and ❹Netscape Navigator for Linux releases, and older ❺Netscape Communicator and ❻Netscape Navigator releases. These packages are closely related, and there's no point in cluttering the already-busy /usr/ports/www directory with six almost-identical pieces of software.[1]

You'll find similar subcategories for some of the popular window manager suites, such as KDE and Gnome.

Finding Software

With over 2,000 ports, how could you possibly find anything? The file /usr/ports/INDEX contains a complete list of all ports in the tree, in alphabetical order. Each port is described on a single line, with pipe-delimited fields (|), much like this:

```
fastjar-0.93|archivers/fastjar||Sun JDK's jar command written entirely in C|
archivers/fastjar/pkg/DESCR|Dan Harnett<danh@openbsd.org>|archivers||:devel/gmake||
any|y|y|y|y
```

While this is a convenience format for system tools to access, it's not particularly friendly for human beings. The INDEX file is convenient to find out if a particular piece of software has been ported to OpenBSD, but that's about it. OpenBSD provides a variety of tools to more easily access this information.

If you're interested in an easier-to-read index of all the available packages, you can get a nicely formatted INDEX file by running "make print-index" in /usr/ports. Here's a snippet of the make print-index output for the same port.

```
# cd /usr/ports
# make print-index
...
❶Port:    fastjar-0.93
❷Path:    archivers/fastjar
❸Info:    Sun JDK's jar command written entirely in C
❹Maint:   Dan Harnett <danh@openbsd.org>
❺Index:   archivers
❻L-deps:
❼B-deps:  :devel/gmake
❽R-deps:
```

[1] If you're paying attention, you might wonder why OpenBSD includes Linux and BSD/OS software. OpenBSD can run software from these operating systems with a minimum of work. See "Running Foreign Software" later in this chapter.

The ❶port line gives the official name of the port and the version number of the ported software. The ❷path gives the category and directory where the port can be found. For example, this piece of software can be found in /usr/ports/archivers/fastjar. The ❸info line gives a one-line description of the software. A ❹maintainer is the person responsible for porting this software to OpenBSD and for maintaining the software's entry in the ports collection. The ❺index line contains a list of all the categories that this software is assigned to. Some pieces of software could be considered part of multiple categories, and they are listed here.

The final three entries describe other software that this software depends upon. The ❻L-deps line lists ports that contain libraries that this software uses. This particular software cannot be used if these libraries are not present. The ❼B-deps line lists software that is required to build this port. In this example, the port is built with the "gmake" program available in /usr/ports/devel/gmake. Gmake does not need to be present to run the software, merely to build it. Finally, the ❽R-deps entry lists other non-library software that must be present to actually run this port.

Finding Software by Name

While the index can be helpful, how can you find a piece of software if you know its name?

If you know the exact name of the software package, you can use a simple grep command to pick it out. This is quick and easy, if you know the exact name of the software. For example, to find the "lsof" system-monitoring tool you might enter this command:

```
# grep -i ^lsof INDEX
lsof-4.63|❶sysutils/lsof||list information about open files|sysutils/lsof/pkg/
DESCR|Peter Valchev <pvalchev@openbsd.org>|sysutils||||any|y|y|y|y
#
```

OpenBSD has a port for lsof, and you can find it in the ❶sysutils/lsof directory.

Finding by Keyword

If you don't know the software's exact name, try the ports collection's search feature. The "make search" command scans the ports index, searching either for the name of a port or a port where the word appears. For example, if you're interested in software to support Java Servlet Pages, you might try to search on the keyword "jserv."

```
# make search key=jserv
Port:    jserv-3.2.4
Path:    www/jserv
Info:    Tomcat (Servlet/JSP) - Apache Connector
```

```
Maint:  Reinhard J. Sammer <reinhard@openbsd.org>
Index:  www
L-deps:
B-deps: unzip-*:archivers/unzip
R-deps: jakarta-tomcat-3.*:www/jakarta-tomcat/v3
❶Archs:  i386
#
```

This looks exactly like an index display, with the addition of an ❶architecture category. This particular program only runs on the i386 architecture.

You may have to try several possible keywords for a particular package, as some keywords may have no hits and others may generate too many. For a good example of too many hits, try "make search key=java".

Browsing the Ports Tree

If you prefer to just poke through the ports collection and see what's available, you can build an HTML index and package description tree. Just go to /usr/ports and type "make readmes" to generate an HTML file for every port in the tree. This isn't quick, but you only have to generate the HTML files once to browse them forevermore. (If you upgrade your ports tree, however, you'll need to regenerate these HTML files.)

When you're finished, point your browser at /usr/ports/README.html, which contains links and a description for every category. Each category has its own HTML index, with a brief description of each port in the category, which in turn links to a more detailed description of the port. With nothing but a web browser, you can spend hours clicking through the ports to find both the software you need for your job and software you can waste your time with.[2]

Now that you know how to find software, let's look at actually installing some.

Using Packages

Packages are precompiled software for a particular version and architecture of OpenBSD. We're going to discuss using packages first, as they're generally easier and faster to use than ports. Once you have a grip on packages, we'll proceed to ports. Many of the tools that can be used for packages also work on ports.

Almost every OpenBSD port is available as a package. Some pieces of software cannot be redistributed without various restrictions, so they are only available as ports. Packages are available on the OpenBSD CD-ROM set and via FTP.

Package Files

Each package is available as a single file named after the port it is found in, a version number, and a ".tgz" extension. For example, the windowmaker-0.80.1.tgz port is from the port named "windowmaker," version 0.80.1. A quick search of /usr/ports/INDEX will show that this is a package prepared from the port /usr/ports/x11/windowmaker.

---

[2] If you want to keep your spare time, avoid /usr/ports/games/falconseye and /usr/ports/games/freeciv at all costs!

To install a standalone package, all you need is the package file. You can get the package file from a CD-ROM, from an FTP site, or from anyone who makes it available over the Internet. (The last creates definite trust issues, however!) If your package depends on other packages, you'll need to install those required packages as well. If your packages are all available at the same location, the package installation process will handle these dependencies automatically.

Installing Packages

Once you have your package file, use pkg_add(1) to extract the software and add it to your system. For example, one of the first pieces of software I install on any computer I manage is the emacs text-processing package.

```
# pkg_add emacs-21.2.tgz
#
```

Package installations usually run silently, although you'll occasionally see messages from the package offering advice or instructions. Pay attention to these messages, and take whatever action they recommend.

If your package has library or program dependencies, it will automatically try to install those as well. It will refuse to install incomplete software. While emacs is a standalone program (arguably because it has all possible lesser programs integrated with it), other packages are not quite so simple. For example, the WindowMaker window manager requires several other programs to run correctly. If you download the WindowMaker package on its own and try to install it without the correct versions of the required packages, the install will fail.

```
# pkg_add windowmaker-0.80.1.tgz
pkg_add(windowmaker-0.80.1): add of dependency `libiconv-1.8' failed!
pkg_add(windowmaker-0.80.1): add of dependency `libiconv-1.8' failed!
pkg_add(windowmaker-0.80.1): add of dependency `libiconv-1.8' failed!
pkg_add(windowmaker-0.80.1): add of dependency `libiconv-1.8' failed!
pkg_add(windowmaker-0.80.1): add of dependency `gettext-0.10.40' failed!
pkg_add(windowmaker-0.80.1): add of dependency `gettext-0.10.40' failed!
pkg_add(windowmaker-0.80.1): add of dependency `libiconv-1.8' failed!
#
```

If I downloaded and tried to install libiconv-1.8 and gettext-0.10.40, I would have come across a variety of other programs that libiconv and gettext need. I didn't download these packages along with WindowMaker, and I don't have them already installed. pkg_add(1) will automatically install dependencies for packages, if it can find them. The simplest thing to do is install the packages from the CD-ROM or configure pkg_add(1) to use a FTP server. Let's look at both.

Installing from CD-ROM

If you have an OpenBSD CD-ROM set, you already have a fairly extensive set of packages. To use them, just mount the CD-ROM and read the package file. Read Chapter 15 for full details on mounting and unmounting removable media; if you're reading the chapters in order, just nod and smile for those bits.

```
# mount /dev/cd0c /mnt
#
```

Your CD-ROM is now available under /mnt. Under the release directory, you should find a directory called "packages," with a subdirectory for each architecture on the CD-ROM. This directory contains a selection of precompiled packages for that release. For example, on the 3.2 CD-ROM /mnt/3.2/packages/i386 contains 182 packages.

Installing WindowMaker from package on CD-ROM is quite simple, as packages for all of the required applications are present.

```
# cd /mnt/3.2/packages/i386
# pkg_add windowmaker-0.80.1.tgz
#
```

That's it! WindowMaker and its dependencies are now installed and ready to configure and use.

Installing from FTP

OpenBSD has thousands of packages for each of its architectures, which would fill up many CD-ROM sets. The OpenBSD disks only contain the most popular packages. If you want to install a package that is less popular, you will need to grab it from an FTP site.

Your first step is to find an OpenBSD FTP server with the packages you want for the release and architecture you're running. The server you installed from is probably your best choice, unless you've found a faster mirror since you installed. Much like the CD-ROM, the "packages" directory is under the "release" directory, and each architecture has a subdirectory.

You could choose to download a package and all its dependencies, but it can be quite a bit of work figuring out which packages a piece of software depends on, and which packages those packages depend on, and so on. It's much better to simply give pkg_add the full location to the package, and let it figure out all of the dependencies for you.

Take note of the full URL to the package directory for your architecture. For example, if you're installing the windowmaker-0.80.1.tgz package from ftp5.usa.OpenBSD.org, the full URL path to the package directory is ftp://ftp5.usa.openbsd.org/pub/OpenBSD/3.2/packages/i386/. You can use this on the command line as part of the package filename, and pkg_add will automatically grab the required packages from the same location.

```
# pkg_add ftp://ftp5.usa.openbsd.org/pub/OpenBSD/3.2/packages/i386/
windowmaker-0.80.1.tgz
>>> ftp -o - ftp://ftp5.usa.openbsd.org/pub/OpenBSD/3.2/packages/i386/
windowmaker0.80.1.tgz
>>> ftp -o - ftp://ftp5.usa.openbsd.org/pub/OpenBSD/3.2/packages/i386/gettext-
0.10.40.tgz
...
#
```

You can watch pkg_add recurse through all the dependencies and subsequently install each one in turn. This is a pain to type, however, and requires that you know the exact package name when you want to install the software. Most people only know that they want "WindowMaker," which happens to be installed as part of the windowmaker-0.80.1 package. You can get around this by installing the package directly from an FTP command prompt.

If you don't know the name of the package you want to install, you can install it from within FTP. This lets you find the name easily enough, but stops pkg_add from automatically installing dependencies. For example, here I've logged in to my preferred FTP server and have wandered down to the package directory for my architecture and checked for any packages beginning with the name "wind."

```
ftp> ls wind*
229 Entering Extended Passive Mode (|||56722|)
150 Opening ASCII mode data connection for '/bin/ls'.
-r--r--r--  1 anonftp  wheel  1583322 Oct 15 05:07 windowmaker-0.80.1.tgz
-r--r--r--  1 anonftp  wheel   202966 Oct 15 05:07 windowmaker-extra-0.1.tgz
-r--r--r--  1 anonftp  wheel   646971 Oct 15 05:07 windowmaker-lang-0.80.1.tgz
226 Transfer complete.
ftp>
```

The first one is my port, although the various WindowMaker add-ons might interest me once I have the main package installed. From within the FTP client, I can download the package and direct it straight to a command.

```
ftp> get windowmaker-0.80.1.tgz "| pkg_add -v -"
```

This dumps the download straight to pkg_add(1). Unfortunately, because pkg_add just sees the package coming in from standard input, it doesn't know where to find the dependencies. You'll see it start to choke almost immediately on the libiconv package.

```
local: | pkg_add -v - remote: windowmaker-0.80.1.tgz
229 Entering Extended Passive Mode (|||49334|)
150 Opening BINARY mode data connection for 'windowmaker-0.80.1.tgz' (1583322
bytes).
Requested space: 400000 bytes, free space: 979604480 bytes in /var/tmp/
instmp.MSNlPE8498
pkg: Handling dependencies for windowmaker-0.80.1
```

```
checking libiconv-* (libiconv-1.8) -> Not found
...
```

At this point, you'll see quite a bit of output complaining about missing packages. You can download those packages separately, install them via FTP, or any combination thereof. You might well find installing the software via ports simpler.

NOTE   *Each time you attempt to install a package from within FTP and the installation fails, the entire package is downloaded, tested, and deleted. In my opinion, if you plan to install a package with many dependencies you're better off downloading the packages to your local hard drive and attempting to install from there rather than trying to install directly from within the FTP client. It might not be as nifty, but it will save bandwidth and time.*

I tend to use an initial FTP query with a Web browser to identify the complete package name and then give pkg_add(1) the full URL to the package and let it sort out the dependencies. You may find some other method more suitable for your circumstances.

Installing from FTP is not quite as secure as installing from CD-ROM. While the OpenBSD release team has verified all the packages on the CD-ROM set, a malicious hacker could have tampered with a random FTP server. You could be installing Trojan horses, backdoors, or worse. Booby-trapped source code has happened often enough to be a realistic concern.

Package Architectures

Every architecture has its own package files. Packages built for one architecture will not run on a different architecture. If you have a package file for WindowMaker on the Alpha platform and install it on i386 hardware, the install process will work. The program will not run, mind you, but the base install will appear to be successful.

For example, I can successfully install the WindowMaker package for Alpha machines on my i386, and pkg_add won't complain at all. If I try to run it, however, I will immediately get an error.

```
# wmaker
/usr/local/bin/wmaker: Exec format error. Binary file not executable.
#
```

This binary format actually *is* executable, just not on i386 hardware. The error you get will differ depending on the hardware you're running on and the architecture the package was compiled for.

Package Contents

Now that your software is installed, how do you find it on your system? There's no Start menu, after all, and no icon is dropped on your desktop. OpenBSD installs almost everything under /usr/local; if /usr/local/bin is in your $PATH, you might just try to run the command and see if it works. If it doesn't, you'll have to check the package installation record.

The directory /var/db/pkg contains a complete record of everything installed by ports or packages on your system: program names, documents, and locations. For example, this system now contains a directory called windowmaker-0.80.1. If you look in that directory, you'll see three files: +COMMENT, +CONTENTS, and +DESC.

The +COMMENT file contains a very brief description of the software. +DESC contains a longer description of the software, including a URL (if available) where you can go for more information. The most interesting file is +CONTENTS, which lists every file installed by the package. The file is quite long, but we'll look at the start of it.

NOTE *You may have difficulties trying to view these files with more(1) or less(1). The plus sign is a special character. To view the file, try specifying it by full path (i.e., "more /var/db/pkg/windowmaker-0.80.1/+CONTENTS") or, if you're in the directory, by giving a leading period and slash (i.e., "less ./+CONTENTS").*

```
# more ./+CONTENTS
❶@name windowmaker-0.80.1
❷@pkgdep libiconv-1.8
@pkgdep libiconv-1.8
...
```

Any line beginning with an @ symbol is a comment. The +CONTENTS file begins by listing ❶the package it belongs to. You'll then find several lines describing each of the packages this package requires, marked by the ❷pkgdep keyword. Continue down the list, and you'll find several more entries of interest.

```
...
❶@cwd /usr/local
❷@src /usr/ports/x11/windowmaker/w-windowmaker-0.80.1/fake-i386/usr/local
❸@comment ❹subdir=x11/windowmaker ❺cdrom=yes ftp=yes
@comment ❻libdepend iconv.3.0:gettext-0.10.40:libiconv-*:libiconv-1.8
...
```

The ❶cwd (change working directory) keyword indicates where this software is installed. WindowMaker is installed under /usr/local. The ❷src label shows where the package was built. The ❸comment keyword is used for general notes about a package. We can see the ❹port the package was built from, and if the package will be on the ❺CD-ROM or on the FTP site. The ❻libdepend comment shows all of the libraries that the port depends on.

```
...
@comment ❶newdepend gettext-0.10.40:libiconv-*:libiconv-1.8
@comment newdepend windowmaker-0.80.1:gettext->=0.10.38:gettext-0.10.40
❷@comment $OpenBSD: PLIST,v 1.25 2002/07/23 07:58:05 wilfried Exp $
...
```

You may have noticed that some packages appear repeatedly in the dependencies list. When a package depends on many other packages, and those other packages have their own dependencies, it's very easy for a single package to be listed as a dependency several times. The ❶newdepend comment strips this down to the bare minimum of packages that are absolutely required, hiding the complex chain of dependencies. Finally, the ❷exact version of the port this package was created with is shown.

After all of this, we finally get to the list of files contained within the package.

```
...
❶GNUstep/Apps/WPrefs.app/WPrefs
❷@comment MD5:146e8da921092c048731ea2827aa5879
GNUstep/Apps/WPrefs.app/WPrefs.tiff
@comment MD5:a47a7110635258aecf2d2744be8b485e
...
```

Most of the remainder of the file is a list of files that are contained within the package. For example, ❶we can see that the package includes the file "GNUstep/Apps/WPrefs.app/WPrefs." Each file is listed relative to the directory tree given at the top of the +CONTENTS file. For example, this whole package is installed under /usr/local, so the WPrefs file is actually available as /usr/local/GNUstep/Apps/WPrefs.app/WPrefs.

Most files installed in a "share" directory are either documentation or data intended for internal use by the program. Files installed in a "bin" directory are programs, and files installed in a "man" directory are manual pages. Some programs, such as WindowMaker, have their own directory hierarchy and do whatever they want. Still, a "grep man ./+CONTENTS" will quickly give you a list of all the man pages the program includes, which will give you a start on learning about a program.

Next, we see a ❷MD5 checksum for the file. The package-handling tools use this checksum to verify that a file has not been damaged in transit or by operator error. Checksums allow you to verify later that a file is the same as what was contained in the original package (see Chapter 10).

At the very end of the package list, we'll see a few instructions for uninstalling the package. These really aren't very useful for day-to-day systems administration, so we'll skip them.

Uninstalling Packages

So, after all this, suppose you don't want to keep the software on your system? That's simple enough with pkg_delete(1). Just give pkg_delete(1) one argument, the full name of the package you want to uninstall, and the program will remove the package from your system.

```
# pkg_delete windowmaker-0.80.1
#
```

If you try to uninstall a package required by other packages, pkg_delete will complain loudly. You might have a very legitimate reason for doing so, but pkg_delete will try to keep you from cutting off your own feet. If you insist, however, the "-f" flag will let you force an uninstall of a package even if it is required by other packages. Don't expect software that requires this package to work once you've uninstalled it, however! For example, if I delete the libiconv package my WindowMaker desktop will almost certainly not run.

Packaging Problems

The package system is fast, efficient, and reliable, and absolutely wonderful for many people. The system has a few problems, however — specifically lags in the software-porting process, software-synchronization requirements, and the support for newer packages on older versions of OpenBSD.

Each version of OpenBSD only supports the packages that it was built with. If you have an OpenBSD 3.2 machine, and you have a package from OpenBSD 3.3 that you want to install, you're on your own. It may work, or not; it will probably fall into a gray area where most of the functions work, but enough doesn't that you'll get quite frustrated. You may be able to compile a port instead, however.

The overwhelming majority of packages are software produced by third parties, who release their software on a schedule completely independent of OpenBSD. Some time after the software developers release an updated version of their software, the OpenBSD package is updated. There is a delay between the release of an original software package and the porting to OpenBSD. A popular package might be updated in hours, while large or less frequently used packages can languish at an older version for days or weeks. These packages are not officially available until the next release of OpenBSD, so you may be running less-than-perfectly-new software for a few months. In almost all cases, this is not a problem.

Also, packages are interdependent, and many rely on others in order to function properly. Those other packages must be of the correct version. If I tried to install a package that depended on windowmaker-0.80.1, it wouldn't work if I had windowmaker-0.80.2 or windowmaker-0.80 installed.

All of this goes away if you install your software from an OpenBSD CD-ROM or only use packages from a particular release of OpenBSD. You only experience these problems if you try to mix and match packages from different OpenBSD versions. Even if you do this, however, you will not be able to install custom-compiled software from a package. You'll have to use a port for that.

Using Ports

Installing software via the ports system takes longer than installing it via packages, and the ports system requires a live Internet connection. The ports system can produce better results for a given situation than packages, however, which more than compensates for these issues in most cases.

What makes ports so interesting is the level of automation they implement. With one command a port can find the source code for a program, fetch that code over the Internet, verify the integrity of the downloaded source code, patch the code to run properly on OpenBSD, integrate any changes required by your system setup, build the code into actual program binaries, and install it, without further human intervention. If you have compiled software on other platforms, you'll quickly realize what a time-saver this is.

Let's take a look at a port. Here's one of my non-negotiable requirements for comfortable systems administration, the tcsh shell.

```
# cd /usr/ports/shells/tcsh/
# ls
❶CVS        ❷Makefile    ❸README.html ❹distinfo  ❺patches   ❻pkg
#
```

As you'll see everywhere else, the ❶CVS directory contains revision control information.

The ❷Makefile contains the basic instructions needed to build this port. If you were to look at the Makefile, you would find that it's pretty minimal compared to the Makefiles found in almost all other software. Rather than target definitions, it contains variable definitions and an instruction to include another Makefile, bsd.port.mk. You'll find the real guts of the ports system in bsd.port.mk. (While you don't have to understand bsd.port.mk, or even look at it, some time when you have free time you might want to peruse this file and see just how the ports system hangs together.) This Makefile only contains settings of interest to this particular port, rather than global settings used by the ports system as a whole.

❸README.html is a basic description of the port, generated by the "make readmes" command in /usr/ports (see "Browsing the Ports Tree").

The ❹distinfo file contains a variety of checksums for the source code of the port. The ports system uses this information to verify the integrity of downloaded source code. We discuss checksums in Chapter 10, but the ports system performs automatic checksum verification.

The ❺patches directory contains any patches necessary for the software to compile and run properly on this particular release of OpenBSD.

Finally, the ❻pkg directory contains various information about the port itself. Let's take a look.

```
# ls pkg/
CVS      DEINSTALL DESCR    INSTALL    PLIST     SECURITY
#
```

The DEINSTALL file contains a message that will be displayed when you uninstall the software, either through the ports mechanism's uninstall tool or pkg_delete(1).

DESCR contains the original long description of the port in plain text, including the home page and any flavors the port supports (See "Flavors").

INSTALL contains a message that is displayed when the port or the package built from the port finishes installing.

PLIST contains a list of all the files contained in the completed port.

Finally the SECURITY file contains a list of known security issues with the port. The OpenBSD team does not subject ports to the same level of security scrutiny that it inflicts upon the base system, but does audit third-party software as time permits. Because add-on software is maintained outside OpenBSD, their project team's ability to secure distributed software is limited by the producers of the add-on software.

Combined, the files in the ports directory create the tools and instructions needed to build a port.

Installing a Port

You have probably noticed that we didn't see any actual source code in the port directory. Sure, there are patches to apply to source code, and scripts to run on source code, and notes about source code, but no actual code! You might rightly ask how this is supposed to run without the source code.

When you activate a port, your system automatically downloads the appropriate source code from an approved Internet site. It then checks the downloaded code for integrity errors, extracts the code to a working directory, patches it, builds it, creates a package, and installs the package. If the port has dependencies that are not already installed, it will interrupt the build of this software to build those dependencies. To trigger all this, all you have to do is go to a port directory and type

```
# make install
```

When you do, you'll see lots of text scroll down your terminal window, ending with a "Installing" message. If you have a good Internet connection, this can be easier than using packages!

What the Port Install Does

Let's dissect a port installation. I need tcsh much in the same way I need oxygen or caffeine, so we'll build that.

```
# make install
===>  Checking files for tcsh-6.12.00
>> tcsh-6.12.00.tar.gz doesn't seem to exist on this system.
>> Attempting to fetch /usr/ports/distfiles/tcsh-6.12.00.tar.gz from ftp://
ftp.astron.com/pub/tcsh/.
...
```

If the source code for this particular version of tcsh was in the /usr/ports/ distfiles directory, make would have found it. Because it isn't there, make(1) tries to download the source from a list of approved sites stored in the ports system or in the port itself. You will see various chunks of FTP output where the ports system download the file, then continues with the building process.

```
...
❶>> Checksum OK for tcsh-6.12.00.tar.gz. (sha1)
❷===>  Extracting for tcsh-6.12.00
❸===>  Patching for tcsh-6.12.00
❺===>  Configuring for tcsh-6.12.00
creating cache ./config.cache
checking host system type... i386-unknown-openbsd3.2
...
```

Make ❶compares the downloaded source code with the integrity information available in the distinfo file and finds that the downloaded file matches the one the OpenBSD port maintainer used. That means that the port will treat the file as intact and correct — presumably the port maintainer verified that the code they used did not contain any backdoors! It then ❷uncompresses the source code, ❸applies any local OpenBSD patches, and ❹starts the build process. (Observant and knowledgeable readers know that "configure" is not the same as "build," but if you keep your eyes open you'll also see a "build" statement later.) You will see many lines of build output — this particular program contains a few dozen, but a large program such as KDE can build for hours and have thousands of lines of make output. Eventually, however, you'll see a message like this:

```
...
===>  Faking installation for tcsh-6.12.00
install -c -s -o root -g bin -m 555 /usr/ports/shells/tcsh/w-tcsh-6.12.00/tcsh-
6.12.00/tcsh /usr/ports/shells/tcsh/w-tcsh-6.12.00/fake-i386/usr/local/bin/tcsh
...
```

The ports system is installing the software in a temporary location, so as to correctly build a clean package. This is called a "fake" installation because, well, it isn't the real installation that will end up on your hard drive. Once the fake install is complete, you'll see packages being built and then the real install.

```
...
===>  Building package for tcsh-6.12.00
Creating package /usr/ports/packages/i386/All/tcsh-6.12.00.tgz
Using SrcDir value of /usr/ports/shells/tcsh/w-tcsh-6.12.00/fake-i386/usr/local
Creating gzip'd tar ball in '/usr/ports/packages/i386/All/tcsh-6.12.00.tgz'
===>  Installing tcsh-6.12.00 from ❶/usr/ports/packages/i386/All/tcsh-6.12.00.tgz
...
```

The important thing to notice here is the ❶location of the package file. You may want to grab this package to install on other machines. This package will contain any local optimizations you may have added to the system, so you can use it to quickly install an utterly identical version of the software on any other OpenBSD systems of the same release and architecture.

Finally, the port spits out a message before returning you to a command prompt.

```
+---------------
| For proper use of tcsh-6.12.00 you should notify the system
| that /usr/local/bin/tcsh is a valid shell by adding it to the
| the file /etc/shells.  If you are unfamiliar with this file
| consult the shells(5) manual page
+---------------
```

This message is important enough that an overworked OpenBSD ports developer spent a few moments to make it appear. Read it. In this case, you have to make some manual changes to /etc/shells (see Chapter 14) for this port to work correctly. In general, OpenBSD ports do not make drastic system changes that can affect system integrity or security; they require the sysadmin to do that himself. Remember, any piece of software you install impacts system security in some way, and even something as innocuous as a shell program might have programming errors that provide a back door into a system. OpenBSD may provide a large-caliber gun and high-explosive armor-piercing bullets, but if you want to shoot yourself in the foot you must pull the trigger yourself.

The interesting thing about this process is that the port build process can actually be stopped at any of these steps. If you want to do some custom work on a port as it builds, you can carefully control the build process.

Port Build Stages

The port installation process includes several stages, which can all be called separately. Each stage performs all of the stages before it — the final stage, "make install," calls all of these. We'll discuss each stage and some of the customizations that can be made during this process.

Many port-building customizations are performed via variables. You can set these variables in the environment of the person building the program, on the command line, or if you want them to be used by all users or by every port you can set them in /etc/mk.conf. You can set these environment variables on any target that includes the target you're running — for example, if you need to use a special command to download files, you can use the variable to set that command during "make install."

Make Fetch

The "make fetch" process checks to see if the source code for the port is available locally. This source file is called a *distfile*. The location it will check is defined by the environment variable DISTDIR, or /usr/ports/distfiles if DISTDIR is not set. For example, if you have a central software source code repository on your network mounted over NFS as /central/sourcerepo, you could set "DISTDIR=/central/sourcerepo" and use that location instead. This allows you to share the downloads among as many machines as you like and reduces external bandwidth usage.

If the software is not available locally, "make fetch" tries to download it from the Internet. The source code location is specified in the port's Makefile as the variable MASTER_SITES. (See "Customizing Download Sources" for some more hints on this variable.) By default, make fetch uses ftp(1) to grab the software.

The ftp(1) program might have problems in certain environments, however. If you need to change the command used, you can do that with the FETCH_CMD variable. For example, I frequently download software from behind a SOCKS5 proxy; I can set FETCH_CMD='/usr/local/bin/runsocks /usr/bin/ftp' to have things work transparently. Alternately, if I'm in a location where a simple ftp program does not work properly, I could use wget (/usr/ports/net/wget) and try FETCH_CMD='/usr/local/bin/wget - - passive-ftp' with whatever other wget options (usernames, passwords, etc) are necessary to grab my source code files.

I said earlier that you could use this sort of variable during any make command, and it would be used at the proper stage. Here's an example of that in action:

```
# make FETCH_CMD='/usr/local/bin/wget - - passive-ftp' install
```

We're trying to run the "make install" command, which runs "make fetch" at an earlier stage. Setting FETCH_CMD or DISTDIR will affect "make fetch," but not interfere with later commands.

The "make fetch" command is very useful when you have certain times that you can download more easily than others. For example, I have a laptop which has a great deal of bandwidth available at certain locations and almost no bandwidth elsewhere. I can run "make fetch" on several ports where bandwidth is available and then unplug from the network and let them build.

Make Checksum

The "make checksum" command confirms that the distfile has not been corrupted, either maliciously or during download. A checksum is the result of a mathematical computation on a file and is discussed in great detail in Chapter 10. If you change the file, the checksum will be changed. Because it is theoretically possible to "pad" an altered file so that a particular checksum will be matched, OpenBSD checks each distfile against three different sorts of checksum: MD5, RMD160, and SHA1. A hacker could alter a bunch of source code and pad the files so that the MD5 checksum would be unchanged, but he couldn't change it so that all three checksums would be met!

After downloading the software, "make checksum" computes all three check-sums for the downloaded distfiles. If the checksums match those given in the "distinfo" file in the port, the port build continues. If the checksums do not match, the build immediately aborts and does not continue until you find a dist-file that matches the checksums. This might seem overly paranoid, but checksum matching quickly alerted the public when an intruder placed a Trojan in the official OpenSSH source code distribution.

If your port download fails, it might be because the software distributor updated the source file without changing the version number. This is endemic in the free software world. It can also happen if an intruder compromises a mirror site where the software is distributed. You can set the REFETCH variable to "yes" to make the ports system try to fetch a distfile from ftp.OpenBSD.org, if the original file fails the checksum match. This will get around both of these problems.

If you have downloaded the file, and you are certain it is correct, but the checksums still do not match, you can define NO_CHECKSUM to have OpenBSD skip the checksum computation and continue. This is an extraordinarily bad idea. At the time the port was made, the files had the checksum given in the port. If the checksum doesn't match, that means that the software is changed in some manner. Perhaps the file was corrupted, or changed by a hacker, or updated by the distributor, or any number of other problems. The simple issue is, the source code does not match what the port was made for. Perhaps the patches included in the port will not apply cleanly any more, or maybe the software will not run on OpenBSD, or you could even be installing a back door inviting a hacker to store his kiddy porn collection on your hard drive. You're on your own if you insist on compiling software after a checksum mismatch.

Make Depends

The make depends target confirms that all the dependencies of the port are available and builds them if they are not. For example, our WindowMaker package required two other packages. If we had built WindowMaker from ports, the WindowMaker port build would have triggered builds of those other ports at this stage. It will recurse through any dependencies and build them all.

You can set NO_DEPENDS to "yes" to skip this stage, but your port may not compile or run if you do so.

Make Extract

The ports system needs to uncompress and extract the source code from the distfile before the port can be built. Source code is extracted in the port directory, in a subdirectory with a w- prefix but named after the software's name and version. For example, the tcsh port we built earlier, tcsh version 6.12.00, was extracted in the directory /usr/ports/shells/tcsh/w-tcsh-6.12.00. Look in this directory for the actual code that is being compiled.

Make Patch

Now that you have the source code, the ports system can apply the local OpenBSD patches from the "patch" directory.

If you want to apply your own patches to the code, or if you want to review the code before compiling it, run "make patch" first. Your patches might conflict with the OpenBSD patches if you apply them first, or cause compilation failures, or any number of other things. By running "make patch" first, you get to see the code as OpenBSD will compile it.

Make Configure

The "make configure" command runs any precompilation configure scripts included in the software. If you want to edit the configure script, do so before letting this step run! If there is no configure script, the port system silently skips it.

Make Build

This step actually builds the extracted, patched, and configured software. Any customizations you want to make need to be finished before you run this step! When it is completed, you will have the finished program binaries in the port's work directory.

Make Fake

This command installs the software in a subdirectory of the work directory, laid out exactly as it would be if was actually installed. This directory is generally named with the word "fake" and the name of the architecture it was built for, e.g., "fake-i386." You can look through this directory to see what will be installed.

Make Package

This command bundles up the port's fake directory, adds in packing and installation instructions, and ties it all up in a package exactly like those available on CD-ROM. The package will be stored under /usr/ports/packages, in a subdirectory by architecture, in a further subdirectory by port category. For example, the package built from the tcsh port is stored in /usr/ports/packages/i386/shells/tcsh-6.12.00.tgz. You can build packages on a machine without installing it on the local machine.

You can then install this port on other architectures, or use it to verify the integrity of installed software.

Make Install

This final step performs some sanity checks and runs pkg_add(1) to installs the package compiled from the port.

Tracking Port-Building Information

How does the ports system know what has been run before? If you run "make patch," edit the source files, and then run "make install" to complete the port installation, why doesn't the port start over at the beginning? The ports system keeps track of completed make targets with hidden files in the ports work directory. These files begin with a period so they don't show up in a normal directory listing, but they show up easily up easily with "ls -a". Let's look at the tcsh work directory after the build is done.

```
# ls -a
.                    ❶.configure_done    ❷.patch_done      pkg
..                   ❸.extract_done      bin               tcsh-6.12.00
❹.build_done         ❺.extract_started   fake-i386
#
```

The ❶.configure_done file indicates that "make configure" has been successfully run. Similarly, ❷.patch_done means that make patch has been run, ❸.extract_done means that the make extract has finished, ❹.build_done means that the port has been built, and ❺.extract_started means that the make extract process has been finished.

You can use this to your advantage. Suppose you don't want to apply the OpenBSD patches to a port. (This isn't a good idea, but presumably you have reasons other than wanting a bullet in your foot.) You could run "make extract," create a file called ".patch_done" in the work directory, and then run "make install." The "make install" process would then think that the patches had been applied and continue on its merry way. You can do something similar to run your own configure process or make any other changes you like. Of course, if you do this you're completely on your own if the software breaks or has a security issue.

Port Flavors

While control of the build process gives a great many possibilities for software customization, where the OpenBSD ports system really shines is in its use of flavors. A *flavor* is a specific customization of a port, which allows you to build a custom package in a predefined way. Many pieces of open-source software are extremely flexible, and can be built with support for many different tools. The OpenBSD ports team has integrated these build options with the ports system, so that by setting a flavor you can tell the port to build in particular ways.

Let's look at a particular example. One of my favorite tools for network management is the Snort (http://www.snort.org/) intrusion detection system. Snort can examine every packet that comes across a network interface and sends alerts if the packet appears to be part of an attack. Snort can send messages to the system logger syslogd(8), or if you compile it properly it can send alerts to databases or Windows workstations, and even attempt to kill hostile connections. These fancy options require add-on software and special compilation settings, however. OpenBSD sets these as flavors. Each port's DESCR file lists any flavors that the port supports, so let's check out /usr/ports/net/snort/pkg/DESCR. At the end of this file, you'll see:

```
...
Available flavors:
        postgresql - enable postgresql database logging support
        mysql      - enable mysql database logging support
        smbalert   - enable samba logging support
        flexresp   - enable dynamic connection killing support
```

If you want to know more about how these features work, you'll need to check out the documentation for the software itself. For example, to learn how to set up SMB alerts for Snort, I'll go check out the Snort home page. In this case I want to log Snort output to a Postgresql database, send alerts to help desk technicians, and cut off connections of certain types. These features are controlled by the flavors "postgresql," "smbalert," and "frexresp."

Whenever a port builds, it looks for flavors in the environment variable FLAVORS. You probably don't want to define these environment variables permanently, but they're easy enough to include on the command line when building the port.

```
# env FLAVOR="postgresql smbalert flexresp" make install
```

The port will make the necessary changes to the code (generally, adding flags to compilation or configure instructions) and add the appropriate dependencies to enable these functions.

The completed port and package name will include the flavors chosen. For example, this port will show up in /var/db/pkg as "snort-1.8.6-postgresql-smbalert-flexresp," and the package in /usr/ports/packages/i386/net will be called "snort-1.8.6-postgresql-smbalert-flexresp .tgz."

This makes it very simple to build many different flavors of a single package. Perhaps you have some systems where you want Snort to run without any of these add-on features or with only one or two of these. You can build many different packages on one high-powered workstation and then install the packages on the system you want it to run on.

Uninstalling and Reinstalling

One nice thing about the tight integration between ports and packages is that you get all the advantages and flexibility of installing via source, but the package-handling tools work perfectly. You can uninstall a port with pkg_delete(1) and learn about it with pkg_info(1). Because the port's installation is recorded under /var/db/pkg/, you can go through the contents file.

You could also uninstall a port from the ports directory with the "make deinstall" target. For example, you might find that you want to experiment with several different versions of the Snort port before finally settling on one you like. You'll need to specify the flavor you want to uninstall in the environment, or the port will not be able to find the installed package you want to uninstall. For example, if I wanted to switch my Snort setup from a Postgresql database over to a MySQL database, I could do this:

```
# env FLAVOR="postgresql smbalert flexresp" make deinstall
# env FLAVOR="mysql smbalert flexresp" make install
```

This would also leave me with two different flavors of the port in /usr/ports/packages/i386, so I could switch back and forth easily.

Customizing Download Sources

Many pieces of popular software are available scattered all over the Internet. If you want to download the source code to the KDE window manager, for example, a manual search would find dozens of mirrors. One of them is probably very close to you. Some collections of software are mirrored as a whole and have a collective name. For example, official GNU software is generally distributed on GNU mirrors, many pieces of software are available in the widely redistributed Sunsite collection, and so on. Many ports use these mirrors as the authoritative source for distfiles.

The location of these mirror collections changes over time, and this month's most reliable mirror will not necessarily be good six months from now. Continually updating all the ports that use these sites would be a very difficult task. Instead, the OpenBSD ports team uses a series of macros to define these sites and has the ports call the macros to learn where to get the software. You can use these macros yourself to choose convenient places to download the software.

Each port Makefile includes a definition for MASTER_SITE, a URL where the source code can be downloaded. For example, the Makefile for /usr/ports/shells/tcsh contains the following line:

```
MASTER_SITES=    ftp://ftp.astron.com/pub/tcsh/
```

If you go look at this FTP site, you'll find the source code for this particular release of tcsh.

Other ports rely on a mirror site macro to get their download locations.

```
MASTER_SITES=             ${MASTER_SITE_WINDOWMAKER:=source/release/}
```

The WindowMaker window manager source code repository is widely mirrored, contains a great deal of software, and is well known enough to rate having its own name. You can call something "an official WindowMaker mirror," and people will generally know what you're talking about.

OpenBSD includes a set of macros that defines the common mirror collections and lists servers that mirror that content. A port will try the mirrors in order until it can find one where it can download the code. As with any collection of mirror sites, some will respond more quickly to you than others. You may find that the mirror site at the top of the list is painfully slow and that there's a more responsive mirror that you'd like to try first. That's fairly easy with OpenBSD.

If you look at the file /usr/ports/infrastructure/templates/network.conf.template, you'll find a whole list of MASTER_SITE_ variables, including MASTER_SITE_WINDOWMAKER, MASTER_SITE_KDE, MASTER_SITE_SUNSITE, and, yes, MASTER_SITE_OPENBSD. Don't directly edit this file — it's considered an OpenBSD system file and will be overwritten when you upgrade your system. Instead, copy it to /usr/ports/db/network.conf and make your changes to the copy.

For example, you'll find the following entry in network.conf:

```
...
MASTER_SITE_SOURCEFORGE+=        \
      http://us.dl.sourceforge.net/ \
      http://eu.dl.sourceforge.net/ \
      ftp://us.dl.sourceforge.net/pub/sourceforge/ \
      ftp://ftp.kddlabs.co.jp/sourceforge/ \
      ftp://ftp.chg.ru/pub/sourceforge/
...
```

This is a list of the SourceForge mirrors that the OpenBSD ports system knows about. When you install a port that downloads from a SourceForge site, the port first tries to grab the software from http://us.dl.sourceforge.net/. If the software is not available there, it then tries http://eu.dl.sourceforge.net/, and then proceeds on down the list to other U.S., Japanese, and Russian SourceForge mirrors. If you happen to be in Europe, you might rightly think that trying a US site first is rather dumb. Edit the list and put your preferred mirror site first, making sure to preserve the trailing slash on the URL and the final trailing backslash on the line, so that the port will try the other sites if the first one doesn't work. You can also add a mirror not on the list, if that works well for you.

Running Foreign Software

Traditionally, operating systems have had to have software written for them, and a piece of software would only run on the platform it was designed for. Many people have built a healthy business changing software for one platform so it will run on another operating system, a task filled with many potential problems. OpenBSD has the ability to run binaries built for certain other operating systems, however, through a process called ABI implementation. This is most commonly used for running software native to Linux and FreeBSD.

The ABI (Application Binary Interface) is the part of the kernel that provides services to programs, including everything from sound-card access to reading files to printing on the screen — all the things a program needs to run. As far as programs are concerned, the ABI is the operating system. By completely implementing the ABI from a different operating system on your native operating system, you can run non-native programs as if they were on their native platform.

The OpenBSD kernel includes modules that implement ABIs for Linux, FreeBSD, SVR4, SCO, and BSD/OS. When you attempt to run a Linux program, for example, the kernel picks out that the program is actually a Linux binary and directs it at the proper ABI.

One large limitation of ABI implementations is that they can only handle the kernel features, not the underlying hardware. A program only works if the binary is built for the same architecture that it is being run on. You can run a Solaris 2.6 binary built for an i386 system on OpenBSD running on i386, but you cannot run a Solaris Sparc binary on an i386 system.

Of course, programs require a little more than just a kernel to run on. They also require the dynamic libraries that they link against, if nothing else. OpenBSD provides these shared libraries for Linux (/usr/ports/emulators/redhat) and FreeBSD (/usr/ports/emulators/freebsd_lib). Because BSD/OS, SVR4, and SCO are proprietary operating systems, the OpenBSD project cannot easily provide easy-to-install ports for their shared libraries. You must have access to the proper operating system to grab the libraries. If you're interested in how to install these libraries see compat_bsdos(8), compat_svr4(8), and compat_ibcs2(8) for details.

In most cases, however, the Linux and FreeBSD ABIs "just work" and are reliable enough that many ports depend on them. Quite a few people use the Linux Netscape port, for example. Using an ABI implementation requires no configuration, once you have the shared libraries installed. If you install software from ports, you may be using Linux mode without even realizing it!

Between add-on native software and foreign ABI implementations, OpenBSD can support a wide variety of software packages. OpenBSD also includes a variety of basic UNIX software, most of it configured through files in /etc. We'll look there in the next chapter.

14

/ETC

You are in a maze
Of twisty little configs
No two are alike

The /etc directory is the heart of any UNIX-like operating system. /etc contains the files that tell the system how it works, what it does, and how it behaves under any circumstances. The first thing I do on any unfamiliar UNIX breed is check out the /etc directory and see what make it tick; it's like kicking the tires and checking under the hood of a used car before taking it for a test drive.

If you've never done this before, I highly recommend sitting down and reading the contents of /etc of almost any UNIX system. This is one of the best ways to earn your journeyman grade in systems administration. If you can read everything in /etc and explain what it does, you have a good grip on the next rung up in the professional ladder.

Understanding /etc is especially important when upgrading OpenBSD, as /etc must be updated to include files and entries from the new version. In many cases the contents of existing files change, so you must understand what the files do in order to make proper decisions on what should be edited and what should be completely replaced. While mergemaster(8) will help identify files that have been added or changed, the actual decision-making process cannot be automated.

You won't find every single file in /etc discussed in this chapter. OpenBSD supports a wide variety of functions, and many of them have configuration files in /etc. We are going to discuss in depth the general-purpose files that are in use in almost every system, however, as well as some files that System V and Linux users probably haven't encountered before.

Some files are used for specific subsystems that we don't cover in this book. For example, /etc/exports is used for NFS. Thick books have been written about NFS, and any overview I could provide within this chapter would be incomplete. If you've set up NFS, however, you already know about /etc/exports, and you'll know that if you overwrite it during an upgrade you'll be restoring from backup later that day. Files like this are mentioned, but only with a brief description and a pointer to further information.

Similarly, files that are discussed in other chapters are only mentioned, and a pointer is provided to the chapter.

/etc/adduser.conf

This file configures adduser(8). We discuss it in great detail in Chapter 7.

/etc/afs/

OpenBSD supports AFS, a distributed file system much like NFS. If you're interested in setting up AFS, check out afsd.conf(8).

/etc/amd/

The automounter daemon automatically loads NFS file systems upon request. If you're interested in using this function, check out amd(8).

/etc/authpf/

This directory contains the configuration for packet filter authentication. We cover this in detail in Chapter 19.

/etc/boot.conf

This file controls the system's basic booting process, as discussed in Chapter 6.

/etc/bootptab

The /etc/bootptab file controls the Bootstrapping Protocol daemon bootpd(8). Diskless clients rely upon a bootpd server to provide their operating system, file system, and so forth. If you're interested in diskless operations with this bootstrapping protocol, check out bootpd(8).

/etc/ccd.conf

This file describes the configuration for concatenated disks, or CCD. Concatenated disks are not supported in OpenBSD's GENERIC kernel, which means that support for them is minimal. If you're interested in using CCD, check out ccd(4).

/etc/changelist

This file contains a list of important system files that are to be checked each day by the system security check script /etc/security. Each file is listed by full path, on its own line. Every day, these files are backed up into /var/backup and compared to the version of the file that existed yesterday. Any changes to these files are mailed to root. Feel free to add any files you like to this list.

For more details on how the security check works, see /etc/security.

/etc/csh.*

The /etc/csh.* files contain system-wide defaults for csh (and tcsh, if installed). When someone using csh logs in, the shell executes any commands it finds in /etc/csh.login. Similarly, when the user logs out, /etc/csh.logout is executed. You can place general shell configuration information in /etc/csh.cshrc.

/etc/daily

The /etc/daily script is run once per day, from root's crontab, and performs very simple system checks and maintenance. The results of this check are mailed to root. The /etc/daily script performs the following actions:

- Removes temporary files, such as old X11/SSH lockfiles, accounting records, and so on.
- Checks disk status.
- Generates network statistics.

The script will also perform some basic maintenance on certain other systems, if those systems appear to be active and configured. For example, if /etc/distfile exists, /etc/daily will run rdist(1). This script also runs the /etc/security script. The /etc/daily script also has additional functionality that can be turned on or off through the use of environment variables in root's crontab or in /etc/daily.local.

Root Filesystem Backups

One nice feature OpenBSD provides is the ability to back up the root file system each day. While you can lose most of your partitions and have some hope of recovering, losing the root file system will make it almost impossible to boot your system. You'll have to provide a partition to put this backup root file system on, the same size as your existing root file system and almost certainly on another disk. The backup root file system has the same location limitations as the standard root file system (see Chapter 3).

List your backup root file system in /etc/fstab, with a mount type of "xx", like this.

```
/dev/sd3a /altroot ffs xx 0 0
```

You won't be able to mount this file system as you could any other files ystem listed in /etc/fstab, as "xx" is not a valid mount type. The /etc/daily script will recognize this as an alternate root partition, however, and overwrite the entire contents of this partition with your root drive. To make this work, set ROOTBACKUP=1 in either /etc/daily.local or in root's crontab.

Daily Filesystem Integrity Check

You might want to perform a very simple fsck(8) on your hard drives to see if any obvious errors appear. While OpenBSD cannot perform an intrusive fsck(8) while the system is running, it can perform a basic integrity check to see if anything is obviously out of whack. To enable this, set CHECKFILESYSTEMS to 1 in root's crontab or in /etc/daily.local.

/etc/daily.local

This file is reserved for local scripts that you want run every day, with the /etc/daily script. Output from these scripts will automatically be included with regular the /etc/daily mail. You can put any special-purpose scripts you like here, to check whatever functions the server should be reporting.

/etc/dhclient.conf

OpenBSD includes the Internet Software Consortium's DHCP client, which allows you to fine-tune how you accept DHCP offers. In most cases you will not need to do this, but when it's necessary it's extremely helpful. For average use, /etc/dhclient.conf can be empty.

Entries in /etc/dhclient.conf resemble C code and generally include a variable declaration followed by a value. Each line ends in a semicolon.

Prolonging Lease Requests

DHCP clients can have trouble when the network suffers from lag, and requests for configuration information time out before a valid offer makes it way back. Frequently, just rebooting and trying again suffices to get an answer back from the DHCP server — that's what they do in Windows support, after all — but you can do a little better. The dhclient(8) program can configure the amount of time it spends on each part of the process.

When dhclient(8) starts, it requests the last IP address it used (leased) and, by default, spends ten seconds trying to get that address. The reboot time is the number of seconds the client will spend trying to get the old address reissued. To change this waiting time, use the "reboot" statement.

```
reboot 20;
```

If the client cannot get its previous address in the reboot time, it will request a new one instead.

Rejecting Bad DHCP Servers

One of dhclient(8)'s more interesting features is its ability to reject bad DHCP servers. For example, some networks allow just about anyone to hook just about anything to them. If you've ever gone to a security conference, you've probably seen someone throw up a rogue DHCP server as a prank. If your system receives a lease from one of these servers, your connection may not work or you may be funneling all of your traffic through a packet sniffer. Nifty, no?

Ideally, you can just ask the network administrator for the correct IP address of the DHCP server. If you can't get that information, examine the leases you have received in /var/db/dhclient.leases. This file lists all the leases your system has ever received, including the bad one. Identifying a bad DHCP server is a matter of trial and error. Get the IP address of each DHCP server and then reject each server one at a time until you get a working configuration. To reject a DHCP server and refuse any further offers from it, list its IP with the "reject" keyword.

```
reject 192.168.1.84;
```

If you find a rogue DHCP server on your network, rather than patching around it with reject statements you should identify the rogue server, disable it, and deal with the person running it appropriately. (Despite any inclinations to the contrary, "appropriately" in this case does not involve chainsaws.) On foreign networks, you don't generally have the privilege to do that.

Announcing Host Information

If you are on someone else's network and feel friendly toward the local network administrator, add a "send" statement to your dhclient.conf. The DHCP server will record the information you put in your "send" statement in its lease database. The local network administrator can use this information to find you if your system starts misbehaving. You might not think this is a good thing, but making yourself easy to find is much better than making the administrator hunt you down.

```
send host-name "mwlucas-laptop.bigcompany.com"
```

Of the many other options in dhclient.conf, most are relatively useless under normal circumstances. You can, for example, refuse lease offers that don't include information you want — but if you refuse the lease, you won't get on the network at all. For detailed information on these options, see dhclient.conf(5).

/etc/dhcpd.conf

In addition to a DHCP client, OpenBSD includes the Internet Software Consortium's DHCP server. It is configured exactly like the ISC DHCP server running on any other operating system. For details on how to administer the DHCP server, see dhcpd(8).

/etc/disklabels/

The systems administrator can use this directory to store backup copies of disklabels. If you have a server with several hard drives, it is a good idea to keep backups of your partition information on hand. This will make emergency restoration far simpler.

/etc/exports

The /etc/exports file system shows which file systems have been exported via NFS. For details, see exports(5) and the related manual pages, then grab a copy of *Managing NIS & NFS* from O'Reilly and Associates.

/etc/fstab

The file system table is discussed in great detail in Chapter 15.

/etc/ftpchroot

Any user who is listed in /etc/ftpchroot is automatically chrooted into their home directory when they log in via FTP. See ftpd(8) for full details.

/etc/ftpusers

Any user who is listed in this file cannot log in via FTP. See ftpd(8) for full details.

/etc/groups

This lists which users are in which groups, as discussed in Chapter 7.

/etc/hostname

The /etc/hostname.interfacename files are discussed in Chapter 8.

/etc/hosts

The /etc/hosts file matches Internet addresses to host names. While the hosts file is very simple, its contents are only reasonably effective on a single machine. Hosts files are most useful on small private networks behind a Network Address Translation device. For example, the hosts file works quite well if you have one or two servers and some other company manages your public nameservice. If you have more than a couple servers, however, it's generally simplest to set up an actual DNS server.

Each line in /etc/hosts represents one host. The first entry on each line is an IP address, and the second is the fully qualified domain name of the host. Following these two entries you can have an arbitrary number of aliases for that host. I can add comments at the end of each line by starting them with a comment. For example, I have a small home network with four computers. One is the proxy server, one is my wife's desktop, one is my crash machine, and one is my laptop. The hosts file looks somewhat like this.

```
192.168.10.1   ❶nat.blackhelicopters.org      ❷firewall gateway
192.168.10.8    liz.blackhelicopters.org       liz  ❸#don't crash!
192.168.10.200 crashbox.blackhelicopters.org  ❹test
192.168.10.250 laptop.blackhelicopters.org     michael
```

The machine ❶"nat.blackhelicopters.org" also has the names ❷"firewall" and "gateway." I've put in a ❸note to remind myself to not run Nessus against my wife's desktop machine. The machine "crashbox" is also called ❹"test." And if I put in one more full-time computer at home, I'm building a DNS server.

Any machine with this hosts table could find any machine listed in the hosts table by name; I could run "ping liz" or "ssh crashbox" and actually reach the desired machine.

/etc/hosts.equiv

This file is used by the various "r" protocols, such as rcp(1) and rlogin(1). They are a relic of an earlier age, when Internet security was not so great a concern, and should not be used today. There should be no uncommented entry in this file unless you specifically put it there. If you're really interested in this, check out hosts.equiv(5), rshd(8), and rlogind(8).

/etc/inetd.conf

The inetd(8) daemon handles connections for less frequently used Internet services. For example, because most systems don't have a steady stream of incoming FTP requests, there's no need for the additional overhead of a FTP daemon listening when it's going to be idle 99.9 percent of the time. Instead, inetd(8) listens on the FTP port. When a FTP request comes in, inetd starts up the FTP daemon and hands it the request. The inetd.conf file configures which port inetd listens on, what service it handles, which programs are started to handle incoming requests, and how those programs are started. Each service has its own line.

Inetd also handles functions that are so small and rarely used that they're easier to implement within inetd rather than write an external program for them. This includes things such as the "echo" service, which just repeats anything you send to it, or the "daytime" service that just prints out the date. These are disabled by default, but can be enabled if you wish. The standard /etc/inetd.conf provides entries for many of the integrated programs included in OpenBSD, such as the pop3 daemon popa3d.

Most daemons have separate configuration lines for IP and IPv6, so if you're not running IPv6, you can ignore all those entries. Let's look at the provided pop3 daemon configuration.

```
❶#❷pop3  ❸stream  ❹tcp     ❺nowait  ❻root  ❼/usr/sbin/popa3d    ❽popa3d
```

First, the ❶pound sign shows that this entry is commented out; it will not have any effect until it is uncommented and inetd(8) is restarted.

Service Name and Address

Then we have the ❷service name and address. The name must match a name in /etc/services. Inetd relies upon the service name to determine which TCP or UDP port to bind to.

As an OpenBSD-specific feature you can specify an address or host name before the service name, separated by a colon. This tells inetd(8) which IP address to bind to. For example, to run the POP3 service on 192.168.87.44, we would use something very much like the line above but specify the address with the service name.

```
192.168.87.44:pop3  stream tcp  nowait  root  /usr/sbin/popa3d    popa3d
```

You can provide multiple addresses, separated by commas, on a single line. If you don't specify a host name or address, inetd will bind to all available IP addresses on the specified port.

If you want inetd to only listen on a specific IP address for all services, you can specify that IP address on a line by itself, followed by a colon. This will then become the default IP address where inetd(8) listens on for all following connections. For example, putting this at the top of your file tells inetd to attach to only the given unless told otherwise.

```
192.168.87.44:
```

You can actually change the default IP address inetd listens on partway through the file. Suppose you have several inetd services that you want to listen on the IP address 192.168.87.44 and several others that you want to listen on the IP address 192.168.87.45. You could do this in your configuration:

```
192.168.87.44:
...
[configure inetd services that listen on 192.168.87.44 here]
...
192.168.87.45:
...
[configure inetd services that listen on 192.168.87.45 here]
...
```

You can override these defaults on any single entry just by specifying your preferred IP. If you want to explicitly tell inetd(8) to listen on all available IP addresses, give an asterisk as the IP address. Following lines will obey the default.

Network and Daemon Configuration

The next field gives the ❸socket type. All TCP connections are type "stream," while UDP connections are type "dgram." There are other possible values, but these are the most common.

We then have the ❹protocol, which must be a valid protocol from /etc/protocols. The most common are "tcp," "udp," "tcp6," and "udp6." The tcp6 and udp6 protocols are explicitly for IPv6 connections. The "udp" and "tcp" protocol types are used for the default networking protocol the system supports, generally IPv4.

The ❺next field indicates whether inetd(8) should wait for the particular service to accept the connection, or just start the program and go away. As a general rule, TCP programs use "nowait," while UDP programs need "wait." Check the documentation for your particular program to be certain. You can rate-limit a daemon will accept by putting a dot and the number of connections per second after the wait or nowait statement. The default limit is 256 connections per service per second. Here, we limit our pop3 to 128 connections per second.

```
pop3  stream  tcp    nowait.128  root  /usr/sbin/popa3d    popa3d
```

You can rate-limit connections across all of inetd(8) by starting the service with the "-R" option, as discussed in the manual page.

The next field lists the ❻user the daemon runs as. The POP3 server must run as root, because it must access files belonging to many different users. We then have the ❼full path to the program that inetd(8) will execute. Finally, we give ❽how the program is called. If you want to use any command-line arguments for the service program, put them here.

For full information, see inetd(8).

/etc/hosts.lpd

This file lists the host names or IP addresses of systems that may use the local system's Line Printer Daemon, lpd(8).

/etc/kerberosIV

This directory contains the highly sensitive information for Kerberos version 4. To start to learn about Kerberos, check out kerberos(1).

/etc/kerberosV

This directory contains the server information for the Kerberos service, version 5. Once you understand Kerberos version 4, check out kdc(8) for an introduction to version 5.

/etc/ksh.kshrc

This file is intended as a global ksh configuration file. Unlike csh(1), ksh(1) does not automatically source this file. Users must manually include it in their .kshrc.

/etc/localtime

This file is a symlink to the actual time zone file. To change the system's time zone, change the symlink. See Chapter 5.

/etc/locate.rc

The locate(1) program finds all files of a given name. For example, to find any files with the string "mozilla" in their name, run this command:

```
# locate mozilla
/usr/ports/www/mozilla
/usr/ports/www/mozilla/CVS
...
```

You'll see that many files include the string "mozilla" in their path, all under the directory /usr/ports/www/mozilla.

Once a week, your OpenBSD fires up the script /usr/libexec/ locate.updatedb, which scans the system's disks, builds a list of everything it finds, and stores that list in a database. The list-building program uses the values contained in /etc/locate.rc to determine which directories and file systems to scan.

Two values that control how the search works are SEARCHPATHS and FILESYSTEMS. SEARCHPATHS is usually set to "/", so that the entire system is scanned. If you want to search only a subsection of the system, you could change this to another directory. This would seriously alter locate(1)'s expected behavior and is not recommended. FILESYSTEMS, on the other hand, lists the type of file systems that locate.updatedb scans. It defaults to searching only FFS and UFS, but if you have a multiboot system you might want to list your foreign file systems here as well. After all, the ability to locate(1) your MP3 collection on your

Windows slice is a vital system function. On the other hand, listing NFS file systems can be dangerous; if all of your clients start searching your central NFS server at the same time, performance will be poor.

The only caveat with these two variables is that SEARCHPATHS must be a directory on a file system listed in FILESYSTEMS; if you give a SEARCHPATH that's on a file system that isn't in FILESYSTEMS, the locate(1) database will be empty.

You might also want to exclude directories from the locate update. The PRUNEPATHS variable includes the directories you don't want checked. This defaults to the standard temporary directories.

/etc/login.conf

This file controls user account login behavior. For full details, see Chapter 7.

/etc/lynx.cfg

OpenBSD ships with the lynx(1) web browser. Lynx is endlessly configurable; see the manual page for details. Settings in /etc/lynx.cfg affect all Lynx users on the system, so you can save yourself a lot of trouble by configuring your proxy server settings here.

/etc/magic

Many files include a "magic number" that identifies what sort of file they are. The file(1) program uses these magic numbers to identify the file type, using /etc/magic as an index of magic numbers. Do not manually edit /etc/magic, as it is automatically generated by compiling file(1).

/etc/mail/

The /etc/mail directory contains the configuration files for sendmail(8), the standard UNIX mail transfer agent. The aliases(5) file also lives here; while it's technically a part of Sendmail, many other mail server programs recognize and use the aliases file.

If you are interested in using a MTA other than Sendmail, check out /etc/mailer.conf.

/etc/mail.rc

This is the global configuration file for the mail(1) mail-reading program. While mail(1) has been almost completely superseded by more advanced mailers, it's worth mastering because almost any UNIX system will have it installed.

/etc/mailer.conf

Traditionally, the only mail server program available for any UNIX was sendmail(8). As such, a huge amount of add-on software expects to find /usr/sbin/sendmail and expects it to behave in a certain manner. What's more, sendmail(8) behaved differently depending on what name it was called with. Some common alternate names are send-mail, mailq, and newaliases. Programs expected to find all of these names as well and expected that these commands would behave appropriately. Sendmail is such a standard that newer mail server programs have been forced to call themselves "sendmail," and to behave exactly as Sendmail does, just to maintain compatibility with this vast installed base. This causes problems when using a different mail program, as you may be stuck wondering exactly which mail program the "sendmail" command calls.

Also, OpenBSD includes classic Sendmail as part of the base system. When you upgrade, sendmail(8) is reinstalled. If you overwrote Sendmail with your preferred mail server, upgrades would cause no end of annoyance.

The /etc/mailer.conf file does an end-run around all this mess by eliminating /usr/sbin/sendmail as a mail program. Instead, "sendmail" is just a wrapper that checks /etc/mailer.conf and redirects the request to the mail-sending program indicated there. Entries in /etc/mailer.conf are just a list of program names, along with the path to the actual program to be called. Sendmail proper is actually installed as /usr/libexec/sendmail/sendmail, for example. To run an alternate mail server, just give the actual command name and the full path to all of the appropriate binaries. This happens automatically when you install a new MTA from a port or package.

/etc/man.conf

The man.conf file tells man(1) how to find and present manual pages. If you install software in nonstandard locations, this file will be quite helpful to let you access documentation transparently. For example, in some environments add-on software is installed under /usr/pkg or /opt. By editing /etc/man.conf, you can access the manual pages in that directory tree just as you can base system documentation. The file has several sorts of entries, each set off by keywords or section names.

Search Index

The "_whatdb" keyword gives the full path to a whatis(1) database, as used by whatis(1) and apropos(1), allowing users to easily search and cross-index the manual. These databases can be created by makewhatis(8). Here, we tell the manual system to check the file /usr/pkg/man/whatis.db when you run apropos(1) or whatis(1):

```
_whatdb        /usr/pkg/man/whatis.db
```

Manual Page Location

Manual pages are scattered in directories all over the system. To tell man(1) which directories to check by default, use the "_default" keyword. You can group directories by using brackets.

For example, here's the standard default directory listing:

```
_default       /usr/{share,X11R6,X11,contrib,gnu,local}/{man,man/old}❶/
```

We have a massive group of directories here. The brackets are used to combine multiple directories associatively — for example, this entry means that we check /usr/share/man, /usr/share/man/old, /usr/X11R6/man, /usr/X11R6/man/old, and so on. Note that this entry ends with a ❶slash; this indicates that this entry has subdirectories. To add /usr/pkg/man to the default locations, just add "pkg" in amongst the directories like so:

```
_default       /usr/{share,X11R6,X11,contrib,gnu,local,❶pkg}/{man,man/old}/
```

By adding in the ❶pkg directory name here, we've added the directories /usr/pkg/man and /usr/pkg/man/old to the directory list.

The "_subdir" keyword contains a list of subdirectories to be searched under other directories. Only use one _subdir entry. These directories will be searched in order.

```
_subdir        ❶cat1 ❷man1 cat8 man8 cat6 man6 cat2 man2 cat3 man3 cat5 man5
cat7 man7 cat3f man3f cat4 man4 cat9 man9 cat3p man3p
```

For example, our search starts in /usr/share/man, as defined by our _default list. Man(1) will check in ❶/usr/share/man/cat1 for a manual page of the desired name, and then proceed to ❷/usr/share/man/man1, and go on down the list. The user will see the first matching manual page.

Displaying Manual Pages

Manual pages are distributed in a wide variety of formats, depending on the software distributor's preferred format. Each different format must be displayed using a different command. Fortunately, each different format also has a different filename suffix, which can be used to determine how to display the file. The "_build" keyword defines a filename suffix and the command used to display that file. Here are a couple simple examples:

```
_suffix        ❶.0
_build         ❷.0.Z           ❸/usr/bin/zcat ❹%s
...
```

Our first examples, files ending in ❶.0, do not need any special formatting command; the file is simply dumped directly to the pager. Our second entry, files ending in ❷.0.gz, need to be processed by ❸zcat first. The ❹%s is a macro for the file containing the manual page.

Section Names

The final function handled by man.conf is dividing the manual into sections. We saw in Chapter 1 that you can search the manual by particular sections to get certain man pages. These sections are nothing more than directories identified in /etc/man.conf. For example, here's where we define the manual pages included in section 1:

```
1          /usr/{share,X11R6,X11,contrib,local}/{man/,man/old/}{cat,man}1
```

There is no trailing slash, because we are not searching any subdirectories; these are the actual directories containing section 1 man pages. You can define arbitrary section names in /etc/man.conf. While it's a good idea to stay away from section names beginning with an underscore, to avoid confusion with man.conf's keywords, you could do just about anything else. The default man.conf has a few section names defined, much like this one for the "local" section.

```
local          /usr/local/man/
```

If you only want to search the man pages for locally installed software for the command "test," you could run "man local test." You could easily add a local section name for your developer manual pages.

/etc/master.passwd

This file contains usernames and passwords. When you log in, the password you type is compared with the encrypted hash of your password in this file. As such, this file is absolutely vital for system security.

If you're considering editing this file directly, *stop*. Go back to Chapter 7. Read it again. See if there's another way to make your desired change. Damaging /etc/master.passwd can prevent people from logging in at all and might render your system unusable. If you must edit the password file directly, there's a special program just for that. Vipw(8) calls up the text editor from $EDITOR, allows you to make changes, and checks the file syntax before saving it. Vipw(8) also updates /etc/passwd and the password databases /etc/pwd.db and /etc/spwd.db. This prevents many of the more basic mistakes and helps ensure data consistency, but if you're really bent on corrupting /etc/master.passwd, vipw(8) will make your task more difficult but won't stop you.

Many programs need access to the information in /etc/master.passwd — for example, shells and home directories must be public information. Rather than allowing anyone to read this file and try to reverse-engineer the hashed password, OpenBSD (and most other UNIXes) provide globally readable bits of this file in /etc/passwd, and a database of this data in /etc/pwd.db.

Fields

Each line in /etc/master.passwd contains ten fields, separated by colons. These are described next.

Username

The first field in a line is the username. This is either an account created by the administrator and used by a real user, or a user created to provide some system user. OpenBSD includes a variety of system accounts such as "named," "nobody," "_portmap," and so on. Various programs run as these other users.

Hashed Password

The second field is the hashed password. System users don't generally have a password, so you can't log in as them. User accounts have a string of random-looking characters here.

One simple way to temporarily disable a user account is to edit the password file and put an asterisk(*) in front of the password. While the account will still be active, nobody will be able to log in to it. I've used this to great effect when a client is behind on a bill; while they ignore overdue payment notices, they call quite quickly when they cannot check their mail. To re-enable the account with the same password they had before, just remove the asterisk.

User ID Number

The third field is the user ID number, or UID. Every user has a unique UID.

Group ID Number

Similarly, the fourth field is the group ID number, or GID. This is the user's primary group, as discussed in Chapter 7. Usually, this is the same as the UID, and the group has the same name as the username.

User's Class

The next field is the user's class, as defined in /etc/login.conf (Chapter 7). You can change a user's class by using chsh(1) or vipw(8).

Password Expiration Date

The expiration date is given in the number of seconds since midnight, January 1, 1970. (This is the "epoch" of UNIX, considered the Beginning of Time, and many different programs use it.) You can convert dates to seconds by using date(1).

Account Expiration Date

This is the number of seconds since the epoch until the system account expires.

Gecos

The gecos field contains the user's real name, office number, work phone number, and home phone number, all separated by commas. Do not use colons in this field; colons are reserved specifically for separating fields in /etc/master.passwd itself.

User's Home Directory

The ninth field is the user's home directory. While this defaults to being under /home, you can move this anywhere you like. You'll just need to move the actual directory when you change this field in /etc/master.passwd.

User's Shell

Finally, the tenth field gives the user's shell. If this field is empty, the user gets boring old /bin/sh.

/etc/mk.conf

The /etc/mk.conf is used by make(1), most frequently when building ports. See Chapter 13.

/etc/moduli

The file /etc/moduli contains Diffie-Hellman moduli for use by sshd(8). You should never have to edit this file, although it may be enhanced by new OpenSSH releases.

/etc/monthly

The /etc/monthly shell script is run once per month to handle basic system administration. By default, it does almost nothing except run /etc/monthly.local. This script does contain a command to provide monthly user login time accounting, but it is commented out. To activate it, just uncomment the lines around "login accounting." This was very important back when computer time was a valuable resource that needed to be accounted for, but is less so now. It can be useful to see which users access the system most frequently, however.

/etc/monthly.local

This file is run by /etc/monthly. If you have any commands that you want run on a monthly basis, you can include them in this file. The output of the commands will be mailed to root each month along with the /etc/monthly output.

/etc/motd

The motd, or message of the day file, is displayed to users upon login. You can put system notices in this file, or other information you want shell users to see. This is a good place to put legal notices or acceptable-use policies.

/etc/mtree

This directory contains a list of all the directories in the base system, their owners, and their permissions in a format suitable for mtree(8). The system upgrade process most often uses this. While you really don't need to edit these files, it's nice to know that they're here.

/etc/myname

The /etc/myname file contains the host name of the system, as discussed in Chapter 5.

/etc/netstart

This script starts the network, as discussed in Chapter 6.

/etc/newsyslog.conf

Log file growth is one common cause of disk space shortages. By rotating your logs, the system compresses older logs, makes room for new logs, and discards the oldest logs. OpenBSD's log file rotation program, newsyslog(8), can handle all this and more. Cron runs newsyslog(8) once per hour. The /etc/newsyslog.conf file tells newsyslog(8) under which conditions a log should be rotated and what actions should be taken upon rotation.

The /etc/newsyslog file uses one line per log file, and each line has between five and eight fields. For example:

```
/var/log/messages                    644   5    30    *    Z
```

Log File Path

The first field is the full path to the log file to be processed, /var/log/messages in this example.

Owner and Group

The second field is optional and does not actually appear in the example above. You can list an owner and group for the rotated log file, separated by a period (such as "root.wheel").

Newsyslog(8) can change the owner and group of old log files. By default, log files are owned by root and are in the wheel group. While it's not common to change the owner, you might have to use this ability on multi-user machines.

You can choose to change only the owner or change only the group. In these cases you must use a period, even though nothing appears on the other side of it. For example, ".customer12" will change the file to be owned by the group "customer12," while "customer15." will change the owner to be customer15.

Permissions

The third field (644) in the example gives the permissions mode, in standard UNIX three-digit notation. See chmod(1) for details.

Count

Next is the "count" field, which represents the number of old log files that newsyslog(8) will keep — sort of. Newsyslog(8) starts counting archived log files at 0. Many computer systems start numbering at 0, but newsyslog(8) includes 0 as well as the count number. With the default count setting of 5 for /var/log/messages, /var/log/ includes the following files:

```
/var/log/messages
/var/log/messages.0.gz
/var/log/messages.1.gz
/var/log/messages.2.gz
/var/log/messages.3.gz
/var/log/messages.4.gz
/var/log/messages.5.gz
```

This is six backups, not five, plus the current log file! The oldest backup log is numbered 5, which is what newsyslog(8) uses the count for. While it's better to have too many logs than not enough, if you have a space shortage you might need to reduce the number of logs you keep. The important thing is that you understand what actually happens when you specify a number of logs to retain.

Size

The fifth field (30 in our example) is the file size. When newsyslog runs, it compares the size listed here with the size of the file. If the file is larger than the given size (in kilobytes), it is rotated. If the file size doesn't affect when you want to rotate the file, list an asterisk in this field.

Time

This is the number of hours that must pass before the logs will be archived again. If you put 24 here, the logs will be rotated once per day. If you put an asterisk here, the age of the file will not be considered when deciding when to rotate the file.

Flags

This optional field tells newsyslog(8) of other actions it should take. OpenBSD supports four flags.

Flag	Meaning
Z	Compress the file with gzip(1) or compress(1)
B	Do not include the "log file turned over" message in the log (for binary files)
F	Follow symlinks
M	A user is monitoring this log

Monitoring User

Newsyslog(8) can notify users when a log file they are interested in is rotated. To do this newsyslog(8) must be run with the "-m" option and the "M" flag must be set on the log file. Next, list the username of the user who will be notified. This entry is optional.

PID File

Some programs record their process ID in a file. Newsyslog can send a signal to a process when the log file has been rotated, so the program knows to start a new log file. List the full path to the PID file next on the line. By default, newsyslog sends a SIGHUP; if you want to use a different signal, specify a signal name in the next field. This entry is optional.

Signal Name

If you don't want to send a SIGHUP to a process with a PID file, you can use a different signal name instead. The signal name must begin with SIG- and must be specified by name. You can get a full list of signals in signal(3). This field is optional, but requires a path to a PID file appear previously.

Command to Execute

Rather than sending a signal to a process, you can have newsyslog(8) run a command when it has finished rotating logs. The command must be given in double quotes. While this field is optional, it cannot be used with a PID file and a signal entry.

/etc/passwd

Many programs require access to user information such as shell, real name, and so on. In older UNIX systems, this was stored in the /etc/passwd file, along with the actual hashed password, and everyone could read this file. This became a problem as UNIX spread into universities. Computer science students had great fun trying to crack hashed passwords, and regretfully they succeeded on too many occasions. Hackers targeted the password file, which was easy to read because of the sloppy permissions. Eventually, the hashed passwords were moved to /etc/master.passwd. The /etc/passwd file remained as an information source for other programs, but was sanitized to remove any sensitive information.

The /etc/passwd file is generated from the /etc/master.passwd file by stripping out the class, change, and expire fields. The hashed password is replaced with an asterisk. The fields that remain are:

- username
- password (asterisk)
- user ID number
- group ID number
- gecos

- home directory
- shell

See /etc/master.passwd for details on these fields.

/etc/pf.conf

This is the master configuration file for PF. See Chapter 19 for an introduction to this high point of OpenBSD.

/etc/phones

Back in the dark ages of the early 1980s, systems connected to each other via phone lines speaking UUCP (Unix-to-Unix Copy Protocol). This functionality still lingers in OpenBSD, much like your veriform appendix. While it is expected to work, its usefulness is greatly limited. See tip(1), remote(5), and phones(5) for details if you're interested in computer archeology.

/etc/portal.conf

This file is used to configure the Portal File System. PFS provides the ability to open TCP/IP connections as files. While this is quite nifty functionality, it's not widely used. See mount_portal(8) for details.

/etc/ppp/

The /etc/ppp directory contains information on configuring dial-up network connections, as covered in Chapter 8.

/etc/printcap

UNIX printing is one of those black magic topics; those who understand it think it's straightforward, while those who have never worked with it cower in fear and hope it will just go away. Setting up a printer attached directly to an OpenBSD system can be very difficult. I strongly recommend that you investigate apsfilter (http://www.apsfilter.org/). This will help you install all necessary software and configure /etc/printcap for your printer.

/etc/protocols

The /etc/protocols file lists all of the standard Internet protocols your OpenBSD system knows about. Each protocol has an assigned number, and various programs use these numbers to determine how they handle transactions. Almost all Internet transactions happen over TCP or UDP. Most people don't realize that TCP is protocol 6, UDP is protocol 17, and there are dozens of other protocols. Some protocols are very heavily used in particular environments, and others are so outdated that you'll almost certainly never encounter them. As a systems administrator you don't have to be intimately familiar with every piddly little protocol out there, but you should know that the world is bigger than TCP/IP. Each protocol has its own line in /etc/protocols. The first entry on a line is the official name. The second entry is the protocol number. Following that are any aliases for the protocol. Finally, comments are set off with a pound sign. Just for amusement, here's a snippet of /etc/protocols.

```
tcf      87     TCF           # TCF
igrp     88     IGRP          # IGRP
ospf     89     OSPFIGP       # Open Shortest Path First IGP
```

Some of you may have heard of OSPF, and a few of those may have even heard of IGRP. I have absolutely no clue what TCF is, and even the almighty Google leads me only to a thousand copies of /etc/protocols when I ask about it. If I was really interested, I could research and find out, but at the moment I don't particularly care. If protocol number 87 shows up knocking at my firewall one day, however, I can at least put a name to it before starting the journey.

/etc/pwd.db

The /etc/pwd.db file is a database version of the public /etc/passwd file. As a computer program can access a database file much more quickly than it can parse a text file, /etc/pwd.db is updated every time /etc/master.passwd changes.

The password database files are the reason why it's so important that you use tools such as chsh(1) and vipw(8) to edit the password file. When the edits are complete these tools automatically run pwd_mkdb(8), keeping the database files in sync. If your /etc/passwd, /etc/master.passwd, and password database files are not synchronized, weird problems will result.

Unless you are a real systems guru and skimming over this chapter because you know everything already, you shouldn't edit /etc/pwd.db directly. Let the password tools do the work for you.

/etc/rbootd.conf

This file configures HP diskless clients. If you're interested in diskless clients, start by reading diskless(8).

/etc/rc.*

All of the /etc/rc files are used for system initialization, as discussed in painful detail in Chapter 6. Go look there.

/etc/remote

Older UNIX systems had extensive support for serial ports, and OpenBSD retains this support. It is most commonly used for serial consoles (Chapter 6), as well as configuring network devices with a serial port. The file /etc/remote contains descriptions of a wide variety of serial connections. These commonly used entries are found at the very end.

If you're interested in writing your own serial port configurations, take a look at remote(5).

/etc/resolv.conf

The resolver helps map host names to IP addresses, and vice versa, and is configured via /etc/resolv.conf. While OpenBSD's /etc/resolv.conf supports a wide variety of options, two basic sorts of entry are sufficient to get the system working properly: a domain or domain search list, and nameserver entries.

Domain or Domain Search Settings

When you're working on machines on your own network, you don't want to have to type the whole hostname. If you have 30 web servers, after all, typing "ssh www23.mycompany.com" gets old. The "domain" and "search" keywords tell the resolver the default domain.

Specifying the Local Domain

The "domain" keyword tells the resolver one domain to check. For example, to specify AbsoluteOpenBSD.com as the local domain, enter this:

```
domain     AbsoluteOpenBSD.com
```

Once the local domain is specified, any command that would ordinarily require a domain name, but doesn't get one, will assume that it's within AbsoluteOpenBSD.com instead. Were I to type "ping www", the resolver would append the domain name to the query and tell ping(8) to try the IP address of www.AbsoluteOpenBSD.com.

Specifying a List of Domains

Alternatively, I can use the "search" keyword to specify a list of domains to try. I own several domains and use them for different parts of my work, and I might want the system to try them all.

```
search AbsoluteOpenBSD.com blackhelicopters.org stenchmaster.com
```

In this case, the resolver will check all three of these domain names in the order they appear, until it finds a match. For example, if I enter "ping petulance" it will try to find petulance.AbsoluteOpenBSD.org. If that fails, it will search for petulance.blackhelicopters.org, the next domain in the list. Finally, it will check for petulance.stenchmaster.com. If no such host exists in any of these domains, the command will eventually fail.

The Nameserver List

Now that the resolver knows which domains to check by default, you need to tell it which nameservers to use. Nameservers should each be listed on a single line, in the order of preference. The nameservers will be tried in order.

```
nameserver 127.0.0.1
nameserver 192.168.170.3
nameserver 209.88.133.4
```

Note that the first entry on this list is the loopback IP, 127.0.0.1 and means "localhost." You'll need this entry if the machine is a nameserver, because it tells the resolver to look at the local machine. While in some instances you might not want to use the local nameserver, in most cases it's a waste of network bandwidth to do otherwise.

With a domain or search keyword and a nameserver list, your machine will be able to match host names and IP addresses. For more on /etc/resolv.conf, check resolv.conf(5).

/etc/rpc

The /etc/rpc file maps human-readable Remote Procedure Call names to protocol numbers. It's used in NFS, NIS, and other RPC-based services. For details on the format, see rpc(5).

/etc/security

The /etc/security file is a straightforward shell script run each day for /etc/daily. It performs a variety of very simple system security and integrity checks. It does not solve any security problems, but it may make you aware of them. The complete list of checks performed by /etc/security grows from one release to the next, but here are some of the biggies:

- Check /etc/master.passwd for suspicious entries.
- Check root's environment for suspicious entries.
- Check ownership on vital system files, disks, file systems, and important user files.
- Check for content changes in files listed in /etc/changelist.

If nothing has changed, the output from this program is extremely short. If something has changed, you really will wish you had been reading your daily security reports.

/etc/services

This file lists many commonly used network ports. See Chapter 8.

/etc/shells

/etc/shells contains a list of all legitimate user shells, by full path, one per line. If you install a shell from package or port, add an appropriate entry to /etc/shells. Various programs check /etc/shells to try to sort out legitimate requests from bogus ones — for example, ftpd(8) will not allow a connection from a user if his shell is not listed in this file.

/etc/skel/

This directory contains the default user dotfiles, as discussed in Chapter 8.

/etc/skeykeys

This file contains the necessary information for the server side of the S/Key one-time password system. Check skey(1) for a good introduction.

/etc/sliphome/

Here you'll find the configuration information for SLIP, the Serial Line Internet Protocol, the predecessor to PPP. While SLIP has largely been superseded by PPP, OpenBSD retains its SLIP support. Check sliplogin(8) and its related pages for an introduction to SLIP.

/etc/spwd.db

Much like /etc/pwd.db, this file is a database hash of the /etc/master.passwd file. As it contains all user information, including the hashed passwords, it must be closely protected. See /etc/master.passwd and /etc/pwd.db for details.

/etc/ssh/

This directory contains the configuration instructions for the OpenSSH server and client. See ssh_config(5) and sshd_config(5) for up-to-date details.

/etc/ssl/

This directory contains the global configuration information for OpenSSL. See openssl(1) for details.

/etc/sudoers

The /etc/sudoers file tells sudo(8) which permissions to give to which users. See Chapter 7 for a full sudo(8) tutorial.

/etc/sysctl.conf

The kernel run-time tunables are set in /etc/sysctl.conf. For more information, see Chapter 11.

/etc/syslog.conf

The UNIX logging system uses /etc/syslog.conf to sort log messages into their proper files. Each program that wants to log sends log entries to the logging system and marks each message with a facility and a level. The syslogd(8) program receives these messages and sorts them according to the matching entries in /etc/syslog.conf. Each entry has two sections: a message identifier consisting of a facility and a level, and an action for matching messages. You must separate the action from the facility/level statement with tabs, not spaces.

Facilities

A facility is a log-entry source, generally a program, that sends messages to syslogd. This is an arbitrary label, just a text string used to sort one program from another. In most cases, each program that needs a unique log needs a unique facility. Many programs have a facility dedicated to them, such as mail, ftp, and cron. Syslogd also has a variety of generic facilities that can be used by any program. Programs can use facilities that aren't meant for them, but you'll be able to track them down by finding their name within the message. The standard facilities are:

auth	Publicly accessible information about user authorization, such as login and su attempts
authpriv	Private information about user authorization, accessible only to root
cron	Messages from the system scheduler, cron(8)
daemon	A catch-all for system daemons that lack their own facility
kern	Messages from the kernel
lpr	Messages from the printing system
mail	Messages from the mail system
mark	This puts an entry in a log every 20 minutes, useful for timing other logs
news	Messages from Internet News daemon
syslog	Internal logging system messages
user	The default message recipient
uucp	Logs from the UNIX-to-UNIX Copy Protocol
local0 through local7	Reserved for administrator use

Levels

A log message's level represents its relative importance. While programs send all their logging data to syslogd, most syslogd configurations only record the important stuff. Everyone has a different view of "important," however, and that's where levels come in. OpenBSD, like every standard-compliant UNIX, provides eight levels, which you can use to tell syslogd what to use and what to discard.

emerg	System panic. Messages are flashed on every terminal. The system is down. Read crash(8).
alert	The system can continue to operate, but requires immediate attention.
crit	There are critical errors, but not as bad as the "alert" level. You may have a hard drive going bad, or serious software issues. You can continue running, if you're brave.

err	Errors that should be fixed, but will not endanger your system.
warning	Assorted errors that should be fixed in your copious free time, as someone will notice them, eventually.
notice	General information that probably doesn't require any action on your part.
info	Individual transaction and program activity information, such as individual messages sent or received on a mail server.
debug	Very detailed information, mostly of use when trying to debug problems. May contain information that violates user privacy.
none	Don't log anything from this facility here.

Actions

Syslogd(8) will take any of several actions upon matching a message. If you give an action of a full path to a file, messages are appended to the file. If you give the "@" symbol followed by the name of a host, messages will be forwarded to the syslogd(8) on that host. If you list users, separated by commas, the message will be sent to the terminal windows of any of those users who are logged in. Finally, if you put an asterisk, every user who is logged in will get the message on his terminal window.

Creating syslog.conf Entries

The first entry on each line describes the information to be logged, by facility and level. All messages sent that use that facility, and that level *or higher* will match the entry. The second tells the action to be taken when a log message matches the description. Syslogd compares each submission to the entries in /etc/syslog.conf and, when it finds a matching entry, processes the log entry in the manner described. Take a look at this line from /etc/syslog.conf:

```
auth.info                          /var/log/authlog
```

This tells syslogd(8) to record messages that use the "auth" facility in /var/log/authlog, if the message has a level of "info" or higher.

Wildcards

You can use wildcards in the message description. For example, to log all messages from the mail system you could use this entry.

```
mail.*                             /var/log/maillog
```

To log everything from everywhere, use two wildcards.

```
*.*                                /var/log/everything
```

Multiple Information Sources

You can send multiple information sources to a single action by separating them with semicolons.

```
*.notice;auth.debug                                  root
```

Local Facilities

Many programs can choose which facility to use for their logging. Most add-on programs can be told which facility to use. The various "local" facilities are reserved for these programs. For example, you might tell a program to log to "local5". Exactly how you set these facilities varies from program to program. Once you have the program's facility set, however, logging these messages works exactly like logging any other messages.

```
local3.debug                              /var/log/programlog
```

Logging Hosts

If your network has a loghost where all systems send their logs, you can specify it as an action by using the at symbol (@). Here, we dump all the messages from the local host to the logging host.

```
*.*                               @loghost.AbsoluteOpenBSD.com
```

The /etc/syslog.conf on the log host determines the final destination for the messages it receives. Fortunately, each log message includes the host name.

Logging to User Sessions

You can send a message to a user, if he is logged in. List multiple users by separating them with commas. To send a message to all users, give an asterisk. For example, here I really annoy Chris, Phil, and Don, but notify all users of real emergencies.

```
*.debug                           chris,phil,don
*.emerg                           *
```

Logging by Program Name

If you're out of facilities, you can use the program's name to handle logging. An entry for a name requires at least two lines: the program name with a leading exclamation point and then a line with the logging information. For example, to log the output of (8), you would use this entry:

```
!chat
*.*                    /var/log/chatlog
```

/etc/systrace/

Here you will find systrace policies for use by systrace(1), as discussed in Chapter 10.

/etc/termcap

This file describes all the various sorts of terminals that OpenBSD supports. With the introduction of wscons(4), pretty much every OpenBSD device will support the standard vt220 terminal. If you want to start playing with terminal descriptions, read termcap(5) and *Termcap & Terminfo* from O'Reilly and Associates.

/etc/ttys

The /etc/ttys file configures terminal devices attached to the system. You can enable, disable, and manage physical terminals here. "Physical terminals" are either on the keyboard and monitor attached to the computer or on a console over a serial line. Historically, a UNIX terminal device resembled a teletype; that's where the "tty" label comes from. You'll see all sorts of UNIX architectural decisions that descend from this bit of trivia. Each of these attached terminal devices can be configured differently through /etc/ttys.

Terminal Types

You'll see a few different sorts of terminal devices in /etc/ttys: the console, keyboard and mouse console, serial ports, and pseudo-terminals. The console is where console error messages are sent and where the system can be managed during boot. It's usually sent to the keyboard and mouse console, although you can send it out the serial port instead. The console uses the device node of /dev/console.

The standard keyboard and mouse are usually called the "console," but that term isn't strictly correct — the console is an abstraction that just usually happens to be pointing at your physical keyboard. On the i386 architecture, OpenBSD supports several multiple virtual consoles. If you hit CTRL-ALT-F2, you'll see brand-new login screen. CTRL-ALT-F1 will take you back to the main console. You can have as many virtual consoles as you have function keys. These virtual consoles have device names beginning with "ttyC" and ending in a hexadecimal number.

Serial ports can be used as login devices, once you attach either an old-fashioned serial terminal or a null-modem cable and another device with a serial port, just like a null-modem cable. Each serial port can have one terminal attached to it. Serial port terminals have device names of "tty" and end in a hexadecimal number.

Finally there are pseudo-terminals, which are used for remote connections such as SSH. Even though your remote xterm has no physical hardware for it, OpenBSD treats it in some ways as a teletype. These pseudo-terminal connections use two types of device nodes, masters and slaves. Master pseudo-terminal devices are named "pty," a letter p through q, and a hexadecimal number. Slave pseudo terminals have names starting with "tty," but have the same ending as their matching "pty" device. For example, /dev/ptyq0a is tied to /dev/ttyq0a. The slave terminal appears in /etc/ttys.

Configuring /etc/ttys

Each terminal has an entry in /etc/ttys, containing at least three entries and possibly up to five.

❶console ❷"/usr/libexec/getty Pc"   ❸vt220   ❹off ❺secure

The first entry is the ❶device name, without the leading /dev.

The second entry is the ❷name of the program that configures the terminal. Physical devices must have a program that handles setting up the system to communicate with that physical device. The standard program for handling terminals is getty(8). You can use multiple words in the second entry, as we have here, by including the entire entry in quotes. While getty(8) is the standard program for this purpose, you could choose to replace it. Pseudo-terminals do not require a terminal configuration program and use a "none" in this space.

Then ❸define the terminal type used for this terminal device. The keyboard and mouse virtual consoles all use the "vt220" terminal type, as documented in /etc/termcap. Other physical terminals will have their own terminal type, which will usually be documented with the terminal. If you specify a terminal type of "unknown," the user will be prompted for their terminal type. Pseudo-terminals, which are accessed over the network, have a terminal type of "network."

After these three required fields, you can list flags that modify the terminal's behavior.

Physical terminal devices need an "on" or "off" flag, showing if the particular terminal is usable or not. If the terminal is off, you cannot access it. If the terminal is on, you can access it. For example, here's the /etc/ttys entry for the eighth virtual console, accessible by hitting CTRL-ALT-F8.

ttyC7   "/usr/libexec/getty Pc"   vt220   off   secure

If you hit CTRL-ALT-F8, nothing will happen. This console is off. Change the "off" to an "on," and the next time you reboot your system this console will be usable.

If you use the flag "secure," this terminal can be used for direct root logins. Note that every physically attached device in /etc/ttys has the secure flag set. Anyone with the root password can walk up to the system and log in. This might not be desirable.

If you use serial consoles, you might find it useful to be able to log in to the system via that same serial connection. The entry for the serial ports looks much like the entry for the virtual consoles; the getty command is slightly different, and the device name has changed, but it's basically the same. If you're using the first serial port as your serial console, change the "off" to an "on," and you will be able to log in to the system via the serial console connection.

/etc/weekly

The /etc/weekly shell script is run once a week, in a similar manner to /etc/daily and /etc/monthly. Its major purpose is to update the locate database and to run /etc/weekly.local.

/etc/weekly.local

This file is reserved for local commands that you want run every week. Output from these commands will automatically be included with regular the /etc/daily mail. You can put any special-purpose scripts you like here, to check whatever functions the server should be reporting.

/etc/wsconsctl.conf

This file contains configuration instructions for the machine-independent wsconsctl(8) console management program. Use this system to configure the keyboard-and-mouse console attached to your computer. Entries in /etc/wsconsctl.conf are simple variable assignments. While the default wsconsctl.conf file contains several examples, here are some of the more commonly used choices.

Change Keyboard Encoding

The default keyboard is the U.S. standard. You can specify a different keyboard layout with the keyboard.encoding variable. For example, to set your keyboard to Russian, just set this:

```
keyboard.encoding=ru
```

To get a complete list of all keyboard encodings supported by your release of OpenBSD, run "kdb -l". You should recognize your local keyboard layout easily enough.

Idle Screen Blank

If the system has been idle for some time, you might want the monitor to go blank to prevent burn-in. By default, the monitor will remain on; to have the screen blank automatically, you must define the conditions for the monitor to re-activate. You have three choices: mouse activity, keyboard activity, and monitor activity. Just set the appropriate value to "on" in /etc/wsconsctl.conf.

display.kbdact	Wake on keyboard activity
display.msact	Wake on mouse activity
display.outact	Wake on monitor output

For example, to have the monitor go blank but reactivate when you hit a key, just enter this in /etc/wsconsctl.conf:

```
display.kbdact=on
```

The display.screen_off variable sets the length of time until the screen goes black, in milliseconds. Here, we set it to 120 seconds.

```
display.screen_off=120000
```

Blanking a screen can be accomplished in two different ways: Turn the screen to black or use the "power saver" mode. A black screen will reactivate immediately upon demand, but it will use more power. A monitor that's set on power saver mode will take a few seconds longer to start back up. You can set power saver mode by turning display.vblank to "on." Of course, if you have an old monitor that doesn't believe in saving power, this won't work.

15

DISK AND FILE SYSTEM MANAGEMENT

Oh, my head hurts bad.
Rings of ones and zeros, ouch!
File systems hide them.

Disk management is one of a systems administrator's most vital duties. Disk flexibility and reliability are paramount to any operating system, and understanding how to manage, tune, and optimize disks and file systems is unquestionably a necessary skill. OpenBSD can handle several different sorts of disks and file systems, and in this chapter we'll discuss many of them.

Device Nodes

A *device node* is a special file that provides a logical interfaces to a piece of hardware. By using a command on a device node, sending information to a device node, or reading from a device node, you're telling the operating system to perform an action on a piece of hardware or, in some cases, a "logical" device. The action taken varies widely from device to device — for example, writing to a disk drive produces very different results than writing data to the screen! OpenBSD stores all device nodes in /dev and actually mounts other file systems in such a way that device nodes cannot be used on them. Many disk-management programs expect to be given a device name as an argument. Device node names are frequently cryptic and vary widely between operating systems, even operating systems that are closely related and run on similar hardware. The following table lists the device node names for OpenBSD disk devices.

Device node	Description
/dev/fd*	floppy disk (block)
/dev/rfd*	"raw" floppy disk
/dev/wd*	IDE disk (block)
/dev/rwd*	"raw" IDE disk
/dev/sd*	SCSI disk (block)
/dev/rsd*	"raw" SCSI disk
/dev/cd*	CD-ROM device, either IDE or SCSI (block)
/dev/rcd*	"raw" CD-ROM device

Device names also have a number, indicating which instance of that device it refers to. For example, /dev/wd0 is your first IDE hard drive, /dev/wd1 is the second, and /dev/cd1 is your second CD-ROM drive.

Remember from when we installed OpenBSD that each partition has a letter: The root partition was "a," the swap area was "b," the whole disk was "c," and so on. Each of those partitions has a separate device node, given by adding the letter to the device name for the hard drive device. For example, /dev/wd0a is the root partition on the first IDE hard drive, and /dev/sd3b is the swap partition on the fourth SCSI hard drive.

Raw and Block Devices

Raw devices are neither crunchy, healthy, nor full of vitamins, but are just a different way of accessing the same device. If you're not interested in an explanation, all you need to know is that certain programs expect to access a device through the standard device node and others expect to access the raw device node. Programs designed to work with raw device nodes will not work on the standard device node, and vice versa. Raw devices are sometimes called *character devices*, because they access the hard drive a character at a time. If you must control exactly how the data is laid down on the disk, such as when creating a file system in the first place, use a raw device.

A "standard" device node is more properly called a *block device*. Data transmitted to or from the device is *buffered*, meaning that chunks of data are collected until there is enough data to make it worth the trouble to access the device. A block device is occasionally called a *cooked device*. Block devices are generally considered more efficient than raw devices.

In contrast, a raw device does no buffering. If you tell a system to write to a file via a raw device, the data is immediately transmitted to the device. This works best when running a program that provides its own input/output buffering or has a particular way it wants to arrange disk data.

Here's an easy way to remember the difference between block and raw throughput. Spill a bottle of aspirin. You might pick up the aspirin with your right hand and collect them in the left, until your left hand is comfortably full and you can dump a bunch into the bottle at once. You're buffering your aspirin transfers in your hand. (If it's buffered aspirin, then this is buffered buffered aspirin transfers. But let's not go there.) If you pick up each aspirin individually and deposit it directly in the bottle, it's considered an unbuffered or raw transfer.

Raw devices have an "r" in front of their name, but they refer to the same physical hardware as the block device. If a program opens /dev/wd0a, it's accessing the root partition on the first IDE hard drive in block mode; however, if it asks for /dev/rwd0a, it's accessing the same partition in raw mode.

The File System Table: /etc/fstab

The file system table lists every configured file system on your computer's hard drives, where that file system is mounted, and any special options used to mount that drive. Each separate file system appears on a separate line in /etc/fstab, as shown in the following example:

```
/dev/wd0a / ffs rw 1 1
/dev/wd0g /home ffs rw,nodev,nosuid 1 2
/dev/wd0d /tmp ffs rw,nodev,nosuid 1 2
/dev/wd0f /usr ffs rw,nodev 1 2
/dev/wd0e /var ffs rw,nodev,nosuid 1 2
```

The first field in this listing gives the device node for the partition, as discussed under "Device Nodes."

The second field lists the mount point, the directory where this file system is found. Swap space, when it's listed, has a mount point of "none." (Swap space is not necessarily listed here.)

Next is the file system type. The standard OpenBSD partition uses type "ffs," the UNIX Fast File System. Other options include, but are not limited to, "msdos" (FAT partitions), "mfs" (Memory File System), and "cd9660" (CD-ROM).

The fourth field shows the mount options used on this file system. We'll discuss mount options in detail later in this chapter.

The fifth field tells the dump(8) program if it should back up this file system. If this field equals 0, dump will not back up the system. Otherwise, the number given is the minimum dump level needed to back up the system.

The last field, the *pass number*, tells fsck(8) when it should check the system during the boot process. The file systems with a 1-pass number are checked first, file systems with a 2-pass number are checked second, and so forth. If you set this to zero, fsck(8) will assume that the file system does not need to be checked.

The Fast File System

The OpenBSD file system, the Fast File System (FFS), is a direct descendant of the file system shipped with BSD4.4. Even today one of the original people who worked on BSD is still making improvements to the file system, and those improvements are frequently imported into OpenBSD. FFS is sometimes called UFS for UNIX File System, and many system utilities call FFS partitions UFS. This Fast File System made its way back into AT&T UNIX; from there, it slipped into many other commercial versions of UNIX. If a UNIX vendor doesn't specifically state that they have a "new and improved file system," they're almost certainly using FFS.

FFS is designed to be fast and reliable. OpenBSD ships FFS configured to be as widely useful as possible on each architecture, but you can choose to optimize it for trillions of small files or a half-dozen 30GB files, if you choose. You don't have to know a huge amount about FFS's internals, but you must know about inodes, blocks, and fragments.

Files are broken up into *blocks* and *fragments*. Blocks are large chunks of data, while fragments are smaller chunks. Generally, a file fills as many blocks as possible and uses a fragment or two for leftover touches of data. As a file grows, the system allocates additional blocks for the information.

Inodes contain very basic information about the file, including a list of the blocks and fragments that the file uses but also the permissions and size of the file. Information in an inode is called *metadata*, which is a fancy word for "data about data." Inodes index the file on disk.

FFS Mount Options

Unlike the Windows or Macintosh file systems, FFS partitions can be treated in several different ways depending on how they're mounted. The manner in which a partition is mounted is called the mount type. You can change the mount options on a standard partition by entering the appropriate options to the fourth column in its /etc/fstab entry.

Read-Only Mounts

If you only want to look at the contents of a partition, and not write to it, you can mount the partition as read-only (or "rdonly"). This is unquestionably the safest way to mount a disk and one of the useless most of the time. The purpose of disks is to store data that you enter, after all!

Many systems administrators mount the root partition, and perhaps even /usr, as read-only to minimize any potential system damage from a loss of power or an intruder. Even if you lose the physical hard drive due to a power surge or some other hardware failure, the data on the platters remains intact. That's the advantage of read-only mounts; the disadvantage is that it makes maintenance far more difficult. Read-only mounts are also useful when you're trying to read a damaged file system that you do not want to damage further.

Read-Write Mounts

You can read to the disk. You can write to the disk. Read-write mounts are abbreviated "rw." This is the standard mount, but I recommend that you use soft updates instead if your architecture supports it.

Soft Update Mounts

Soft update, or "softdep," mounts organize and arrange disk writes so that the file system metadata on the disk remains consistent, and it comes close to giving the performance of an "async" mount with the reliability of a "sync" mount. While that doesn't mean that all the data will be written to disk — a power failure at the wrong moment will still lose datat — using soft updates will prevent a lot of problems. It's not the default only because some older, smaller architectures do not have enough memory to support it. On i386, I strongly recommend enabling soft updates for all your FFS partitions.

Synchronous Mounts

Synchronous (or "sync") mounts are the old-fashioned way of mounting a file system. When a disk is synchronously mounted you can read from it as fast as the disk can feed data to the operating system, but writes run more slowly. The kernel will write a chunk of data to the disk, wait to receive a confirmation from the disk that the data has actually been accepted and written to the disk, and then will tell the program that requested the data write that the data is on disk.

Synchronous mounts provide the greatest data integrity in the case of a crash, but they are slow in terms of computer speed. Consider using synchronous mounting when you want to be truly pedantic about data integrity, but in most cases it's overkill.

Asynchronous Mounts

For faster data writing at a much higher risk of data loss, mount your partitions asynchronously ("async"). When a disk is asynchronously mounted, the kernel sends data to the disk and immediately tells the program that the write was successful without waiting for the disk to confirm that the data was written. As you can probably imagine, a data loss or system failure will result in corrupt data and confused software. Asynchronous mounts are fine on disposable machines, but don't use them when you care about your data.

No Access Time Mounts

FFS records the last time a file was accessed, meaning the last time it was executed or read by any means. These updates consume a small but measurable amount of time and disk performance. By mounting your disks "noatime" you can conserve that shred of time. In most cases, if you're using this option, you should invest in a faster disk instead.

On machines where power is a concern, however, noatime is very useful — the hard disk and the screen are the two most power-hungry devices on a laptop, and if you can reduce the amount of time your laptop's hard drive spins you will extend battery life.

No Device Nodes Mounts

Using a "nodev" mount tells the system to not interpret any device nodes on the file system. This is useful for security reasons, and is especially useful if you have hard drives from a different operating system on the computer. For example, on your dual-boot OpenBSD/Linux computer, you do not want to accidentally try to access a Linux device node instead of your native OpenBSD device node! In most cases, there is no reason to have a device node on any partition except that containing the root file system.

Noexec Mounts

The "noexec" mount option prevents any binaries from being executed on the partition. Mounting /home noexec can help prevent users from installing and running their own programs, but for it to be effective, be sure to also noexec mount any shared areas (such as /tmp).

Nosuid Mounts

The "nosuid" option disallows setuid behavior from programs on this file system. Many partitions should not have setuid files, and this is an easy way to disrupt them. Like noexec mounts, you must carefully place this option on all user-writable directories for it to be effective.

Noauto Mounts

The "noauto" mount isn't actually a mount, but a way of marking partitions that should not be automatically mounted at boot time. I frequently create /etc/fstab entries for my floppy and CD-ROM drives, but the system should not attempt to mount these at boot. The boot will hang if a partition the system needs is not available, and I don't want my computer to refuse to complete the booting process just because there is no CD-ROM in the tray!

Using FFS Mount Options

You can specify multiple mount options in a comma-separated list on a partition's /etc/fstab entry. Here's an entry with several options for reference.

```
/dev/wd0g /home ffs rw,softdep,nodev,nosuid,noexec 1 2
```

You can also specify these options when you mount partitions on the command line, as we'll discuss shortly.

What's Mounted Now?

How can you determine what file systems are mounted on your system and how they are mounted? Start by running mount(8) without any options, which will give you a list of all mounted file systems.

```
# mount
/dev/wd0a on / type ffs (local, softdep)
/dev/wd0g on /home type ffs (local, nodev, noexec, nosuid, softdep)
/dev/wd0d on /tmp type ffs (local, nodev, nosuid, softdep)
/dev/wd0f on /usr type ffs (local, nodev, softdep)
/dev/wd0e on /var type ffs (local, nodev, noexec, nosuid, softdep)
❶/dev/cd0c on /mnt type cd9660 (local, read-only)
#
```

This is also a quick way to get the device names for your partitions. In addition to the /etc/fstab entries we saw earlier, we have a ❶CD-ROM mounted. If you're using NFS, MFS, or other file systems, they will also show up here.

Corrupt FFS Partitions

If you have a system crash while writing to disk, the disk is considered *dirty*. It's in a kind of limbo: The operating system has requested that information be written to disk, but the data is not yet completely written out. Part of the data block may have been written, the inode might have been edited but the data not written, or any combination of the two. You need to identify and resolve these inconsistencies before the system will let you mount a disk read-write. OpenBSD includes a powerful FFS checking tool, fsck(8).

When a rebooting system finds a dirty disk partition, it automatically checks the disk and tries to clean everything up. Any data that was not written to the disk before the failure is lost, of course, but fsck does its best to clean up the data that remains. If successful, everything should be right where you left it – except for that unwritten data.

Failed Automatic Fscks

Occasionally a reboot will fail, and you'll be left staring at a single-user prompt asking you to run fsck manually. At this point, you have a few choices: run fsck, run fsck in automatic mode, backing up the damaged partition, or debugging the file system.

Running Fsck

If you enter "fsck", fsck will check every block and inode on the disk. It will probably find any number of blocks that have become disassociated from their inodes and will make a good guess as to how they fit together and how they should be attached. This can take quite a while on the huge disks that are so common these days.

When fsck finds a problem that it isn't absolutely sure about, it will ask you if you want to perform a fix it suggests. You have two choices, yes or no. If you answer "y," fsck will rebuild the disassociated file and place it in a lost+found directory on the partition, such as /usr/lost+found. If you answer "n," the file will be lost. Files in the lost+found directory have a number for a name. Use grep(1) to scan these files for missing data.

Running Fsck in Automatic Mode

If your disk was in the middle of a very busy operation when the system failure occurred, you could end up with many, many disassociated files. Rather than spending an hour typing "y" over and over again to tell fsck(8) to attempt to recover these files, you can just run "fsck -y" at the single-user prompt. This tells fsck(8) to assume that you're answering "y" to every question; this is much easier than typing "y" repeatedly.

In most cases it is. It's possible for the entire contents of the disk to migrate to the lost+found directory thanks to fsck -y. Recovery becomes difficult at that point.

Backing Up the File System

You can use dump(8) to grab a copy of the damaged file system and place it somewhere for further work. This gives you the luxury of being able to try various ways to restore the data, while leaving the possibility of starting over. Chances are, if you have to try this, you didn't have an adequate backup process in the first place.

File System Debugging

OpenBSD includes the powerful system debugging tools fsdb(8) and clri(8), which allow a skilled user to debug the file system and redirect files to their proper locations. These tools work on a block-and-inode level, and many partitions have hundreds of thousands of both. You need a very good understanding of FFS to be able to use these tools, so it's not an option for most people. The best way to learn how to use them is to fsdb(8) and clri(8) your way through a few corrupt file systems, sadly.

Mount(8) and FFS

The mount(8) command attaches disk partitions to mount points on the system. Boot your OpenBSD system into single-user mode and follow along.

When the system boots it mounts the root partition read-only, which gives the operating system enough information to do basic setup and get core systems running before mounting the rest of the file systems. You'll only have the programs in /bin and /sbin available. If you're comfortable editing files with ed(1), you may be just fine. If not, you'll want to mount some of your other file systems.

Mounting Standard File Systems

To mount a single file system that is listed in /etc/fstab, such as /usr or /var, give the file system mount point as an argument to mount(8).

```
# mount /usr
#
```

This mounts /usr exactly as /etc/fstab describes it, with the same options.

Mounting with Options

To use a different option that is not specified in /etc/fstab for that file system, use the options flag "-o." We discussed the available FFS options earlier, in the "FFS Mount Options" section. For example, to mount /var as read-only, enter this:

```
# mount -o rdonly /var
#
```

A read-only mount is very useful for a damaged file system. In the past, I've had file systems that were so badly damaged that fsck(8) choked on them. These were Usenet news servers with hundreds of thousands of articles, and I generally did something to cause such problems. If you just want to pull some information off the disk without risking further damage to data, you can mount the partition as read-only and copy to your heart's content. (This isn't true in the case of physical disk damage, mind you; if one of the platters is coming apart, your data is doomed.)

Forcing Read-Write Mounts

If a partition is marked dirty, fsck(8) it before mounting it read-write. I hate to say that you should *ever* skip the fsck(8) step before trying to read-write mount a partition, but someone would inevitably point out some circumstance involving a blue moon, cows in tutus dancing down Broadway, and a Libertarian presidential victory, under which you could safely or intelligently write a damaged partition read-write. So, for completeness, you can use the "-f" flag to force a dirty file system to mount read-write. This may crash your system, damage your data further, or any combination of the two.

```
# mount -f /tmp
#
```

Mounting All Standard File Systems

To mount all the file systems as listed in /etc/fstab, use the "-A" option.

```
# mount -A
#
```

This will not mount file systems with the "noauto" option set.

Mounting Partitions at Other Mount Points

You can mount partitions at arbitrary locations if you have the block device name and the mount point. You might use this when you're installing a new disk, so you can copy the contents of the old partition onto their new location, or you can use this to mount temporary file systems. Here, we mount a partition on a SCSI disk under /mnt.

```
# mount /dev/sd0a /mnt
#
```

Unmounting FFS File Systems

When you need to disconnect a mounted file system, you can unmount it with umount(8). The only argument you need is the mount point. Here, I'm unmounting that same SCSI disk — although it could be anything that is mounted at /mnt.

```
# umount /mnt
#
```

If you cannot unmount a drive, you're probably accessing it in some way. If you are reading or writing a file on a partition, you cannot unmount it. You cannot even have a command prompt sitting idle in a directory on that partition if you want to unmount it. If you think that you have nothing in a file system, but you still get complaints that the file system is busy, use fstat(1) or install /usr/ports/sysutils/lsof to identify the problem.

Mounting Foreign File Systems

For our purposes, any partition that doesn't have an FFS file system is a foreign file system. Fortunately, OpenBSD includes extensive support for these foreign file systems, with the caveat that only those functions supported by the file system will work. FAT doesn't set security permissions, for example. You can set file system security flags on a FAT file system all you want, but they won't change anything.

Each file system has its own unique mount program that handles the vagaries of that file system, and each file system needs support in the kernel. To make your life a little easier, mount(8) can recognize the standard file systems and can call the correct mount program as needed. Also, every file system reliably supported by OpenBSD is in the GENERIC kernel.

Using Foreign Mounts

To mount a foreign file system you need the same information you would need when mounting an FFS file system: a device name and a mount point. You may also need to know the type of file system you'll be mounting.

For example, let's mount a CD-ROM. Our system has one CD-ROM drive, /dev/cd0. A CD-ROM has only partition on it, and that partition takes up the whole disk, so we want the whole-disk partition, or "c." The device name for a CD-ROM partition is /dev/cd0c. We'll let mount(8) try to figure out what sort of file system this is.

```
# mount_cd9660 /dev/cd0c /cdrom
#
```

This may take longer than a hard disk mount, simply because the CD-ROM must spin up the disk before the kernel can mount it.

Mount(8) may be smart, but it cannot always guess correctly. It's easy to determine that a file system in a CD-ROM is a CD-ROM file system – the chances that it will be a network file system or a UNIX file system are really pretty slim. Other guesses are not so easy. Here, I'm trying to mount a floppy disk of unknown format.

```
# mount /dev/fd0c /mnt/
mount_ffs: /dev/fd0c on /mnt: Inappropriate file type or format
#
```

Mount(8) guessed that this was an FFS floppy, which is apparently not correct. If I explicitly use the program to mount FAT file systems, it works just fine.

No matter what sort of file system you have mounted, umount(8) can unmount it.

```
# umount /mnt/
#
```

Vnodes, Foreign File Systems, and FFS

Earlier we discussed inodes and blocks, the building blocks of FFS. This worked well in the early days of UNIX, but as years passed it became normal to swap disks between different machines and different operating systems. CD-ROMs, with their unique file system, became popular; floppy disks converged on FAT32 as a standard; and other UNIXes developed their own file systems. Because BSD needed to speak to all these different systems, another layer of abstraction was needed.

That abstraction was the *virtual node*, or *vnode*. You never directly manipulate vnodes, but you'll see references to them throughout the system documentation, so it's important to know what they are. The vnode is a translator between the kernel and whatever sort of file system you have mounted. Every tool that reads and writes to disks actually does so through vnodes, which map the data to the appropriate file system for the underlying media. You'll see references to inodes only when dealing with FFS file systems, but you'll see vnodes when you deal with any file system.

When you write a file to a FFS file system, the vnode talks to an inode. When you write a file to a Microsoft-style FAT32 file system, the vnode talks to the file allocation table. Vnodes are actually used for far more than just interacting with the file system, but we won't get into that here. To learn more about vnodes, read vnode(9).

Foreign File System Types

Here are some of the most commonly used foreign file systems, along with a brief description of each and the appropriate mount command.

MS-DOS

OpenBSD supports FAT, FAT16, and FAT32 file systems, the standard DOS/ Windows format commonly used in dual-boot systems and on floppy disks. You can format a floppy disk in FFS, however, so you cannot assume that all floppy disks are MS-DOS formatted. If you try to mount a floppy disk and it won't work as an MS-DOS disk, try to mount it as an FFS disk. Personally, my only use for floppy disks is to transfer files to and from a Windows machine that I don't control — for example, for taking files to the print shop. I make it my personal standard to always format floppy disks in MS-DOS format.

The mount command is mount_msdos(8).

```
# mount_msdos /dev/fd0c /mnt
```

If you work with a lot of MS-DOS file systems check out /usr/ports/sysutils/ mtools, a collection of programs for working with MS-DOS partitions that offers you the ability to access MS-DOS disks without mounting them. While mount_msdos(8) works reliably, if you want a prettier interface this is for you.

ISO-9660

ISO-9660 is the standard data CD-ROM file system. OpenBSD reads CD-ROMs, and also has integrated tools to write to CD-ROM (mkisofs(8)). Just about every CD-ROM you will ever encounter has ISO-9660 format. The mount command is mount_cd9660(8), although mount(8) is very good about autodetecting this file system.

```
# mount_cd9660 /dev/cd1c /cdrom
```

ext2fs

The standard Linux filesystem, ext2fs, supports many of the same features as FFS and can safely be written to and read from without any problems. You may need this in a dual-boot Linux/OpenBSD machine, or if you need to get information off of a Linux hard drive. The mount command is mount_ext2fs.

```
# mount_ext2fs /dev/wd0l /linux/usr
```

File System Permissions

Different file systems have different permissions schemes. For example, both FFS and ext2fs store permissions in the file system, mapping them to user ID numbers (UIDs). Because ext2fs normally behaves much like FFS, and all the permissions information it needs is available within the file system, OpenBSD respects its permissions. The UIDs might not match up to what you have on your OpenBSD system, which can cause a wide variety of separate problems, but the permissions *are* respected.

MS-DOS file systems, on the other hand, have no permissions scheme. You can use the "-u" and "-g" flags to set the user and group ownership of mounted MS-DOS file systems. For example, to mount a MS-DOS disk to be owned by the user "phil" and the group "staff," mount it as such.

```
# mount_msdos -u phil -g staff /dev/fd0c /mnt
```

Removable Media

The two most common tasks with removable media are mounting CD-ROMs and floppies, and formatting floppy disks. We'll discuss how to simplify both of them.

Removable Disks and /etc/fstab

Typing long commands for mounting common media can be tedious and annoying. I usually edit /etc/fstab to make life a little easier. If a removable filesystem has an entry in /etc/fstab, you can drop the device name when mounting it and you can just use mount(8) instead of the file system–specific command.

```
# mount /mnt
```

That's far easier than typing "mount_msdos /dev/fd0c /mnt" every time, isn't it?

Here are some sample entries for /etc/fstab to mount MS-DOS floppies on /mnt and CD-ROMs on /cdrom. (OpenBSD does not create a /cdrom directory during the install, so you must create that directory before this will work.)

```
/dev/cd0c /cdrom cd9660 ro,noauto
/dev/fd0c /mnt msdos rw,noauto
```

Formatting Floppies

What most Windows users think of as "formatting a floppy" is actually a multi-stage process that includes performing a low-level format, giving it a disklabel, and creating a file system. You must do all of these tasks to make a usable floppy in OpenBSD.

Start by doing a low-level format of the floppy disk with fdformat(8). This program only requires one argument, the floppy's device name.

```
# fdformat /dev/fd0c
Format 1440K floppy `/dev/fd0c'? (y/n): y
```

When you type y, fdformat(8) will start running a low-level format to prepare the disk to receive a file system. Low-level formatting is the slowest part of making a floppy usable.

Once you have formatted the disk, you can decide to put either a FFS or MS-DOS filesystem on the floppy.

MS-DOS File Systems

To swap data between a Windows machine and your OpenBSD box, format your floppy with the MS-DOS file system. The OpenBSD program newfs_msdos(8) provides this functionality.

```
# newfs_msdos /dev/rfd0c
/dev/rfd0c: 2840 sectors in 355 FAT12 clusters (4096 bytes/cluster)
bps=512 spc=8 res=1 nft=2 rde=512 sec=2880 mid=0xf0 spf=2 spt=18 hds=2 hid=0
#
```

That's it!

FFS File Systems

FFS file systems need a valid disklabel on every disk, even something as simple as a floppy. disklabel(8) can grab predefined disklabels from /etc/disktab and copy them to a disk, which simplifies the process considerably. While disklabel(8) can also create partition information or mark a disk as bootable, this is all overkill for a floppy disk. You can do all the required labeling by just running:

```
# disklabel ❶-w ❷/dev/rfd0c ❸floppy
```

The ❶"-w" option tells disklabel(8) to write to the raw disk device ❷/dev/rfd0c, using the ❸"floppy" label from /etc/disktab.

Now that you have a label, you can create a file system with newfs(8).

```
# newfs /dev/rfd0c
/dev/rfd0c:     2880 sectors in 80 cylinders of 2 tracks, 18 sectors
        1.4MB in 5 cyl groups (16 c/g, 0.28MB/g, 64 i/g)
super-block backups (for fsck -b #) at:
 32, 640, 1184, 1792, 2336,
#
```

That looks much more interesting than the MS-DOS file system–creation output, doesn't it? FFS is a more complex file system than any variant of FAT. The various MS-DOS file systems are more interchangeable between machines, however, being something of a lowest common denominator these days. You need to decide what best suits your needs.

Adding New Hard Disks

When you first install OpenBSD, the install program handles formatting and partitioning your hard disks and walks you through partitioning and mounting them. When you have to add disks to an existing system, you'll need to run the commands to perform these actions. The good news is, if you can install OpenBSD you already know how to work the commands — the only hard part will be learning which commands to run.

We'll cover two examples: creating an empty /usr/obj partition for upgrading your system and moving /home to a new disk. Just as if you were starting an install, write down how you want your new hard drive to be partitioned.

NOTE *Before you start, be absolutely certain you have backed up your system!*

fdisk

Do you want your new hard drive to be dedicated to OpenBSD? If so, fdisk(8) will easily let you initialize the MBR partition table. Here, we're dedicating the first SCSI hard disk to OpenBSD partitions. fdisk(8) requires access to the raw device, and we want to work on the entire disk, so we're using device node /dev/rsd0c.

```
# fdisk -i /dev/rsd0c
        -----------------------------------------------------
        ------ ATTENTION - UPDATING MASTER BOOT RECORD ------
        -----------------------------------------------------
Do you wish to write new MBR and partition table? [n] y
#
```

Answer "y", and your disk will be updated. If you're not certain, enter "n" to cancel.

If you have a multiboot system, you may want to split your hard drive between multiple operating systems. Just as if you're doing an install, you want to use an operating system's native tools to create MBR partitions for that operating system.

```
# fdisk -e /dev/rsd0c
Enter 'help' for information
fdisk: 1>
```

This is the same fdisk(8) prompt we saw during a multiboot installation. See Chapter 4 for detailed instructions on how to use it.

Once you have MBR partitions on your disk, you can proceed to assign OpenBSD partitions.

Partitioning

If you used fdisk to dedicate this hard drive to OpenBSD, the drive automatically has one large "a" partition that covers the entire drive. If this is what you want, you're done. If not, you must use disklabel(8) to divide the hard disk into partitions. You can use disklabel(8) to partition the drive in two ways: a straight text menu or the same interactive process that we used during the install.

If you know exactly what you want and are comfortable with cylinder/head/sector calculations, you can jump straight into a text editor and make the changes directly to the label. The "-e" flag to disklabel(8) will bring up a text editor containing the current disklabel, letting you make whatever changes you like.

```
# disklabel -e /dev/rsd0c
```

Personally, I find calculating cylinder boundaries to be a waste of time when disklabel(8) will do it for me. The "-E" flag will dump you in the same interactive disklabel(8) editor we used in the install.

```
# disklabel -E /dev/rsd0c
# using MBR partition 3: type A6 off 198 (0xc6) size 8302932 (0x7eb154)

Treating sectors 198-8303130 as the OpenBSD portion of the disk.
You can use the 'b' command to change this.

Initial label editor (enter '?' for help at any prompt)
>
```

This should look fairly familiar from Chapter 3.

Once you're done, you can check your work by asking disklabel(8) to print out the complete label on the disk. Running disklabel with only one argument, the disk name, will print out the label currently on the disk.

```
# disklabel /dev/rsd0c
```

Once you're satisfied with your partitioning, you can create a file system on the new partitions.

Creating File Systems

Use newfs(8) to create file systems on each of your new OpenBSD partitions. If you're an very experienced UNIX administrator, you may wish to specify your own block and fragment sizes, and fdisk(8) describes the flags you need to use for that. (On the other hand, if you're an experienced UNIX administrator, you know better than to specify your own block and fragment sizes on most hardware most of the time.) The rest of us can just run newfs(8), telling it the device name for the partition we want to format.

```
# newfs /dev/rsd0a
/dev/rsd0a:    8302932 sectors in 8387 cylinders of 5 tracks, 198 sectors
        4054.2MB in 525 cyl groups (16 c/g, 7.73MB/g, 1856 i/g)
super-block backups (for fsck -b #) at:
 32, 16080, 32128, 48176, 64224, 80272, 96320, 112368, 126752, 142800, 158848,
...
```

You will see quite a few lines giving alternate superblocks for this drive, as newfs(8) crawls over the disk and prepares the file system. Once it's finished, you have a file system and the disk is ready to use.

Mounting Your New Drive

If this new disk is going to be placed on an empty mount point, just mount it! In this case, I'm using this old SCSI disk for my /usr/obj directory.

```
# mount /dev/sd0 /usr/obj
```

Then you just need an appropriate entry for /etc/fstab, and you're done.

Moving Data to a New Partition

If this drive is intended to hold data that is elsewhere on the drive, you'll need to move the data before mounting the drive. (Read "Stackable Mounts" later this chapter for more notes on this.) If the files are in use (e.g., log files), you'll need to boot into single-user mode to move them.

Start by mounting your new partition at a temporary location.

```
# mount /dev/sd0a /mnt
```

You can then use tar(1) or cpio(1) to copy the files to the temporary location. Here, I'm moving /usr/ports to the partition temporarily mounted at /mnt.

```
# ( cd /usr/ports && tar cf - . ) | (cd /mnt && tar xpf - )
```

This does not delete the files from their original location. Once you're certain that they've been copied correctly, use "rm -rf" to remove them. Once the new mount point is empty, you can unmount the drive from /mnt and mount it at its permanent home. Be sure to update /etc/fstab for the new drive.

Stackable Mounts

OpenBSD file systems are stackable, which means that you can mount one partition over another. Suppose you have followed the example above, and copied /usr/ports onto a new partition, and then mount the new partition without removing the data from the old one. The old partition will not gain any free space; the data from the old /usr/ports is still there! Because your new partition is mounted "above" the old disk you cannot access the old data, but it's still there. Unmount the new /usr/ports and remove the old /usr/ports to gain the space back.

Memory File Systems

OpenBSD's memory file system, or MFS, allows you to create a "virtual hard disk" out of RAM. Essentially, you can use system memory as a hard drive. You can write files to this virtual hard disk just like any other hard disk in your system. Because files on a MFS partition are already in memory, they can be accessed with a memory-to-memory copy. This is extremely fast compared to a disk-to-memory copy. As with everything else in memory, however, you lose all data on that partition when the computer goes down or if you unmount that partition.

You can even use MFS as a "scratch" partition to compile, compress/decompress, or manipulate files rapidly. If you have enough RAM, a MFS /usr/obj will vastly accelerate "make build." Some people even store news server history files or database lockfiles on MFS to noticeably enhance performance.

MFS and Swap

MFS is effective in situations where the system swaps regularly. The kernel keeps any information being actively used in memory, while transferring unused information to swap. This is excellent for partitions like /tmp in which small files that are used frequently can be accessed quickly. Files that are less frequently accessed end up in swap, with performance roughly similar to standard UFS. You can even have a MFS partition larger than your physical memory, although if you run short on combined memory/swap your system will still be in deep trouble.

Creating an MFS Partition

Let's start by creating a temporary MFS partition on the command line with mount_mfs(8). Like the other mount commands, mount_mfs(8) takes two arguments, the physical device and a mount point. Memory doesn't have a device name, however, so we use the device name of the system swap space. If you have multiple swap partitions, just pick one.

```
# mount_mfs /dev/wd0b /tmp/db/
```

This creates a partition of a size a little bit less than the swap space you chose as a device. It's generally a good idea to specify a maximum size on an MFS partition, so that you will have some memory and/or swap available in case the MFS partition fills up. You can specify the size with the "-s" flag, giving an argument in sectors. A sector is 512K, which isn't exactly a useful measurement these days; multiply the size of your desired MFS partition in megabytes by 2,048 to get the number of sectors. For example, a 256MB partition uses 524,288 sectors. Here, we create a 256MB /tmp/db MFS file system.

```
# mount_mfs -s 524288 /dev/wd0b /tmp/db/
```

Mounting MFS Partitions at Boot

You can automatically create a MFS partition at boot time by making the proper entry in /etc/fstab. All you need is the device name of your swap partition, the mount point, and the number of sectors you want this partition to use. You'll make an entry in /etc/fstab, much like those discussed earlier, but with some minor tweaks.

| ❶/dev/wd0b | ❷/tmp/db | ❸mfs | ❹rw,async,-s=524288 | ❺0 | ❻0 |

First we have the ❶device name and the ❷mount point, exactly as in an /etc/fstab entry for a standard UFS file system. The ❸file system type is MFS. Our ❹options are a little different than those used by a FFS partition, however. We can safely mount an MFS partition "async," to enhance performance, because a system crash will result in complete and total data loss on this partition anyway. You might also want "nodev" and "nosuid" options on this partition. We also specify the maximum size of the partition with the "-s" option. Make sure you have the equal sign between the -s and the number of sectors the partition fills; /etc/fstab uses spaces to separate fields, and without the equal sign you'll be dumping this disk at dump levels of 524,288 or higher!

Because the data on a MFS partition is disposable, you usually don't want to back it up, so you can set the ❺dump level to 0. And you should never have to fsck(8) a MFS partition at boot, so the ❻fsck pass number can also be zero.

This entry is the only change you have to make for a MFS partition to appear at runtime.

Mounting Disk Images

You can mount a disk image and access the image just as you would a disk partition. This is very useful for those times you want to extract a few files from an ISO image, without burning the image to CD-ROM and mounting it, or if you want to edit a floppy disk image. Mounting a disk image file has two steps. First, you need to attach disk image to a device node. Then, you can mount that device node as you would any other device.

OpenBSD provides the vnconfig(8) program to attach disk images to device nodes. Remember, a vnode is an abstraction layer between the kernel and a file system. vnconfig(8) tells the kernel that a file should have vnodes attached to it and which device node those vnodes should be accessible through.

Vnode Device Nodes

OpenBSD provides both standard and raw device nodes for vnode devices. The standard buffered vnode device nodes are /dev/svnd*, while the raw vnode device nodes are /dev/vnd*. All of the mount programs use buffered device nodes, so that's the sort of node you want to use.

If you look at the device nodes in /dev, you will notice that each of these device nodes has partition letters after it. Once the image is associated with a vnode, partitions within the disk will be available at the usual partition letters under the device node. For your initial steps, you will want to use the "c" partition that represents the whole disk, just as in disklabel(8).

The GENERIC kernel has four vnode devices. If you need to mount more than four disk images simultaneously, you will need to build a custom kernel.

Running vnconfig(8) and mount(8)

Vnconfig(8) takes two arguments, the node you want to use and the disk image you want to mount. Here, we mount a the floppy disk image /tmp/floppy33.fs on the vnode device /dev/svnd0.

```
# vnconfig /dev/svnd0c /tmp/floppy33.fs
```

This disk image is now tied to the device node /dev/svnd0.. You can mount it just as you would any other floppy disk device node.

```
# mount /dev/svnd0c /mnt
```

You can now access the contents of the disk image under /mnt.

Mount(8) cannot guess what sort of image is inside a disk image, so you must use the correct mount command. For example, if you're mounting an ISO, you *must* use mount_cd9660(8) instead of vanilla mount(8).

Disconnecting Disk Images

The svnd0c device will remain attached to this particular image until you tell it otherwise. You can mount and unmount the same image repeatedly using the same vnode device, but you cannot use the same vnode device for another file. Disconnect a vnode device from any disk image with vnconfig's "-u" flag.

```
# vnconfig -u /dev/svnd0c
```

You can now attach this vnode device to another image.

Encrypted Partitions

One of vnconfig(8)'s more interesting features is the ability to associate an encryption key with a vnode device. This means that you can create an encrypted disk partition image on your hard drive. It's not quite as direct as having the partition encrypted directly on the disk, but it's quite effective at protecting your data. To create an encrypted partition you need a file to use as the partition, an encryption key, and the same tools used for mounting disk images.

Creating a Partition File

Our partition file must be the exact size of the file system we want and can initially contain any information we want. We'll have to newfs(8) this new partition anyway, after all! For quickest results, just copy /dev/zero into a file of the size you require. Here, we create a 128MB file.

```
# dd ❶if=/dev/zero ❷of=/home/mwlucas/images/encrypted.image ❸bs=1024
❹count=131072
131072+0 records in
131072+0 records out
134217728 bytes transferred in 16.954 secs (7916179 bytes/sec)
#
```

We've used dd(1) before, but because you'll have to make some decisions here we'll dissect this command. The ❶if argument gives the input file we're copying from, and the ❷of argument tells dd(1) where to put the copy. The "bs" argument gives the size of each block copied. The default is 512 bytes, but I'm tired of multiplying everything by half a K, so I've set this to 1,024 bytes or 1K. The ❹count is the number of times the copy from /dev/zero is made. We want to create a 128MB file, and each megabyte is 1,024 bytes, so we copy 131,072 blocks.

Be conservative in sizing the file for your encrypted filesystem image. Each action on this file system must be run through the blowfish(3) encryption engine, so huge encrypted file systems containing everything on your hard drive are not necessarily optimal solutions to data security problems. If you only have a few megs of files that you need to encrypt, you don't need to create a 500MB encrypted disk image!

Partition File Setup

Now, associate that disk image file with a vnode device, much as you would a regular disk image. The only difference is the additional -k argument, which tells vnconfig(8) to request and use an encryption key.

```
# vnconfig -ck /dev/svnd0c /home/mwlucas/images/encrypted.image
Encryption key:
```

The vnconfig(8) command will pause until you enter an encryption key. Like passwords, encryption keys should contain a mix of alphanumeric and symbol characters and should not be recognizable words. Encryption keys can contain spaces. Because vnconfig(8) has no idea about what the contents of the file should be, you can enter an incorrect encryption key, and vnconfig(8) will run correctly. You won't know that the key is wrong until you attempt to use the image as a disk partition and cannot mount the partition or access the information in it.

Now that you have a file attached to the vnode device, you can run disklabel(8) on that image and partition it. By default, it will be one large "c" partition.

```
# disklabel -E /dev/svnd0c
❶disklabel: Can't get bios geometry: Device not configured
Initial label editor (enter '?' for help at any prompt)
>
```

You will see a ❶warning that disklabel(8) cannot get BIOS information for this disk device. That's to be expected — this disk device has nothing to do with the BIOS! disklabel(8) this image file as you would like. For most applications, a single large partition is suitable. Once the image is labeled correctly, create a file system on it.

```
# newfs /dev/rsvnd0c
```

Remember, newfs(8) works directly on the disk, not through the buffer, so you need to use the raw device. Your encrypted partition is now an actual partition instead of a bunch of disk space, so you can mount it as you would any other disk image.

```
# mount /dev/svnd0c /mnt
```

The encrypted partition will remain until you unmount the image file and unconfigure the vnode device.

```
# umount /mnt
# vnconfig -u /dev/svnd0c
```

If you unmount the partition, but do not unconfigure the vnode device, the vnode device will still remember the encryption key! The next person who can mount partitions won't need to bypass your encryption key, he can just mount the vnode device you're so kindly left unlocked and configured for him. If you need encrypted file systems, you also need to remember to unconfigure your vnode devices.

Unclean Shutdowns

If your system crashes, the encrypted partition will be forcibly unmounted just like the standard partitions. This means that the partition may have disassociated files or some other problems. Unfortunately, the system will not to fsck(8) this partition upon a reboot. You must perform the fsck(8) manually, which isn't too hard.

First, attach your image file to a vnode device with vnconfig(8) normally, making sure to enter the correct encryption key. Before you run mount(8), however, run fsck(8) by hand to clean up any possible damage.

```
# fsck -t ffs /dev/svnd0c
```

This will run a standard fsck(8) on the partition, just as if the partition was a usual FFS partition on disk. You must specify the file system type with the "-t" flag, however, as fsck(8) cannot readily identify a disk image file's file system.

Incorrect and Changing Keys

Vnconfig(8) has no idea what the data underlying a file is supposed to be; it just ties that data to a bunch of vnodes and attaches the whole mess to a vnode device. After vnconfig(8) prompts you for an encryption key, all transfers to and from that image file are passed through an encryption cycle with that key, whatever it is. This means that you will have no warning that you entered the incorrect encryption key until you attempt to mount the image file.

```
# mount /dev/svnd0c /mnt
mount_ffs: /dev/svnd0c on /mnt: Inappropriate file type or format
#
```

Mount(8) has tried to examine the data on the vnode device and found only garbage. Unconfigure the vnode device and reenter your encryption key.

Sadly, vnconfig(8) has no provisions for changing the encryption key used on a file system image. (To be pedantic, vnconfig(8) is very much the wrong place to implement such a change because the encryption really has very little to do with vnconfig(8).) If you need to change your encryption key, create a new partition with the desired key, copy the data to the new partition, and erase the old encrypted file.

Now that you understand everything you must about working with disks under OpenBSD, let's take a look at upgrading your operating system.

16

UPGRADING OPENBSD

The latest source code?
Fugu extraordinary!
Be brave and swallow.

System upgrades can make even seasoned systems administrators wish they had a simpler job, such as taming rabid weasels. While you can probably deal with a bit of odd behavior in a desktop system after an upgrade, your network firewall and servers must behave as expected. Many sysadmins avoid the whole issue by delaying upgrades as long as possible, until the system is old enough that it can be replaced with a new machine running a clean install of the new release.

Not only is this expensive, but it's very bad from a security standpoint. Computer systems must be patched, maintained, and upgraded, or an intruder will almost certainly compromise them.

The OpenBSD upgrade process isn't nearly as difficult as that used by many other UNIX-like operating systems, and is far more reliable than that used by many other operating systems. With proper preparation, you can upgrade your OpenBSD systems with a minimum of difficulty.

Why Upgrade?

The simplest answer to this good question is: because you don't have a choice. Security researchers, programmers, and skilled intruders continuously discover new ways to break into computers. While OpenBSD has gone for over seven years with "only one remote root hole in the default install," that doesn't mean that a two-year-old version of OpenBSD is secure. The OpenBSD Project only provides security updates for the two most recently released versions of its software. For example, when OpenBSD 3.5 comes out, OpenBSD 3.3 will be "end-of-lifed" and gradually lose support from the developer community. If a way to break into an OpenBSD 3.3 machine is discovered after version 3.5 comes out, the Project is not obliged to provide patches to fix the hole. You may be able to adjust new security patches to work on the older versions of the code, but backporting these patches will become increasingly difficult.

The good news is that various OpenBSD releases are usually binary-compatible. The MySQL install that you have running on your OpenBSD 2.9 machine will probably run just as well as ever on OpenBSD 3.3. You will probably want to upgrade that software as well, but the software wouldn't refuse to run just because you upgraded the operating system underneath it. This isn't guaranteed, but is common. You may need to reconfigure your software in some way or provide some other special support for it, however.

Applying security patches can also be considered an upgrade. Just because there isn't an exploitable problem in a default OpenBSD install doesn't mean that an exploitable problem doesn't exist in a feature that you turn on. For example, while OpenBSD 2.8 was out and current, a security hole was discovered in the telnet daemon. OpenBSD does not ship with telnetd enabled, so this wasn't a hole in the default install — but it is certainly a security problem in a function you might have chosen to enable! You must understand how to apply security patches, either by applying the patch in and of itself or by upgrading the entire system.

Versions of OpenBSD

Developers from around the world are continually making minor changes to the master OpenBSD source code repository. If you download the OpenBSD source code in the morning and download it again in the afternoon, you'll get two slightly different versions of the source code. This makes the traditional release numbering used by proprietary software less than practical. At any given moment, you can get a few different versions of OpenBSD: releases, -current, -stable, and snapshots.

Current

OpenBSD-current is simply the most recent development version of OpenBSD and contains code that is just making its public debut. OpenBSD-current is where much initial public review takes place and, at times, -current sees radical changes of the sort that give experienced systems administrators headaches. If a change in current temporarily breaks Web browsers, games, and database programs running on -current, but the change is for the long-term good, that's perfectly fine. These programs will work again before the next release of OpenBSD, but there's no requirement to have every program working perfectly at all times.

OpenBSD-current is available to the public at large, but it is intended for use by developers, testers, and interested parties. Support for generic UNIX user questions about -current is rather slim, because users are expected to be able to read the source code, fix problems, and contribute their work back to the community. If you can't read C, shell, and Perl, or don't feel like debugging your computer whenever something behaves in a manner you don't expect, or just don't like being left hanging until some volunteer somewhere finds the time to fix something that broke, -current is not for you.

Current is expected to work at all times, however. While it might break on occasion, those breaks are considered serious problems, and the OpenBSD team loses sleep over them. You might have to recompile your Web browser, but the project team requires a functioning core operating system at all times.

So, with all this, why would you want to run -current? One excellent reason to run -current is to test the operating system in your environment. If your new OpenBSD-current system panics under certain conditions, the OpenBSD group wants to know about it. You certainly run a risk by doing this, but the only way the operating system can be enhanced is when volunteers test the improvements in a variety of environments. If you can provide a good bug report, the developers want to hear about your crash.

If this doesn't sound like your idea of a good time, then don't run -current.

Snapshots

Every few days, the OpenBSD team builds a release from the latest -current code and puts it up on a FTP server. This interim release is a *snapshot* and is identified only by the date it is made available. There's nothing special about a snapshot, as compared to -current; it's just the state of -current at such-and-such a time. While the developers make a reasonable effort to not build a snapshot on a day that -current is utterly unusable, it may have any of the usual problems you'll see in tracking -current. There is no real quality-assurance process for snapshots.

Snapshots are mainly provided for installation convenience. It's much easier to upgrade to the latest OpenBSD-current from the most recent snapshot than it is to upgrade to -current from the most recent release.

Releases

Every six months, the pace of OpenBSD-current development is deliberately slowed. New features are polished and thoroughly tested, and public requests are made for beta testers of the latest snapshots. When the OpenBSD team is satisfied as to the quality of the software, a CVS tag (see CVS) is laid down, and a high-quality snapshot is built from that tag. This snapshot is called a *release* and is issued a number. This is almost certainly what you initially installed.

OpenBSD releases are numbered sequentially, starting with 2.0 and incrementing .1 with every release. Unlike most software products, a .0 release has no special meaning; it's just a point along a long path.

Once you have a release installed, you can start to follow the OpenBSD-stable patch branch.

Stable

OpenBSD-stable is simply OpenBSD-release with very minor patches. These patches are generally the "errata" for the release, including security fixes, things that are of great importance, or things that affect a lot of people. OpenBSD-stable is expected to be calm and reliable, requiring little user attention. According to Theo de Raadt, "The -stable tree must never get worse. It must never break. The fixes must be simple, even if hackjobs. They must not fail." This is an excellent choice for a production environment.

The only way to get OpenBSD-stable is to update the system from source. You can get effectively the same OS as -stable by applying the errata for a release, however.

Which Version Should You Use?

This release system gives users the best features of open source development and commercial releases. As a user, you have access to both the bleeding-edge experimental code and the stable, polished releases. You have everything you need to choose which release you want.

If you're running OpenBSD in a production environment, either use a release with the security errata or track stable.

If you're a network administrator evaluating OpenBSD for use in a production environment, install the version you plan to use — almost certainly a release with the security errata, or perhaps stable.

If you're just learning UNIX, use a release and apply the security errata.

If you're an operating system developer or experienced programmer, feel free to jump right into current. You should be able to handle any problems you encounter or use those problems as an excuse to expand your knowledge of UNIX programming.

Lastly, if you're a hobbyist, you can run anything! Just remember the limitations of the branch you're using. A release is a good place to start, but you can gradually upgrade your system to stable and then to current as your OpenBSD, UNIX, and programming understanding expands.

Errata

The public and security community closely scrutinizes each release of OpenBSD — again, there's nothing like claiming to be the best to make people try to knock you down. Bugs are frequently found after a release, but most of these bugs are trivial. If a bug is bad enough, the OpenBSD team will issue an *errata*. An errata is a fix for a serious bug that affects system security, reliability, or stability. (They may be issued for other reasons as well, but those are the most popular.) Errata are announced on the OpenBSD website, under the "Patches" link, and on the security-announce@OpenBSD.org mailing list. I highly recommend subscribing to security-announce, so that you can be notified of errata immediately when they are available.

Evaluate each errata for its impact on your environment, and decide how quickly you need to apply: Do you need this fix as soon as possible, or can it wait for a maintenance window? If an errata comes out for a part of the system you are not using, it isn't necessary to rush the patch into production. On the other hand, if an errata applies directly to a system component you are using, you should apply it as soon as possible. If you're experiencing a problem that can be explained by a new errata, you certainly want to install it immediately if not sooner!

Here's a typical errata entry for OpenBSD 3.2 from the website:

```
❶# 004: RELIABILITY FIX: November 6, 2002
❷A logic error in the pool kernel memory allocator could cause memory corruption
in low-memory situations, causing the system to crash.
❸A source code patch exists which remedies the problem.
```

Each errata has a ❶unique number within the release; the sample shown is errata #4 for OpenBSD 3.2. You'll also get a ❷brief description of the problem, and a ❸link to the patch that solves the issue. The information presented is generally enough to decide if you need to worry about the issue. Any errata that discusses system crashes should certainly be applied!

As I write this, OpenBSD 3.2 has four errata. Two are "reliability fixes," one of which is shown above. The other is a patch for OpenBSD systems configured as bridges that are also using PF scrubbing. The other two issues are security problems, one affecting the Sendmail restricted shell smrsh(8) and the other affecting the Kerberos administration daemon. If you're using these features, you need to apply the patches as soon as possible. If you're not using the features you should still apply the patches, but you don't need to rush them into place.

Errata should be applied in order, as a later errata can touch a piece of code affected by earlier errata. For example, if you have two errata that affect a single program, the second errata assumes that the first has been applied. You might get unpleasant results by applying errata out of order.

Errata Prerequisites

Before you can use any of the errata, you need to have both the kernel and the system source code available and ready for use on your system. If you read Chapter 5 and did as suggested, you have everything you need. If not, go back to Chapter 5 and install the source code for both the userland programs and the kernel on your system before trying to continue.

Applying Errata

Download the indicated source code patch for the errata and review it. Each errata has instructions at the top and actual code below. The instructions for kernel patches are usually the simplest, while patches for userland programs go into more depth. That's largely because the kernel has its own build process, which we cover in great depth in Chapter 12, and you're assumed to know it. Still, let's look at both. Here are the instructions for OpenBSD 3.2 errata #4.

```
Apply by doing:
    cd /usr/src
    patch -p0 < 004_pool.patch
And then rebuild your kernel.
```

Let's see what happens. The only possible complication here is that you need to give the full path to the errata file. In this case, I've stored the patch under /home/mwlucas/errata.

```
# patch -p0 < /home/mwlucas/errata/004_pool.patch
Hmm...  Looks like a unified diff to me...
The text leading up to this was:
```

You'll then see the instructions for applying the patch, as patch(1) separates them out from actual code. The program will generate comparisons between the patch and the file(s) being patched and should eventually try to apply the patches directly to the source code. If the errata patch is successful, you will see something like this:

```
Patching file sys/kern/subr_pool.c using Plan A...
Hunk #1 succeeded at 1.
Hunk #2 succeeded at 1947.
Hunk #3 succeeded at 1962.
Hunk #4 succeeded at 1982.
done
#
```

The patch examined four different parts of this file and was able to successfully alter each section of the file as it should. Your source code is now patched, and you can just rebuild the kernel.

Suppose something goes wrong? Here's what you look for to see if a patch fails:

```
Hunk #1 succeeded at 1.
Hunk #2 failed❶ at 2470.
Hunk #3 succeeded at 2507.
Hunk #4 succeeded at 2525.
1 out of 4 hunks failed--saving rejects to sys/net/if_bridge.c.rej❷
```

Part of the patch ❶failed to apply, which means that either your patch was damaged during the download or the system source code on your system is damaged in some way.[1] More likely you didn't apply some previous errata, or someone has edited the source code. Patch(1) will tell you ❷where the failed piece of the patch is saved, so you can try to identify the problem.

Compiling Kernel Errata

If you're running in the default configuration, you just need to rebuild and reinstall the GENERIC kernel. The following commands will rebuild and reinstall a GENERIC kernel when you're logged in as root.

```
# cd /sys/arch/i386/conf
# config GENERIC
# cd ../compile/GENERIC/
# make depend
# make
# cp /bsd /bsd.old
# cp bsd /bsd
# reboot
```

We discuss compiling kernels from source in great detail in Chapter 12.

Compiling Userland Errata

Userland errata are slightly more difficult to compile than kernel errata, if only because the process is unique to each patch. Follow the instructions in the errata *exactly*, performing all tasks as root. The errata includes the exact commands to run. If you do not follow the instructions precisely, you will have problems afterward.

Upgrading OpenBSD

An OpenBSD upgrade has three distinct phases: installing the newer versions of binaries and files on disk, updating the local configuration information, and updating obsolete add-on software packages. Each is a separate process and must be handled independently.

Upgrade Prerequisites

Before you upgrade, back up any data you actually care about. The upgrade process extracts new files over the existing system, and it's entirely possible that you might overwrite something important. Back up your data!

---

[1] Both of these are very rare. To write this demonstration, I had to deliberately damage the patch file.

To update your configuration files you must have the system source code for the version you are upgrading to available in /usr/src, even if you upgrade from a CD-ROM or over the network. If space is at a premium you could install only the contents of /usr/src/etc, but you must be able to compare the contents of your old /etc/ directory with what should be in the new version and make the appropriate changes. You can keep the source code for the old version of OpenBSD around if you wish, but it must not be under /usr/src.

Once you have backups and the system source installed, you need to decide which distribution sets you want to install during the upgrade. As a rule, you must install any distribution sets that were previously installed, but you can choose to install additional sets if you desire.

Upgrading Base Software

The OpenBSD base system includes everything that is in one of the distribution sets you originally installed. The base system does not include add-on packages, nor any software you installed by hand. This is the very heart of the system upgrade. In this section, we're going to discuss upgrading to a release of OpenBSD from a CD-ROM or over the network; however, the exact same process applies to upgrading to a snapshot. Much of this information also applies to building and upgrading the system from source code, but building from source is a far more complicated and risky process and is covered in its own section.

The Upgrading Mini-FAQ

Basic system features change as OpenBSD evolves. This wouldn't be a big problem, except when interdependent changes create a chicken-and-egg or "bootstrap" problem. If you just blindly run the upgrade process and don't handle any other required changes, you'll find that your system suffers from a variety of errors. If you're building the new system from source, you may find that these problems prevent the build from completing. All of the problems should be solvable by anyone who should be building the system from source, but it's nice to have them documented in a single place. The Upgrading Mini-FAQ (http://www.OpenBSD.org/faq/upgrade-minifaq.html, or linked off the main FAQ page) documents these problems to make upgrades easier.

The Mini-FAQ is divided into chunks describing the changes necessary to upgrade from a particular release. For example, to upgrade from 3.1 to 3.2 check under "Upgrading from 3.1." There it gives several programs that must be built and installed before you can begin an upgrade from source, and several users and groups that must be added before you begin any sort of upgrade.

Before you start to upgrade your system, take a look at the Upgrading Mini-FAQ. Some of the changes only apply if you are upgrading via source code, while other types of upgrades require you to make different changes. Generally speaking, the instructions that apply for the build clearly say something along the lines of "to install this library, run these shell commands." Other upgrade requirements are typical systems administration duties: adding users and groups, adding entries to /etc/ files, or changing permissions on directories.

Upgrade instructions fall into these general categories.

New Users and Groups

Add any new users or groups before beginning the upgrade. Updated programs will expect to be owned by these new users and groups, and if the user isn't there the programs will behave in unexpected ways or will flat-out refuse to install.

Install Programs

When bootstrap tools such as gcc(1) and perl(1) are upgraded, the new system generally expects to be built with the upgraded tool. If you are upgrading from source code, you must install these bootstrap tools before beginning to compile the new version of OpenBSD. The Upgrading Mini-FAQ notes which programs must be upgraded and how to build and install them.

Uninstall Programs

Sometimes programs are removed from the base OpenBSD distribution. For example, in OpenBSD 3.2 the at(1) program was merged into cron(1), so the Mini-FAQ recommends changing /etc/crontab and removing the binaries and man pages when upgrading from 3.1. These changes can be taken after the upgrade.

System Configuration

You might have other general system configuration changes to make, such as entries in various /etc files. These changes might be required either before or after updating the installed programs. In general, read the Mini-FAQ and follow what it recommends. Your programs may not run as expected if you do not make these changes, so be sure to follow them!

Customized Upgrades

The upgrade process supports the same custom siteXX.tgz file discussed in Chapter 3. What's more, it also supports running custom post-upgrade scripts as part of the upgrade process. When the rest of the upgrade process finishes, the upgrade program checks for a script "upgrade.site" in the root directory. If it finds this script, it executes it as the last step of the upgrade.

You can create /upgrade.site on the system before starting the upgrade, which makes it much simpler to use than the equivalent install.site functionality discussed in Chapter 3.

Installing Updated Base Software

Once you complete the necessary pre-upgrade steps as described in the Upgrading Mini-FAQ, you can install the updated userland and kernel. The very simplest way to do any of this is from a CD-ROM or network server. (You can also install the updated system from a locally compiled source tree, but that's part of the upgrade from source process, which we cover separately.) Whichever method you choose, the process bears a great deal of resemblance to the initial installation process.

Prepare boot media for the version of OpenBSD you want to upgrade to; if you're running OpenBSD 3.4, and you want to upgrade to 3.5, you need an OpenBSD 3.5 boot floppy or CD-ROM. Do not attempt to use a boot disk from the wrong version of OpenBSD, or you will be exceptionally unhappy with the botch of a system you'll end up with. Boot off this new boot media. You will see the usual OpenBSD boot messages scroll past, concluding with the original prompt you saw at the beginning of the install.

```
erase ^?, werase ^W, kill ^U, intr ^C, status ^T
(I)nstall, (U)pgrade or (S)hell? u
```

This time, we want to upgrade. Enter "u". You'll see the same welcome-to-the-install message we saw in Chapter 3, with the word "upgrade" substituted for "install." Many of the instructions displayed at the beginning of the upgrade program are absolutely the same as those from the install program, so I'll just refer you back to Chapter 3 for questions on what they mean.

```
Specify terminal type: [vt220] ❶
Do you wish to select a keyboard encoding table? [n] ❷

IS YOUR DATA BACKED UP? As with anything that modifies disk contents, this
program can cause SIGNIFICANT data loss. ❸

NOTE: once your system has been upgraded, you must manually merge any changes
to files in the 'etc' set into the files already on your system. ❹



Proceed with upgrade? [n] y❺
```

We discuss the ❶terminal type and the ❷keyboard encoding table in Chapter 3. You can almost certainly accept the defaults for both of these.

I warned you about backups, and ❸now the installer has warned you. Is your data backed up? If you're not certain, stop now and check!

The ❹warning about your /etc/ files is fairly small, for what is generally considered the most difficult part of the upgrade process; we'll cover that in "Merging /etc" later this chapter.

If you're ready, ❺enter "y" to continue with the upgrade.

```
Available disks are: sd0 sd1 wd0.
Which one is the root disk? (or done) [done] wd0❶
Root filesystem? [wd0a] ❷
```

By ❶"root disk," the upgrade program means "which disk has your root partition on it?" If you followed standard installation practice, the upgrade program should be able to ❷guess which partition on your disk is your root partition. If you did put your root partition somewhere other than the "a" partition, enter the device name for your root partition. OpenBSD will perform basic file system checks on the root partition and, if all is well, proceed.

```
Enable network using configuration stored on root filesystem? [y]
```

You only need to enable the network if you plan to upgrade your base system via FTP, HTTP, or some other network protocol. If you enable the network you'll see several screens of network configuration information flow by as OpenBSD reads the system configuration and the installer prints out everything it finds as it sets up the system.

```
Do you want to do more, manual, network configuration? [n]
```

You'll get a chance to alter the network configuration manually if something doesn't look right, but if this system was on the network previously the setup should be correct as is.

The upgrade program now inspects /etc/fstab (see Chapter 14) and identifies the file systems that the root partition knows about. The installer will display /etc/fstab, and you'll see a series of warnings and notices about disk partition usage during the upgrade. Read those messages carefully. In general, only your OpenBSD partitions will be mounted read-write. Known partitions of other types, such as FAT32 and ext2fs, will be mounted read-only. NFS partitions and partitions labeled "noauto" will not be mounted. The program will give you a chance to edit a temporary copy of the file system table before proceeding, allowing you to not mount a partition you don't want to touch or make any other changes you like. You should be able to just take the default and continue.

```
Edit the fstab with ed? [n]
```

The installer performs basic fsck(8) checks on all the file systems and mounts them. Now you can tell the upgrade program where to find the upgraded you want to install. The process should look very familiar from Chapter 3.

```
Sets can be located on a (m)ounted filesystem; a (c)drom, (d)isk or (t)ape
device; or a (f)tp, (n)fs or (h)ttp server.
Where are the upgrade sets you want to use? (m, c, f, etc.)
```

The next several dialogs are exactly identical to the install process. You can pick a FTP or HTTP server, or just install from CD-ROM. You'll be asked for directory information, and a username and password if necessary. You'll then be asked about which sets you want to upgrade. You must reinstall all of the sets you installed previously!

Once you have chosen all of your distribution sets, the system will ask you if you're ready to proceed. Up until this point, you have done nothing irreversible; you can interrupt the process and reboot into an untouched system. Once you enter "y" here, however, you're committed.

```
Ready to upgrade sets? [y]
```

The upgrade program extracts all of the distribution sets you chose and over-writes the corresponding programs on the system.

```
What timezone are you in? ('?' for list) [EST]
You have selected timezone 'EST'.
```

While the installer remembers which time zone you had previously chosen, you might want to change it. The upgrade program rebuilds a variety of system settings, such as device nodes and bootblocks, and finally spits out a completion message that closely resembles the "successful installation" message. Just as you do on an install, enter "halt" to unmount your disks cleanly.

You could now restart your system and be running on an updated userland and kernel. Do *not* do it yet, though — you still have to deal with the /etc/ changes your upgrade caused.

Merging /etc

The /etc/ directory contains system and program configuration information. When a program is changed, the configuration file format or syntax may also change. If you try to run a program on an obsolete configuration file, the program might not run correctly. You absolutely must update /etc before running your system! We covered /etc/ in expansive detail in Chapter 14 and particular pieces of /etc/ throughout this book. If you're not familiar with UNIX, you may want to keep this book at hand as a reference when trying to update /etc/.

No automated process can know how your machine is supposed to behave, so you must handle any changes to /etc/ yourself. You'll have to compare almost every file under /etc/ to its counterpart under /usr/src/etc and handle any changes that you find. This is a very tedious process to do by hand, but OpenBSD has tools to make this much simpler.

Preparations

After running the upgrade program, remove the OpenBSD boot media from your system and reboot your computer into single-user mode (Chapter 6).

```
boot> boot -s❶
booting hd0a:/bsd:
...
Enter pathname of shell or RETURN for sh: /bin/sh❷
#
```

You can set any ❶other boot-time flags that don't interfere with a single-user boot, such as setting a tty to boot with a serial console. To get an actual shell prompt in single-user mode, you can just ❷hit ENTER or enter a full path to a shell other than sh. This alternate shell must be statically linked, as shared libraries are not yet available on the system. I recommend always sticking with /bin/sh in single-user mode.

Once you have a command prompt, perform some basic system setup. First, mount all of your usual partitions so you can have access to their files. Set a terminal type as well, so you can use vi(1) to edit system configurations.

```
# mount -a
# TERM=vt220; export TERM
#
```

You might also want to run df(1) to confirm that all your expected partitions are available.

Annoyingly, the "etc.tgz" distribution also contains the documentation for OpenBSD's integrated Apache web server. The program that is used to integrate changes to files within the /etc/ directory, mergemaster(8) will pick up these changed files as part of its comparison process and by default will ask you about each of these files. This can be extremely annoying, to say the least, and can make the /etc/ merging process much longer and far more tedious. The simplest way to get around this is to install the updated documentation from the installed source code, so that mergemaster(8) detects that the documents are up-to-date. Just run:

```
# cd /usr/src/usr.sbin/httpd
# make -f Makefile.bsd-wrapper distribution
```

Installing Mergemaster

The mergemaster(8) program compares the files in /etc/ to the files in the source code for /etc/, displays any differences, and allows you to update your /etc/, reject the changes, or manually merge the two files together.

You want to be certain to have the latest version of mergemaster before running it, however. This generally means that you want the version that's available for the version you just upgraded to. Check your installation media for the mergemaster package, and check /var/db/pkg/ to see if you already have mergemaster. If you have the latest mergemaster installed, you're ready. If you have an older version than that available on your installation media, uninstall it with pkg_delete(1). You can then install the mergemaster script from a package or port (/usr/ports/sysutils/mergemaster).

The Network in Single-User Mode During an Upgrade

You may notice that your network connection doesn't come up in single-user mode, which is a problem if you need to grab mergemaster from a FTP server. The script /etc/netstart should bring up your network, but that script is written for the older version of OpenBSD on your system. I recommend trying the following things in order to configure the network. First, try running /etc/netstart, which will probably function as expected.

```
# /bin/sh /etc/netstart
```

This might fail if some of the network configuration commands have changed to expect different arguments. If so, try running the new version of /etc/netstart from the source code on your local system.

```
# /bin/sh /usr/src/etc/netstart
```

This may still fail, because the configuration files in /etc/rc.conf are not synchronized with what that script expects. If so, you need to bring up the network by hand. See ifconfig(8) and route(8) for some hints. If the two previous methods failed, you might have most but not all of your network set up and only have to add a route or add a flag to an ifconfig(8) statement.

This sort of headache is typical of the sort of things you can expect to have to deal with until your /etc/ directory is fully updated.

Running Mergemaster

Once installed, mergemaster(8) can be found in /usr/local/sbin. The script will create an up-to-date "shadow" root directory in /var/tmp/temproot, and then compare the contents of the existing /etc/ directory. This can take quite some time, and generates a huge amount of output.

```
# /usr/local/sbin/mergemaster
*** Creating the temporary root environment in /var/tmp/temproot
 *** /var/tmp/temproot ready for use
 *** Creating and populating directory structure in /var/tmp/temproot
...
```

This sort of thing will go on for quite some time but eventually, mergemaster starts to compare the files.

```
*** Beginning comparison

 *** Temp ./dev/MAKEDEV and installed are the same, deleting
```

Here, mergemaster found a file that was the same on the installed system as it was in the source code. Because these files are identical, and either keeping the old file or installing the new one makes no difference whatsoever, it doesn't waste your time and deletes the temporary copy. This is actually not uncommon. Files with differences between versions are much more interesting, however.

```
 *** Displaying differences between ./etc/ssh/sshd_config❶ and installed version

--- /etc/ssh/sshd_config      Sat Apr 13 16:04:49 2002
+++ ./etc/ssh/sshd_config     Mon Nov 11 12:27:59 2002
@@ -1,7 +1,7 @@
❷-#     $OpenBSD: sshd_config,v 1.49 2002/03/21 20:51:12 markus Exp $
❸+#     $OpenBSD: sshd_config,v 1.59 2002/09/25 11:17:16 markus Exp $
```

Here, we're examining the installed ❶/etc/ssh/sshd_config and the version of sshd_config found in the latest source code. Lines from the two different files are intermixed, but lines from the old (currently installed) version have a leading minus sign, while lines found in the new version have a leading plus sign. This example shows us that the version number of this file changed from ❷1.49 to ❸1.59. Although this is a trivial change, it indicates that later in the file we will find quite a few additional changes. For example, later in the mergemaster output we'll see this entry.

```
-#LoginGraceTime 600
+#LoginGraceTime 120
```

Here, the LoginGraceTime variable has been reduced to 120 in the newer version of OpenBSD. You'd have to look in the sshd(8) documentation to see what this variable means, but the important thing for our example is that information in this file has changed. You need to decide if you want to update to the new configuration, or if you rely upon the behavior in your old configuration.

Once you reach the end of the file, mergemaster will present you with several options.

```
Use ❸'d' to delete the temporary ./etc/ssh/sshd_config
Use ❶'i' to install the temporary ./etc/ssh/sshd_config
Use ❷'m' to merge the temporary and installed versions
Use 'v' to view the diff results again

Default is to leave the temporary file to deal with by hand
How should I deal with this? [Leave it for later]
```

If the updated file can safely be plugged into your system as is, you want to ❶install it. Other files contain only system-specific information (i.e., master. passwd), and should not be replaced during an upgrade. You can just ❸delete the temporary copy of the new version of the file. The default is to not do anything and leave the file in the temporary directory, so you can later install this file by hand.

Some files have modifications local to the system, however, and replacing them will destroy the system configuration. This includes files such as /etc/rc. conf, which will include both local changes and new configuration options. I generally recommend that new users leave the new versions of these files in the temporary root directory (/var/tmp/temproot), and go back and merge the changes by hand. Mergemaster has the ability to create these files on the fly, however, using the ❷merge feature.

Merging Changes

The merge function in mergemaster is actually not that difficult to use, but requires close attention to detail. A mistake here can leave your system unbootable or damage data. We're going to walk through a merge of

/etc/rc.conf when upgrading a system from 3.1 to 3.2. Once you view the differences between the two files, hit "m" to begin the merge. Lines with differences will be presented side-by-side.

```
#     ❶$OpenBSD: rc.conf,v 1.72 2002 | #     ❷$OpenBSD: rc.conf,v 1.79 2002
%
```

Both entries are severely truncated by being displayed side-by-side, but they're still usable. The entry on the ❶left is currently installed in /etc, while the entry on the ❷right is the one from the new version of OpenBSD.

Mergemaster will walk through the entire file, creating a new file to install in /etc. Lines that are identical in both versions will be automatically entered into this file, and you can choose between the left and right entries on lines that have differences. Enter "r" to choose the entry on the right, and "l" to choose the entry on the left.

```
rdate_flags=NO          # for normal  | rdate_flags=NO          # for normal
%
```

On an entry such as this you could probably guess that the difference lies on the far right side of the line, as part of the comment. In this sort of case, you want the most recent version of the line — otherwise, the next time you upgrade, merge-master will complain about the line again! Enter "r".

```
photurisd_flags=NO      # for normal  <
%
```

Here, there's an entry on the left but none on the right. This entry has been removed from the file, so no /etc/rc scripts will be looking for this function. Delete the line by choosing the entry on the right — enter "r".

You don't always want the latest entry in /etc/rc.conf, however.

```
portmap=YES             # almost alwa | portmap=NO              # Note: inetd
%
```

The portmap daemon was set to YES, but the default is now NO. If you need portmap, don't turn it off during the upgrade! Choose "l".

Once you've processed the entire file, mergemaster(8) will give you some choices for your new file.

```
❶   Use 'i' to install merged file
❷   Use 'r' to re-do the merge
❸   Use 'v' to view the merged file
   Default is to leave the temporary file to deal with by hand

   *** How should I deal with the merged file? [Leave it for later] v
```

If you want to double-check your work, enter ❸"v". If you're satisfied with the results, you can enter ❶"i" to install the file you created. If you made a mistake, you can start over with "r".

Some file changes, such /dev/MAKEDEV, require other commands be run after updating the system. Mergemaster will ask you if it may run these commands. Let it. If you say no, your system may not work as desired.

```
*** Comparison complete

Do you wish to delete what is left of /var/tmp/temproot? [no]
```

If you have chosen to leave some files in /var/tmp/temproot to compare manually, you need to leave the directory. Otherwise, tell mergemaster to delete it. You never want to reuse the same /var/tmp/temproot between different upgrades.

Once all of your /etc files have been updated, reboot the system. You could theoretically just exit from single-user mode and boot into the new userland with new /etc/ files, but there is a small possibility for error. An extra reboot is a small price to make sure that your system starts perfectly cleanly.

Updating Ports and Packages

Now that your main system is updated, you can worry about the ports tree and the related packages installed on your system. While they're closely related, we'll consider the ports tree first and then evaluate how to upgrade installed packages.

One important thing to remember is that the ports and packages tree are closely tied to a version of OpenBSD. The ports tree for 3.2 will not run reliably on 3.3, and packages compiled for an older version may not run on a newer version. They might run, and probably will run, most of the time, for most purposes, usually. That's too many potential problems for my tastes, however. Whenever possible, I recommend starting over and reinstalling all software on the system from ports or packages built for the release you are using. That may be a luxury for some users, so we'll discuss some of the problems in upgrading packages.

We'll start by updating the ports tree.

Updating the Ports Tree

If you're installing from CD-ROM or FTP, you can update the ports tree simply by removing the old ports tree and extracting the new one. You might want to keep one old ports tree around for reference, simply because it contains the packages for the software you have installed at the moment. It's always nice to have the option to fall back a software version, in case the latest version has some horrible flaw.

```
# cd /usr
# mv ports ports-3.2
# tar -xzf /mnt/ports.tar.gz
#
```

That's it. (If you're installing from source, there are other ways to do this. We'll discuss those when we discuss source installs.)

Updating Installed Packages

The cleanest way to update your installed software is to remove everything you have installed already, and install everything from new packages for the release you are using. This frequently turns out to be far less work than updating everything piecemeal.

Some packages look like reinstalling would be a lot of work for no real gain. For example, the "gmake" package on both OpenBSD 3.1 and 3.2 is at version 3. 79.1. Why rip it out and replace it with something that looks the same? The package for 3.1 was built on an OpenBSD 3.1 system and various system infrastructure has changed since 3.2. Among other things the compiler has been upgraded, which means that although the program name and version is unchanged the actual binary the OpenBSD 3.2 gmake package installs may be quite different than that installed by the 3.1 package. For maximum safety, remove the 3.1 package and install the 3.2 package. On the other hand, the differences probably won't keep it from functioning. You could probably quite easily live with this older package for a few releases until it broke unexpectedly.

Finding Obsolete Packages

Perhaps you want to live with packages that were compiled on an older version of OpenBSD if their version is up-to-date and only upgrade obsolete packages. The biggest problem in this case is finding out which packages are obsolete. This is just tedious on a simple Web server with few packages, but can become a nightmare if you have dozens of packages installed. The simplest way to identify obsolete packages is with the up-to-date script available in /usr/ports/infrastructure/build.

```
# ./out-of-date
>>> Is /usr/ports/INDEX up-to-date ?❶
>>> Otherwise, this script will find out outdated flavors of packages
>>> compared to your installed packages...
❷Update tcsh-6.10.00-static to one of ❸tcsh-6.12.00 tcsh-6.12.00-static
Update png-1.2.1 to png-1.2.4
...
#
```

If you installed the ports tree by extracting the ports.tar.gz for the release of OpenBSD you are currently running, you can ignore the ❶warning about /usr/ports/INDEX; it only applies if you update your ports tree using CVS.

The script then lists every piece of packaged software on your system that has a newer version available in the ports tree. For example, the ❷tcsh shell has been upgraded from 6.10.00 to 6.12.00. Those changes may or may not be worth updating the package for, but when in doubt, upgrade. The script also lists all the ❸available flavors of the updated package.

Dependencies in Updated Packages

OpenBSD packages that depend on other packages require the exact version of dependent packages. For example, if a package requires tcsh-6.10.00, and you install tcsh-6.12.00, you may find that the other package will not run or will not behave properly.

One problem comes from the fact that packages that are required by other packages record the names of the packages that need them in a file in their /var/db/pkg/ directory, called +REQUIRED_BY. The package tools check for the existence of this file, and will refuse to uninstall a package if it is required by other packages. You can force pkg_delete(1) to uninstall a package by using the "-f" flag to "force" the uninstall, but this will destroy the entire /var/db/pkg entry, included the +REQUIRED_BY file. You can maintain entries in this file by hand, but that is difficult and tedious.[2]

With this maze of documentation for interdependent programs, you're better off just reinstalling all your packages after an upgrade. Your data will stay; just your programs will change.

Upgrades from Source

Upgrading from source is intended only for advanced users who are not afraid of compiling C, debugging problems, and restoring from backup. It's also the only way to get the very latest development and stable versions of OpenBSD, so it's worth learning about.

When you upgrade from source, you are essentially building the distribution sets that you installed during the CD-ROM or FTP install. They aren't bundled up as distributions, but the contents are the same. You'll still have to run mergemaster(8), and you will still need to update your installed software. The only thing building your system from source gets you is the latest version of the branch you're using.

Source Code Distribution

The first task you need to perform when building the system from source is getting the source code. The OpenBSD Project uses CVS (Concurrent Versions System) to maintain its source code repositories. When a developer implements an improvement he integrates this change into the CVS repository, which is distributed and mirrored across the world in a matter of hours. The master CVS server tracks source code, all changes made to it, and who made those changes;

---

[2] If you search on the Internet, you will find a few different scripts that are designed to recurse through the ports tree and rebuild all outdated applications and their dependencies. These scripts are not yet mature enough that I'm comfortable recommending any of them, but people are hard at work on this.

developers can "check in" new code, and users can "check out" the latest versions. As a user on any OpenBSD architecture, you can use CVS to get the latest version of the source code.

CVS is a decent tool for source-code management, but is a lousy tool for source-code distribution: It requires huge amounts of system resources and bandwidth and tends to chew up the server's hard drive. CVS has a more efficient older brother, CVSup — a combination of CVS and sup, the Software Update Protocol. Compared with CVS, the CVSup protocol is much faster, more efficient, easier on the servers, and generally nicer when supporting millions of users scattered around the world. It also only runs on the i386 architecture as of this writing. (Unfortunately, CVSup is written in Modula-3, which is difficult to port to new architectures.)

Because i386 is by far the most popular OpenBSD architecture, we'll consider both methods. Before that, however, let's look at some of the terms that both CVS and CVSup share.

Source Code Repositories

OpenBSD's source code is divided into *repositories,* or collections of code for particular subsystems. You only need to download and synchronize the collection that you want to use. The five repositories included in the OpenBSD include the following.

- **src** contains all the source code for the OpenBSD core operating system.
- **X11** contains the XFree86 release 3, adapted for OpenBSD (mostly obsolete).
- **XF4** contains XFree86 release 4, as adapted for OpenBSD.
- **ports** contains the OpenBSD ports tree.
- **www** contains the OpenBSD website.

You only need to update or install the collections for the components you want to use. For example, if you only want to update your base system and your ports tree, grab just the "src" and "ports" repositories. If a new version of X is released, you may wish to grab the X11 and/or XF4 collections. Only those people interested in editing the OpenBSD website need the www collection.

If at all possible, you want to start with a recent version of these collections from the most recent release. This will save considerably on download time and bandwidth when making your first update; it's quickest to update a collection of source code that exists, rather than downloading the whole collection a piece at a time. We've already discussed installing the system source code and ports collection in Chapter 5, and the www collection is not generally available as part of a release, but the XFree86 version 4 source code is available as a tarball with each release. Just grab the XF4.tar.gz tarball from the FTP site or the CD-ROM and extract it directly under /usr. Here, we take the XF4 collection right off of the CD-ROM.

```
# cd /usr
# tar -xzf /mnt/XF4.tar.gz
#
```

Tags

A *tag* is a label for a particular version of a collection of the "src" repository. Each different branch of OpenBSD-stable has a tag indicating which set of code it represents. When you update your source code, you will want to be absolutely certain that you use the correct tag!

For example, OpenBSD 3.3-stable has a tag of OPENBSD_3_3. The tag is just the word "OPENBSD," with the version numbers separated by underscores. This is expected to be consistent in the future — even though it isn't released yet, we can easily guess that the tag for OpenBSD 3.8 stable will be OPENBSD_3_8. OpenBSD-current has no tag.

Using the correct tag is very important. If you use the wrong tag, you will get the source code for the wrong version of OpenBSD. For example, if you're trying to get the source code for the latest OpenBSD-stable but do not include a tag, you'll get OpenBSD-current instead. If you use a tag that does not exist — e.g., try to get OPENBSD3_4 instead of OPENBSD_3_4 — you'll delete all the files in your local copy of that repository.

Mixing Repository Versions

Tags are not used for the XF4, X11, ports, or www repositories. These are assumed to be synchronized to OpenBSD-current at all times. Once a version of OpenBSD is released, these tools are assumed to be complete for that release and are not updated further.

Only the src repository is branched into stable and current. The ports tree is tightly tied to the version of OpenBSD and is synchronized to current. A current ports tree will not work reliably on an OpenBSD-stable system and can in fact cause much grief. It doesn't matter if the ports tree repository is only a few months older than the source repository; compiler and header changes can render it dysfunctional or useless. If you mix repository versions, you're on your own.

Similarly, the XFree86 collections track current, not stable.

You can update the www collection at any time, but the documentation it contains is assumed to track current as well. Incorrect documentation can cause as many headaches as incorrect code.

In short, if you're tracking stable, only update the src repository!

Source-changes@OpenBSD.org

Every change made to any source code repository, on any branch, is announced on the source-changes@OpenBSD.org mailing list. If you are running OpenBSD-current, you really need to read this mailing list, as often this is the only announcement of new features, bugs, or other points of concern. An OpenBSD developer may well break some vital system function and announce it only via the source-changes mailing list. If you miss the update here, you can destroy your data or render the computer unbootable until you get the information you should have read in the first place!

Here's a typical message sent to source-changes for a major change:

```
CVSROOT:        /cvs
Module name:    src❶
Changes by:     henning@cvs.openbsd.org 2002/11/18 15:49:15❷

Modified files:
        sbin/pfctl      : Makefile parse.y pfctl.c pfctl_parser.c
                          pfctl_parser.h❸
Added files:
        sbin/pfctl      : pfctl_altq.c pfctl_altq.h❹

Log message:
altq and pf merged❺

this isn't 100% done yet: the print_ stuff isn't finished, some features
will be added later, and there is no documetation yet, but committing now
enables a few more people to work on. ❻

print_altq_node stuff hacked by Daniel at euroBSDcon; lotsa stuff from kjc,
debugging help also pb and camiel. lots of good ideas by theo.❼

"commit now" theo philipp daniel❽
```

The first important thing we see is ❶which repository this change affects. This message represents a "src" repository change. To get this update, you would update your local src repository. We are also shown which ❷committer made the change, at which time. We're shown which files are ❸modified by this chang and which have been ❹added. If files had been removed, we would see those as well. Then there's the real meat of the message: the ❺nature of the change. Many commit messages end here, but this one goes on to explain some of the ❻problems and missing pieces in the commit. Various people are given ❼credit for their work on this feature. Finally, we are told why this incomplete work is being placed in the main tree — the committer was ❽urged to do so by a whole list of people. Not all commit messages are this complete, but not all commits perform this sort of wholesale surgery to a major system component.

If you were updating from source to the latest version of OpenBSD and were using altq or pf, this commit would have made your life very difficult. While the missing functionality will be restored, later, at the moment you are stuck. Even if the functionality you need is still there, the way it is used has changed. If you were reading the source-changes mailing list, you can decide if you want to upgrade or not. If you weren't, you're going to have a very bad day.

CVS Setup

To use CVS, you must be able to connect to an anonymous CVS server. You can get a complete list of official anonymous CVS servers at http://www.OpenBSD. org/anoncvs.html. This list includes the physical location of the servers, how often the server is updated, and the appropriate environment variables needed to connect to it.

While CVS can be very complicated if you're using every feature it offers to its fullest extent, to update your source code from an anonymous CVS server you only need to configure the client portion. The simplest way to use cvs(1) for our purposes is to set the environment variables CVSROOT and CVS_RSH, which will make the commands you have to type much shorter and simpler.

CVS_RSH instructs cvs(1) to use the correct network protocol when it issues commands to the CVS server and then how to transmit the patches back to the client. This defaults to "ssh," so if your anonymous CVS server permits this protocol, you don't need to set this to anything. Almost all OpenBSD anonymous CVS servers support SSH. If you cannot SSH out of your network (unlikely, but possible) you might try to use CVS_RSH=rsh instead. Updates will not be encrypted as they cross the network, but this is not generally a concern for source code updates.

CVSROOT tells cvs(1) where to go to fetch source code updates. Despite how long this variable can be, the actual interpretation is fairly simple:

```
username@server:directory
```

Some anonymous CVS servers support a protocol called "pserver," which runs on TCP port 2401. This protocol is most commonly used when firewalls block both SSH and rsh. You do not have to set a CVS_RSH variable to use this; instead, the pserver method is specified in the CVSROOT variable. You'll see examples on those few servers that only support the pserver method.

In general, if you leave CVS_RSH at the default and just set CVSROOT from the anonymous CVS mirror listing, you will be able to update your repositories.

Running CVS

Once you have chosen an anonymous CVS server, running CVS itself is trivial.

```
# cd /usr
# cvs -q get -P -rtag❶ repository❷
```

You just need to fill in the CVS ❶tag and the ❷repository you want to grab. Note the lack of a space between the -r and the tag. For example, to grab the latest OpenBSD 3.2 source repository, you would run:

```
# cvs -q get -rOPENBSD_3_2 -P src
U src/gnu/usr.sbin/sendmail/smrsh/smrsh.c
U src/kerberosV/src/kadmin/version4.c
U src/lib/libc/net/getnetnamadr.c
```

```
U src/share/zoneinfo/datfiles/southamerica
...
```

Each file listed has been updated since the last time I updated this source code. In this case, I'm updating the source code as distributed with OpenBSD 3.2 to 3. 2-stable. You'll also notices as CVS finds files that have been removed from or added to the repository.

Be warned; there may be a delay of several minutes between starting the command and seeing updates start to arrive. The cvs(1) program is not a very well-optimized tool for downloading source code. If you want the latest and greatest downloading tool, and you're on i386 hardware, run cvsup(1) instead.

CVSup Setup

If you're running on the i386 architecture, update your repositories with CVSup instead of CVS. CVSup is much faster and more efficient than CVS, is easier on the server, and consumes less bandwidth than vanilla CVS. You can install CVSup from /usr/ports/net/cvsup.

CVSup uses a configuration file, also called a *supfile*, which identifies which repositories it should update, the servers it should use, and how the updates should be made. This supfile is generally stored as /etc/supfile. Once you have created a supfile, you can continue to use it forever. The supfile has the following basic entries:

```
❶*default release=cvs
❷*default delete use-rel-suffix
❸*default umask=002
❹*default host=cvsup.usa.openbsd.org
❺*default base=/usr
❻*default prefix=/usr
❼*default tag=OPENBSD3_2
❽*default compress
❾OpenBSD-src
```

Generic configuration options begin with an asterisk. The ❶first entry tells CVSup that it is talking to a CVS repository. While this is the most common sort of repository to be used with CVSup, it is possible to use CVSup with other sorts of repositories. We then tell CVSup that it is to ❷delete files that are no longer in the master repository and that all of the directories specified are relative instead of absolute. We set a ❸umask of 002 for the times that we do touch files.

You then need to set a ❹CVSup server. CVSup is not the same as CVS, and you cannot run CVSup off of a CVS server. You can find a complete list of official OpenBSD CVSup mirrors at http://www.OpenBSD.org/cvsup.html. There are far fewer CVSup mirrors than CVS mirrors, but the CVSup mirrors do far less work to service each user, so things even out.

The ❺base is the location where CVSup keeps its status files, including a list of updated files, so it can accelerate further updates. It will create a directory called "sup" under this directory for these files. If you set this to /usr (the default), your updates will be stored in /usr/sup.

The default ❻prefix is the directory tree where the repository you've chosen will go. If you want to use the standard OpenBSD locations of /usr/src, /usr/XF4, and so on, set this to /usr.

The ❼tag is the CVS tag you want to use. In this example, we want to grab OpenBSD 3.2-stable. Remember, tags are only used for the main src collection; the other repositories only have a current branch! If you do not specify a tag, CVSup will assume you mean current.

The default ❽compress keyword tells CVSup to compress data before sending it across the network. If your connection is a T1 or faster, compressing the data isn't that important, and you can remove this entire line, which will reduce the CPU load while increasing the bandwidth needed. Because today's processors are usually much cheaper than bandwidth (in North America, at least), there are very few circumstances where not using compression makes sense.

Finally, we tell ❾CVSup which repository to update. Not all CVSup mirrors carry all the repositories, so be certain you check the mirror list! You have the following choices:

OpenBSD-src	The src repository
OpenBSD-www	The www repository
OpenBSD-ports	The ports repository
OpenBSD-x11	The XFree86 version 3 repository
OpenBSD-xf4	The XFree86 version 4 repository
OpenBSD-all	All available OpenBSD repositories

If you want to track OpenBSD-current, do not define a default tag in your supfile. Remember, you can choose to track stable, in which case you only want to update your src repository, or you can choose to track current, in which case you can update any repository.

Running CVSup

Now that you have a configuration, you can run cvsup(1).

```
# cvsup /etc/supfile
```

If you're running X, cvsup(1) will open a GUI on your display. (The "-g" option tells cvsup to not open the GUI, but just print its results on the terminal.) If you have the GUI you must hit the green arrow to start the update process, but with the "-g" flag cvsup(1) just starts going. The output is similar to that from cvs(1), but the whole process runs much faster.

Standard Source Build Process

Now that you have the latest source code for the version you want, you can try to build it. If everything goes well, building from source is completely routine. (If something goes wrong, you're stuck relying on your brain, which is a situation I personally prefer to not be in.) We'll first document how the process should work and then proceed to discuss some of the issues you might encounter.

First, be completely certain that you have backed up any data that you or your users might still feel attached to, as upgrading from source adds an additional layer of risk to the upgrade process. If in doubt, back up!

Review the Upgrading Mini-FAQ very closely for the version you're upgrading to, as discussed earlier in this chapter. Generally speaking, there should be no issue with upgrading to an newer version of the same release of OpenBSD-stable — for example, no special preparations should be necessary to upgrade from OpenBSD 3.2-stable as of December to OpenBSD 3.2-stable as of March. If you are upgrading to a newer release of OpenBSD or to OpenBSD-current, you must follow all of the steps listed in the Upgrading Mini-FAQ.

Working as Root

While you can use sudo(1) for everything while upgrading your system, it's simplest to actually become root before starting the upgrade. Running these operations as root may not fit with your security stance, however. Add an entry like the below for sudo in /etc/mk.conf, and the build process will call sudo(8) at appropriate times.

```
SUDO=/usr/bin/sudo
```

You will still need to add sudo(8) calls to the various preparatory commands — for example, "make obj" will become "sudo make obj." If your build machine is slow, you may have to enter your password repeatedly. You can get around that by not requiring a password to run commands as root, but that also may not fit your security stance.

For the rest of this section, I will assume that you are logged in as root.

The Build Commands

First, make sure you have a /usr/obj directory. This is where the build process will store the actual binaries, and pieces thereof, that it creates. You do not want the system to build the binaries under the /usr/src directory! If you do not have a /usr/obj directory, create one.

Now go into the /usr/src directory. All commands from this point on will be run under /usr/src, unless specified otherwise.

If you have compiled errata on this system, or if you have previously upgraded from source, you might have old binary objects scattered throughout your source tree. These binaries will interfere with the upgrade process, and need to be removed. To be absolutely certain you have eliminated all binaries from your source tree, run the following command.

```
# find . -type l -name obj | xargs rm
# make cleandir
# rm -rf /usr/obj/*
```

Now that you have blown away any binaries lurking in the source tree, create a new directory hierarchy for the new binaries.

```
# make obj
```

You will see several screens of output as make(1) builds a directory tree under /usr/obj and sets appropriate symlinks from the source tree to those new directories.

Before you can install your freshly built software, you must tell the system to create any necessary directories for new programs. The /etc/ directory frequently needs new directories as programs are enhanced. You can do this as we show here.

```
# cd /usr/src/etc
# make DESTDIR=/ distrib-dirs
```

Make(1) will spit out a few lines about directories and links it creates.

Now that you have some basic preparations, build a new GENERIC kernel from source and install it. You could use a custom kernel for this, but if something goes wrong you will have to try to decide whether your kernel or your source code is at fault. Play it safe, use the GENERIC kernel. This new kernel must be considered experimental; keep your old kernel as an emergency backup! Fortunately, building the whole operating system from source code is an excellent stress test of a kernel.

Reboot on your new kernel. Do not attempt to build a new system on an old kernel, especially when upgrading to OpenBSD-current, or you may find the build failing because of missing or incompatible system calls.

Once your system has rebooted on the new kernel, go to /usr/src and type:

```
# make build
```

This one command will build the entire system from source and install it on the system! On an Athlon 1800+, the build takes less than an hour. On a Pentium 50, this can take days. Eventually, you'll see something like the following:

```
.....
cd /usr/src/share/man && exec make makedb
/usr/libexec/makewhatis /usr/share/man
#
```

The last stage of the build process is to run makewhatis(1) on the manual page collection, so the new man pages can be easily searched.

The system is now in a state similar to what it would be after installing the new distributions from a CD-ROM or FTP. You still need to merge /etc/ and take care of any actions recommended in the Upgrading Mini-FAQ. I recommend the following process. First, install the updated Apache manual.

```
# cd /usr/src/usr.sbin/httpd
# make -f Makefile.bsd-wrapper distribution
```

Check the Upgrade Mini-FAQ, and remove any programs or files it targets, then run mergemaster(8). Reboot one last time, and if the system comes back up you have successfully upgraded!

Source Upgrade Problems

If the upgrade from source process does not work, you need to fire up your brain cells and debug it. Start by reading the error message you received, and try to figure out what it means.

Don't forget, there is a delay between the appearance of an issue and the Upgrade Mini-FAQ being updated. Definitely search the mailing list archives for other people having this issue. Frequently, new users or groups that are added to the system cause upgrade problems; you can easily work around these problems by adding the user or group.

It is also possible that you grabbed the system source at a moment when some committer was in the middle of a large commit or on one of those rare occasions when the build process was broken. Wait a day, update your source repository again, and try to build the source code once more.

If you hack on the source code yourself, perhaps you broke the upgrade process. Try removing your changes and start again from a clean source code tree.

If all else fails, follow the standard troubleshooting process discussed in Chapter 1. People upgrading from source are generally expected to be able to troubleshoot compilation problems, however.

If you have trouble, remember you can always upgrade to snapshots and releases from CD-ROM. Upgrading from source is only for the advanced user; if you're not yet an advanced user, this is something to work toward.

17

BASIC PACKET FILTERING

The name's Pond, James Pond.
Alpha PPK loaded,
licensed to filter.

Packet filtering and manipulation are among
the most basic tools in network security.
OpenBSD includes a very powerful in-kernel
packet filter, pf(4), that not only performs
standard stateless and stateful packet filtering, but can
also inspect and reassemble packet fragments in several
ways, redirect connections, translate addresses in several
different directions simultaneously, authenticate users,
and manage bandwidth.

PF is one of the high points of OpenBSD, and we're going to spend a few chapters discussing it. PF allows you to do some things that commercial firewall vendors still cannot manage reliably.

PF is still undergoing very active development, and new features are added almost weekly. We are only going to discuss those features that are mature and stable. By the time you read this, PF will have features that aren't covered here. Be sure to read the pf.conf(5) man page for details on the nifty features available in your version of OpenBSD.

Firewalls

The word *firewall* has been tortured into horrendous contortions over the last few years, until it has ceased to mean much of anything. You can buy a firewall for your cable modem for under a hundred dollars, and you can purchase an enterprise firewall for a hundred thousand dollars. What's the difference? They're all firewalls — much as cats, elephants, and llamas are all mammals, but some are welcome in your home and some most certainly are not. (Which of course, is a matter of personal preference.)

What differentiate firewalls are the features that they offer, the hardware they run on, and the robustness of the software. Your basic home firewalls perform the bare minimum to allow users to surf the web and keep outsiders out. Your enterprise firewall may do exactly the same thing, but also include application proxies and a hefty support contract. Some breeds of either type are quite resilient, while others can be out-thought by drunken squirrels. Frequently, price and quality have no sensible relationship to each other.

OpenBSD can be used as the basis for a full-featured firewall. The integrated packet filtering software can perform any of the packet-level tasks that any commercial firewall provides. If you want application proxies, however, OpenBSD does not include them (with the exception of a FTP proxy, which is necessary for normal FTP operations through a packet filter, as discussed in Chapter 18). Several popular application proxies run quite well on OpenBSD, but they are not part of OpenBSD. I've used Squid (/usr/ports/www/squid) quite easily to proxy the most common Internet applications and an assortment of other proxies to manage just about everything else.

A firewall is what you make it. You can send all your network traffic through a simple OpenBSD packet filter and honestly say you have a "firewall," or you can set up application proxies, authentication, and so on, and still say you have a "firewall." Remember this the next time someone says that they have a firewall.

To build an effective firewall, you absolutely must understand TCP/IP. If you don't understand as much TCP/IP as you'd like, allow me to recommend Stevens's *TCP/IP Illustrated*, volume 1 (Addison-Wesley).[1] While you can set up a basic firewall knowing only the basics of TCP/IP, you're going to find that debugging problems can be quite difficult.

Throughout this section, we're going to talk about using your OpenBSD system as a firewall. This assumes that you have two or more network cards, and you want to pass traffic between them. While this is a popular application for OpenBSD, everything discussed here works just as well to protect an OpenBSD machine sitting naked on the Internet. Don't be afraid to implement packet filtering on your web server!

---

[1] I also recommend volumes 2 and 3, but for different reasons.

Enabling PF

PF is enabled at system boot by the following two /etc/rc.conf variables:

```
pf=YES
pf_rules=/etc/pf.conf
```

By changing the pf value to "NO," you disable the packet filter. Similarly, you can choose a different boot-time PF configuration file by changing the pf_rules variable. If something is wrong with your PF configuration file and it won't parse, the OpenBSD startup routine will install some basic PF rules that will block almost all traffic to the machine, with the exception of SSH. You'll be able to connect to the machine and correct your rules, but that's about it. (And, as anyone who administers firewalls remotely can tell you, this ability is enough to save a lot of pain.)

If you want to forward packets between multiple interfaces (i.e., be a "firewall"), you need to tell OpenBSD to do this with the net.inet.ip.forwarding sysctl MIB. There's a commented-out entry for this in /etc/sysctl.conf.

```
#net.inet.ip.forwarding=1
```

Just remove the pound sign and reboot!

If you want to have stop and start packet forwarding without rebooting your system, you can do this easily with sysctl(8), as discussed in Chapter 11. Setting this MIB to 0 stops packet forwarding; setting the MIB to 1 enables it. If you want to perform some basic system maintenance that may interfere with your network in some way you can stop packet forwarding, do your work, and restart forwarding.

What Is Packet Filtering?

Packet filtering is just comparing packets to a list of rules and accepting or rejecting the packets on the basis of those rules. As network administrator, you decide which packets are naughty and which are nice. When you filter packets for a single host, you could legitimately call that host hardened. (The word "hardened" means almost exactly what "firewall" means — i.e., nothing.) When you force all packets on your network through a single host that filters packets, you have a basic firewall.

A basic packet filter may only allow you to filter based upon TCP or UDP protocol number. Some don't even allow you to filter by ICMP type or cannot cope with nonstandard protocols. PF can cope with almost anything you throw at it. If some client wants a host behind your firewall to speak IP protocol number 184 to their development server, PF will let you do that. Many commercial firewalls won't let you pass such traffic or claim that they will but throw a tantrum if you actually try to do it.

Basic Packet Filtering Concepts

In Chapter 8, we mentioned that TCP connections can be in a variety of states. (If you don't remember that, go back and reread that chapter.) A TCP connection that is just opening goes through a three-way handshake process. A client first requests a connection by sending a special "connection synchronization request" or SYN packet to the server. The server responds by sending the client a "synchronization acknowledgment" or SYN+ACK packet, which contains some basic information about how to connect this particular TCP session. Finally the client responds with an "acknowledgment" or ACK packet, which tells the server that the client understands and accepts the connection requirements. Every part of this three-way handshake must be completed for any actual data to be transferred between the two machines. Your packet filtering rules must permit each part of the three-way handshake and the data transmission itself to complete. Allowing your server to receive incoming messages is useless if your packet filter rules do not permit it to send back an acknowledgment.

In the early 1990s, packet filters compared each packet to a list of static rules. If a packet matched a rule, it was allowed to pass. The system did not record what came before and had no idea if a packet was part of a legitimate transaction or not. For example, if a packet arrived marked SYN+ACK and addressed to a machine in the middle of the network, the packet filter would let it pass. Such packets had to pass for internal systems to successfully establish outbound TCP connections. Because the packet filter didn't know who had sent a SYN packet, it couldn't reject such illegitimate packets. As a result, intruders could forge SYN+ACK packets and use them to circumvent seemingly secure devices. Once intruders got packets into the network they could usually trigger a response from some device and then start to worm their way in. This is just one example of a whole host of problems caused by such simple packet filtering. PF can do this sort of packet filtering, but you really don't want to bother with it.

Stateful inspection counteracts this problem. Packet filters that use state inspection maintain a table of every connection running through the firewall. When a client sends out a SYN packet, it records that packet in a table and waits for a corresponding SYN+ACK packet. If a SYN+ACK packet arrives at the packet filter, but no matching SYN packet was sent requesting such a response, the SYN+ACK packet is rejected. This also had the pleasant result of simplifying packet-filtering rulesets considerably. PF performs excellent stateful packet inspection, and it's much easier to manage, so we're going to spend most of our time focusing on that.

UDP is technically stateless, but some applications expect a certain amount of state. When your system transmits a UDP packet, the application might well expect a UDP packet or ten to flow back in response, or no packets, depending on the application. DNS queries are a popular example of UDP packets flowing back and forth; while UDP has no state, DNS certainly does. ICMP behaves similarly. You can tell PF to expect and accept ICMP replies, or to disallow them, as you choose. While UDP and ICMP have no state, telling PF to certain types of replies with these protocols is also called stateful inspection.

Packets can be mangled during transit, usually by fragmentation. Part of a packet filter's job is to reassemble those packets in a sensible manner. PF can reassemble and rationalize packets in a variety of ways, depending upon your needs, by using the *scrub* function.

One of the essential concepts in packet filtering is the question of *default accept* versus *default deny*. A *default accept stance* means that you allow any type of connection except for what you specifically disallow. A *default deny stance* means that you only allow connections from specific parts of the Internet; all other connection attempts are refused. Once you have chosen your default, you can adjust your rules to hide or reveal network services as you desire. This choice is really between whether you are offering services to the world or only to a select few. If your system is a corporate web server, you might want to make it only visible to the company network. If so, you've adopted a default deny security stance. This is especially appropriate when building firewalls to protect a company network — users should not be able to run web servers on their desktops! On the other hand, if you have a sitting out on the Internet, and only want to block a few certain services from a select handful of locations, you're using a default accept stance.

In addition to packet filtering and packet reassembly, PF has several other important features: network address translation, connection redirection, bandwidth management, and authentication. We will consider each separately, although they are all configured in /etc/pf.conf and managed with pfctl(8).

Packet Filter Control Program

All packet filter management is handled via pfctl(8). This program will show you the current packet filtering settings, connections that are being processed by PF, the current state of various TCP/IP transactions, debugging information, and any other information you might possibly want to know. Here and there, you will see discussion of how the packet filter control program can be used in conjunction with various sorts of rules. Much of Chapter 19 is devoted to pfctl(8).

/etc/pf.conf

All PF features are configured in /etc/pf.conf. You're going to be very good friends with this file before we're through, but we'll start with an overview. The /etc/pf.conf file contains statements and rules, whose format varies with the feature they configure. As the PF features manipulate packets in very specific ways, not only is the order of rules extremely important but also the order in which the features are configured matters greatly. If you try to do stateful inspection before you reassemble packet fragments, for example, things will not work properly.

The default /etc/pf.conf has the sample rules in order by feature, but if you're in the slightest danger of becoming confused, I suggest that you put large comment markers between them, in capital letters if necessary. (Use standard pound signs to comment /etc/pf.conf.) The features must[2] be entered in /etc/pf.conf in this exact order:

- Macros
- Tables
- Options
- Traffic normalization
- Bandwidth management
- Translation
- Redirection
- Packet filtering

No matter what section a particular rule may be in, it will have this general format:

```
❶pass ❷in ❸on fxp0 proto tcp from any to 192.168.1.1 port 22 keep state
```

The first word is a ❶keyword labeling what sort of rule this is. Each sort of rule has its own keywords. This particular rule is a packet-filtering rule. ❷"in" is the direction the packet is traveling. ❸"on fxp0" labels which interface this packet is crossing. The remainder of the rule line varies with the sort of rule it is. This particular example happens to be a packet-filtering rule.

In and Out

Two keywords that appear in many sorts of PF rules are "in" and "out." When you're building a firewall, the word "in" usually means "traffic coming into the protected network," and "out" means "traffic leaving the protected network."

Your OpenBSD system does not magically know which side of your network is protected and which is not. As far as your packet filter is concerned, it is just controlling traffic from one interface to another. The keyword "in" means traffic flowing into the machine from the network," while "out" means "traffic leaving the machine for the network."

When you see the word "in" or "out" in a PF rule, do not think about your network as a whole. Imagine that you're very small and sitting on your CPU, toasting marshmallows over the heat sink and watching packets enter and leave the computer. You cannot see what lies beyond the computer case, just the packets as they come and go. Packets marked with an "in" are coming toward you, while packets marked with "out" are leaving.

---

[2] Technically, macros and tables can appear anywhere in the rules, as long as they are defined before they are used — but scattering macros and tables throughout your ruleset is a good way to confuse yourself!

"My Network Can Do No Wrong"

While we're on the subject of which way is in and which is out, let's spend a moment and ponder in and out of the network as a whole. Many network administrators who build a firewall carefully filter and restrict incoming traffic, but only apply minimal restrictions on outgoing traffic.

While control of incoming traffic is among the most in-your-face issues of network management, control of outgoing traffic is also quite important. Even if you trust your users, viruses or Trojans can convert a salesperson's workstation into a garbage-spewing pest. Do not assume that your network can do no wrong — it can be malicious, and one day it will, but careful traffic control can minimize the damage you will inflict upon your neighbors, clients, and customers. And believe me; even if the system that wreaks havoc is the Windows 98 workstation that a senior company officer refuses to give up, the mayhem it causes will be considered the fault and responsibility of the network administrator.

Logical Operators

Many application protocols use a range of network ports, or you may want rules that apply to a particular group of hosts with one or two exceptions. FTP, for example, is notorious for connecting over random high-numbered ports. PF makes it easy to specify ranges and groups by including a variety of logical operators.

In the examples here we're going to look at some sorts of rules you haven't yet seen, but don't let that worry you. Just keep the logical operator examples in mind as we go on.

=	Equals exactly this (default)
!=	Does not equal this
<	Is less than
<=	Is less than or equal to
>	Is greater than
>=	Is greater than or equal to this
><	Anything between two numbers, exclusive
<>	Anything outside two numbers, exclusive

The equal symbol is the implicit default in PF rules. Our previous example could have been written like this:

```
pass in proto udp from 10.15.3.8 port ❶= 53 to 192.168.1.5 port ❶= 53
```

Note the ❶equal signs in the middle of the port declaration. This makes absolutely no functional difference, but some people find such rules more readable.

The not-equal symbol can be used to exclude a port, host, or interface from a rule. For example, here we allow traffic to enter the system from any interface except fxp3:

```
pass in on !fxp3 from any to any
```

We could also block traffic from going to particular ports. Here, we allow the world at large to connect to any service on this machine except SSH. (In most cases you would write a block rule instead, but this is certainly a legitimate way of doing it.)

```
pass in from any to 192.168.1.5 port != 22
```

The other logical operators all apply only to port numbers. The > (greater than) and >= (greater than or equal to) operators can be used to specify a port above a certain range. Either can be used in most situations. For example, both of the following rules allow any packets to a port numbered 1024 or greater to pass:

```
pass in proto tcp from any to any port  > 1023
pass in proto tcp from any to any port  >= 1024
```

Similarly, you could prevent anyone with a UID 1100 or greater to make outbound connections. This can be helpful if you give your system administrators and trusted users a UID less that 1100, and untrusted users and customers higher UIDs.

```
block out proto tcp from any to any user >= 1100
```

You can also specify a range of ports with the ">< " operator. This takes two arguments, the low port number and the high port number. This following rule allows TCP traffic on any port above 5000 but below 6000. Port 0 through 5000 will not be allowed, and ports 6000 or greater will also be rejected.

```
pass in proto tcp from any to any port 5000><6000
```

The "<>" operator matches ports that are not within a specific range. The following example allows access to TCP ports 0 through 5000, and ports 6000 and greater:

```
pass in proto tcp from any to any port 5000<>6000
```

Combining Entries with Braces

You may have a regular pattern of rules for certain hosts or ports. Perhaps you want a particular group of TCP ports open to a particular group of hosts, and your rule entries would just be repetitions with one minor change on each rule. Opening port 80 and 443 to a server requires two rules. For example, a set of 30 web servers means you have 60 rules that are almost identical. Curly braces allow you to write these rules briefly and efficiently, thereby greatly reducing the risk of misconfigurations. (Again, while some of these examples make reference to rules that we haven't discussed yet, keep these examples in mind as we go on.)

Each entry within the braces creates a separate rule. This is easier to understand by example. For example, DNS queries run over UDP port 53, while zone transfers run over TCP port 53. You could write a UDP port 53 rule and a TCP port 53 rule like this:

```
pass out proto ❶udp from any to any port 53
pass out proto ❷tcp from any to any port 53
```

These rules are almost identical, with the exception of the ❶UDP and ❷TCP keywords, so you can combine them with braces:

```
pass in proto {tcp, udp} from any to any port 53
```

When the PF rule parser examines this entry, it will automatically expand it into a set of rules. You only have to write one rule, which is easier to maintain than two.

```
pass in proto tcp from any to any port = domain
pass in proto udp from any to any port = domain
```

While this example is trivial, it quickly becomes quite useful when you have a large number of hosts with similar rules.

You can use multiple braces within a line. Suppose that you have two web servers, 192.168.1.4 and 192.168.1.5, that need clients to access them on ports 80 and 443. Two servers, two ports, for a total of four rules. You could write rules for both protocols and both servers, much like this:

```
pass in from any to 192.168.1.4 port 80
pass in from any to 192.168.1.4 port 443
pass in from any to 192.168.1.5 port 80
pass in from any to 192.168.1.5 port 443
```

There's nothing wrong with this, but you can write the rule a little more easily using braces. The previous rules compress down to this:

```
pass in proto tcp from any to {192.168.1.4,192.168.1.5} port {80,443}
```

Again, when you load your PF rules into the kernel, the line above will be expanded to the full number of rules.

Macros

Macros are variables you can define for use within PF rules. They help keep your rules more maintainable, readable, and manageable. A macro name must begin with a letter, but can contain letters, numbers, and underscores. Frequent uses of macros include interface names, network numbers, and host names.

For example, network interfaces are generally identified by the name of the network card driver the interface uses: fxp, xl, ne, and so on. If you change your network card, you would have to rewrite all the rules that use that network card. By using a macro, you can change the interface name in one place and have it propagate throughout your rules.

```
External_if="fxp0"
```

If the IP addresses behind your firewall were 209.69.69.0 through 209.69.69.255, you could define a macro for these addresses. If you added more addresses, you could just add them to the macro.

```
Internal_ip="209.69.69.0/24"
```

Similarly, you can define macros for each IP address on your firewall, in case you have to renumber your network. Also, when reading PF rules, it's much easier to read well-named macros than dozens and dozens of IP addresses. Is fxp0 the internal or external network card? You'd have to look it up, but "$External_Int" is unambiguous.

When a rule needs the term represented by the macro, just use the macro instead. This makes it easy to change information consistently throughout your rules and greatly reduces the risk of typos.

```
block in on $External_int from $Internal_ip
```

Similarly, you could write macros for groups of machines. You can easily group machines by purpose and trivially give them the same rulesets.

```
Webservers="{209.69.69.8, 209.69.69.12, 209.69.69.87}"
```

When you have a new web server, or one of your old web servers dies, just edit the macro appropriately to have your firewall rules apply to the correct machines. Similarly, we will keep repeating the port numbers 80 and 443 (the standard web ports) throughout our rules. Instead, you can just do this:

```
webports = "{80, 443}"
```

Macro names cannot contain any characters other than letters, numbers, and underscores, and they cannot consist entirely of a PF keyword such as "pass," "block," or "scrub." You could name a macro "nat1," but not "nat."

Combined with braces, macros can make your rules much simpler. Here, we write one rule to allow access to all appropriate ports on all of our web servers:

```
pass in proto tcp from any to $webservers port $webports
```

When you add a new web server, you just have to add its IP address to the list in the "webservers" macro. This trivial example doesn't do the concept justice, but once you have dozens of servers with many rules applying to them, you'll see the usefulness of macros.

Tables

PF can store long lists of network addresses (both hosts and netblocks) in tables. These tables can be defined in /etc/pf.conf or can be kept in external files.

For example, say you have a list of IP addresses of known spam sources that you don't want to allow to talk to your mail server. Such lists tend to be thousands of entries long and would be difficult to maintain inside /etc/pf.conf. Instead, you can create a table with a name like "spamhosts," load your list into this table, and keep your main pf.conf quite simple.

PF checks IP addresses in a table much more quickly than it handles checking against a list of IP addresses in braces. Tables are handled in a slightly different way than lists, however, and can actually be edited by using pfctl(8) while the firewall is running.

In general, you should use lists of hostnames for your standard network equipment such as your corporate web servers, and use tables for integration with other network programs such as spam-blockers or intrusion detection systems. (Of course, if your network has hundreds of web servers, you might want to use a table for those as well!)

Defining Tables

While you can create and edit tables entirely with pfctl(8), such usage is fairly advanced (and one we'll consider in Chapter 19). To define a table entirely within /etc/pf.conf put the name of the table in angle brackets, list the contents of the table in braces like so:

```
table <❶rfc1918> {❷10.0.0.0/8, 176.16.0.0/12, 192.168.0.0/16}
```

This creates a table called ❶rfc1918 that contains the ❷private IP addresses that should never appear on the public Internet. You can use this table name later in your ruleset much as you would use a macro.

If you have a long list of IPs to add to a table, you can just list them in an external file and direct /etc/pf.conf to pull the table from that file. Here's how we would specify that exact same list, using an external file:

```
table <rfc1918> file "/etc/rfc1918list"
```

In /etc/rfc1918list, list one IP address or network block per line. Any line with a leading pound sign is a comment. Here's a file containing the RFC1918 IP addresses:

```
#rfc1918 addresses
#These should never arrive at the outside of our firewall!
```

```
10.0.0.0/8
172.16.0.0/12
192.168.0.0/16
```

This particular example is very simple, but you might have lists of IP addresses that you update on a regular basis, including spam blacklists and client IP addresses. You could simply download the new list to the firewall device, update the list, and reload the table without having to touch your carefully tuned /etc/pf.conf.

You can also specify multiple files in a single table statement like so:

```
table <illegaladdresses> file "/etc/rfc1918list" file "/etc/weird-ip-list"
```

This single table includes every IP and network listed in each file.

NOTE *If you list a hostname in the file, PF will do a DNS lookup and get all of the IP addresses for that host and enter them in the table. For example, www.yahoo.com has eight IP addresses; if you list www.yahoo.com in your file, all eight IP addresses will be added to the table.*

Table Attributes

By default, tables can be dynamically edited, added, or even removed. This may well conflict with your desired use for the table. Fortunately, PF allows you to modify this behavior with the special attributes *const* and *persist*.

Some tables should never change. And since the RFC1918 address space is not going to increase or decrease any time soon, you wouldn't expect to see that table change. The *const* keyword prevents anything from changing the table via pfctl(8), and is used as follows:

```
table <rfc1918>  const {10.0.0.0/8, 176.16.0.0/12, 192.168.0.0/16}
```

When you load a ruleset into PF, the system automatically parses the file and performs some optimization. Tables that are not referred to in any rules are deleted before they are fed to the kernel. You can tell PF to keep these tables even when rules refer to them by using the *persist* keyword:

```
table <intruders>  persist
```

An empty table like this might be used by your intrusion detection system, allowing an OpenBSD firewall to dynamically block questionable traffic. (We'll discuss adding entries to these tables in Chapter 19, but getting your IDS to issue the proper commands will vary widely with the type of intrusion detection system you have.)

Exclusions

You can specifically exclude a section of network numbers from a table by using the negation (!) operator. This lets you make tables easily with entries such as "Every IP address beginning with 10, except for the 10.8.8.0/24 block."

```
table <remote> {10.0.0.0/8, !10.8.8.0/24}
```

You can also use a similar entry in a file:

```
10.0.0.0/8
!10.8.8.0/24
```

What's more, these can be cascaded, with increasingly smaller areas being negated and included:

```
❶10.0.0.0/8
❷!10.0.0.0/16
❸10.0.0.0/24
❹!10.0.0.1
```

In this example, the ❶first line puts IP address that begins with 10 into the table. We then deliberately ❷exclude any entry that begins with exactly 10.0, effectively making 10.1.0.0 the first entry in this table. Then we complicate things further by putting ❸any IP that begins with exactly 10.0.0 in the table, and removing the ❹specific IP 10.0.0.1. This sequential inclusion and exclusion lets us build very complicated lists of IP addresses in a few lines of text.

Using Tables in Rules

Tables can be used in rules just like macros, network numbers, or braces. When you define a table, specify the table name in angle brackets:

```
block in from <intruders> to any
```

You can also use multiple tables within braces, like so:

```
block in from { <rfc1918>, <intruders> } to any
```

And tables can be used for packet source or destination, for NAT rules, or for scrub rules. You cannot, however, use tables for routing rules or for the NAT redirection address.

Options

Basic settings that affect how PF performs basic actions, such as "how long does PF keep state on a TCP connection in the SYN+ACK state" and "do we have logging on?" are classified as *options*. All option rules start with the "set" keyword.

Timing Options

You can exhaustively tweak the global timeouts for stateful inspection on TCP, UDP, and other protocols. For most users, this is just a complicated way to get a truly impressive migraine. Adjusting TCP timeouts is a very tricky subject, and it generally causes network administrators more problems than it solves. Timeouts are all interrelated, and adjusting one without adjusting the others will not achieve your desired results unless you know exactly what you're doing and why. Similarly, PF's defaults for other protocols are almost certainly correct for the standard Internet.

Problems certainly do happen when you're not running on the standard Internet, however. You might be behind an overloaded link, or perhaps you have a satellite connection between you and the rest of the world. PF includes a set of precalculated network timing options for particular sorts of networks. You can set these with the *optimization* keyword. OpenBSD supports four different sorts of timing optimization: normal, high-latency, aggressive, and conservative.

The *normal* setting is for use on a system connected to the Internet via a modem, cable modem, T1, OC192, or other fairly standard method. If you don't specify an optimization, this is the default — in fact, "default" is an alias for "normal."

The *high-latency* optimization option is for systems connected to the Internet via satellite or other extremely slow methods. Timeouts are turned up very high. "Satellite" is an alias for "high-latency."

Aggressive optimization quickly discards idle connection information. This saves memory and CPU time, at the possible expense of cutting off legitimate connections. If you are on a high-speed network and have limited memory on your system, or you don't want people leaving idle connections hanging around to systems on the other side of the firewall, you might want to use aggressive optimization.

Conservative optimization extends timeouts coherently so as to not cut off any legitimate connections if at all possible. This can use more CPU time and memory.

Setting the optimization is very easy:

```
set optimization high-latency
```

If you're a real TCP/IP stud, feel free to look at pf.conf(5) for the "set timeout" keyword, and adjust the timeout on each individual stage of the protocol negotiation process as you see fit.

Enabling Logging

PF's logging functions can be enabled on an interface-by-interface basis with the "loginterface" keyword. Each interface that you want to enable logging on should be specified by this option:

```
set loginterface fxp0
```

You can disable logging entirely, on any interface, by setting the interface name to "none."

PF Memory Limits

One problem with filtering network traffic is that you may have very little control over how much traffic you receive. One day Slashdot might post a link to a web page behind your OpenBSD firewall, and you would start to receive tens of thousands of connections per minute. OpenBSD can handle this, if you have the proper hardware, but it may consume all your system memory if your hardware is inadequate. The two features that are most likely to use memory are stateful inspection and fragment reassembly. By limiting the amount of memory you will allocate to these, you can guarantee that your system will have memory left for such trivial things as a command prompt. The "set limits" keyword configures these limits. You can limit the number of connections you are performing stateful inspection on by using "set limits states" and limit the number of fragments with "set limit frags":

```
set limit states 5000
set limit frags 10000
```

To make your rules slightly shorter, you can set both of these on a single line using braces.

```
set limit { states 5000, frags 10000 }
```

Yes, you can use queuing to limit outbound traffic, but that won't help you if your system runs out of memory.

Generally, speaking, one state uses about 1KB of memory, so a machine with 64MB RAM could handle about 65,000 states. The amount of memory used by fragments depends on the size of the fragments, but is generally quite small.

Blocked Packet Policy

When PF blocks packets, it can either send back an error message to the originating system or refuse the traffic without returning any errors. Configure this with the "set block-policy" keyword.

It is generally considered polite to return an error, as clients will immediately realize that they cannot make this connection and (usually) tell the user that the connection has been refused. Your security policy may or may not involve politeness. The "return" option tells PF to return polite errors: an RST for TCP connections and an ICMP unreachable message for UDP connections. All other connections will be silently dropped anyway, but this covers most situations:

```
set block-policy return
```

By default PF silently drops blocked packets. If your silently drops the traffic, applications will have to wait for the network protocol timeout to elapse before realizing that they cannot connect. The "drop" option tells PF to silently drop packets:

```
set block-policy drop
```

This blocked packet policy can be overridden on individual filter statements.

Packet Normalization

Packets can be shredded in transit, and processing these shards of data can increase system load. The system at one end of the connection might have a habit of breaking up transmitted packets into tiny bits, or perhaps some router in the middle thinks that your packets are too large and splits them up to digest them more easily. In either event, instead of nice whole packets your network will receive small bits, or fragments. Different operating systems reassemble packets in slightly different ways. While these differences are usually trivial, a skilled attacker can use them to exploit the client operating system. PF's "scrub" rules allow you to decide how to handle packets, or even to perform some rearrangement of your own. (Other people "mangle" packets, but you "normalize" them.) PF's goal is to hand the client operating systems complete packets, so that the client doesn't have to do the work of reassembling the packet and so you don't have to worry about possible attacks on the client's packet reassembly code.

Packet normalization is done via "scrub" rules. The easiest way to perform the most common packet-fragment handling is to just put in a basic scrub rule:

```
scrub in all
```

This affects all packets entering the computer. While PF won't fragment or change packets unless you tell it to, you might want to also use a "scrub out all" rule. If you have a complex internal network some internal device might well mangle the packets. You could also add interface names to this rule, to only normalize packets coming from one network. In most cases, not scrubbing your own packets is an example of "My network can do no wrong."

```
scrub in all on fxp0
```

Customizing Fragment Handling

By default, a scrub rule reassembles fragments. The bits and pieces of each packet are cached locally until the entire packet arrives, and then the completed packet is passed on down to later rules. This simplifies the writing of rules and makes it easy for your clients to receive more complete packets than they would otherwise. If you are using network address translation, you *must* use fragment reassembly. While this is the default behavior for scrub rules, you can explicitly set it with "fragment reassemble."

```
scrub in all fragment reassemble
```

You could also choose to crop fragments. One packet can be partially repeated in a few different fragments. Cropping eliminates all duplicates and trim out any content overlap within fragments. This results in one and only one copy of each piece of data traveling on down the rules and onto the network. PF normally keeps a very small cache of recent fragments for comparison purposes. Cropping reduces PF's memory requirements, which may be important if you're running on very old hardware. In most cases, reassembling packets is a better choice.

```
scrub in all fragment crop
```

If you're really short on memory (e.g., running OpenBSD on a VAX), you might want to perform even more drastic fragment trimming. You can drop overlaps and fragments alike with the "drop-ovl" scrub rule. If you're this desperate for memory, however, buy a Pentium 100 to do your packet filtering instead. If you're running thousands of states simultaneously, you can certainly afford a machine with more RAM!

```
scrub in all fragment drop-ovl
```

In addition to handling fragmentation, scrub rules can perform some other basic packet checking and manipulation. One common setting on network packets is the "don't fragment" flag, which indicates that either the client or the server did not want this particular packet broken up. On occasion, however, a particular system or program will do something odd such as send a fragment with the don't-fragment flag set. This can confuse other computers on the network. You can choose to unset the don't-fragment flag on all packets that pass through PF by using the "no-df" modifier:

```
scrub in all no-df
```

Every IP packet has a time-to-live, or TTL. You can insist that all packets that pass through your packet filter have a minimum TTL. You would probably want two different scrub rules for this, as packets that you are sending should probably have a very high TTL, while packets entering your network should have a TTL large enough to let them reach their destination within your network. Set this with the "min-ttl" modifier:

```
scrub in on fxp0 min-ttl 5
scrub in on fxp1 min-ttl 30
```

Finally, you can adjust the maximum segment size of packets that pass through PF. Some networks have a problem with an unusual maximum segment size, so use the "max-mss" option with care.

```
scrub in all max-mss 1500
```

You can combine scrub rules on a single line, or break them up by interface, or any combination of these. Here, we have a scrub rule that applies to all packets, and separate rules that apply to packets that enter the system on particular interfaces:

```
scrub in all max-mss 1440 fragment reassemble
scrub in on fxp0 min-ttl 5
scrub in on fxp1 min-ttl 30 no-df
```

Avoiding Fragment Processing

Fragment caching and reassembly uses memory, of course, and you might think that you can reduce memory usage by not reassembling fragments. Don't do this. Buy memory instead. Fragments are generally the maximum size as the physical protocol allows, which is frequently much smaller than a large TCP/IP packet. Each fragment relies on information available in the first few fragments, such as the destination and source ports.

This means that if you do not reassemble fragments, you will not be able to filter based on source or destination port, or on ICMP message or code. This means that you cannot use stateful inspection on fragments, which immediately increases the size of your rule base dramatically. Packet descriptions that rely only upon source and destination IP address and protocol will catch fragments, but once you mention a port number the fragment will not match the rule. You can choose to either let all the packets in or block them without referring to port number, both of which dramatically reduce your security options. Do *something* with your fragments!

Packet Filtering

While packet filtering rules come last in /etc/pf.conf, understanding packet filtering is essential to using PF. People use PF without going near address translation, redirection, or any of the other nifty PF features, but packet filtering is the destination for many people. You could say that the entire function of PF is to "filter packets": allow packets with this TTL or higher, sieve out fragments, and so on. In this context, however, packet filtering has a very specific meaning: providing access control for network packets by source, destination, protocol, and other packet characteristics.

What Packet Filtering Doesn't Do

Packet filtering controls network connections based entirely on TCP/IP protocols and protocol characteristics, such as ports. If you want to stop all connections coming from a particular block of IP addresses, packet filtering is your friend. If you only want to allow connections to a particular TCP/IP port, packet filtering will work for you. If you want to allow entrance only to packets with the ECN flag set, but no other flags, PF will do that without even questioning why you would want to do such a weird thing. You can also filter other protocols that operate at a logical protocol layer such as IPSec, SKIP, VINES, and so on, but only on the logical network protocol. If it's a different protocol layer, PF cannot even see it.

One common question is, "How do I use PF to filter based on Ethernet MAC addresses?" The answer is, "You don't." MAC addresses are part of a physical protocol and are in a different layer. You might as well ask how one could use PF to filter dial-up connections. (Also, don't forget that MAC addresses are easily changed, and filtering based on them is more trouble than the security gained in almost all environments.) Mind you, OpenBSD does have a tool to filter based on MAC address, brconfig(8). But it's not part of PF.

Also, PF doesn't know anything about applications or application protocols. If you allow TCP/IP connections to port 25 on a server within your network, you might think you're allowing connections to the mail server on that host. Actually, you're allowing the connection to whatever daemon happens to be running on port 25 on that host! PF does not and never will recognize a SMTP data stream; it only sees that the connection is going to port 25 on that host, and allows it.

At one time, I had a system on the Net running an ssh daemon on ports 25 (email), 80 (web), 110 (POP3), 443 (secure web), and several other popular TCP/IP ports so that I could saunter past whatever packet-filtering firewall I happened to be behind that day. It made a very effective demonstration of exactly why I thought that company's security system could stand improvement.

Packet Filtering Rule Design

We took a brief look at the design of a PF rule earlier this chapter. Let's completely dissect this same rule to identify each piece.

```
❶pass ❷in ❸on fxp0 ❹proto tcp ❺from any ❻to 192.168.1.1 ❼port 22 ❽keep state
```

The ❶first part of the rule is the keyword that tells PF how to process this particular rule. Every packet-filtering rule begins with either "pass" or "block." We then state if this rule applies to packets ❷entering (in) or leaving (out) the system. This rule applies to a ❸particular interface.

We then have several statements to define the characteristics of the connection that this rule matches — a regular expression for TCP/IP, as it were. This rule applies to ❹TCP connections ❺from any IP address, if the connection is made ❻to the IP address 192.168.1.1 on ❼port 22. Finally, if the rest of the rule matches and the connection is allowed, we ❽keep state for the connection.

Each sort of rule has a slightly different syntax, depending on the type of protocol being filtered. For example, ICMP has no port numbers, so the rules are written slightly differently. Their own modifiers can follow some keywords. We'll see examples of all of these throughout this chapter.

Pass and Block

Each packet-filtering rule begins with one of two keywords: *pass* or *block*. Pass rules allow traffic that matches the pattern specified in the rule to continue. The trick lies in specifying the pattern that matches only the packets you want to pass.

Block rules are similar, but they have a wide range of possible responses. What, exactly, should happen when a packet is rejected? PF can give several types of responses, depending on the protocol you are using and your desired behavior.

The default is to silently drop rejected packets, but this can be adjusted on a global level by the block-policy option (see "Blocked Packet Policy"). You can also decide how to respond to blocked packets on a rule-by-rule basis.

Dropped packets are simply rejected without notifying the client. The effects of this vary widely depending on the sort of connection and the type of client. In most cases, the client will wait until the protocol times out and then complain that it could not make a connection or that the connection was lost. While this is the default, you can set it explicitly to override a default policy.

```
block drop in all
```

You can make your system respond politely to TCP requests and say, "No, I'm not going to accept that connection" by using the "return-rst" response. As it implies, this returns a RST (reset) for any matching attempted connection. This only works for rules that only match TCP packets — if you do not specify the protocol, you will get a syntax error. The following example sends a RST for every incoming TCP connection request:

```
block return-rst in proto tcp all
```

This only affects TCP packets, however. PF includes the "return" keyword, which returns an RST for TCP connections and an ICMP UNREACHABLE message for UDP requests and silently drops everything else. This is the same as the "block-policy" option.

```
block return in all
```

You can also specify particular types of ICMP responses for matching packets. This defaults to the standard "port unreachable" ICMP type 3 message, but you can choose to override it and return a more specific ICMP code. The effects of this will vary depending on the error code returned; if you are not conversant with ICMP error messages, either take the default and like it or learn the proper ICMP code to return in each circumstance. Getting this wrong is an excellent way to announuce that you have a misconfigured firewall, you don't know what you're doing, and would some kind hacker please show you the error of your ways?

ICMP Code	PF Name	Description
0	net-unr	Network Unreachable
1	host-unr	Host Unreachable
2	proto-unr	Protocol Unreachable
3	port-unr	Port Unreachable
4	needfrag	Fragmentation Needed

ICMP Code	PF Name	Description
5	srcfail	Source Route Failed
6	net-unk	Destination Network Unknown
7	host-unk	Destination Host Unknown
8	isolate	Source Host Isolated
9	net-prohib	Destination Network Administratively Prohibited
10	host-prohib	Destination Host Administratively Prohibited
11	net-tos	Network Unreachable for Terms of Service
12	host-tos	Host Unreachable for Terms of Service
13	filter-prohib	Communication Administratively Prohibited by Filtering
14	host-preced	Host Precedence Violation
15	cutoff-preced	Precedence Cutoff in Effect

If you just want the standard "icmp unreachable" message, use the "return-icmp" statement.

```
block return-icmp in all
```

Alternately, if you know which ICMP code you want to return, you can specify the code name or number in parenthesis after the return-icmp statement. If you to return a polite message telling clients that they may not connect to your network, for example, you might want to use ICMP code 13, "filter-prohib."

```
block return-icmp(filter-prohib) in all
```

If you're seriously interested in ICMP filtering, uses, and the effect of filtering and returning various sorts of ICMP responses, I recommend you check out Ofir Arkin's "ICMP Usage in Scanning" at http://www.sys-security.com/html/projects/icmp.html.

Default Pass or Default Block

Out of the box, PF uses a "default pass" stance. This is very simple to change with two rules at the beginning of /etc/pf.conf.

```
block in all
block out all
```

Now, nothing will go in or out unless you explicitly create a rule allowing it.

Additional Actions in Rules

You can use a couple of keywords here to specify actions that the PF system should take upon matching a packet to a rule. If you specify the "log" keyword immediately after the "in" or "out," a log message is sent to the pflogd(8) daemon (see "PF Logging"). If pflogd is not running, no log is kept. If this rule includes a "keep state" or "modulate state" statement; only the packet that establishes state is logged. If you want to log all the packets in stateful inspection connections, use the "log-all" option instead of just plain "log." All packets that match that rule, not just the initial packet, will be logged.

```
block return in log-all
```

You can tell PF to stop processing the rules when a packet matches a particular rule. Remember, rules are processed in order: If you have a rule that allows a connection and a later rule that disallows that connection, you can use the "quick" keyword to prevent PF from ever reaching that later rule. This makes it safe to have a "block all" rule last in /etc/pf.conf, and it can accelerate PF on long rule lists. Remember, all rules are processed in order.

```
pass in quick proto tcp from any to $ext_if port 22 keep state
```

The "quick" keyword must appear after the "log" or "log-all" keyword or the "direction" keyword if you are not logging. The PF developers discourage use of the quick keyword, as you should be able to achieve the same results with a properly-written ruleset.

Packet Pattern Matching

One of the most intensive parts of PF is the syntax used to describe packets. The next several terms in a rule describe particular sorts of packet by protocol, port, direction, and various other characteristics. PF will compare each arriving packet to these rules. If the rule matches the packet description, it will be treated as you decide. These terms must be specified in the order presented here. A term can be skipped, but the terms that appear must be in order.

Interface Matching

The "on" keyword describes an interface that this rule applies to. You must specify an interface, either explicitly or with a macro. If you want a rule to match every interface on the machine, you can use the "all" interface name. Here we stop all traffic coming in on interface fxp0 and allow traffic out on whatever interface is represented by the macro $external_if:

```
block in on fxp0
pass out on $external_if
```

Address Families

You could list an protocol address family, either "inet" for IPv4 or "inet6" for IPv6, to state that this rule only applies to packets in that type of address. The inet address family includes the IP, ICMP, TCP, and UDP protocols. The inet6 family includes the IPv6, ICMPv6, TCP, and UDP protocols. While TCP and UDP are common to both families, IPv6 and ICMPv6 are extremely different from IP and ICMP. The following rules allow standard IP traffic but deny IPv6 traffic:

```
pass in inet
block in inet6
```

Network Protocol

In addition to the inet and inet6 families, PF can recognize almost any network protocol by number or name. The "proto" keyword tells PF to filter by protocol. Network protocols can be listed by name, as given in /etc/protocols, or by protocol number. For example, here is a rule that allows SKIP traffic (protocol 57) to pass through the packet filter:

```
pass in proto 57
```

Obviously, this functionality somewhat overlaps the inet and inet6 statements — you could have a statement that explicitly allowed the IP, ICMP, TCP, and UDP protocols.

Address and Port

The next set of statements is the most commonly used type of packet-filtering rule, identifying source and destination addresses and ports. The syntax is very simple:

```
from source-address port source-port to destination-address port destination-port
```

Addresses here can be specific IP addresses or netblocks in CIDR notation (such as /24, /22, and so on, as discussed in Chapter 8). You could also use the keyword "any," meaning "any address." For example, this rule allows connections from anywhere on the Internet to the IP address 192.168.1.5:

```
pass in from any to 192.168.1.5
```

You could also specify an address as "no-route," meaning "any address which is not currently routable." If your OpenBSD machine does not know how to get to an IP address, the no-route address matches. It's usually a good idea to drop packets for unreachable hosts — even if they are legitimate, your system cannot respond to them. (This can only happen on systems without a default route, of course.) See Chapter 8 for a discussion of routing.

Interface and host names can also be used in the address space. PF will automatically translate these to IP addresses when loading the rules. Here, for example, we are allowing the machine 192.168.1.200 to connect to anything on the fxp0 interface:

```
pass in from 192.168.1.200 to fxp0
```

When you activate these rules and check them within PF, you'll see that the live rules contain the actual IP addresses on interface fxp0.

Ports can be specified as numbers or as names as found in /etc/services. Port numbers exist only in the TCP and UDP protocols, so when you specify a port you must specify the protocol being used. Use of the port keyword is optional in both source and destination; if you don't care which port a connection is coming from or going to, do not include a port statement. Here, we tighten the previous rule to specify that only TCP connections to port 22 are permitted:

```
pass in proto tcp from any to 192.168.1.5 port 22
```

Remember, this is *not* the same as only allowing SSH connections! PF doesn't know what application protocol you're using; it only knows about the TCP/IP port you are permitting.

If you know the source port of a connection, you can easily specify that on the rule line. For example, many old firewalls make all of their outbound DNS queries from UDP port 53. Here, we allow the nameserver running on our PF-protected host to make queries of our ISP's nameserver. We're also specifying that packets may return back to this service:

```
❶pass out proto udp from 192.168.1.5 port 53 to 10.15.3.8 port 53
❷pass in proto udp from 10.15.3.8 port 53 to 192.168.1.5 port 53
```

Note that we specify ❶"pass out" in the first rule so that packets can leave this system and ❷"pass in" on the second rule so that the responses may come back. As DNS queries run over UDP, we restrict this to UDP queries only. (In a little bit, we'll see how to write this sort of rule more securely and as a single line with stateful inspection.)

User and Group

PF allows you to filter by the user and group of the socket opened by the program trying to access the network. This functionality can only work when connections originate with or terminate at the PF device; you cannot use this on a network-protecting firewall to protect hosts within the network. In other words, if you're running a web server on your OpenBSD machine, you can use PF only allow connections to port 80 if the web server user has opened the connection, but if you're using your OpenBSD machine to protect another web server the user and group ID will not work. Also, this only works with TCP or UDP protocols; if you try to filter other protocols such as ICMP by user, the restriction will be ignored.

A "user" or a "group" keyword followed by a name or UID/GID activates this functionality, such as:

```
user username
```

Add this after your packet address and port statement. For example, here we allow anyone in the wheel group to make outbound SSH connections from this machine:

```
pass out on fxp0 proto tcp from any to any port 22 group wheel
```

Be careful restricting user functionality; you might be surprised what sorts of connectivity a shell user might need! If you don't have interactive shell users, and none of your users should be running programs on the server, you might consider a rule such as this:

```
block out on fxp0 proto tcp from any to any group customers
```

In the event of a user account compromise, or if some FTP-only customer even manages to break out into a shell, he won't be able to initiate any outbound connections from your system. This will seriously restrict the intruder's ability to use your server to attack other servers, which is always nice. The downside is, he'll have time to spend trying to break root on your server instead. Are you *certain* all of your programs are secure?[3]

Packet Flags

PF allows you to filter based upon TCP packet flags. A *packet flag* is a flag that indicates the state of the connection that the packet claims to be a part of. For example, when a client sends a SYN packet to a server, that packet includes a flag that says "I'm a SYN packet." The returning SYN+ACK packet will have two flags set, the SYN flag and the ACK flag. TCP packets have many different possible flags, each with its own purpose.

If you're going to start complex filtering based on TCP flags, you must be completely intimate with TCP/IP. You will see many sites on the Internet that claim that if you filter on such-and-such flags, you will get a particular useful behavior. Research these claims carefully. The problem is that every TCP/IP stack has been modified by vendors for their own purposes[4] and behaves in a slightly different way. You may find a description of a neat filtering-on-flags trick that can prevent port scans from working, for example, but then discover that some of your desktop systems crash whenever they try to access the Internet. If you want to really get into flag-based filtering, get a copy of all three volumes of *TCP/IP Illustrated* and don't just read it; assimilate it, live it, commune with it, become one with it. Ambitious flag-based filtering is of questionable efficacy, and (in my opinion) the single part of firewall construction most laden with uncertainty, error, and superstition.

---

[3] Of course, if the user account can use CGI programs, the intruder could just run a program with the permissions of the "www" user. Isn't security *fun*?

[4] I have been told that this purpose is *not* "Make Michael's life difficult," but am still awaiting hard evidence to back this assertion.

Simple flag-based packet filtering help manage multi-interface firewalls. If you want to filter connections through one machine to your sales office, your financial network, your DMZ, the factory in Shaolin China, and the public Internet, the only way to differentiate traffic flows is on which flags are set in each packet. PF recognizes the following flags.

Flag	Name
F	FIN
S	SYN
R	RST
P	PUSH
A	ACK
U	URG
E	ECE
W	CWR

We will discuss certain precise combinations of flags that can be used in various situations. Using other combinations of flags leaves you on your own.

The general syntax of a flag statement is:

```
flags ❶set / ❷list
```

This rule matches a packet that has certain flags ❶set out of a ❷list of flags. One popular example is:

```
flags S/SA
```

PF will check the "S" and "A" flags on every packet. If the "S" flag is set, and the "A" flag is not set, this rule matches. This rule doesn't care if, say, "R" or "E" or any other flag is set, because it's not in the list. This is a typical "connection creation" rule; packets that are sent by one machine requesting access to a another have the SYN flag set, but the ACK flag not set. This is commonly referred to as a "SYN packet."

You can also specify lists that cannot be set, such as this:

```
flags /SFRA
```

A matching packet has none of the flags S, F, R, and A set.

If you're only concerned about one flag, you can specify it on both sides of the slash. Here, matching rules have the SYN flag set, and the other flags are irrelevant:

```
flags S/S
```

Add the flag statement after the address and port statement in your PF rule. Here, we are allowing any machine on the Internet to request a TCP connection to our web server:

```
pass in proto tcp from any to 192.168.1.5 port 80 flags S/SA
```

If the packet has the SYN flag set, and the ACK flag is not set, the connection will be allowed. If both the SYN and ACK flags are set, this rule does not match.

Filtering on Flags and Port Scanners

In most cases, filtering based on flags is just over-engineering with very little net benefit. One popular use for flag-based filtering is to confound network scanners such as nmap that use the characteristics of an operating system's responses to bad packets to identify an operating system. While this is of questionable efficiency — the intruder will just use some other method to identify the operating system — PF can provide some basic protection against these sorts of probes with the following rules:

```
block in quick proto tcp all flags SF/SFRA
block in quick proto tcp all flags SFUP/SFRAU
block in quick proto tcp all flags FPU/SFRAUP
block in quick proto tcp all flags /SFRA
block in quick proto tcp all flags F/SFRA
block in quick proto tcp all flags U/SFRAU
block in quick proto tcp all flags P
```

ICMP Types and Codes

Much like TCP flags, ICMP has types and codes. Despite what you might hear, it is not proper to unilaterally block ICMP. ICMP has a vital role to play in many sorts of connections. Fortunately, most ICMP needs are handled very easily by the provided block policies.

You can allow particular types of ICMP traffic with the "icmp-type" keyword.

```
icmp-type type code code
```

For example, here's how you allow incoming ping requests. This doesn't allow the responses, but it will let the requests into your system. (Adding stateful inspection would let the transaction complete, but we haven't discussed stateful inspection yet.)

```
pass in inet proto icmp icmp-type 8 code 0
```

Everything I said about filtering by TCP flags applies doubly to filtering ICMP. You must really understand TCP/IP before you start playing with ICMP filtering.

IP Options

Unless you specifically allow packets containing IP options, PF will block them. The "allow-opts" keyword tells PF to accept matching packets if they contain IP options.

With the packet description language presented here, you can describe almost any TCP/IP packet and give basic descriptions of packets of most other protocols. While passing and blocking is theoretically all you need to do with packets, PF includes some options to make managing packets easier.

Type of Service

Every TCP packet includes a Type of Service field. The setting of this field varies with the application protocol; each application requests a particular Type of Service setting. You will need to study your particular application to determine what Type of Service your application uses (or, just drop a packet sniffer on the network and see what it says). PF can match packets on Type of Service with the "tos" keyword. Here we allow an application protocol to pass when it has a Type of Service of 0x10, but reject it when it has a Type of Service of 0x08:

```
pass  out on fxp0 proto tcp from any to any port 88 tos 0x10
block out on fxp0 proto tcp from any to any port 22 tos 0x08
```

Applications can change the requested Type of Service after the connection is set up, making filtering based on Type of Service very tricky. In "Bandwidth Management," we'll see an example of using Type of Service to offer different service levels to different parts of an application.

Labels

Your /etc/pf.conf file should certainly be well commented, with labels for each major section describing the desired effect so your coworkers can have some idea what was going through your mind when they get paged at 3 a.m. to diagnose a problem. But you can also use labels visible to pfctl(8). These labels have no operational effect whatsoever, but can help you manage your system. Labels can be useful for parsing rule output for billing purposes, for example. To use a label, add the "label" keyword and a label name to the end of your rule.

```
pass out proto tcp from any to any port 22 ❶label ❷ssh
```

We have the label at the ❶end of the rule and a simple ❷label name. In addition to these simple text names, you can use macros within label names. PF provides several macros for label names. When you use a macro, the label name must be in double quotes (").

$if	Interface name
$srcaddr	Source IP address
$dstaddr	Destination IP address
$srcport	Source port description

$dstport	Destination port description
$proto	Protocol name
$nr	Rule number

These macros are parsed when the rules are first loaded; you can't dynamically build a list of labels from the packets that pass through your firewall. If a macro references a field with an "any" value, the macro also shows up as "any." For example, our sample label rule above doesn't list an interface name. Let's use the $if macro in the rule name:

```
pass out proto tcp from any to any port 22 label "$if:ssh"
```

When you load the rules and run them, the label will show up as "any:ssh." The rule doesn't mention an interface, so the rule applies to any interface, and the label macro knows it. Macros for IP address and port are most useful when applied to macros for groups of servers or ports: Each generated rule will be separately labeled.

```
pass in proto tcp from any to $Webservers port 22 label ❶"ssh:$dstaddr"
```

This will generate a separate rule for each web server, each with its own label named after the IP address of the web server.

One thing to note is that you can use the same label multiple times within a rule. I could put the string "label ftp" in several FTP-related rules, and they would each show up as a separate lines with the same name when viewing the statistics, like this. Or, if I have a rule with brackets to allow multiple protocols or addresses, it will expand to have multiple rules with the same label. For example, this rule creates multiple labels called "web":

```
pass out proto tcp from ($ExtIf) to any port {80, 443} label web
```

If you want separate labels for these, try combining the label with the macro for the destination port, like this:

```
pass out proto tcp from ($ExtIf) to any port {80, 443} label "web:$dstport"
```

This would create two labels, called "web:80" and "web:443."

Anchors and Named Rulesets

PF supports the ability to add attachment points for rules. You can define an attachment point, or *anchor,* so that when a packet reaches the anchor point in the rules list, the rules in that attachment point are interpreted. At first glance, this seems rather pointless — why not just put the rules you want to have executed where you want them executed, instead of using an attachment point and some fancy redirection?

The clever bit is that outside programs can add rules into anchor points! Your IDS can add rules to block an IP address when it detects an attack, although with the current state of IDS technology this tends to block legitimate activities too frequently. Your mail server can use this to block known spam sources (see spamd(8)). Your authentication system can add rules to your firewall when a user logs in. We discuss OpenBSD's integrated authpf(8) features in Chapter 19, which makes heavy use of anchors. Most of these functions require a bit of programming, or at least shell scripting.

PF supports the following types of anchors.

nat-anchor	An anchor for NAT rules
rdr-anchor	An anchor for redirection rules
binat-anchor	An anchor for bi-directional NAT rules
anchor	An anchor for packet-filtering rules

In pf.conf, an anchor appears like this:

```
anchortype anchorname
```

For example, an anchor called "intrusion-detection" would appear as:

```
anchor intrusion-detection
```

You cannot put anchors within anchors.

We'll look at an example of anchor use in Chapter 19.

Rules, Interfaces, and DHCP

All PF rules are set at the time the rules are parsed. This can be a problem if you're using DHCP or PPP, where your IP address will change frequently enough to cause annoyance. Your computer may be up for some time and change IP addresses several times. By putting the interface name in parentheses, you tell PF to adjust the rules whenever the IP address changes.

```
block in on (fxp0) from any to any
```

Using Stateful Inspection

You can now match particular sorts of packets, and allow them in or out. You can even set rules that will identify the first packet in a TCP/IP request. If you can identify the first packet of a permitted data stream, you can tell PF to not only allow that packet but to allow all packets related to that first packet.

For example, suppose a SYN (connection request) packet arrives at port 80 on your OpenBSD web server. If you have a rule allowing stateful inspection, PF will examine that packet and record the source IP, source port, and various other connection characteristics such as sequence number. This information is stored in a *state table*, or a list of existing permitted connections. When your web server replies, PF will run that packet through the state table. When it sees that a permitted connection exists between the web server and the client requesting access, and that this packet matches the information it has for this connection, it allows the packet to pass without running it through the rules table. If an ICMP message related to a particular TCP connection arrives, stateful inspection will match the message to the proper connection and let it through. If the connection is properly terminated, or if no traffic goes over it for a reasonable length of time, the entry in the state table is discarded.

You enable stateful inspection with the "keep state" keyword at the end of your rule.

```
pass in proto tcp from any to 192.168.1.5 port 80 ❶flags S/SA ❷keep state
```

Not only can packets arrive at your web server now, but also with the addition of ❷stateful inspection your web server will be able to respond. Note that this rule only matches ❶initial TCP connection requests, so an intruder would not be able to send a packet that appeared to be part of an outgoing connection instead, or any of the other wide range of TCP/IP tricks that intruders have used through the years. (Without this flag, you could clear your state table and PF would automatically rebuild it from existing connections. We'll talk about that in "Managing Stateful Inspection.")

UDP State

UDP traffic is stateless, but in some cases you may well expect a response packet. As the firewall administrator, you must know if a particular application protocol that runs over UDP will send a response or not. If you are expecting a response, you can use stateful inspection to match based on hostname and port. Because UDP packets don't have any of TCP's fancy flags, that's the best any filter can do. For example, systems expect replies to DNS queries, and you should know that. In this example, we allow anyone within the firewall to access the ISP's nameserver and receive the replies.

```
pass out proto udp from any to 10.0.0.5 port 53 keep state
```

With all the caveats, UDP stateful inspection might seem to be risky. The risks are not as high as they might seem, however. To breach UDP stateful inspection, the intruder would have to send UDP packets to port 53 on a particular client that appeared to be from port 53 on the nameserver, and do this before the stateful inspection timed out, and be able to use that packet to compromise the client in some way. Can it be done? Yes. Is it very difficult? Absolutely.

In an ideal world, you would never permit UDP through your firewall. But that isn't very likely given the current design of the Internet.

ICMP States

While ICMP messages that are part of TCP connections are handled by stateful inspection in the TCP connection, ICMP messages used for connections such as ping(8) and traceroute(8) have separate stateful requirements. PF is aware of the most common of these and can use stateful inspection to allow the proper replies. We earlier saw how to allow ping requests into a packet filter; now, we can easily allow the replies:

```
pass in inet proto icmp icmp-type 8 code 0 keep state
```

State Modulation

State modulation is much like stateful inspection, but provides additional security enhancements for poor TCP/IP stacks. Every connection request contains an initial sequence number, or ISN, that the client and the server both use to track individual connections. If you can guess this ISN, you can hijack the connection and feed the client any information you like. This might sound unlikely, but the most common TCP/IP stack in the world chose astonishingly poor ISNs, making ISN hijacking a popular technique.

State modulation replaces the ISN sent by every machine involved in a connection by a highly random ISN, and translates that ISN as needed for each client. While it only works for TCP connections, it provides a much greater level of TCP protocol security than the naive TCP stack found in the most common desktop operating systems.

You enable state modulation with the "modulate state" keyword. This includes stateful inspection. Here, we enable state modulation for web browsing on every client behind our network:

```
pass out from any to any port {80, 443} flags S/SA modulate state
```

Inspection and Modulation Options

Stateful inspection and state modulation have two settings that can be tweaked: the number of states a particular rule will match and the timeouts for the state table. Each option should be given in parenthesis after the "keep state" or "modulate state" statements.

You can use the "max" keyword to limit the number of entries in the state table. You might be low on system resources and want to conserve memory, but this is also useful for connection rate limiting. If someone posts the script for the next Harry Potter movie on your web server, you could find your bandwidth devoured by hordes of rabid fans. The max keyword will restrict the state table to that many entries in the state table. Additional packets that would match the rule and keep state are rejected. When an existing connection times out or terminates, another connection may be opened. This example limits port 80 to 100 simultaneous connections:

```
pass in proto tcp from any to 192.168.1.5 port 80 flags S/SA keep state (max 100)
```

You can use this same technique to implement rate limits to any port, and it is much simpler than limiting rates via the program itself or by using bandwidth managers. I personally prefer to return requested information quickly for the users that are lucky enough to get in and get them off my server so I can serve other people, as opposed to making everyone's connections unbearably slow via bandwidth queues. Your preferences or requirements may be different, of course.

Timeouts can be adjusted on a per-rule basis, much as the global stateful inspection timeouts can be set (see OPTIONS). While I find the defaults perfectly sensible for almost all situations, there are occasional rules where adjusting them makes sense.

You can view the current timeout settings with "pfctl -s timeouts." This will spit out the stateful inspection timeouts for every state of a TCP connection. By default, idle TCP sessions time out after 24 hours. Here I tell TCP connections to port 80 on my web server to time out in only one hour, or 3,600 seconds:

```
pass in proto tcp from any to 192.168.1.5 port 80 flags S/SA keep state (tcp.
established 3600)
```

This is generally not necessary, but you might have special circumstances.

Stateful inspection is absolutely necessary if you are using NAT (see "Network Address Translation"). Without stateful inspection, your packet filter will be unable to match translated addresses to real addresses.

Filtering Spoofed Packets

One common way to defeat a less intelligent packet filter is to send fraudulent packets with a source address within the firewall. In theory, the firewall will pass those packets on into the network. If the intruder does everything exactly right, he could compute the likely response packets from packets he sends and compute the packets he would need to send in response to those, eventually building a sequence of packets to issue commands to a target machine without receiving any responses from it. This attack has been used before and will probably be used again.

To prevent this, filter out packets from interfaces that they couldn't possibly be coming in legitimately. For one very typical example, suppose you have an OpenBSD machine with two network cards. One card has the IP address 192.168.1.1/24 and is connected to your internal network, while the other is connected to the Internet and has whatever IP address your ISP has assigned. Packets with a source address beginning with 192.168.1 should not be entering your network from the card attached to the Internet. Similarly, packets with a source address of 192.168.1.1 should not be entering the firewall from either network card. You could write rules for this, but this is such a common situation that PF includes a statement for it, "antispoof." Here we block spoofed packets on the fxp0 interface:

```
antispoof for fxp0
```

This statement automatically adds rules that block the Ethernet network directly attached to the interface from coming in on any other interface and that block the actual IP on that card from coming in over any network.

It's a good idea to provide antispoof protection for every network interface on your firewall, including the loopback interfaces. Providing antispoof protection on loopback interfaces can cause problems if software on your system attempts to communicate with the system via a local IP address. You'll need to add rules to bypass the antispoof protection in this instance. For that reason, I also suggest logging spoofed packets by adding the "log" keyword.

```
antispoof log for fxp0
```

Now that you have a grip on the basics of packet filtering, let's consider some of PF's more interesting traffic-management abilities, which are discussed in the next chapter.

18

MORE PACKET FILTERING

Office net seems slow,
Thanks to MP3 swapping.
Let's stop that right quick!

Now that you have a basic understanding of how to keep undesired traffic out while permitting acceptable traffic, let's look at some ways you can rearrange and manipulate network traffic.

A common trick to make one IP address seem like many is Network Address Translation (NAT), a very popular feature among small network administrators. NAT requires the ability to arbitrarily redirect network connections, so we'll discuss that next. Another useful feature is the ability to manage bandwidth for particular tasks, which OpenBSD supports through queuing.

Network Address Translation

Network Address Translation is like making soup out of a bone; it makes what you have go much further. If you only have a handful of IP addresses, or only one, you can use NAT to place a whole bunch of private IP addresses behind the public address and attach dozens, hundreds, or thousands of computers to the Internet with one "real" IP. NAT can cause problems — some VPN protocols do not work well with NAT, and it really confuses anyone who is trying to control machine access by IP address — but in general it solves more problems than it causes. If some of your machines cannot use NAT for whatever reason, you must give them real IP addresses (or possibly use binat, as discussed in "Bi-directional NAT").

All you need to know to configure NAT is the external interface, the addresses you want translated, and the address you want to translate them to.

```
nat on external-interface from internal-network to any -> external-interface-or-
real-IP-address
```

For example, if your external interface is fxp0, your internal IP addresses are 192.168.1.0/24, and your real IP address 10.0.5.4, you would write:

```
nat on fxp0 from 192.168.1.0/24 to any -> 10.0.5.4
```

PF rewrites outbound packets to give them a source IP of 10.0.5.4 and keep a state table of outgoing connections. When packets return it uses port numbers, IP addresses, and ISNs to match the returning packets to the real machine, rewrites the packets to give them the proper destination address, and send them back to the client.

If you only have one IP address, and that address changes when you connect to the Internet, you may not want to hard-code the interface name in your rules. That's fine. Instead of using the IP address as the translation address, use the interface name. PF will learn the IP on that interface and use it.

```
nat on fxp0 from 192.168.1.0/24 to any -> fxp0
```

If you're using DHCP to get your IP address, the IP may change while the system is still connected to the Internet. Just as you can put the interface name in parentheses to have a filter rule reevaluated when the IP address changes, use parentheses for NAT as well.

```
nat on fxp0 from 192.168.1.0/24 to any -> (fxp0)
```

You can also specify that NAT will take place only from certain networks or to certain networks. This is useful if you have several internal networks and don't want to translate traffic between them.

As a NAT device many different devices sharing one IP address, and rewrites outbound and inbound connecting ports and IPs as necessary, it is nearly impossible to write packet-filtering rules that will properly redirect responses back to the correct client. As such, a NAT rule automatically implies stateful inspection to all connections made out through that rule. You do not need to specify "keep state" on rules going out through the NAT, as that is applied automatically by the NAT. If you want to modulate state, you must specify that. But standard stateful inspection is enforced by the NAT rule.

NAT Rule Order

Unlike packet-filtering rules, NAT rules are processed on a first-fit basis. In most cases, you only have one NAT rule. If you're using binat rules (see "Bi-directional NAT") or if you have some special circumstances that require multiple NAT rules, keep this in mind. Put binat rules and exclusions before your default rule.

Private NAT Addresses

In theory, you could use any addresses behind your NAT device. If you just grab some IPs and use them, you won't be able to reach whoever has those IP addresses out in the real world. It's highly advisable to use some of the IP addresses reserved for private use. Those IP addresses are:

     10.0.0.0/8, (10.0.0.0-10.255.255.255)
     172.16.0.0/12 (172.16.0.0-172.31.255.255)
     192.168.0.0/16 (192.168.0.0-192.168.255.255)

You can subnet and rearrange these IP addresses in any way you wish, so long as you don't try to route them on the public Internet.

Exclusions from NAT

You may have a block of IPs that you do not want to allow to NAT, or a particular server that you do not want to allow on the Internet, or a protocol that chokes on NAT (such as IPSec). You can specifically exclude addresses or protocols from undergoing NAT by using the "no" keyword before the rule. Remember, in NAT the first matching rule is applied immediately! In this example, we first exclude protocol 51 (the AH protocol used in IPSec) from the NAT, then NAT everything else:

```
no nat on fxp0 proto 51 from 192.168.1.0/24 to any
nat on fxp0 from 192.168.1.0/24 to any -> 204.92.77.100
```

Bi-directional NAT

It's not uncommon to have several real IP addresses available, but need more than you have available. Many ISPs will happily issue a block of 8 or 16 IP addresses to a company, and expect them to use NAT for most of their hosts and use the remainder of the address for DMZ hosts, nameservers, and so on.

You may have some hosts behind a firewall with special address-translation needs. Perhaps you need to allow Microsoft RPC[1] through your firewall to a particular host or some other protocol that uses a wide range of almost-random port numbers. You want all of your protected hosts on the same network. Bi-directional NAT might solve your problem. Bi-directional NAT allows one system to monopolize a single real IP address in a one-to-one relationship. Incoming requests to that IP are always directed to the bi-directional NAT host, and outbound packets from that host are always translated to have the monopolized IP address.

For example, suppose your firewall has two IP addresses bound to it — 10.0.5.4 and 10.0.5.5 — and you are using 192.168.1.0/24 for your machines. All of your office client machines and most of your servers use NAT through 10.0.5.4, but you reserve 10.0.5.5 for one special-purpose host at 192.168.1.66. Packets sent to 10.0.5.5 are directed to this 192.168.1.66, and packets from 192.168.1.66 are translated to have a source IP of 10.0.5.5. This allows you to make broad, sweeping port redirections and other rules that simply are not possible under many-to-one NAT. This is done via a "binat" rule.

```
binat on external-interface from private-ip to any -> real-ip
```

To continue our earlier example, if the external interface is fxp0, your private IP 192.168.1.66, and your reserved public IP 10.0.5.5, your binat rule would look like this:

```
binat on fxp0 from 192.168.1.66 to any -> 10.0.5.5
```

Put binat rules before other NAT rules.

Using a binat rule is not necessary if you want to redirect particular connections to hosts within your NAT network; they're only helpful if you need broad swaths of ports open and you don't want to overlap other services provided by your main NAT IP. Use redirection to send the occasional port to servers inside your NAT.

Packet Filtering and NAT

You need a packet-filtering rule to allow traffic to a host behind the firewall. Use the actual, not translated, IP addresses for such rules. Here, we allow inbound connections to SSH to a server behind our NAT:

```
pass in on fxp0 proto tcp from any to 192.168.1.200 port 22
```

While this rule will allow the traffic, how will the firewall know to route new requests to this machine? That's where connection redirection comes in.

---

[1] Allowing RPC to a host is almost saying "Here I am, hackers, take me now!" Get rid of the RPC box, tunnel RPC over HTTPS, or get a new job. With that box on your network, you'll be looking for a job soon anyway.

Connection Redirection

Many networks lurk behind a single IP address; their mail server lives on one machine behind the NAT, their web server is on another machine, and so on. You can use connection redirection to aim incoming TCP/IP connection requests to the appropriate machines, allowing an IP address the global DNS calls "www.mycompany.com" to handle any incoming service. Connection redirection is useful for situations other than just NAT, but NAT is the first place it's needed. You need to know the port number and the IP address that you want to show to the world, and the port number and IP address of the daemon on the hidden machine that you want the connection to go to.

```
rdr on external-interface proto protocol from source-ip to public-ip port public-
port -> destination-port port real-destination-port
```

For example, we might have a NAT firewall with an external IP address of 209.69.178.18, with an SSH server lurking behind it on 192.168.1.200. We want incoming TCP requests on port 2022 to be redirected to this SSH server. I'm not using the standard SSH port, 22, because the OpenBSD firewall also runs sshd. PF will intercept incoming connection requests before they ever reach the local SSH daemon, which means I wouldn't be able to log in remotely.

```
❶rdr ❷on fxp0 ❸proto tcp from ❹any to ❺209.69.178.18 ❻port 2022 ->
❼192.168.1.200 ❽port 22
```

All redirection rules start with the ❶rdr keyword.

Then we have ❷the interface that the redirection applies to. Any packets that cross this interface and that match the rest of the packet description will be redirected as the rule says. Including the interface in a redirection rule is optional if you have only one interface doing NAT. If you're doing different sorts of NAT on different interfaces, you'll need to include this. If I didn't include this rule, however, any packet from anywhere would be redirected to the internal SSH server. I'd like to be able to SSH into my firewall from the inside network, so I specify the outside interface.

Every redirection rule must include a ❸protocol statement. You can use braces to include multiple protocols, which is useful for applications such as DNS, but most applications run over a single network protocol.

Just as with packet-filtering rules, redirections allow you to specify a ❹source address and/or port. You can choose different servers to redirect to based on source IP address.

The destination ❺IP and ❻port are actually the IP address visible to the outside world. The IP address is bound to the external network card. Then we have the actual destination IP and port. In this example, connections to port ❻2022 of the IP address ❺209.69.178.18 are forwarded on to port ❽22 on the IP address ❼192.168.1.200.

Put redirection rules after NAT rules.

Redirecting Ranges of Ports

PF can also redirect entire ranges of ports to a single port or a range of ports, as you desire. The configuration is done entirely by changing how you specify the public port and the real destination port.

To specify a range of public ports, list the lowest and highest ports, separated by a colon. For example, many Microsoft RPC-based network services require access to random ports above 1024. To redirect the entire range of network ports from 1024 to 65535 to an internal host, use a public port statement like this:

```
1024:65535
```

On the destination side, if you want all of the redirections to arrive at a single port, just list the port number as usual. Here, we redirect the entire range of ports from 1024 to 65535, inclusive, to a single machine:

```
rdr on fxp0 proto tcp from any to 209.69.178.18 port 1024:65535 -> 192.168.1.200
port 1024
```

Much more likely is that you would need to redirect a range of ports to another range of ports, e.g., port 1024 on your public IP goes to port 1024 on your private IP, port 1025 on the public IP goes to port 1025 on the private IP, and so on. Do this by specifying the start port, a colon, and an asterisk, like this:

```
1024:*
```

For a working Microsoft RPC service, you would redirect the entire range of ports like this:

```
rdr on fxp0 proto tcp from any to 209.69.178.18 port 1024:65535 -> 192.168.1.200
port 1024:*
```

This, of course, provides a whole wide variety of holes for an intruder to gleefully exploit. It will provide you with a solid background in intrusion response and recovery, however.

Redirection and Proxies

You can use redirection to provide transparent proxy services. One common application proxy is the Squid HTTP cache (/usr/ports/www/squid). You could run around from desktop to desktop and reconfigure all the web browsers to point at the proxy server, or you could just do this redirection at the firewall. For example, if you want to send all of the web requests from 192.168.1.0/24 to the Squid proxy running on port 8080 of the firewall, you would just do this:

```
rdr on ❶fxp1 proto tcp from 192.168.1.0/24 to any port 80 -> 127.0.0.1 port 8080
```

The first tricky thing here is that we need to specify the ❶internal interface rather than the external interface. Requests that should be proxied will only be coming in on the internal interface. This will also prevent things such as some clever user installing a port 80 sshd(8) on his home machine just to bypass the packet-filtering firewall.

This works well if your proxy server is on your firewall, but what if you have a separate cache machine? The cache machine must be able to make outbound requests to port 80, but you almost certainly want to protect it behind your firewall. You can specifically exclude one machine from this redirection by using a "no" rule. In the following example, 192.168.1.12 is our Squid machine. As the first rule matches, this machine can go out to the Internet and browse web pages directly. Other machines that attempt to access the Web are instead redirected to the Squid machine's cache on TCP port 3128.

```
no rdr on fxp1 proto tcp from 192.168.1.12 to any port 80
rdr on fxp1 proto tcp from 192.168.1.0/24 to any port 80 -> 192.168.1.12 port 3128
```

You can use a similar technique to allow particular machines to bypass the Web proxy. At times, allowing a single machine to bypass the proxy can be useful for troubleshooting purposes.

Redirection and Packet Filtering

You might need a packet-filtering rule to allow traffic to a redirected port. Use the port number visible to the world in these rules, not the redirected port number. For example, if you are redirecting all traffic on port 80 to port 8081 on a different machine, your packet filtering rules must allow access to port 80, not port 8081.

FTP and Firewalls

Modern application protocols run over a single network connection. If you make a Web request your Web browser requests a connection to port 80, transmits a request for information over that channel, and receives the answer over that same channel. SSH opens a single connection over port 22 and sends all its information over that connection. Experience and experiments with older protocols taught the wisdom of this approach. FTP is an older protocol, and it provided a wealth of education on this subject.

The original version of FTP (called *active FTP* today) required the client to send a connection to the server on TCP port 21. The server would then open a connection back to the client from port 20 to some random high-numbered port on the client. This is called a *backchannel*. On a network protocol level, however, no connection exists between the initial request and the backchannel. There's no way for a firewall to use stateful inspection to sort out if such a connection is allowed. Worse, if the client is behind a NAT device, there's no way to determine which actual IP an incoming FTP response should go to!

On a technical level a better choice is to use passive FTP, an updated version of the protocol that only uses one TCP connection. Not all clients support passive FTP, however, and this can lead to an endless round of user education and increased help desk load. As help desk people are usually pretty close to the breaking point anyway, increasing the pressure on them isn't a good move.

OpenBSD works around this by including an active FTP application proxy, ftp-proxy(8). Once configured, when a user makes a FTP request that request is redirected to the application proxy. The proxy keeps track of the FTP protocol transactions, receives the incoming active FTP data stream, and redirects it to the appropriate client. The proxy requires two parts: the proxy application and the redirect rules.

Configuring the FTP Proxy Application

Ftp-proxy(8) daemon runs out of inetd(8). We discuss inetd.conf in Chapter 14, so if you want full details on how this configuration works look there. First, be sure that inetd is running on your system. Not only should "inetd" appear in the system process list, but also you should have a line like this in /etc/rc.conf.

```
inetd=YES
```

Now you'll need to add an entry to /etc/inetd.conf for this daemon.

```
127.0.0.1:8021❶ stream tcp nowait root /usr/libexec/ftp-proxy ftp-proxy❷
```

Here, we're running the proxy on port ❶8021 of the firewall machine. We're also running the ftp-proxy command as "ftp-proxy," without any command-line arguments. If you want to change the command-line arguments, edit them at the end of this line.

For full details on ftp-proxy(8), read the man page. Here are some of the most useful features.

Anonymous FTP Only

You might want to only allow anonymous FTP, especially in situations where data theft is a possibility. (While there are other ways to get data out of a network, FTP uploads are perhaps the easiest.) The "-A" flag tells ftp-proxy to only allow FTP connections with the server logins of "anonymous" or "ftp."

NAT Mode

The proxy must run slightly differently when using NAT. The "-n" flag tells ftp-proxy that it is running in a NAT environment and to make the appropriate protocol changes.

Timeouts

By default, the proxy does not time out. On a long-running firewall with sloppy clients, this can result in a gradual increase of firewall resource use. Use the "-t" flag to specify a number of seconds after which an idle connection will be disconnected. This will only affect people who leave an FTP session open without doing anything in it. For example, to set a timeout of 300 seconds (5 minutes), you would add this to /etc/inetd.conf.

```
127.0.0.1:8021 stream tcp nowait root /usr/libexec/ftp-proxy ftp-proxy -t 300
```

FTP Logging

You might want to log which particular transfers your users make. The "-V" flag will log everything the users do to syslogd(8), which you can redirect as you wish using /etc/syslog.conf (see Chapter 14).

FTP Proxy PF Rules

To use the proxy, you must have three sets of rules: a redirection rule for clients, a rule to allow the proxy to speak to the desired FTP servers, and a rule to allow the backchannel connections to reach the application proxy. The client redirection rule is very similar to the example we saw for Squid.

```
rdr on ❶fxp1 proto tcp from ❷192.168.1.0/24 to ❸any ❹port 21 -> ❺127.0.0.1 port 8021
```

We're redirecting all incoming traffic on our ❶internal interface from our ❷internal network that tries to go to the ❹FTP command port of ❸any server on the Internet, to the FTP proxy running on port ❺8021 of the firewall itself.

Your firewall may or may not allow connections out to the world. If you have a "default deny" security stance, you will need to explicitly allow the firewall to connect to outside FTP servers.

```
pass out of fxp0 proto tcp from fxp0 to any port 21 keep state
```

Now we need to allow backchannel connections to the FTP proxy itself. Presumably you're blocking all inbound connections by default. How can you possibly know which port a connection will be coming back in on? Here you can take advantage of the fact that ftp-proxy(8) runs as the user "proxy." Remember, PF has the ability to allow connections to or from particular users on the firewall itself.

```
pass in on fxp0 proto tcp from any to fxp0 user proxy keep state
```

You can, of course, use any other PF features you like in combination with ftp-proxy(8): Restrict certain users from using FTP, only allow access to particular FTP sites, and so on.

Load Balancing

OpenBSD's load balancing integrated with PF allows you to share multiple NAT addresses among multiple users, both entering and leaving the network. This lets you both make multiple application servers show up as a single host, or even share several IP addresses amongst your NAT users. This is also called "address pooling," because several IP addresses are in a common pool.

In many situations, IP-based load balancing is more akin to "load scattering"; traffic is almost randomly sprayed across the addresses pooled together. OpenBSD includes the ability to specify exactly how you want your load balancing to work.

Types of Load Balancing

PF supports four distinct types of load balancing: round-robin, random, source-hash, and bitmask.

The default, round-robin, sends each connection to a different IP address in the group, looping back to the beginning once it has gone through every IP. The first incoming connection goes to the first address in the pool, the second to the second address, and so on. This is quite quick and easy to implement, but may not be suitable for all applications being load-balanced. You may have problems if using round-robin load balancing for SSL web servers or certain web applications that track user information by IP address. (A properly written enterprise-level web application won't do that, but those applications are not as common as you might think.) The advantage to round-robin load balancing is that you can use any combination of IP addresses in your pool. For example, you could have three identical web servers with IP addresses of 192.168.0.2, 192.168.0.8, and 192.168.0.9 behind your OpenBSD firewall, and want them to share the IP address of 209.69.178.26. This is the textbook application for load balancing.

Random load balancing sends each connection to a random IP address in the pool. This has all of the disadvantages of round-robin load balancing, with the additional restriction that the address pool must be a proper network block instead of just a list of IP addresses. You can use an address pool of 192.168.1.1/26, but not the IP addresses 192.168.1.2, 192.168.1.3, and 192.168.1.44 — the latter is not a network block. See Chapter 5 for a reminder of network blocks and netmasks. For example, if you have four identical Web servers behind your firewall, with IP addresses of 192.168.1.4, 192.168.1.5, 192.168.1.6, and 192.168.1.7 (also known as the netblock 192.168.1.4/30), you could use random load balancing to assign these to a single public IP address.

Source-hash load balancing uses a hash of the IP address to assign connection requests to a pool address. This means that every machine that connects is always assigned to the same address, which will alleviate many application problems of round-robin and random load balancing. The catch is that the address pool must be a proper network block, just as in the random example. PF by default uses a random hash value each time you reload the ruleset, but you can specify a static hash value if you like. Using a fixed hash value means that each client gets an identical IP address even across firewall reloads.

The bitmask load-balancing method isn't actually load-balancing, but instead a way of doing NAT or redirection across two blocks of IP addresses of identical size. This might look similar to bi-directional NAT on a massive scale, but doesn't map connections in the other direction and only works if you have two network blocks. Technically, this "grafts" the network portion of one address onto the host portion of the other. In practice, this means that the first address of one block is permanently mapped to the first address of the second block. The second address of the first block is mapped to the second address of the second block, and so on. For example, you might have several servers on the inside of your firewall, all with IP addresses in the range 192.168.0.16/28. If you want to "static NAT" all of these servers to the public IP addresses 209.69.178.16/28, you could use bitmask load-balancing. 192.168.0.16 would be visible at 209.69.178.16, 192.168.0.22 would be at 209.69.178.22, and so on. While I chose these network numbers to be easy to understand, you could just as well map addresses between wildly different blocks such as 192.168.0.224/28 and 209.69.178.16/28; 192.168.0.224 (the first number in the first block) would become 209.69.178.16 (the first number in the second block) in that case.

Now that you understand what sorts of load balancing are available, let's see how they work in practice.

Outbound Load Balancing

OpenBSD's default NAT conceals an entire network behind a single public IP address, which is suitable for most home offices and small businesses. Each TCP/IP connection uses a unique port number, however, and a single IP address has only 65,536 ports. If you have a large network with a lot of active Internet users, you may run out of TCP/IP ports on that single IP! That's where you need to implement outbound load balancing.

For round-robin load balancing the syntax is very similar to the standard NAT rules, but you specify your public IP addresses in brackets.

```
❶nat on ❷fxp0 from ❸10.0.0.0/8 to any -> { ❹209.69.178.25, ❺209.69.178.26 }
```

We use the standard ❶nat keyword to indicate that this is a NAT rule, and give our ❷external interface name and the ❸internal IP address range. The last part of the rule is the new part, where we list ❹❺both of our public NAT IP addresses in brackets. Outbound traffic on this network will undergo round-robin NAT.

As discussed under the round-robin load balancing discussion earlier, this can cause problems for programs that track connections by IP address. If you have enough client computers that you must use outbound load balancing, some user almost certainly has a business-critical Internet application that will have grief with this setup. Random load balancing will cause the same problem, and if you have this many IP addresses in use bitmask load balancing is absurd. Using hash load balancing will give a simulation of persistence, assigning each NAT client to the same public IP address. Specify source-hash at the end of the configuration line to use source hashing. Remember to use only a valid network block for your translated addresses, or you will get an error like this.

```
# pfctl -f pf.conf
pf.conf.lb:8: only round-robin valid for multiple redirection addresses
pfctl: Syntax error in file: pf rules not loaded
#
```

Instead, drop the brackets and just list the network block.

```
nat on fxp0 from 10.0.0.0 to any -> 209.69.178.18/31 source-hash
```

Each time you load the ruleset, OpenBSD will hash your private IP address with a random value and use the result to assign the client a public IP address. If you want the client to always get the same public IP address, you can specify a hash value. This hash can either be a string, or a hex number. If you use hex, the value must be 32 characters, but you can use a string of any length.

```
nat on fxp0 from 10.0.0.0 to any -> 209.69.178.18/31 source-hash
SomeRandomHashString
```

Outbound bitmask-style load balancing looks very similar, even though the effects are quite different.

```
nat on fxp1 from 10.0.1.0/24 to any -> 209.69.178.0/24 bitmask
```

This will map each IP address beginning with 10.0.1 to an IP address beginning with 209.69.178.

Inbound Load Balancing

The most common use for incoming load balancing is to balance load between several Web or application servers, concealing them behind a single IP address. For example, No Starch Press could have four high-capacity web servers providing their content and ordering site, all behind the public web server at 66.80.60.21.

```
rdr on fxp1 proto tcp from any to 66.80.60.21 port 80 -> { 192.168.1.4,
192.168.1.5}
```

While this quickly gets long when you have many web servers, you can of course use macros to simplify it.

```
$webservers = { 192.168.1.4, 192.168.1.5, 192.168.1.6, 192.168.1.7 }
rdr on fxp1 proto tcp from any to 66.80.60.21 port 80 -> $webservers
```

This defaults to providing round-robin load balancing. The good part about this is that you can easily change the servers in the pool. If one of your content servers fails, you can remove its IP from the pool, reload your ruleset, and business will proceed normally. This is an excellent trick to meet high service level agreements for Windows web servers. The catch is, with round-robin redirection your application might have problems, and SSL may also have problems. You can work around the latter problem by using a SSL accelerator to provide session negotiation, but rewriting your application may be more problematical.

If you have an even number of web servers, you can use the source-hash option to get around some of these problems. The catch with these is that you won't have the ability to easily move servers in to or out of the pool — while you can renumber application servers, or give one server multiple IP addresses, it's not nearly as simple as just editing the configuration file and rebooting. Still, it's an option. Here, we split the load on http://www.nostarch.com amongst application servers at 192.168.1.4, 192.168.1.5, 192.168.1.6, and 192.168.1.7, using source-hash load balancing:

```
rdr on fxp1 proto tcp from any to 60.80.60.21 port 80 -> 192.168.1.4/29 source-hash
```

Again, you could add a static hashing value to make every application client always visit the same web server.

Unlike some commercial load balancers, PF does not check to confirm that individual application servers are up and running, and will not automatically remove failed application servers from the pool. There is wide interest in implementing this functionality, but it hasn't happened yet. It may be available by the time you read this, so I advise you to check pf.conf(5) and the OpenBSD mailing list archives to learn the latest.

Bandwidth Management

One common task for a firewall to perform is bandwidth management. Not only do you want to be able to control how much bandwidth is used for certain tasks, you need to be able to reserve bandwidth for vital functions. If someone really does load the next Harry Potter script on your web server you need to be able to SSH in, find out why your server is running so slowly, and fix the problem. PF includes a large chunk of the ALTQ bandwidth management system. While some aspects are not yet completely integrated as this is written, work is in progress. We will only discuss those portions that are integrated and stable as of this writing. As with the rest of PF, check the manual pages for the latest details.

The most important thing to remember with bandwidth management is that you cannot control how much traffic enters your network. Traffic can be stopped at the first point it enters the network, but it cannot be stopped before it enters your network. You might restrict your web server to serving 1.4MB/second with ALTQ, but that won't stop ten thousand people a second from clicking on a link to that server. The best you can do is restrict how you respond to those requests.

The only way to restrict incoming traffic is to block it before it reaches you. If you control the routers upstream of this web server (e.g., if you're in an ISP environment), you may be able to implement bandwidth controls there.

NOTE   *While memory and hard disks are usually measured in multiples of bytes, network traffic is almost always measured in bits. One byte is eight bits. Do not confuse bits and bytes!*

Queues

ALTQ manages bandwidth in queues. A *queue* is just a list of packets waiting to be processed. By breaking your traffic up into separate queues, and processing those queues under different conditions, you can manage server bandwidth. Queues are somewhat like the checkout lines at the grocery store; some lines are for ten packets or less, and supposedly get you out quickly, while others are for people whom only shop once a month but fill up three carts. You can define just about any characteristics for packet queues, as if you could create a "meats only" or a "white wine with fish" register. (Unlike grocery store customers, packets have no choice but to respect the queues they're assigned to.)

Queue Types

Queues can be handled in any number of different ways, and the most proper method for any situation is a very thorny topic. TCP/IP quality of service queue handling is one of those topics that makes small children cry and fish fly over mountains in an effort to escape the discussion. By default, OpenBSD (and all BSD-based systems) use First-In First Out queuing, where packets that are received first and processed first. Newer packets wait in a queue for their turn to be processed.

OpenBSD also supports Priority Queuing (PRIQ), where packets of a certain type are considered to have "priority" and are processed first. This means that if you assign web packets highest priority, all web packets gets to jump to the head of the queue. Packets of lower priority may never be processed at all under this scheme.

In almost all operational settings where you want to regulate bandwidth, however, Class-Based Queuing (CBQ) is appropriate. CBQ allows the network administrator to allocate a certain amount of bandwidth to different type of traffic through hierarchical classes. Each class has its own queue, with its own bandwidth characteristics. You can assign different sorts of traffic to different classes — SSH traffic to one class, HTTP traffic to another, and so on. One of the nice features of CBQ is that its hierarchical nature allows lower classes to borrow bandwidth from classes above it, if the bandwidth is available.

PRIQ and CBQ are mutually exclusive; you cannot enable both sorts of queues on a single interface. Both CBQ and PRIQ require a parent queue to define basic facts about how traffic passes through the system.

Queue Options

OpenBSD can process queues in a variety of ways through the use of options. Options allow a queue to decide how to respond to a variety of bad network conditions and bandwidth availability.

Default

Every parent queue must have one and only one default child. If a packet is assigned to no other queue, it is assigned to the default queue.

Control

This queue is used for network control packets, such as ICMP, IGMP, RSVP, and so on.

Red

Random Early Detection is a method for handling packet loss when a queue is full. If you fill up your queues, packets will start to drop. By enabling RED, PF will drop packets proportionately to the queue length. Data streams with long queues will drop more packets than data streams with short queues. The net effect is that short transfers, such as HTTP requests and interactive SSH sessions, will respond more quickly, while larger transfers will become slower. Random Early Detection is a very complicated system, however, and don't think that it will solve all your interactive connection problems. Before you begin implementing RED everywhere, I strongly suggest reading "Random Early Detection (RED) Gateways for Congestion Avoidance" by S. Floyd and V. Jacobson. Your favorite search engine will lead you to a dozen copies of this classic paper, but a good site is at http://www.icir.org/floyd/papers/red/red.html.

ECN

Explicit Congestion Notification is an addition to RED that allows devices along a connection path to notify the client and the server that the network is experiencing congestion and to slow down transmission rates. Not all devices speak ECN, however, so it's best to know that everything involved in transactions along this queue won't have trouble with ECN before enabling it. For full details on ECN, read RFC3168.

Borrow

The "borrow" option is only available in CBQ. A queue with the "borrow" option may borrow bandwidth from its parent queue, if the bandwidth is available. For example, you might have a queue reserving 20 percent of your bandwidth for HTTP. If you don't have that much HTTP traffic at the moment, the parent will have excess traffic available. Other queues could "borrow" bandwidth from that allocation. The second you need that bandwidth for HTTP traffic, the bandwidth loan is revoked and the HTTP traffic gets priority. This option is what makes CBQ so desirable in most circumstances.

ALTQ Parent Queue Setup

Before you can set up either sort of queue, you must tell PF where to place the parent queue. The parent queue is attached to a network interface, generally the Internet-facing interface. Queue rules go in /etc/pf.conf between the scrub and NAT rules. Not all of the components are necessary, but here's the full ugly syntax:

```
❶altq on ❷interfacename ❸queue-type bandwidth ❹bandwidth qlimit ❺qlimit tbrsize
❻tbrsize ❼queue {❽queue2, ❾queue3}
```

All altq parent queue definitions start with the ❶altq keyword. You then state the ❷interface that this queue is attached to. Each interface can have no more than one parent queue.

Then state the ❸queue type you've chosen. You must state the total amount of ❹bandwidth in the parent queue. PF recognizes the following case-sensitive bandwidth labels.

b	bits per second
Kb	kilobits per second
Mb	megabits per second
Gb	gigabits per second

The ❺qlimit parameter gives the number of packets to hold in the queue. This defaults to 50, which is suitable for almost all cases. You can decide to not include the qlimit value.

The ❻tbrsize, or Token Bucket Regulator size, dictates how quickly packets can be removed from the queue (transmitted). This parameter is optional, and defaults to the wire speed. You're better off using the bandwidth option to regulate bandwidth, as the effective usage of tbrsize is to control if packets are transmitted based on device driver interrupts or the kernel clock. On any vaguely modern system, either comes extremely quickly.

We then identify this as the ❼parent queue, and list the child queues ❽queue2 and ❾queue3.

Defining Priority Queues

As priority queueing is much simpler than class-based queueing, we'll look at that first. Use an entry like the following to enable PRIQ on your system's Internet-facing Ethernet interface.

```
altq on fxp1 ❶priq bandwidth ❷100Mb queue {❸ssh, ❹other}
```

We define ❶PRIQ on this interface, so any other queues on this interface are also priority queues. We have ❷100 MB to work with, which we want to split into the queues ❸ssh and ❹other.

Each queue under the parent queue must have a unique name. While you can use any names you like, it's best if they actually mean something. If you have a special queue set aside for SSH, then you could do worse than naming the queue "ssh."

Child queues are defined in a similar manner:

```
queue queue-name ❶priority priority ❷priq(options)
```

❶Priorities in PRIQ run from 0 to 15, with 0 being "no priority" and 15 being "maximum priority." Traffic with a priority of 15 will be handled before traffic of any other priority. If there is no priority 15 traffic, priority 14 traffic will be handled, and so on.

We can also enable ❷options on the queue, such as "red" or "default" (see "Queue Options"), by listing "priq" and the option name in parenthesis. If you have no options for a particular queue, you do not need this term.

Here, we define two PRIQ child queues. In PRIQ, child queues cannot have children of their own.

```
queue ssh ❶priority 15
queue other priority 8 ❷priq(default)
```

In this case, we're going to use priority queueing to give SSH traffic ❶priority over everything else. As SSH traffic is generally only used by the system administrator, but is usually only a small amount of traffic, this gives a quick-and-dirty method of prioritizing emergency logins while not interfering too badly with the applications. Every other application is placed in the default queue.

Defining Class-Based Queues

Class-based queueing is much more interesting than priority-based queueing. Start by enabling CBQ on your system's Internet-facing Ethernet interface:

```
altq on fxp1 ❶cbq bandwidth ❷100Mb queue {❸local, ❹t1}
```

As we state that we're using ❶CBQ on this interface, all child queues are also CBQ queues. This particular queue has ❷100Mb of bandwidth, and two child queues: ❸local and ❹t1. We do not bother defining tbrsize or qlimit.

Once you have a parent queue, you can define the children. CBQ queues are defined with the following syntax:

```
queue queue-name bandwidth bandwidth priority priority cbq(options) {child-queue4,
child-queue5}
```

Like PRIQ, each queue must have a unique name.

The bandwidth term uses the same bandwidth labels that the parent queue uses, but the value cannot exceed the total amount of bandwidth available on the parent queue. Child queues can also use a percentage value for bandwidth, indicating the percentage of the parent queue that this queue can consume. Bandwidth and queue are the only mandatory terms in a child queue description. Here we set the "local" queue to have a bandwidth of 98,456Kb[2]:

```
queue local bandwidth 98456Kb
```

The total bandwidth of all child queues should add up to the bandwidth of the parent. The parent queue is 100 megabits per second, or 100,000,000 bits per second. We have a comparatively small amount of bandwidth remaining for our other queue:

---

[2] 98,456 kilobits per second? What sort of half-baked bandwidth limit is that? It's a hundred megabit, minus a T1. You do want to treat your Ethernet outside the firewall differently than the T1 bandwidth, no?

```
queue t1 bandwidth 1544Kb
```

Anyone who has worked on a WAN should recognize the size of the bandwidth queue here — 1,544 kilobits per second is the maximum throughput of a standard T1 circuit. The Ethernet card on the outside of our firewall might be able to handle a hundred megabits a second, but the circuit to our Internet provider almost certainly cannot. We have lots of local bandwidth to our local Ethernet, however, so we want to handle that separately. You could easily edit these numbers to fit your particular situation. We will make further queues for Internet traffic, all children of the t1 queue. But first, let's look at our local queue.

We set aside a queue for systems on our local Ethernet but outside our firewall, so that the bandwidth limits we placed on the circuit will not affect our connections to hosts outside our firewall. Let's expand this rule to make it do what we want.

Then we can assign a priority to a queue. CBQ priorities run from 0 to 7, with 7 being the highest. The default priority is 1. A CBQ queue with a higher priority does not run to the exclusion of other queues, but it is processed more quickly than other queues. Going back to the grocery store analogy for a moment; if you give a queue a high priority, it's like assigning a faster cashier to that line. Each packet will pass through the queue more quickly than it would get through another queue, but other queues will still be processed. We don't really need to assign a priority to our local queue.

We then have options for how CBQ behaves, as discussed in "Queue Options." To enable an option, put the algorithm it applies to, and then the options in parenthesis. For example, our "local" queue can borrow extra bandwidth from the parent queue, if it is available.

```
queue local bandwidth 98456Kb cbq(borrow)
```

This queue is now complete. If you wanted to allocate bandwidth on that local network you could do so, but generally this is a waste of time. We just need to write a PF rule that will direct all connections to the local network outside the firewall to this queue. We'll see how to do that in "Queue Assignment."

Subdividing a CBQ Queue

Before you write your rules, decide how you want to divide your Internet bandwidth. While you could use bits per second to measure bandwidth, generally speaking percentages are easier to deal with for such things. Here's how I might divide up Internet bandwidth for a small company. Start by writing down your desired results, and then assign a name to each queue.

- 5% of our bandwidth is reserved for SSH sessions (ssh).
- 25% of our bandwidth is reserved for inbound HTTP requests (http-in).
- 25% is reserved for outbound HTTP request, with Random Early Detection (http-out).

- 20% is reserved for email (mail).
- 4% is reserved for DNS (dns).
- 20% is reserved for FTP (ftp).
- 1% is reserved for any other traffic (misc).
- All of these connections may borrow from their parent queue.

Because all of these are children of the t1 queue, the t1 queue is their parent. Just as we did with the initial parent queue, list these children in braces at the end of the rule;

```
queue t1 bandwidth 1544Kb {ssh, http-in, http-out, mail, dns, ftp, misc}
```

Now create a definition for each child queue:

```
queue ❶ssh bandwidth ❷5% ❸priority 7 ❹cbq(borrow)
```

We start with the ❶queue name and the ❷bandwidth percentage we've selected. This percentage is taken from the parent of this particular queue, so we've allocated 5 percent of 1544 Kb per second, or about 77 Kb per second. This is faster than a 56 Kbps modem, and should be enough to do any interactive task in the event of a bandwidth flood. Because this queue is the most likely to be vitally needed in case of emergency, we're going to increase its ❸priority dramatically. Finally, we allow this queue to ❹borrow available bandwidth from other queues. We can use more than 77 Kb/second for SSH, but that much will always be available at the server.[3] Given this example, our other queues are very simple to create:

```
queue http-in bandwidth 25% cbq(borrow)
queue http-out bandwidth 25% cbq(borrow, red)
queue mail bandwidth 20% cbq(borrow)
queue dns bandwidth 4% cbq (borrow)
queue ftp bandwidth 20% cbq(borrow)
queue misc bandwidth 1% cbq(borrow)
```

Now that we have rules to describe our desired maximum bandwidth usage, we have to somehow get the traffic into these queues.

Assigning Traffic to Queues

Assign particular sets of traffic to a queue in the packet filtering rules with the "queue" keyword. The queue comes at the very end of the rule. For example, to allow all SSH traffic and assign it to the queue named "ssh," you would use a rule like this:

```
pass in proto tcp from ❶any to ❷any port 22 keep state queue ssh
```

---

[3] Of course, if other sorts of requests (such as a denial-of-service attack) flood the circuit itself, this SSH connection queue is useless. Never forget that.

By setting both the ❶source and ❷destination to "any," we set incoming and outgoing SSH traffic into this queue. If we wanted to break up traffic over one port into two separate queues, we would need to write a separate rule for each. Here, we establish separate queues for incoming and outgoing HTTP traffic:

```
pass ❶in proto tcp from any to fxp1 port {80, 443} keep state queue ❷http-in
pass ❸out proto tcp from fxp1 to any port {80,443} keep state queue ❹http-out
```

The first rule only covers traffic coming ❶into the firewall, assigning all that traffic to the queue ❷http-in. The second rule only matches ❸outgoing traffic and assigns everything to the ❹queue http-out.

In our CBQ example we created two queues, "local" and "t1." Don't forget to set up a rule to direct traffic on the local Ethernet through the local queue, so it isn't captured by one of the other rules. Put this near the end, so it will be caught by all matching packets. Assuming that the network outside our firewall was 209.69.178.16/28, we would have a rule like this:

```
pass out from fxp1 to 209.69.178.16/28 queue local
```

Any traffic through the firewall to a local IP address will go through the local queue, giving almost unlimited bandwidth.

You can repeat this setup for any rules that you want. We give a detailed example in Appendix B.

Queuing by Type of Service

Applications can request a Type of Service from the IP stack, reflected in the Type of Service flag in the IP packet. Routers, firewalls, and other network infrastructure devices can choose to examine this flag and act appropriately — or not. Read the application's documentation to determine if and how that application supports IP Type of Service.

Queuing can specifically recognize the Types of Service flags "lowdelay" (or "0x10"). These packets are considered especially vital. If you assign multiple queues to a rule, the second applies only to packets with a "lowdelay" Type of Service. For example, the SSH application protocol requests that interactive sessions be assigned a Type of Service of "lowdelay," but requests a ToS of "throughput" for data transfers (sftp, scp). A delay of a few seconds is perfectly tolerable when uploading or downloading a large chunk of data, while a delay of a few seconds between keystrokes on a remote server is intolerable. We don't want to divide our SSH bandwidth between the two types of connection, just have one react more quickly than another. That means we want prioritize our queues:

```
queue ssh bandwidth 5% cbq(borrow) {❶ssh_interactive, ❸ssh_bulk}
queue ssh_interactive ❸priority 7
queue ssh_bulk ❹priority 0
```

Here we've split the ssh queue into two chunks, ❶ssh_interactive and ❸ssh_bulk. The ssh_interactive queue has no further bandwidth restrictions, but is assigned the ❸highest priority, 7. The ssh_bulk queue also has no restrictions on bandwidth beyond the 5 percent reserved for the main SSH queue, but has the ❹lowest possible priority, 0. Now, let's split up our SSH traffic in the packet-filtering rule.

```
pass in proto tcp from any to any port 22 keep state queue {ssh_bulk,
❶ssh_interactive}
```

The ❶second queue listed is only used for packets with the Type of Service of "lowdelay," meaning that our keystrokes will appear more quickly in a high-congestion situation. If you know the nitty-gritty details of how your network protocol works, this can be extremely effective.

Rule Optimization

Comparing packets to complicated packet filter rulesets can be expensive in terms of CPU and memory usage. Some packet filters use rule grouping and the equivalent of a "goto" statement to reduce the number of rules an individual packet must be compared against. Instead of using groups, PF performs an automatic ruleset optimization called *skip-steps*. By simply putting your rules in the correct order, you can vastly accelerate PF's packet processing. Basically, PF can count ahead to see how many rules have similar parameters and can skip processing rules that are sufficiently similar if they fail to match.

Let's see how this works in practice with the following simple ruleset:

```
❶block in quick on fxp1 from 10.0.0.0/8 to any
❷block in quick on fxp1 from 172.16.0.0/12 to any
❸block in quick on fxp1 from 192.168.0.0/16 to any
❹pass in quick on fxp1 from 209.69.178.16/28 to any
❺block in quick on fxp0
❻pass in on fxp0 from 192.168.1.0/24 to any port = 22 keep state
❼pass in on fxp0 from 192.168.1.0/24 to any port = {80, 443} keep state
❽pass in on fxp0 from 192.168.2.0/24 to any port = 22 keep state
```

Assume that we have a packet crossing the fxp0 interface, with a source address of 192.168.2.8, bound for a SSH server somewhere. Let's see how PF optimizes crossing the rules in this instance.

Our first four rules cover packets going over the fxp1 interface. When a packet enters the packet filter, it is compared to the ❶first rule. If this packet is crossing the fxp0 interface, the first rule does not apply. PF can count ahead and see that rules ❷, ❸, and ❹ all involve the fxp1 interface, so the packet does not have to be compared to these rules. The packet is immediately compared against rule❺.

Our packet is crossing the fxp0 interface, so rule❺ does apply. It doesn't have a source address of 192.168.1.0/24, however, so rule❻ doesn't match. PF looks ahead and sees that rule❼ also involves fxp0 and the 192.168.1.0/24 source address, so it can skip that rule.

Finally, at rule❽, we have the fxp0 interface and a source address of 192.168.2.0/24. This matches, and the packet is allowed to proceed. We have crossed eight rules, but have only done full packet comparisons on three of them thanks to skip steps! If you had arranged your rules any which way, skip steps would not work.

PF computes skip steps based on the following fields:

- interface
- protocol
- source address
- source port
- destination address
- destination port

The best way to optimize PF is to have a neat and orderly ruleset.

Now that you have learned to configure PF to do almost anything, let's explore how to activate and manage the configuration that you've set up. You'll learn how to accomplish this in the next chapter.

19

MANAGING PF

Blowfish guard the gates.
You may pass, vermin may not:
"Get your own network!"

Now that you can configure the packet filter, let's take a look at how to actually manage the PF system. The pfctl program does most of the basic management of the packet filter and gives you a window into the entire system. You can examine and edit the state and address tables separately. Finally, PF will allow you to authenticate users to the packet filter, giving Internet access only after a successful login.

pfctl(8)

All PF actions are controlled by the packet filter control program pfctl(8). You can manage your configuration as a whole, or each of the sub-functions independently. You can also kill individual connections or display statistics. Stateful inspection has different management requirements, so we're going to consider those in "Managing State Tables"; here, we'll look at managing every other part of PF.

pfctl(8) has many different functions, which are documented in the manual page. New functions are being added all the time, and the syntax occasionally changes, so be sure to check the manual page if you have trouble.

General Commands

To disable PF and all its functions, run "pfctl -d". Note that this will not turn off packet forwarding, so if you're running a PF firewall without NAT you have just exposed your network to the world. If you're using NAT, of course, disabling NAT turns off your private network's access to the Internet. To enable PF again, run "pfctl -e".

Many pfctl(8) commands produce output when everything runs correctly. To make pfctl(8) run more quietly, only printing errors and warnings, add "-q" to your command line. Similarly, to produce more information add "-v" to the command. You can make pfctl(8) even more verbose by adding a second or third "-v."

Loading Rules

PF handles rule switching in such a way that there is no "window" where the system is not protected by packet filtering, unlike some older packet filters. The rules are loaded into system memory, then the switch between the old ruleset and the new ruleset is made in a single operation. If you want to load an entire rules file, use the "-f" flag and give the name of your rules file. Here, we load in the rules from /etc/pf.conf:

```
# pfctl -f /etc/pf.conf
```

If your configuration file has a syntax error, pfctl(8) will complain and won't load the rules. Your old rules will remain in effect.

```
# pfctl -f /etc/pf.conf
pf.conf:❶6: syntax error
pfctl: Syntax error in file: pf rules not loaded
#
```

In this example, there's an ❶error on line 6 of the configuration. Personally, I like to know that my edited packet filter configuration is correct before the scheduled time to put it into production. (It's quite embarrassing to announce to the development team that "the new firewall configuration will be active during lunch," and then spend the whole time tracking down a misplaced comma or a parenthesis where you should have put in a curly brace.) You can parse your configuration file without loading it into the kernel with the "-n" flag.

```
# pfctl -n -f /etc/pf.conf
#
```

Loading a new ruleset will not remove any existing open connections. If my ruleset allows outbound SSH connections, and I remove that permission from the rules and reload them, existing SSH connections will remain. I can either specifically kill that connection or flush the state table as well.

If you want to reload your packet-handling rules without touching any of the other rules in your configuration file, you can use the "-R" option.

```
# pfctl -R -f /etc/pf.conf
```

This leaves the rules for all options, NAT, and other PF features unchanged, and only reads the packet-filtering rules. You can change filter rules all you want, and the other functions will be unaffected. Of course, if you load rules that are incompatible with the configuration of those other functions, such as referring to nonexistent queues, you'll have other problems.

Similarly, you can load only the NAT rules with "-N," and only the option rules with "-O."

```
# pfctl -N -f /etc/pf.conf
# pfctl -O -f /etc/pf.conf
```

Flushing Rules

You can blow away all the existing configuration information with the "-F" (flush) flag. The "-F" flag takes an argument that indicates which part of the configuration should be flushed.

To flush all the configuration you must add the "all" argument. Your NAT rules will go away, existing state entries will disappear, and your queue configuration will vanish. If this is your firewall, your internal network's access to the Internet will fail and all existing connections will drop. This will pretty much hose your network, your connectivity, and your security. The flush command will identify each component as it flushes the information.

```
# pfctl -F all
rules cleared
nat cleared
altq cleared
states cleared
pf: statistics cleared
#
```

You can also flush only the packet-filtering rules, leaving all traffic free to go in any direction. Although any queues will still be in place, you won't have any rules to direct traffic to those queues. NAT will remain in place. Also, just flushing the rules will not interrupt any existing stateful connections.

```
# pfctl -F rules
rules cleared
#
```

The most common situation where I've had to flush the filtering rules is when troubleshooting a connection problem. It's neither pretty nor secure, but it's nice to have the option.

Flushing queues leaves you without any bandwidth management. PF will not complain if packet-filtering rules direct packets at nonexistent queues, it will just process the packets as best it can. Flush your queues with the "queue" argument.

```
# pfctl -F queue
altq cleared
#
```

If you want to remove your NAT ability, you could flush your NAT rules. This will not interrupt existing connections in the state table, but will prevent further connections that require NAT.

```
# pfctl -F nat
nat cleared
#
```

Finally, PF also keeps statistics that are not part of any rule. You can reset all those counters to zero by running "-F info".

Viewing PF Information

You can check various information PF keeps with the "-s" (show) flag. You might also look at the configuration file to see what you loaded, but this might change if you're using authpf (see "Authenticated Access") or other anchor functions. The show function takes an argument, the part of the system whose rules you want to see.

Viewing Current Packet Filter Rules

To view the current PF rules, run "pfctl -s rules."

```
# pfctl -s rules
scrub in all fragment reassemble
pass in inet proto tcp from any to 192.168.1.4 port = www
pass in inet proto tcp from any to 192.168.1.4 port = https
pass in inet proto tcp from any to 192.168.1.5 port = www
```

```
pass in inet proto tcp from any to 192.168.1.5 port = https
...
```

If you use verbose output ("-v") when viewing the rules, pfctl(8) will show how often a given rule is hit. This is extremely useful when debugging packet filter issues.

```
# pfctl -v -s rules
...
block drop in on fxp1 inet all
[ Evaluations: ❶34984      ❷Packets: 21      ❸Bytes: 16330      ❹States: 0
]
...
```

Each rule is displayed with four numbers: ❶how many times this rule has been evaluated, ❷the number of packets that have matched the rule, the ❸number of bytes that the rule has processed through this rule, and the number of ❹states that are maintained via stateful inspection by this rule. Since the counters were last cleared, this generic "block all incoming traffic" rule has matched 21 out of 34,984 packets, containing 16330 bytes. To see what was in those packets, examine them via tcpdump (see "Logging").

Viewing Current NAT Rules

View the current NAT rules by running "pfctl -s nat".

```
# pfctl -s nat
nat on fxp1 inet from 192.168.1.0/24 to any -> (fxp1)
#
```

If you want to see more on how your NAT rules are processed, add the "-v" flag. The output is almost identical to the rule output, so we're not going to repeat it.

Viewing Current Queues

You can view the current queues with "-s queue". Verbosity has no effect upon viewing queues.

```
# pfctl -s queue
altq on fxp1 cbq bandwidth 100.00Mb tbrsize 12000
queue root_fxp1 bandwidth 100.00Mb priority 0 cbq( wrr root ) {t1, local}
queue  t1 bandwidth 1.54Mb {ssh, http-in, http-out, mail, dns, ftp, misc}
queue    ssh bandwidth ❶77.20Kb cbq( borrow )
...
```

No matter how we specified bandwidth allowances, they are converted to a bits, kilobits, or megabits in this output. If you recall, in our examples we divided up the bandwidth of our T1 by percentages, but here our individual queue sizes are shown in ❶kilobits. PF does all of its internal operations in bits, of course.

Viewing Labels

Back when we set up labels, it was with the promise that you could view rule statistics per label. Do this with the "pfctl -s labels" command.

```
# pfctl -s label
ssh-out ❶38 ❷126 ❸24333
browsing 38 253 59599
browsing 26 0 0
#
```

The ❶first column is the number of times this rule has been evaluated. The ❷second is the number of packets that have been affected by this rule, and the ❸third is the number of bytes that have been affected by this rule.

One odd thing is this output is that we have two labels called "browsing!" What's more, they have different statistics. This can happen when you use braces within a rule and don't use a macro to label the differences between those rules. The "browsing" label was created by this rule.

```
pass out proto tcp from ($ExtIf) to any port {80, 443} label browsing
```

We are allowing two different ports, with two different statistics, and giving them the same label. See Chapter 18 for how to properly differentiate between these connections with labels.

View State and Normalization Statistics

PF maintains statistics for state tables and packet normalization. You can view both of these statistics lists with "pfctl -s info". These statistics may be in terms of packets, or fragments, or entries in a table, or a number of times an action has been performed, as appropriate.

```
# pfctl -s info
Status: Enabled for 0 days 21:49:18❶            Debug: None

❷State Table              ❸Total        ❹Rate
❺current entries              6
❻searches               487527          6.2/s
❼inserts                   1118          0.0/s
❽removals                  1112          0.0/s
```

The "enabled for" entry shows how long PF has been running for. This is usually the time since boot, although if someone has enabled and disabled the packet filter with pfctl(8) commands it will be reflected here as well.

The first half of the output shows the statistics for the ❷state table. We also display the number of ❸items that match a particular entry and the number of ❹items per second that PF processes. While state table entries per second is a largely meaningless value, we can see the number of ❺current state table entries. (We discuss viewing the actual state table entries in "Managing Stateful Inspection.")

The ❻"searches" line indicates the number of times a packet has been compared to the state table. The state table is searched every time a packet passes an interface, so if you're forwarding packets between interfaces this is probably about twice the number of packets your system has passed. (Packets that originate on or terminate at your system are only searched once, of course.)

The ❼"inserts" entry shows how many times states have been created, and ❽"removals" shows how many have been destroyed. The difference between the two should equal the number of current states. As your system stays up the number of insertions and removals should get very close to each other — even if you have a few hundred entries in your state table, that's fairly insignificant compared to millions of states that will be created and destroyed over the state table's lifetime.

```
Counters
❶match                          1847         0.0/s
❷bad-offset                        0         0.0/s
❸fragment                          0         0.0/s
❹short                             0         0.0/s
❺normalize                         0         0.0/s
❻memory                            0         0.0/s
```

The "Counters" section tells how many times a packet has matched a particular rule. For example, the ❶"match" entry says how many packets find a last matching rule in PF. This should be a total of the number of packets that have passed through the system, unless you're relying on PF's implicit "pass all" to manage traffic. The ❷"bad-offset" entry shows how many packets were received with a bad offset, the ❸"fragment" column shows how many fragments have been received, and the ❹"short" entry tells how many unusually short packets were received.

If a packet cannot be coherently reassembled, PF will drop the pieces. ❺"Normalize" shows how many packets have been dropped after scrubbing. Similarly, the ❻"memory" entry shows how many packets have been dropped because PF doesn't have enough memory to hold on to the packet fragments before reassembling them. If you start to lose packets due to memory shortages, you need to increase the memory you have allocated to PF (see "PF Memory Limits").

Viewing Everything at Once

As this command also works for many different functions of PF, to view the entire configuration add the "all" argument.

```
# pfctl -s all
```

This provides a complete listing of the configuration for NAT, packet-filtering rules, queues, and statistics.

Clearing PF Statistics

Finally, PF keeps statistics on just about everything it does. You can clear these statistics with the "-z" (zero) flag.

```
# pfctl -z
pf: rule counters cleared
#
```

Managing Tables

Tables are handled slightly differently than other sorts of rules. The whole point of a table is to maintain a list of network numbers, so pfctl(8)'s table support is concerned with creating, editing, and removing table information. Whenever you work with a table in pfctl(8), you must specify the name of the table you are editing with the "-t" option. For example, if you're working with the "intruders" table, each pfctl(8) command should start with:

```
# pfctl -t intruders
```

If you just run this command like this, pfctl(8) won't actually do anything. You need to tell pfctl(8) what you want it to do with the table, using the "-T" flag before it will actually consult with PF and do something. The "-T" flag takes an argument, the action you want it to take. For example, to display the contents of the table, use the "show" argument.

```
# pfctl -t intruders -T show
   209.69.178.26
#
```

The "intruders" table has one entry, 209.69.178.18.

Add an entry to the table with the "add" argument.

```
# pfctl -t intruders -T add 10.0.0.9
1/1 addresses added.
#
```

You can add entire networks to the table by specifying a netmask.

```
# pfctl -t intruders -T add 88.88.0.0/16
1/1 addresses added
#
```

Also, you can add multiple network numbers at a time.

```
# pfctl -t intruders -T add 88.99.0.0/16 99.99.8.0/24
2/2 addresses added
#
```

If you add entries to a non-existent table, the table is automatically created. (You might use this with anchor rules, or with authpf(8).)

Similarly, you can delete entries from a table with the "delete" argument. You can use any number of network numbers in a single delete statement.

```
# pfctl -t intruders -T delete 99.99.8.0/24
1/1 addresses deleted
#
```

To remove all the entries from a table, use the "flush" command.

```
# pfctl -t intruders -T flush
4 addresses deleted
#
```

The table is now empty. But perhaps deleting entries from a table is not enough, and you want to delete the table itself. Use the "kill" argument for this.

```
# pfctl -t intruders -T kill
1 table deleted
#
```

The next time you add an entry to the "intruders" table, PF will automatically recreate it.

If you're using text files to maintain your tables, you might want to reload the text file into your tables without restarting PF. This might be common with spam blacklists, for example; when you download the latest list of spam-spewing hosts, you want to get this into your system as soon as possible. You also want to remove old entries from the table at the same time. Use the "replace" argument for this, and also use the "-f" flag to specify the file name.

```
# pfctl -t spamhosts -T replace -f /etc/spamhosts
99 addresses added
4 addresses deleted
#
```

You can also check if a particular IP address is inside a table, using the "test" argument. Here, we check to see if a particular IP address is in our running spamhosts table.

```
# pfctl -t spamhosts -T test 209.69.178.26
0/1 addresses match.
#
```

It's not common to have to create and remove tables on the fly, but it's quite possible that you will want different types of tables for different circumstances. You can load table definitions from a file with the "load" argument. Use pfctl(8)'s -f argument to specify a file name.

```
# pfctl -T load -f /etc/pf.conf
```

Table Statistics

PF keeps statistics on each IP address in a table. If you add the -v flag to the "show" argument, you'll get a list of each entry in the table and the number of packets that have passed through it.

```
# pfctl -t rfc1918 -T show -v
   10.0.0.0/8
        Cleared:        ❶Sun May 11 09:55:20 2003
        ❷In/Block:      [ Packets: 0        Bytes: 0        ]
        ❸In/Pass:       [ Packets: 0        Bytes: 0        ]
        ❹Out/Block:     [ Packets: 0        Bytes: 0        ]
        ❺Out/Pass:      [ Packets: 0        Bytes: 0        ]
   172.16.0.0/12
   ...
```

We can see how much data has been ❷blocked coming into the system, how much data has been ❸allowed into the system, how much data has been ❹blocked trying to go out, and how much data has been ❺allowed out. This particular system hasn't seen any traffic from the 10.0.0.0/8 network since ❶May 11 at 9:55 AM, so the counters are all zero.

To reset the counters, use the "zero" argument.

```
# pfctl -t rfc1918 -T zero
1 table/stats cleared.
#
```

PF keeps all sorts of statistics on every part of the system, and can report on almost all of its actions. If you're interested, see pf.conf(5).

Managing State Tables

While PF uses rules to determine which connections may use stateful inspection, the actual state table is generated from the connections created by machines connecting through the firewall. Managing the state table therefore has two aspects: administering the rules for stateful inspection, and viewing and editing the state table itself. The rules for stateful inspection are actually managed as part of NAT and packet filtering, so we're left with viewing the state table itself.

Viewing the State Table

You can see the current contents of the state table with "pfctl -s state." Here's the output from a mostly idle network.

```
# pfctl -s state
❶tcp ❷192.168.1.200:❸51276 -> ❹209.69.178.18:❺51276 -> ❻209.69.178.22:❼22
❽ESTABLISHED:❾ESTABLISHED
#
```

There is only one entry in this state table, for a ❶TCP connection. The host ❷192.168.1.200 has opened port ❸51276 for an outbound connection. At the firewall, this IP undergoes translation to the IP ❹209.69.178.18, port ❺51276. This IP is connecting to the IP address ❻209.69.178.22 on port ❼22. The connection from the first machine to the firewall is in the state ❽ESTABLISHED, and the connection from the firewall to the eventual destination is also in the state ❾ESTABLISHED. While it's possible to have connection states be different on either side of the firewall, this should only appear very briefly. If you have a large enough state table, you'll catch a few of them from time to time.

If you're looking for particular information in your state table, you might want to add the "-r" (reverse lookup) option. This will make the state table perform DNS lookups on every IP address in the table and display host names where possible. This can take much longer than displaying the state table without host names, but is more readable when you're just seeing who is talking to what. "209.81.7.23" doesn't mean much to most of us, but "www.sex.com" might hint that someone's having a little bit too much fun at work.

Removing States

If you just want to clear every entry in your state table, you can just flush the entire state table with "-F state." This will completely erase the state table.

```
# pfctl -F state
states cleared
#
```

Most connections will actually recover from having the state table cleared, if the PF rules allow the connection to continue. For example, if we clear the state table shown earlier and wait a moment, the SSH session will continue, and PF will create a new state entry.

We mentioned earlier that changing your packet-filtering rules to disallow a certain connection did not cut off connections that were already in place. If you clear the state table after loading your updated packet-filtering rules, the existing connections will try to recover. If PF does not allow the connection, the connection cannot recover, and both ends of the connection will time out.

If you are using state modulation instead of stateful inspection, connections *cannot* recover. State modulation changes the initial sequence number of the connection by a random amount, and flushing the table removes that random number. Flushing the state table will destroy all existing connections using state modulation and disconnect everyone accessing the network over that rule.

Killing States

At times, timing out the connection simply isn't good enough. You may want to kill a particular existing connection. You can do this with the "-k" (kill) option. This takes a single argument, the host name or IP address of the traffic source. For example, to delete all state entries for traffic originating from 192.168.1.200, you would use this command:

```
# pfctl -k 192.168.1.200
killed 1 states from 1 sources and 0 destinations
#
```

You could specify a second -k and a second host name or IP address, allowing you to narrow down the state you want to eliminate to those between two particular hosts.

```
# pfctl -k 192.168.1.200 -k 209.69.178.22
killed 1 states from 1 sources and 1 destinations
#
```

These connections can probably recover, however, so the best thing to do is put in a packet-filtering rule that will disallow undesired connections.

Authenticating PF

One common requirement is for a firewall to require authentication before allowing a user to access the Internet. PF includes this functionality through the use of authpf(8). When a user authenticates via SSH, PF will check several files for PF rules to insert into the ruleset via anchor attachment points. When the user terminates the SSH session, the rules are removed. While SSH can intimidate new users, it's very simple to take any of a variety of free SSH clients and set them up on users' desktops as a "double-click here, log in, read the message, and minimize the icon" tool.

To use authpf, you must properly set up user accounts, make sure your server is configured to use authpf, and set up rules.

User Account Setup

Every user who can authenticate to the firewall needs a shell of /usr/sbin/authpf. This shell will not allow users to get a command-line shell; it exists solely for authentication purposes. As these users require almost no system resources, you may wish to use a login class (see Chapter 7) to define the shell and very minimal resource allocation. This is also useful if the user login information is distributed from a central source, such as NIS.

NOTE *Do not add /usr/sbin/authpf to /etc/shells, unless you want your users to be able to FTP to the firewall host.*

Server Setup

Authpf(8) will keep rules in place until the SSH session terminates. An intruder might attempt to hijack an existing SSH connection to gain access out through the firewall. If you're using OpenBSD's integrated OpenSSH, add the following two options to /etc/ssh/sshd_config.

```
ClientAliveInterval ❶15
ClientAliveCountMax ❷3
```

This tells sshd(8) to make a keepalive check every ❶15 seconds and to disconnect after ❷three failed keepalive checks. Because keepalives cannot be faked in a hijacked connection, this ensures that any attacker will be disconnected within 60 seconds.

You might also want to create a file /etc/authpf/authpf.message, displaying text to be displayed upon a successful authpf login. This is an excellent place to put your acceptable use policy, network notices, or anything else you want your users to actually see.[1] This is much like /etc/motd, but only appears for authpf users.

You can also create a /etc/authpf/authpf.problem file, which will be displayed if there is a problem. This is a good place to put your helpdesk phone number or a link to your internal trouble ticket system.

PF Setup

Most authpf(8) configuration is done in /etc/pf.conf and in the /etc/authpf/ directory. You'll need to configure PF to accept instructions from authpf(8) through the use of anchors. In /etc/authpf/, you must at least have a basic configuration file, authpf.conf, and a rules file, authpf.rules.

/etc/pf.conf

Authpf(8) uses anchor attachment points to insert rules into the running ruleset. Your /etc/pf.conf must include anchor rules. By default, these anchors are named "authpf," but you can change this with an entry in /etc/authpf/ authpf.conf. You must include these anchors, in order, within /etc/pf.conf, for authpf(8) to work.

```
nat-anchor authpf
rdr-anchor authpf
binat-anchor authpf
anchor authpf
```

If you are using anchor rules to provide network access, this means that you can also get rid of most general-purpose PF rules. With authpf(8) implementing rules that allow individual workstations out, you can strip your general-purpose PF rules to only those that provide basic network infrastructure support. You'll

---

[1] "You didn't know we were taking the mail server down over lunch? Well, did you use the Internet today? The message appeared when you logged on." No matter how tempted you are, it is not polite to add words such as "loser" or "moron" to the end of such a statement.

want to retain the rules to let the world view your website, for example, and maybe rules that let one or two key management workstations SSH out, but authpf(8) should provide most of your rules.

/etc/authpf/authpf.conf

The authpf.conf file is used to set general authpf(8) options. When a client logs in with authpf(8), one of the first things the program does is check for the existence of /etc/authpf/authpf.conf. If that file does not exist, the program immediately exits. If you don't need to set any authpf options, then simply running "touch /etc/authpf/authpf.conf" will suffice to let authpf(8) run normally. (You'll still need to add rules for your users, mind you, but authpf(8) will run.)

Options in authpf.conf are simple "variable=value" pairs. At the time of this writing, authpf.conf only has one option: choice of anchor name. If you don't want to name your anchors "authpf," you can choose a new name here like this:

```
anchor=newanchorname
```

If you're happy with the default name, however, just touch(1) /etc/authpf/authpf.conf to proceed.

Creating authpf(8) Rules

The file /etc/authpf/authpf.rules contains a generic list of rules that will be added to PF when a user successfully authenticates with authpf(8). These rules are completely identical to those used in /etc/pf.conf, with one minor addition. The macro "$user_ip" is used for the IP address that the user authenticated from. You can use this IP address to write very specific rules for outbound access. For example, here's a very generous authpf.rules that allows an authenticated user complete outbound access from behind a NAT device. This assumes that the only entries you have in /etc/pf.conf are those required by authpf(8).

```
ext_if="fxp1"
nat on $ext_if inet from $user_ip to any -> $ExtIf
pass out log on $ext_if inet from $user_ip to any modulate state
```

You can, of course, use authpf(8) to create far more restrictive rules. One popular use for authpf(8) is to create a secure wireless gateway. In that case, you almost certainly want to only allow secure network protocols such as SSH, SSL, and IPSEC through PF. The authpf(8) man page contains an example of exactly that configuration.

Per-User Authpf Rules

While most of your users should be given access with the standard rule template, it's entirely possible that you'll have one or two users with special needs. The authpf(8) system includes the ability to use per-user configuration files. If a user has a private configuration file, it will be used. If not, the user will get the configuration given in /etc/authpf/authpf.rules.

Per-user authpf(8) configuration files should be kept in the directory /etc/authpf/users/*username*/ and named "authpf.rules." For example, the rules file for the user "chris" would be in the file /etc/authpf/users/chris/authpf.rules.

Do not give users the ability to edit their own authpf.rules files! Remember, the rules in this file are injected directly into the main /etc/pf.conf configuration. If a user was to put in a simple rule that solved all their problems, such as "pass in from any to any keep state," your entire security policy would be eviscerated.

Authpf Access Lists

The authpf(8) system can allow specific users to use authpf, instead of just letting anyone with a system account authenticate to the packet filter. It also includes the ability to ban particular users from using the firewall.

The file /etc/authpf/authpf.allow can contain usernames, one per line. If the file /etc/authpf/authpf.allow exists, PF will only allow users whose usernames appear in that file to use authpf. Without this file, anyone who can authenticate on the firewall machine can get standard user authpf access.

On the other hand, we have the directory /etc/authpf/banned. If the systems administrator does not want a user with an account to use the firewall, he can create a file in this directory with the same name as the username. That user cannot authenticate to the firewall as long as the file exists. For example, once I've had enough of Phil surfing the Net while he should be working I can just do this:

```
# touch /etc/authpf/banned/phil
```

Even if the username "phil" appears in /etc/authpf/authpf.allow, he will not be able to authenticate to authpf(8). A ban always overrides a permit. (If Phil made me cranky enough, I could even use chflags(1) to make the file immutable and hence not removable without a reboot. But that wouldn't be professional.)

PF Logging

PF can be set up to log every packet that it processes, through the "log" keyword of the packet filter rules. Without additional setup, however, those logs go nowhere. You need to start the log capturing program, pflogd(8), to write the log to /var/log/pflog.

If you start PF at boot in /etc/rc.conf, pflogd(8) is automatically started. Otherwise, you will need to start it on the command line. While pflogd(8) has several possible command-line arguments, for the most part you can simply run this:

```
# pflogd
```

One thing to remember is that if you are using stateful inspection, only the first packets that send a connection into the state table are logged. Further packets in the same data stream are not logged. If you want to log all packets in a connection created by stateful inspection, you must use the "log-all" keyword instead of "log" in the rule.

Logging is especially useful when troubleshooting connection problems. If packets are being blocked when you think that they should be being passed, you can easily add "log" keywords to your "block" statements and see which rule is stopping the traffic.

Logs can also be quite large, however, and you may not want to log everything. Perhaps you don't care what websites your users visit, but only care about incoming traffic. Some traffic may not make sense to log or be impossible to log. For example, any network I build has a standalone logging host, where all systems transmit all their logs for centralized management. If you log all traffic coming from your logging host, including the log messages, you will quickly find that PF is logging the transmission of the logs, and then logging the messages logging the transmissions of the logs, and pretty quickly you will be a very unhappy network administrator with a lot of very repetitive logs on your hands!

Reading PF Logs

PF logs its data in tcpdump(8) format, allowing the systems administrator to examine the data through this standard systems administration tool. The tcpdump included in OpenBSD has been modified slightly to recognize the PF-specific fields included in a logged packet.

```
# tcpdump -n -e -ttt -r /var/log/pflog
```

The tcpdump(8) program can be difficult to use and certainly doesn't look friendly. If you don't feel like parsing all the output tcpdump(8) will produce, install Ethereal (/usr/ports/net/ethereal). The port also recognizes the additional fields stored in a logged packet and will greatly simplify the log evaluation process.

```
# ethereal -r /var/log/pflog
```

Real-Time Log Access

The entries in /var/log/pflog are not added in real time; pflogd(8) buffers its input until it thinks it's worth writing a log message. If you want to see PF act in real time, attach tcpdump(8) or Ethereal to the pflog(4) interface with the "-i" flag to either command.

```
# ethereal -i pflog0
```

Congratulations! While PF contains enough features to fill most of a book, the last three chapters should get you started with just about anything you want to do with it. At this point you should know what you need to know to run OpenBSD.

A

i386 KERNEL CONFIGURATION CHOICES

 Each hardware platform has certain options and configuration statements that must be in a kernel for that platform. In this appendix, we're going to focus on i386-specific kernel configuration and discuss almost every common device driver, option, pseudo-device, and configuration instruction.

Because OpenBSD continues to evolve and new versions are released often, it's impossible to write a book that contains extensive and complete documentation on every feature of every device driver for the version of OpenBSD that will inevitably come out six months after the publication of this book. The device names rarely change, however, and much of the related information about using hardware and various options doesn't change either. This appendix provides enough information so that you can find your way around, and includes a manual page reference for each option.

If you're using something other than i386 hardware, you will want to check the GENERIC kernel configuration for that platform.

CPU Configuration

Every kernel needs basic information about your CPU and its associated equipment.

option   I*_CPU

These options tell your kernel how to speak to the CPU. Each type of CPU has its own instruction sets and features, some of which OpenBSD will take advantage. You can see what sort of CPU your system has by checking /var/run/dmesg.boot for information on your CPU. For example, my test system has the following line near the top of /var/run/dmesg.boot:

```
cpu0: Intel Pentium/MMX ("GenuineIntel" 586-class) 166 MHz
```

This is a 586-class CPU, or a Pentium. A kernel that runs on it must include the necessary options for this CPU, or the kernel will not boot!

option I386_CPU	Intel-compatible 386 CPU
option I486_CPU	Intel-compatible 486 CPU
option I586_CPU	Intel-compatible Pentium CPU
option I686_CPU	Intel-compatible Pentium II or better CPU

You might note that there's no differentiation between a Pentium II and a Pentium III. That's mainly because there's no real hardware difference between a Pentium II and a Pentium III, other than size and speed.

option   GPL_MATH_EMULATE

A floating-point unit handles floating-point math. 386-based systems didn't come with a floating-point unit, although one was available as an add-on coprocessor. Many 486-based systems also lack a floating-point unit. Later 486s, Pentiums, and more modern chips all include an integrated floating-point unit.

OpenBSD absolutely requires a floating-point unit. This option provides a floating-point emulator that runs in software. It is slow, but it will allow you to run OpenBSD on an ancient 386 if you really want to.

The option is called GPL_MATH_EMULATE instead of, say, MATH_EMULATE because the GNU General Public License covers this particular section of kernel code; you cannot use this kernel option in a product with a proprietary kernel without releasing the source code to your kernel. Today, even inexpensive embedded systems have a floating-point unit, so this isn't such a big deal.

Miscellaneous Options

The following options are a potpourri of basic configuration instructions:

machine   i386

You must tell config(8) the architecture, or hardware platform, the kernel is intended to run on. This absolutely must be correct; you cannot boot, say, a Sparc kernel on an i386! You do this with the machine keyword.

maxusers   32

The maxusers setting affects a variety of in-kernel memory structure sizes, such as the maximum number of processes that can be run and the maximum number of files that can be open at any given time. (For those of you who read code, take a look at param.c in the kernel configuration directory for the full gory details on how maxusers affects these values.) What's more, these values trickle down throughout the kernel to set a variety of hard limits. The default of 32 is sensible for most occasions.

Many of these characteristics can be altered via sysctls, rather than changing maxusers. For example, the maximum number of files that can be open at one time is shown in kern.maxfiles, while the maximum number of processes is in kern.maxproc.

config   bsd   swap generic

The kernel needs to understand where its root device is, where it will swap, and where it will dump. You can specify all of this with the config keyword. The default config statement covers almost any circumstance, using standardized routines to figure out where each of these components will be.

You can do some very strange things with it if you desire, as discussed in config(8). You simply specify the disk device where you want each of the root, swap, and dump partitions. You can use the word "and" to concatenate multiple instances of one device. In the following example, we explicitly tell the kernel that the root partition is on the device sd3a (SCSI disk three, partition a):

```
config    bsd    root on sd3a
```

We don't tell the kernel anything about the dump or swap partitions, so it doesn't know anything about them. In most cases, your system can find its swap partitions through /etc/fstab, and it will dump automatically to a swap partition.

In this example (shown in the GENERIC kernel configuration, but commented out), we explicitly list the root partition, the swap partition, and the dump device:

```
config    bsd    root on wd0a swap on wd0b and vnd0c dumps on wd0b
```

For most cases you can just let the kernel figure everything out — I've never had a problem with the generic routines the OpenBSD kernel uses.

Common Device Drivers

Knowing that a device driver exists is fine, but what name goes with which hardware? This section lists the common device drivers, and the hardware that they support.

Again, I'm not going to discuss each device driver in detail, but instead provide a reference to the man page where greater detail can be found. The OpenBSD team is meticulous about keeping their man pages up-to-date, and documentation flaws are considered fairly serious bugs.

Not all hardware is unique to i386, but not much is found on all hardware platforms. The ne2000 network card runs on both Alpha and i386, for example, but not on Sparc. For that reason, all hardware device drivers are kept with the hardware, rather than in the cross-platform information.

Busses

Busses are the bolts that hold a computer's components. When a piece of hardware wants to talk to another piece of hardware, the signals travel along a bus. Busses plug into each other. If you don't include the proper busses for your hardware in your kernel, your kernel will not work properly. Perhaps such a kernel won't boot, or perhaps you won't see all of your hardware.

mainbus0 at root

Every lesser bus talks to the main bus, or to some bus connected to the main bus. Every i386 kernel must have this.

bios0 at mainbus0

This is the hardware built-in operating system. It's always attached to the main bus. A BIOS driver is necessary on almost all hardware. You can read all about the BIOS driver in bios(4).

isa0

This is a standard old-fashioned ISA bus. Many so-called "ISA-free systems" actually do have an ISA bus in them; they simply don't have any ISA card slots. Here, we plug the ISA bus into the main bus:

```
isa0    at mainbus0
```

Or, you could plug the ISA bus into a PCI-ISA bridge:

```
isa0    at pcib?
```

You can learn more by reading isa(4).

eisa

The Extended Industry-Standard Architecture bus is not very common these days, having mostly been supplanted by PCI. Here, we show an EISA bus attached to the mainbus:

```
eisa0   at mainbus0
```

You can learn more in eisa(4).

pci

The Peripheral Component Interconnect bus is the modern standard. Generally speaking, it's plugged into the main bus. Here, we show a PCI bus plugged into the main bus. Since PCI is self-configuring, we don't need to hard-code a device number. Here, we have a PCI bus attached to the main bus:

```
pci*   at mainbus0 bus ?
```

A PCI bus can also attach to a PCI-PCI bridge (ppb) or a PCI-Host bridge (pchb). You can get more information in pci(4).

pcmcia

This is the PCMCIA bus, generally used for 16-bit PC Cards as found in laptops.

cbb*   at pci? dev ? function ?

This bus supports 32-bit CardBus cards, most commonly found in laptops.

usb

The USB bus is always attached to a USB controller. It manages all USB devices.

iop

man: iop(4)

This driver incorporates general support for I2O in the kernel. Intelligent Input-Output specification is a newer input-output standard for input/output devices.

i386 Core Hardware

This hardware is common to just about any i386 system.

npx0   at isa? port 0xf0 irq 13

This drives the Numerical Processing Extension, also known as the floating-point coprocessor. All modern hardware has a FPU — on the i386, only 386s and some 486s do not. You must have either the npx device, or the GPL_MATH_EMULATE kernel option in your kernel, or your kernel will not boot. You can find more documentation in npx(4).

isadma0   at isa?

This handles DMA support for disks on the ISA bus.

isapnp0   at isa?

This handles ISA plug-and-play.

pckbc

This is the keyboard controller, the place on the motherboard where the keyboard traditionally plugs in. You almost certainly want this! It is documented in pckbc(4).

pckbd

This is the actual keyboard. Note that while it is possible to remap your keyboard to your local layout at the kernel level, it's almost always better to use wsconsctl(8). If you must remap your keyboard at the kernel level, check out pckbd(4).

pms*   at pckbc?

This is a PS/2 mouse, plugged into the onboard keyboard controller's PS/2 mouse port. You can learn a little more in pms(4).

pmsi*   at pckbc?

man: pms(4)

This driver supports the PS/2 "IntelliMouse" wheeled mice. Wheel usage is handled automatically.

lms0   at isa? port 0x23c irq 5

man: lms(4)

This driver manages the Logitech bus mouse.

mms0   at isa? port 0x23c irq 5

man: mms(4)

This supports the Microsoft-style bus mouse, such as the InPort mouse.

vga

man: vga(4)

This is the classic VGA graphics card found.

pcdisplay0   at isa?

man: pcdisplay(4)

This supports pre-VGA video cards, such as CGA, MDA, EGA, and HGA displays. You'll only find these on extremely old hardware.

lpt

man: lpt (4)

This is a parallel port, also known as a printer port.

Bridges

Bridges connect one sort of bus (or other subsystem) to another.

pchb*   at pci? dev ? function ?

This PCI-Host bridge supports adapter-specific functions on a narrow range of hardware. Among the more interesting of these devices are the i82810/810E, the i82815/815E, the i82820, and the i82840, which supply random numbers to the operating system. See pchb(4) for details on the hardware this driver supports in your version of OpenBSD.

ppb*   at pci? dev ? function ?

This is a PCI-PCI bridge, which attaches one PCI bus to another. It really doesn't need much configuration.

pcib*   at pci? dev ? function ?

This bridge attaches an ISA bus to a PCI bus. Again, it's fairly simple and doesn't need configuration.

Non-SCSI Controllers

A controller is a device that interfaces between a device and a bus. They are commonly used for removable hardware such as laptop cards and USB devices.

fdc

man: fdc(4)

This is the controller for the i386 floppy drive controller. Any standard system (IDE, SCSI, and so on) with a floppy drive will use this controller.

pcic

man: pcic(4)

The pcic devices are common ISA PCMCIA controllers, for 16-bit PC Card devices. This device does not support 32-bit CardBus cards; you need a cardbus device for those.

tcic0   at isa? port 0x240 iomem 0xd0000 iosiz 0x10000

man: tcic(4)

This is a Databook ISA PCMCIA controller. It's disabled by default in the GENERIC kernel, but you can enable it with config -e. It's strictly an ISA controller.

uhci*   at pci?

man: uhci(4)

This is an Intel USB Controller (also known as a Universal Host Controller). It's always plugged into a PCI bus.

ohci*   at pci?

man: ohci(4)

This is the Open Host Controller USB controller, the alternative to Intel's Universal Host Controller. It's always plugged into a PCI bus.

pciide

man: pciide(4)

This driver supports all IDE controllers attached to the PCI bus. It supports the DMA and UltraDMA functions of these controllers.

wdc

man: wdc(4)

This controller supports IDE hard disk controllers on an ISA or Plug-and-Play ISA bus. You might consider trying the 0x01 flag to enable 32-bit negotiation, but this can cause problems on some motherboards.

atapiscsi

man: atapiscsi(4)

This integrates the ATAPI (IDE) system with the SCSI system, so that IDE devices can appear as SCSI devices. See Chapter 15. All CD-ROM devices attach to the ATAPISCSI system automatically, so you can use SCSI-only CD-ROM access programs to access your IDE CD-ROMs.

SCSI Controllers

SCSI controllers are fairly straightforward and don't require much individual documentation. Many drivers support quite a few similar cards, so if you have a card similar to one listed here, check the man page to see whether it is supported. Remember, you must attach a SCSI bus to your SCSI card!

bha	bha(4)	BusLogic ISA BT-445,EISA BT-74x, PCI BT-945/968
aha	aha(4)	Adaptec AHA-1549, most 154x
ahb	ahb(4)	Adaptec 1742
ahc	ahc(4)	Adaptec 274x, 2940x, 2950x, 2940, many others
iha	iha(4)	DTC Domex 3194U Plus, INI-9090U,INI-9100U/UW
isp	isp(4)	Qlogic SCSI or FibreChannel
aic	aic(4)	Adaptec 6260/6360,152x
esp	none	PCMCIA based NCR 53C9X
ncr	ncr(4)	Older NCR 538XX
siop	siop(4)	New NCR 538XX
adv	advansys(4)	Most AdvanSys PCI adapters
adw	advansys(4)	The other AdvanSys PCI adapters
pcscp	pcscp(4)	Tekram DC-390
sea	sea(4)	ST01/02, Future Domain TMC-885/950
trm	trm(4)	Tekram DC-3x5Ux

| **uha** | uha(4) | UltraStor x4f |
| **wds** | none | WD7000 and TMC-7000 |

RAID Controllers

The following RAID controllers all use SCSI interfaces and SCSI drives, so you must attach a SCSI bus to your card to make it work. All RAID functionality is handled by the BIOS on the card.

dpt	dpt(4)	DPT SmartCache III/IV, SmartRAID III/IV
gdt	gdt(4)	All known GDT cards
twe	twe(4)	All known 3ware Escalade cards
aac	aac(4)	All known Adaptec FSA cards
ami	ami(4)	All known AMI MegaRAID
cac	cac(4)	Many Compaq Smart Array cards
ioprbs	ioprbs(4)	I2O controllers

SCSI Interface Devices

The following SCSI devices can be attached to a SCSI bus:

sd

man: sd(4)

This supports all SCSI disk drives.

st

man: st(4)

This handles all SCSI tape drives.

cd

man: cd(4)

This driver handles all CD-ROM drives, both SCSI and IDE.

ch

man: ch(4)

This drives all SCSI autochanger devices, such as CD jukeboxes.

ss

This identifies SCSI scanners. SCSI scanner support is questionable, and you will want to check the mailing list archives closely before purchasing any scanner.

uk

man: uk(4)

This driver attaches to all unidentified SCSI devices. You would need a program to actually access these devices, but at least the kernel shows something when you probe such a device.

Non-SCSI Storage Devices

This catchall category includes everything you can store data on that isn't SCSI.

fd

man: fdc(4)

This is an old-fashioned floppy disk drive, which supports everything from the fancy 2.88MB disk to the huge 360Kb disk.

mcd

man: mcd(4)

This driver supports the Mitsumi CD-ROM drive.

wd

man: wd(4)

This supports IDE hard disks. By default, the drive will attempt to use whatever features (PIO, DMA, and so forth) the drive claims to support. If you find that a hard disk does not function as you expect in the mode it claims to support, you might try hard-coding a slower mode into your kernel. (You would probably be better off acquiring a new disk, mind you.)

wt0

man: wt(4)

This driver supports the QIC-02 and QIC-32 tape drives from Archive and Wangtek.

MII Network Cards

The Media Independent Interface is an abstraction layer to improve code sharing in network cards. Almost all modern network cards use the MII interface. The following table lists these cards. When you use these cards in a kernel configuration, they must be attached to a "mii" entry.

```
exphy*      at mii? phy ?
```

There is no "root" mii entry, however; don't let that confuse you.

exphy	exphy(4)	3Com internal network cards
inphy	inphy(4)	Intel 82555-based cards
iophy	isophy(4)	Intel 82553-based cards
icsphy	icsphy(4)	Integrated Circuit Systems ICS1890/ 1892-based cards
lxtphy	lxtphy(4)	Level One LXT-970, 970A, 971-based cards.
nsphy	nsphy(4)	National Semiconductor DP83840/ DP83840A-based cards
nsphyter	nsphyter(4)	National Semiconductor PHYTER DP83843-based cards

qsphy	qsphy(4)	Quality Semiconductor QS6612-based cards
sqphy	sqphy(4)	Seeq 80220/80221, 80223, 84220-based cards
rlphy	rlphy(4)	RealTek RTL8139-based cards
mtdphy	mtdphy(4)	Myson MTD972-based cards.
dcphy	none	Digital 21143-based cards
amphy	amphy(4)	AMD AM79c873, Davicom DM9101-based cards
tqphy	tqphy(4)	TDK Semiconductor 78Q2120-based cards, 3Com 574 PCMCIA card
bmtphy	bmtphy(4)	Broadcom Mini-Theta BCM5201/BCM5202-based cards
brgphy	brgphy(4)	Broadcom BCM5400, BCM5401, BCM5411, etc, based cards
eephy	eephy(4)	Marvell 88E1000-based cards
xmphy	xmphy(4)	XaQti XMAC-II-based cards
nsgphy	nsgphy(4)	National Semiconductor DP83891/DP83861-based cards
ukphy	ukphy(4)	unknown chipsets, supports basic Ethernet on most other cards

Non-MII Network Cards

The following network cards do not require the MII interface; they're just boring old cards.

we	we(4)	Western Digital/SMC WD80x3, SMC Elite Ultra, SMC EtherEZ
ec	ec(4)	3Com 503 cards
ne	ne(4)	NE1000-compatible and NE2000-compatible cards
eg	eg(4)	3Com EtherLink Plus (505) card
el	el(4)	3Com Etherlink 501 card
ep	ep(4)	3Com Etherlink III card (many types)
ef	ef(4)	3Com Fast EtherLink (515) card
ie	ie(4)	Intel 82586-based cards
lc	lc(4)	LEMAC-based cards (DEC DE203, DE204, DE205)
le	le(4)	AMD Lance-based cards (StarLAN, Kingston 21xx, Novell NE1500T, etc.)
ex	ex(4)	Intel EtherExpress PRO/10
de	de(4)	DC21X4X-based ethernet
fxp	fxp(4)	Intel i82557, i82558, i82559, i82562-based cards (Intel EtherExpress, PRO)
sm	sm(4)	SMC91C9x-based cards
xe	xe(4)	Xircom Ethernet cards

xl	xl(4)	3Com EtherLink XL family (many models)
rl	rl(4)	RealTek 8129/8139-based cards (many inexpensive cards)
tx	tx(4)	SMC EPIC-based cards (SMC EtherPower II)
tl	tl(4)	Compaq Thunderlan
vr	vr(4)	VIA VT3043 Rhine I/VT86C100A Rhine II-based cards
wb	wb(4)	Winbond W89C840F-based cards (assorted inexpensive cards)
sf	sf(4)	Adaptec AIC-6915-based cards
sis	sis(4)	SiS 900/7016, National Semiconductor DP83815-based cards
ste	ste(4)	Sundance ST201-based cards (D-Link DFE-550TX)
dc	dc(4)	"Tulip" Ethernet cards (many inexpensive cards)
ti	ti(4)	Alteon Tigon-based cards

Gigabit Ethernet Cards

Gigabit ethernet cards do not require the MII interface.

skc	sk(4)	SysKonnect GE-984x-based controller
sk	sk(4)	SysKonnect GE-984x-based port
gx	gx(4)	Intel i82542, i82543, i82544-based cards (Pro/1000)
txp	txp(4)	3com Typhoon/Sidewinder-based cards
nge	nge(4)	National Semiconductor DP83820/DP83821-based cards
bge	bge(4)	Broadcom BCM570x-based cards
stge	stge(4)	Sundance TC9021-based cards
lge	lge(4)	Level 1 LXT1001-based cards

Wireless Network Cards

These wireless network cards also do not require the MII interface.

wi	wi(4)	Lucent Hermes, Intersil PRISM-II/Prism 2.5, Symbol Spectrum 24-based cards
awi	aw(4)	Bay Networks BayStack 650 PCMCIA cards
an	an(4)	Aironet Communications 4500/4800, Cisco 350-based cards

| cnw | cnw(4) | Xircom CreditCard Netwave, Xircom Netwave Airsurfer |
| ray | ray(4) | Raytheon Raylink and Aviator2.4/Pro |

Non-Ethernet Network Cards

The following cards are all network cards, but do not speak Ethernet:

fpa

man: fpa(4)

This driver supports all versions of the DEC DEFPA FDDI card.

fea

man: fea(4)

This supports all versions of the DEC DEFEA FDDI card.

tr

man: none

This supports a variety of token-ring cards, including the IBM TROPIC based cards and some 3Com cards.

lmc

man: lmc(4)

This driver supports the Lan Media Corporation's SSI, DS1, HSSI, and DS3 PCI Wide Area Network cards. You can use these drivers to make your own WAN router.

CardBus Devices

CardBus is the 32-bit removable card standard, the successor to PCMCIA. It has two additional devices. All modern laptops use CardBus (even though some marketing literature still calls it a PC Card interface). These really aren't optional; if you have a CardBus interface (the cbb driver), you really need the following two entries to actually use any removable cards.

cardslot

man: cardbus(4)

The cardslot is a particular hardware slot attached to the cardbus.

cardbus

man: cardbus(4)

This device is somewhat badly named; it's the glue between a CardBus card and the CardBus slot on the system.

BIOS Devices

BIOS devices are attached to the system's BIOS, and only to the BIOS. As such, they rate their own section — at least, they don't fit in anywhere else!

apm0   at bios0 flags 0x0000

This supports Advanced Power Management. APM has recently been replaced by ACPI, and is no longer considered quite so advanced.

The APM driver has several options, controlled by flags. Depending on the version of APM you have, you may need to change the flags. You can do this on the GENERIC kernel with config(8), but if you're rebuilding the kernel you might as well set it here. If you don't know which version of APM your hardware uses, check your hardware manual. For more information, see apm(4).

flags 0x0101	APM version 1.1
flags 0x0110	APM version 1.2
flags 0x10000	leave interrupts enabled (required on some IBM laptops)

pcibios0 at bios0 flags 0x0000

The PCI BIOS handles tasks such as assigning memory addresses and IRQs automatically. This gets rid of all the icky plug-and-play crud that plagues ISA cards. Sadly, not all PCI BIOS manufacturers do things correctly, and the OpenBSD driver needs to implement some magic to make problems go away. If you have problems with your PCI bus, definitely take a look at pcibios(4) for a whole list of flags that might address your particular problem.

Serial Ports

Serial ports are some of the oldest computer interfaces. Modems, mice, and terminals have all at one time or another been attached to serial ports.

pccom

man: com(4)

This driver handles standard PC serial ports, generally known as COM ports.

com

man: com(4)

The com driver supports non-i386-specific serial ports, such as those found on multiport serial cards.

puc

man: puc(4)

This driver handles PCI cards that contain standard serial and parallel ports. The ports on these cards cannot usually be used as serial consoles; PCI cards get dynamic hardware addresses, which makes hard-coding the serial console address difficult. (If you can get a serial port on one of these cards to have the same I/O port and memory address as one of the first four i386 serial ports, it would work. None of my cards do this reliably, but yours might.) You can attach pccom and lpt devices to this as necessary to have your kernel recognize your ports.

ast

man: ast(4)

This driver supports 4-port serial cards that use the EIA RS-232C interface. You need a com device attached to this device in your kernel to have the actual ports be recognized.

addcom

man: addcom(4)

This driver supports the Addonics FlexPort 8/S 8-port serial ISA board. It probably works on the 4-port version as well. You'll want to add a com device for each port on the board.

rtfps

man: rtfps(4)

This driver supports the IBM RT boards that multiplex up to four serial ports. You need to attach com devices to this card for it to work.

hsq

man: hsq(4)

This driver supports 4-port Hostess-compatible serial port cards. Attach pccom devices to it to have them recognized.

cy

man: cy(4)

This driver supports the Cyclades Cyclom-4Y, Cyclom-8Y, and Cyclom-16Y multiport serial cards.

cz

man: cz

This driver supports the Cyclades-Z multiport serial cards.

Console Drivers

The drivers here are all part of the platform-independent console system, which is wscons(8). There is no hardware for any of these drivers; they are all abstractions on top of the hardware platform's native keyboard, mouse, and display system. As such, each device needs to be attached to the proper physical hardware.

wsdisplay

man: wsdisplay(4)

This is the display driver that actually places characters on the screen. You must have this device in your kernel if you want to use any sort of monitor.

wskbd

man: wskbd(4)

This driver manages keyboards in the wscons framework. Again, if you want to use your keyboard you need to have this device in your kernel.

wsmouse

man: wsmouse(4)

This driver abstracts mouse hardware. You just have to configure the wsmouse driver via wsconsctl(8), and the wscons framework translates that to the correct instructions for whatever hardware you have.

USB Devices

The Universal Serial Bus is a very popular standard for removable devices. Not only do you need to define your USB bus and USB controller in your kernel, you need to list drivers for any and all USB devices you have. Since it's very hard to tell what might be plugged into a USB controller, I recommend leaving any and all USB devices in your kernel configuration.

uhub

This is a USB hub. Every USB system needs at least one USB hub, plugged into the USB bus like so.

```
uhub*    at usb?
```

The USB hub is one of those rare devices that can daisy-chain onto itself — you can plug a USB hub into another USB hub, as demonstrated here.

```
uhub*    at uhub? port ? configuration ?
```

You can learn more about OpenBSD's USB support in general in usb(4).

uhid

man: uhid(4)

This device supports USB devices that do not have specific drivers. The most common devices of this sort are joysticks and digitizer tablets.

ucom

man: umodem(4)

This is a COM port that runs on the USB modem. Many USB devices, such as modems, Handspring Visors, and serial adapters, need an old-fashioned serial connection. All of these devices actually talk to a ucom device that attaches to the actual device driver.

ubsa

man: ubsa(4)

This is a Belkin USB serial adapter that many ucom(4) devices can connect to, and can behave much like a serial terminal.

umodem

man: umodem(4)

This driver attaches USB modems to the USB subsystem. Don't try to communicate with your modem via the umodem device, however; instead, talk to the ucom device.

uvisor

man: uvisor(4)

Yes, you can plug your Visor into your OpenBSD box and sync it, courtesy of this device driver and some add-on software. This device driver works much like the umodem driver, though; you will actually talk to the ucom driver that automatically attaches to this device.

uftdi

man: uftdi(4)

This supports a variety of USB serial adapters based on the FT8U100AX chipset, such as the D-Link DSB-H4SMK, the Inland UAS111, and the QVS USC-1000. Again, you want to attach a ucom device to this to make it work properly.

uplcom*   at uhub? port ?

man: uplcom(4)

This device driver supports USB serial adapters based on the Prolific PL-2303 USB-to-RS232 chipset.

uaudio*   at uhub? port ? configuration ?

man: uaudio(4)

This supports USB sound cards. A USB sound device needs to have an audio driver attached to it.

ulpt

man: ulpt(4)

This is a USB printer. Unlike the serial-port devices, you can work directly with a USB printer instead of attaching a parallel port on top of it.

ukbd

man: ukbd(4)

This is a fairly boring, common USB keyboard. You'll need to attach the console pseudo-devices to it to make it work.

umass

man: umass(4)

This supports any USB storage devices, such as removable flash disks, digital cameras, and so on. OpenBSD uses a SCSI interface to connect to these devices, so be sure to put a SCSI bus on top of your umass driver. The driver is described in umass(4).

ums

man: ums(4)

These are USB mice. You'll need to attach the console mouse device to this for the mouse to actually work.

aue

man: aue(4)

This support USB Ethernet adapters with the ADMtek AN986 Pegasus chipset. Many different USB ethernet devices use this device. It interoperates with the Media Independent Interface (mii) network system. See aue(4) for a full list of cards supported by this driver.

cue

man: cue(4)

This supports USB Ethernet adapters built with Computer Access Technology Corporation's USB-EL1202A chipset. This includes only a handful of devices.

kue

man: kue(4)

This driver supports USB Ethernet adapters built around the Kawasaki KL5KUSB101B chipset.

upl

man: upl(4)

This is a direct host-to-host connection over USB, much like parallel port "Laplink" connections.

urio

man: urio(4)

The urio device supports the Rio MP3 player. See urio(4) for examples on how to use the Rio on your OpenBSD machine.

uscanner

man: uscanner(4)

This device supports common USB scanners. To actually use the scanner, however, you need to add on a scanner software package. The most popular one is SANE, but people have reported mixed results with scanners on OpenBSD. See uscanner(4) for the list of supported USB scanners.

usscanner

man: usscanner(4)

This driver supports USB scanners that operate via a SCSI interface, such as the HP5300. You'll need to attach a SCSI bus to this device for it to work. Again, scanning under OpenBSD is tricky and will require some work.

uyap*   at uhub? port ?

man: uyap(4)

This device driver supports the YAP Internet phone. At the time of this writing, it's not enabled in the default kernel, but you can choose to add it in.

ugen

man: ugen(4)

This is a driver for "generic" USB devices. Any USB device should attach to the ugen driver. It may not work as you expect, but some experimentation will probably get some functionality out of the device. See ugen(4) for more than you really want to know about generic USB devices.

Multimedia Hardware

OpenBSD supports a wide variety of multimedia hardware, including sound cards, video capture cards, and so on.

pcppi

man: pcppi(4)

This driver supports system speakers in i386 hardware. All systems with sound hardware need this.

sysbeep

man: pcppi(4)

This is a fake "keyboard beep" generated through the pcppi speaker.

spkr

man: speaker(4)

This is a simple interface to the system pcppi speaker, allowing programs to generate basic tones.

midi

man: midi(4)

This driver supports MIDI hardware: external or internal synthesizers, soundcard MIDI port, and so on.

opl

man: opl(4)

This supports the Yamaha OPL2 and OPL3 FM synthesizer chips.

audio

man: audio(4)

This provides a generic interface to any sound card attached to the system.

bktr

man: bktr(4)

This driver supports PCI video capture boards based on the Brooktree Bt848/849-878/879 chip. This includes most of the capture cards on the market.

joy

man: joy(4)

This supports the game controller, which in turn handles up to two joysticks.

The following table lists the common sound card drivers, their man pages, and the cards they handle. You must attach an audio(4) driver to each of these to actually use them.

aria	aria(4)	Sierra Semiconductor Aria-based cards
auich	auich(4)	Intel 82801AA/AB/BA/CA, 82440MX
autri	autri(4)	Trident 4DWAVE-DX/NX, SiS 7018, ALi M5451
auvia	auvia(4)	VIA VT82C686A
clcs	clcs(4)	Cirrus Logis CS4280/CS461x-based cards
clct	clct(4)	Cirrus Logic CS4281-based cards
cmpci	cmpci(4)	C-Media CMI8338A/B, CMI8738-based cards
eap	eap(4)	ES1370, SoundBlaster PCI128-based cards
emu	emu(4)	SoundBlaster Live!, SoundBlaster PCI 512
esa	esa(4)	ESS Allegro-1, Maestro-3-based cards
eso	eso(4)	ESS ES1938/ES1946-based cards
ess	ess(4)	ESS 1788, 1888, 1887, 888 AudioDrive
fms	fms(4)	Forte Media FM801
gus	gus(4)	Gravis UltraSound, GUS MAX
maestro	maestro(4)	ESS maestro 1/2/2E
mpu	none	Yamaha MPU401 and compatible MIDI
neo	neo(4)	NeoMagic 256AV/ZX
pas	pas(4)	ProAudio Spectrum
pss	pss(4)	ESC614/614A ASIC, AD1848/CS4231 codec-based cards
sb	sb(4)	SoundBlaster-based cards

sp	pss(4)	Sound port on pss-driven cards
sv	sv(4)	S3 SonicVibes (S3 617)-based cards
wss	wss(4)	Windows Sound System-based cards
yds	yds(4)	Yamaha DS-XG-based cards
ym	ym(4)	Yamaha OPL3-SAx-based cards

Radio Support

OpenBSD supports a variety of radio tuners.

radio

man: radio(4)

This is a card-independent radio management layer. You need a radio device attached to any radio card in your system.

The following table lists all radio cards supported by OpenBSD, their man pages, and the hardware they support:

mr	mr(4)	Guillemot Maxi Radio FM2000 PCI Radio Card
sf4r	sf4r(4)	SoundForte RadioLink SF64-PCR FM Radio Card
sf2r	sf2r(4)	SoundForte RadioLink SF16-FMR2 FM Radio Card
az	az(4)	Aztech/PackardBell FM Radio Card
rt	rt(4)	AIMS Lab Radiotrack FM Radio Card
rtii	rtii(4)	AIMS Lab Radiotrack II FM Radio Card

Hardware Crypto Cards

OpenBSD supports a variety of hardware cryptographic accelerators. Any OpenSSL system calls will be processed by the crypto accelerator, and not on the main CPU. This greatly aids secure web servers and other crypto-intensive programs.

hifn	hifn(4)	Hifn 7751/7951/7811-based cards
ubsec	ubsec(4)	Bluesteel Networks 5xxx-based cards
ises	ises(4)	Securealink PCC-ISES

i386 Kernel Options

Some kernel options only work on certain hardware platforms, while others are found on all platforms. We'll only discuss the kernel options that work on i386 here. For a fairly complete list of kernel options meant for general use, see options(4).

Bus Options

These kernel options affect how hardware busses and associated hardware behaves.

option   PCIVERBOSE

This option makes the computer print vendor names, chips IDs, and such for all PCI devices in the system when those devices are first detected.

option   EISAVERBOSE

This option makes the computer print vendor names, chip IDs, and so on for all EISA devices at boot-time.

option   USBVERBOSE

Whenever a USB device is detected (either at boot-time, or by plugging into the system), this option makes it print out any information it can get from the hardware.

option   PCMCIAVERBOSE

This makes the boot process give more information about the PCMCIA bus and any attached devices.

option   DEBUG_ISAPNP

As you can probably guess by now, this provides additional debugging information about the ISA Plug-and-Play interface during boots.

Debugging Options

In most cases, system developers are the ones interested in ones interested in debugging options. Many of these options aren't particularly useful to people who just want to run OpenBSD.

option   DDB

This compiles the kernel debugger into the kernel. See ddb(4) for more information.

option   DDB_SAFE_CONSOLE

This allows a developer to call up the debugger before the system finishes initializing. It's useful if you're working on init(8).

makeoptions   DEBUG="-g"

This includes the full symbol table in the kernel. If you are developing an OpenBSD kernel, you probably want this.

makeoptions   PROF="-pg"

This builds a kernel with support for profiling.

option   GPROF

This builds the kernel hooks for the profiling tool, kgmon(8).

option   DIAGNOSTIC

This adds internal consistency checks on kernel data. If a system fails a DIAGNOSTIC check, the kernel panics. You might think this is bad, but it's better than running with corrupt data!

option   KGDB

This compiles in a remote kernel debugger, allowing a kernel developer to use gdb(1)'s remote target features.

option   "KGDB_DEVNAME=\"pccom\""

This sets the device name used by the kgdb option.

option   KGDBADDR=0x2f8

This sets the memory address used by the kgdb option.

option   KGDBRATE=9600

This sets the port speed used by the kgdb option.

Security Options

The following options affect system security.

option   UVM_SWAP_ENCRYPT

This supports encrypted swap space. See Chapter 15 for details.

option   INSECURE

This sets the default securelevel to -1, instead of zero. See securelevel(7).

Userland Syscall Options

System calls are the interface the kernel provides to programs running on the system. Removing these options can cause programs to run badly, or not at all.

option   KTRACE

This provides the kernel hooks for ktrace(1), which allows users to track the system calls made by programs they run.

option   KMEMSTATS

This keeps statistics on how memory is used. It adds overhead to the system calls malloc() and free(), dramatically increasing system overhead for trivial things such as networking and the (unsupported) RAID driver.

option   PTRACE

This adds hooks for the ptrace(2) system call, which allows one process to monitor and control another process.

option CRYPTO

This adds an in-kernel cryptographic engine. The most common user for this is IPSEC, but it's available to other kernel features as well. Se crypto(9) for details.

option SYSVMSG

This supports System V message queues, as documented in msgctl(2), msgget(2), msgrcv(2), and msgsnd(2). If you don't know what this is, you want it.

option SYSVSEM

This supports System V-style semaphores. For details, see semctl(2), semget(2), and semop(2). Again, include it unless you specifically know you don't want it.

option SYSVSHM

If you want to use System V-style shared memory, use this option. You can read about this in shmat(2), shmctl(2), shmdt(2), and shmget(2). Many programs expect to find these features.

option FIFO

These are "named pipes." Many programs use named pipes, and you should always include them. (If you're using OpenBSD in an embedded system, you might know that you don't need them.)

Filesystem Options

These options support the various file systems that OpenBSD can use. If you don't include the option for a filesystem, you cannot access disks formatted in that manner.

option FFS

This is the standard UNIX file system. It is required.

option FFS_SOFTUPDATES

Soft Updates greatly enhance FFS. You almost certainly want this. See Chapter 15.

option QUOTA

This allows you to set quotas on how much disk a user can take up.

option EXT2FS

This is the standard Linux file system.

option MFS

This option allows you to create virtual disks out of memory. Such disks are extremely fast, and excellent for many short-term operations.

option XFS

This supports the AFS-compatible Arla filesystem. See mount_xfs(8) for details.

option   NFSCLIENT

This allows your system to access NFS mounts exported from other machines. See mount_nfs(8).

option   NFSSERVER

This allows your system to export NFS file systems to other machines. See mountd(8) and nfsd(8) for details.

option   CD9660

This supports CD-ROMs. See Chapter 15.

option   MSDOSFS

This tells your kernel how to access MS-DOS formatted disks, which is the default floppy disk format. See Chapter 15.

option   FDESC

This allows programs to access the per-process file descriptor space. This is not needed on most OpenBSD systems, as the fd(4) pseudo-device provides identical functionality.

option   KERNFS

The kernel file system creates a directory, traditionally mounted on /kern, which exports a variety of kernel information. See mount_kernfs(8). If you don't want to use this, don't need it.

option   NULLFS

This lets the kernel "layer" file systems on top of each other, basically re-mounting directories at different locations. This nifty trick is discussed in mount_null(8).

option   PORTAL

The portal filesystem provides a map between the filesystem and the kernel. It allows you to, say, create a TCP connection by opening a file. It is highly experimental; see mount_portal(8).

option   PROCFS

The process filesystem gives details on processes running in system. See Chapter 15.

option   UMAPFS

This is nullfs, plus the ability to remap user ID and group ID numbers. It's useful for mounting foreign file systems where these values are different — say, over NFS. See mount_umap(8).

option   UNION

This is a massively cool, but slightly buggy option where the kernel can create a stackable filesystem where both layers are visible. See mount_union(8).

Networking Options

The following options all alter networking behavior.

option GATEWAY

This option increases NMBCLUSTERS and sets sysctl net.inet.ip.forwarding to 1. These effects can be achieved separately without recompiling the kernel by, well, increasing NMBCLUSTERS and changing the sysctl.

option INET

This gives the kernel basic networking functionality.

option ALTQ

This enables up simple rate-limiting and traffic shaping. See altqd(8).

option INET6

This tells the kernel about IPv6.

option PULLDOWN_TEST

This helps IPv6 handle erratic packet flows. If you're using IPv6, you want this.

option IPSEC

IPSec is the standard built-in security for IPv6.

option KEY

This option supports PFKEYv2. If you have the IPSEC option, you automatically get this. You can read about PFKEYv2 in RFC 2367.

option NS

This option supports the Xerox Network Systems networking protocols. Most people don't need it. See ns(4).

option NSIP

This option supports tunneling XNS over TCP/IP. If you don't need XNS support, you certainly don't need this!

option IPX

This gives the kernel support for the Internet Packet Exchange protocol popular in older Netware environments.

option IPXIP

This lets the kernel support "tunnels" to put IPX over an IP network.

option ISO,TPIP

This supports the ISO protocols that use the ISO addressing scheme, such as CLNP or TP. See ios(4).

option   EON

This lets you tunnel ISO protocols over TCP/IP.

option   NETATALK

This lets the kernel understand Apple's AppleTalk protocol.

option   CCITT,LLC,HDLC

This supports X.25 protocols. It's been neglected for some time, so it's probably scary and certainly buggy.

option   PPP_BSDCOMP

This is the standard compression style for PPP connections. It's only used by pppd(8).

option   PPP_DEFLATE

This is the interface to the zlib library for PPP connections, as used by pppd(8).

option   MROUTING

This supports the kernel part of multicast routing. If you're building a multicast router, you want this. If you don't know what multicast routing is, you aren't doing it. See mrouted(8).

option   TCP_SACK

This enables Selective Acknowledgements allow for faster recovery from interrupted TCP connections.

option   TCP_FACK

Forward Acknowledgements help reduce congestion on TCP networks, but both sides of every connection must understand forward acknowledgements. It can only be used with TCP_FACK.

option   TCP_SIGNATURE

This computes MD5 checksums of TCP packets. While this sounds truly nifty, only Internet backbone routers use it to verify BGP routing information. As such, it's not exactly useful to most people. If you're building a BGP-speaking router out of an OpenBSD box, however, you might find this useful.

Console Options

The following options all affect how the wscons platform-independent console driver behaves.

option   WSDISPLAY_COMPAT_USL

This supports switching between multiple virtual consoles.

option   WSDISPLAY_COMPAT_RAWKBD

This supports raw keyboard code compatibility, without the wscons framework. The X Window System needs this.

option   WSDISPLAY_DEFAULTSCREENS

This is the number of virtual consoles.

option   WSDISPLAY_COMPAT_PCVT

This gives the console compatibility with pcvt, needed for X.

Binary Compatibility Options

These options provide compatibility with other operating systems. Some of these are network compatibility features, but most cover OpenBSD's support for foreign ABIs, as discussed in Chapter 13.

option   TCP_COMPAT_42

You might need this option to connect to systems with a BSD 4.2 TCP stack. You really don't want to communicate with those systems; in fact, such systems should be disconnected from the network, as they're almost certainly insecure and unstable.

option   COMPAT_23

Provides compatibility with older releases of OpenBSD. Older versions of OpenBSD had different msgtcl(2), shmctl(2), and semctl(2) system calls. You only need this option if you're running binaries compiled under OpenBSD 2.3 or earlier.

option   COMPAT_25

The statfs(2), fstatfs(2), and fetfsstat(2) system calls changed after OpenBSD 2.5. If you are using binaries compiled on OpenBSD 2.5 or earlier, you need this.

option   COMPAT_43

This option supports a whole host of system calls from BSD 4.3, in the late 80s. If you have binaries built for BSD 4.3, you need this. These programs almost certainly have security holes.

option   COMPAT_SVR4

This option allows binary compatibility with i386 Solaris (or, if you're running on sparc, sparc Solaris). See compat_svr4(8).

option   COMPAT_IBCS2

This option supports Intel Binary Compatibility Standard 2 binaries, as found in SCO UNIX and SVR3.

option   COMPAT_LINUX

This supports binary compatibility with i386 Linux binaries.

option   COMPAT_FREEBSD

This supports binary compatibility with i386 FreeBSD binaries.

option   COMPAT_BSDOS

This option allows the system to run BSD/OS binaries. You must have
COMPAT_43 in your kernel for this to work. See compat_bsdos(8).

Misc Options

These options are a scattered mix of things that don't fit elsewhere.

option   BOOT_CONFIG

This supports boot-time kernel configuration, as discussed in Chapter 11.

option   NTP

This adds kernel support for a userland daemon (i.e., ntpd) setting the time.

option   USER_LDT

This lets programs set the local descriptor table. It's only necessary if you're using
the Wine win32 emulator.

option   XSERVER

This changes the console driver so that you can use the X windows system on the
local display.

option   APERTURE

This supports VGA framebuffer mapping, so you can run X on the local display.

option   USER_PCICONF

This allows on X server to reconfigure PCI cards.

option   LKM

This supports loadable kernel modules. LKMs are not common in OpenBSD.

Pseudo-Devices

These are things that act like hardware, but have no actual hardware attached.
Most are found on all architectures. If a number appears after a pseudo-device
driver, that is the total number of the particular pseudo-device driver the system
will support.

Disk-Like Pseudo-Devices

pseudo-device   vnd   4

This is a disk-like interface to files, for a variety of filesystem tricks. See Chapter
15.

pseudo-device   ccd   4

This allows you to combine multiple disks into one large concatenated disk. See
ccd(4).

pseudo-device   raid   4

This is the RAIDframe software RAID system. See raid(4).

Networking Pseudo-Devices

These pseudo-devices provide different methods of accessing the network.

pseudo-device   pf   1

This is OpenBSD's integrated packet filter, and is discussed in Chapters 17 through 19.

pseudo-device   pflog   1

This device lets pf log what it does, and is also discussed in Chapters 17 through 19.

pseudo-device   loop   2

This is the loopback device. If you remove it, many programs will break in an entertaining way. See lo(4) for details.

pseudo-device   bpfilter   8

This supports the Berkeley Packet Filter, the standard packet sniffer.

pseudo-device   sl   2

This supports SLIP, the popular pre-PPP dialup protocol.

pseudo-device   ppp   2

This lets you connect to the Internet with dialup connections using pppd(8). I recommend using user-mode ppp, which requires tun devices instead of this. See Chapter 9.

pseudo-device   sppp   1

This supports Synchronous PPP. Most people have no need of it, but see sppp(4) if you're curious.

pseudo-device   tun   2

This is a tunneling network device, used by user-mode ppp and a variety of VPN tools. We discuss using tun with ppp in Chapter 9.

pseudo-device   bridge   2

man: brconfig(8)

Bridging is where two separate Ethernet segments are connected transparently.

pseudo-device   vlan   2

This lets you divide a single Ethernet into two segments, or virtual lans. See vlan(4).

pseudo-device   gre   1

This supports Cisco Generic Routing Encapsulation, a common VPN protocol. See gre(4).

pseudo-device   pty   64

Pseudo-terminals are software terminals. Every remote shell connection needs a pseudo-terminal. See pty(4).

pseudo-device   tb   1

This supports many popular serial digitizers. See tb(4).

pseudo-device   ksyms   1

This lets a programmer pull symbol names from a running kernel. It's very useful for kernel developers; see ksyms(4).

IPv6 Pseudo-Devices

While we're not covering IPv6 in this book, the following IPv6 devices are included in the GENERIC kernel and so should be mentioned.

pseudo-device   gif   4

This is a generic IP tunnel, allowing you to tunnel either IPv4 or IPv6 over IPv4 or IPv6. See gif(4).

pseudo-device   faith   1

This pseudo-device can capture IPv6 traffic and relay it to a userland program. See faith(4).

pseudo-device   enc   1

The encapsulation interface allows the system to send IPv6 traffic through pf(4). See enc(4).

Miscellaneous Pseudo-Devices

The following pseudo-devices really don't fit anywhere else.

pseudo-device   pctr   1

This adds hooks for performance counters, discussed in pctr(1).

pseudo-device   mtrr   1

This pseudo-device provides access to the memory range attributes supported on Pentium CPUs. See mtrr(4).

pseudo-device   sequencer   1

This supports MIDI sequencers.

pseudo-device   wsmux   2

This is a virtual multiplexor for the wscons virtual console framework.

pseudo-device   crypto   1

This provides userland programs a generic interface to hardware cryptographic support through the kernel. See crypto(4).

B

PF EXAMPLE CONFIGURATIONS

Here we give examples for three different sorts of network: a simple home NAT device with no services, a small office with a restricted-capacity web server, and a 3-tier architecture application server farm using load balancing. While these examples are written to be different than those complete examples provided by the OpenBSD Project and related resources, they may well create some similar examples by the time you read this.

These examples are written to be plugged into /etc/pf.conf. All you need to do to use them is enable PF in /etc/rc.conf, and enable packet forwarding.

As typing in examples from a book is quite an annoyance, text files of these example configuration files are available from http://www.AbsoluteOpenBSD.org. Be sure to check there for any updates!

Home Firewall

In this example, we are using OpenBSD to provide very basic NAT, routing, and firewall protection services to a home user with a DSL connection. This home network is not providing any services to the outside world; it's literally as simple as you can get with NAT.

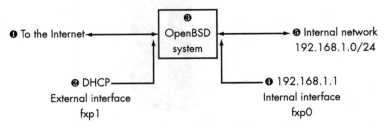

Here, we have an ❸OpenBSD machine attached to the ❶public Internet via a ❷DHCP connection. Our internal network is on the private IP addresses ❺192.168.0.0/24, routing through the ❹default gateway of 192.168.1.1. We don't want anyone to come in from the outside world normally, but we will leave port 22 open so we can SSH to home from other locations.

```
#set our macros
ext_if="fxp1"            #the external interface
int_if="fxp0"            #the internal interface
internal_net="192.168.1.0/24"

#first, normalize packets we transmit and receive
scrub in all

#then, give NAT to our internal addresses
nat on $ext_if from $internal_net to any -> ($ext_if)

#We want outbound FTP to work properly, so let's enable the
#FTP proxy.  Be sure you have ftp-proxy running out of inetd(8)!
rdr on $int_if proto tcp from any to any port ftp -> 127.0.0.1 port 8021

#We're not doing any packet shaping, so let's go directly to the
#packet filtering.  We'll block everything first, and then only
#explicitly allow desirable traffic.

block in log all

#As our client operating systems may be running some godforsaken
#operating system with poor ISN selection, we'll use state modulation.

pass in on $int_if inet from $internal_net to any modulate state

#I'd like to be able to SSH to my network from anywhere
pass in on $ext_if inet proto tcp from any to ($ext_if) port ssh keep state
```

```
#and, don't forget to allow our ftp-proxy program to connect back to
#the firewall!
pass in on $ext_if inet proto tcp from any to ($ext_if) user proxy keep state
```

Small Office Usage

Our small office has a network outside the OpenBSD system and a T1 for
Internet access. Unlike our home network, all the IP addresses for non-desktop
systems are static. Not only do we want to redirect traffic for some internal
servers, we want to restrict bandwidth usage for all of the services we allow.
People will be able to use programs such as streaming audio, so long as
bandwidth is not required for sanctioned corporate activities.

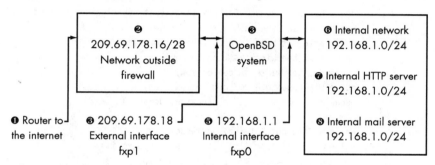

Much like the first example, our ❻internal network is on the private IP addresses
192.168.0.0/24, routing through the ❺default gateway of 192.168.1.1. Unlike the
first example, though, we have a ❶separate router outside our firewall and a
❷network between the two. At this time, all of our services will be attached to a
❸single IP address attached to the ❹OpenBSD system. We also have two servers
inside our network, a ❽mail server and a ❼web server. Bandwidth will be reg-
ulated via class-based queuing.

```
#set our macros
ext_if="fxp1"
int_if="fxp0"

ext_ip="209.69.178.18"
int_ip="192.168.1.1"
ext_net="209.69.178.16/28"
int_net="192.168.1.0/24"

#use macros for our web servers and mail server
webserver="192.168.1.2"
mailserver="192.168.1.3"

#first, normalize packets we transmit and receive
scrub in all

#now, set up our traffic queues
```

```
#
# the parent queue:
altq on $ext_if cbq bandwidth 100Mb queue {local, t1}

#the child queue for communication to our local network outside the
#firewall.  This queue can borrow traffic from the T1, if the T1 isn't
#full.
queue local bandwidth 98456Kb cbq(borrow)

#the child queue for T1 traffic.  This queue cannot borrow traffic
#from the parent; once the T1 is full, it's full!
queue t1 bandwidth 1544Kb {ssh, http-in, http-out, mail, dns, ftp, misc}

#now the child queues for our T1 circuit, shaping our usage the way we want.
queue http-in bandwidth 25% cbq(borrow)
queue http-out bandwidth 25% cbq(borrow, red)
queue mail bandwidth 25% cbq(borrow)
queue dns bandwidth 4% cbq(borrow)
queue ftp bandwidth 20% cbq(borrow, red)
queue misc bandwidth 1% cbq(borrow, default)

#give NAT to our internal addresses
nat on $ext_if from $int_net to any -> ($ext_if)

#We want outbound FTP to work properly, so let's enable the
#FTP proxy.  Be sure you have ftp-proxy running out of inetd(8)!
rdr on $int_if proto tcp from any to any port ftp -> 127.0.0.1 port 8021

#Redirect requests to our external IP address to the proper internal IP
rdr on $ext_if proto tcp from any to $ext_ip port www -> $webserver port www
rdr on $ext_if proto tcp from any to $ext_ip port smtp -> $mailserver port smtp

#Block everything first, and then explicitly allow only desirable
#traffic.
block in log all

#We have incoming connections to our mail and web server.
#Be sure to use the translated IP addresses here!
#Using macros will ensure that you have the correct IP.

pass in on $ext_if proto tcp from any to $webserver port www keep state queue http-
in
pass in on $ext_if proto tcp from any to $mailserver port smtp keep state queue
mail

#Allow our ftp-proxy program to connect back to the firewall!
pass in on $ext_if inet proto tcp from any to $ext_ip user proxy keep state

#The next rules cover traffic from inside the network, going out As
#our client operating systems may be running some godforsaken
```

```
#operating system with poor ISN selection, we'll use state modulation.
#Remember, the last matching rule is attached to the packet

#first, we set up the misc queue, where traffic will go if nothing
#else fits better.  People can use P2P programs if nothing more
#important is running.

pass out on $ext_if from $int_net to any queue misc

#pass out on $ext_if from $int_net proto tcp to any port { www, https } modulate
state queue http-out
#pass out on $ext_if from $int_net proto { tcp, udp } to any port domain modulate
state queue dns
#pass out on $ext_if from $int_net proto tcp to any port { ftp, ftp-data } modulate
state queue ftp
#pass out on $ext_if from $mailserver proto tcp to any port smtp modulate state
queue mail

#lastly, catch all traffic bound for the local exterior network and
#drop it in the big queue; basically unlimited bandwidth on the local
#ethernet, after all!

pass out on $ext_if from $int_net to $ext_net modulate state queue local

#protect against spoofing
antispoof for $int_if
antispoof for $ext_if
```

3-Tier Architecture

This is modeled after a large, commercial web server farm. A real web farm
would have multiple application servers and multiple databases, but that would
just clutter up this example. To add additional servers, just duplicate what exists
here and rename the macros.

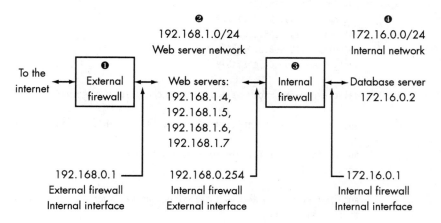

Our ❷application tier is protected from the Internet by a very restrictive set of ❶firewall rules. The only access to the application servers in this environment is on port 80 and 443, plus SSH from a management network. The application servers are not allowed to initiate outbound connections to the Internet, and are are load-balanced so that if one fails it can be removed from the pool without affecting service level agreements. This technique is very popular with Windows web servers in high-availability environments; when you have to reboot a server, just pull it from the load balance pool until you're done.

Most large-scale application servers get their data from a ❹database server. The database server is protected from the application servers by a ❸second firewall that only allows database queries and our management SSH connection from the outside world. Note that the application servers are not allowed to SSH to the database tier; if an intruder successfully compromises a web server, they still cannot stage an attack against the database server except through a very small window. While they can make database queries, anyone who has ever tried to reverse-engineer a complicated database will tell you that this is quite difficult without documentation! This design is quite efficacious against would-be intruders.

In some three-tier network environments, the application servers will have two network cards; one facing the Internet firewall, and one facing the database tier. Not only does this improve performance on the local Ethernet, it also slightly enhances security.

This type of network requires proper routing, which we discussed in Chapter 5 — in fact, we routed this exact example in Chapter 5! We also need configuration files for both the application server firewall, and the database tier firewall.

```
# Application Tier Firewall Configuration
#set our macros

ext_if = "fxp1"
int_if = "fxp0"
ext_ip = "209.69.178.26"
int_ip = "192.168.1.1"
ext_net = "209.69.178.16/28"
int_net = "192.168.1.0/24"
db_net = "172.168.0.0/24"
mgmt_net = "209.69.178.18/32"

#also use macros for our load-balanced application servers

appservers = "{ 192.168.1.4, 192.168.1.5, 192.168.1.6, 192.168.1.7 }"

#normalize all traffic we receive and transmit
scrub in all

#use NAT so we can access internal equipment, such as switches, from
#the outside world.
```

```
nat on $ext_if from { $db_net, $int_net } to any -> $ext_ip

#here, we load-balance our application servers
rdr on fxp1 proto tcp from any to $ext_ip port { 80, 443 } -> $appservers

#
block in log all

#allow traffic from the world to our application server
pass in on $ext_if proto tcp from any to $appservers port { 80, 443 } keep state

#allow packets from our management network (a single IP, in this case) to
#enter the network

pass in on $ext_if proto tcp from $mgmt_net to { $db_net, $int_net } keep state

#lastly, make sure we are spoof-protected
antispoof for $ext_if
antispoof for $int_if

# Database Tier Firewall Configuration

#set our macros

ext_if = "fxp1"
int_if = "fxp0"
ext_ip = "192.168.1.254"
int_ip = "172.16.0.1"
ext_net = "192.168.1.0/24"
int_net = "172.16.0.0/24"
mgmt_net = "209.69.178.18/32"

#our database server

dbserver = "172.16.0.2"

#normalize all traffic we receive and transmit
scrub in all

#Our application tier firewall is doing NAT for us, so we do not need
#to NAT further...

#...but we do need to filter traffic
block in log all

#allow traffic from the world to our application server
#Port 1723 is used by the Oracle listener; each database has its own port~
pass in on $ext_if proto tcp from $ext_net to $dbserver port 1521 keep state
```

```
#allow packets from our management network (a single IP, in this case) to
#enter the network
pass in on $ext_if proto tcp from $mgmt_net to $db_net, $int_net keep state

#lastly, make sure we are spoof-protected
antispoof for $ext_if
antispoof for $int_if
```

AFTERWORD

"Unix for the Practical Paranoid?" What does that mean, anyway?

Back when I got my first email address, the Internet was a military and educational network run by DARPA, with an entirely different security profile. UUNet had not yet appeared, and corporate Internet access was inconceivable. Security was a whole different matter then: All you had to worry about were students and soldiers, and generally all parties were sufficiently interested in the well-being of the network that everyone, for the most part, took care of their own security problems.

Today, any yahoo with an old PC and twenty bucks a month can get a dialup account. We share the network with every country in the world, some of which are quite hostile to each other. The Internet also has a variety of tempting, juicy targets on it: Banking systems, online shopping, and embarrassing personal information are just the tip of the iceberg. Criminals have a lot of incentive to learn how to compromise computer systems. Additionally, script kiddies have their own juvenile reasons for wanting to damage or alter Internet sites. The common point in all of these is that for an intruder to escape unscathed, he needs to compromise an "attack staging" server belonging to an unrelated third party. This leaves the third party with the blame, and the intruder with the profits. While the third party might be able to prove their innocence, the lack of logging and auditing tools on most networks make this unlikely. If your computer is not secure, sooner or later you will be exploited.

The Internet is now a hostile place. While people might not be trying to get your data or your system in particular, some people are trying to break into any system they can get. Even if all you have is a desktop computer on a cable modem, you are a target of opportunity. This should give everyone on the Net a definite sense of paranoia!

Absolutely 100 percent effective security is simple to achieve: Just unplug your computer from the Internet and never plug it in again. Better still, feed the components to a blast furnace. Oh, you wanted to use your system for something? Well, that's a different story. You must rely upon the operating system and application security.

Application programmers have no choice but to rely upon the operating system's features to build their programs, but if that infrastructure is insecure, their programs are inherently and irremediably insecure. The OpenBSD Project develops a computing infrastructure that supports all the standard computing functions in a safe and secure way, giving developers a solid footing. OpenBSD makes paranoia practical in day-to-day life.

How effective is this approach? Well, in 2001, DARPA started a project to fund open-source security and dedicated close to two million dollars to OpenBSD development. This funding was canceled in 2003, without notice. When asked why, the DARPA spokesperson cited "the evolving threat posed by increasingly capable nation-states." I could go on for pages and pages speculating what this means, but there's not much point at this date.

This, of course, leaves the OpenBSD Project in a bit of a bind. The DARPA contract paid for several developers to work full-time on OpenBSD. Those people were left scrambling for jobs, and could no longer devote such intense energy to the project. OpenBSD survived this — after all, it existed for several years before DARPA offered it any money, and it will keep on surviving for years to come. With neither government nor corporate sponsors, OpenBSD is funded entirely by donations and by CD-ROM and T-shirt sales. Their speed of innovation is limited only by their financial resources.

If you're interested in the progress of OpenBSD, the best way you can demonstrate this is to either purchase CD-ROMs and/or related accoutrements, or just give them money. Sadly, donations to OpenBSD are not tax-deductible in the United States. You might be able to write them off as a business expense, however. For more information, check out the "donations" link at http://www.OpenBSD.org.

In the meantime, though, when someone calls you paranoid, just ask them, "Yes, but am I paranoid *enough*?" Then give them an OpenBSD CD-ROM and go on your merry way, secure in knowing that whoever the hackers break in to en route to robbing the Federal Reserve, it won't be you.

INDEX

F

-f argument, 413
-f flag, 210, 251, 305, 406, 407, 413
-F state, 415
facilities, local, 291
facility, 289
fake installation, 254
Fast File System (FFS), 300–304, 306, 310
FAT file system, 37
FAT32 format, 74
fdformat(8), 309
fdimage.exe, 50
fdisk tools, 73
fdisk(8) tool, 45, 76–80, 311
features, /etc/pf.conf, 354
FETCH_CMD variable, 256
FFS checking tool, 303
FFS (Fast File System), 300–304, 306, 310
file flags, 183–85
file format, configuration, 225–26
file fragments, 55
file size, 282
file system management, 297–319
    adding new hard disks, 310–13
    backing up, 304
    corrupt FFS partitions, 303–4
    creating file systems, 312–13
    debugging, 304
    device node, 298–99
    encrypted partitions, 316–19
    fast file system, 300–303
    file system partition, 82–83
    file system table, 299–300
    memory file systems, 313–15
    mount(8) and FFS, 304–6
    mounting disk images, 315–16
    mounting foreign file systems, 306–9
    removable media, 309–10
File Transfer Protocol. *See* FTP (File Transfer Protocol)
files, package, 244–45
filesize resource-limiting login.conf variable, 127
Filesystem integrity check, 268
filter authentication, 266
filter rules, 192
filtering, packet. *See* PF (packet filtering)
filter-prohib, 369
fingerprint, 182
fips.exe tool, 74–75

firewalls, 350
First-In First Out queuing, 396
flag-based filtering, 373–74
flags, 282, 375
    filtering, 211
    routing, 164–65
flags field, 161
flavors, port, 259–60
floppies
    creating, 49–50
    formatting, 309
floppy label, 310
floppy33.fs image, 50
floppyXXB.fs image, 49
floppyXXC.fs image, 49
floppyXX.fs image, 49
flush command, 413
flushing rules, 407–8
foreign file system partition, 82–83
foreign file system types, 307–8
foreign mounts, 306–7
Fortran compilers, 39
fragment column, 411
fragment handling, customizing, 364–66
fragment processing, 366
fragments, 55, 300
free sectors, 54
FreeBSD, 4, 75
    and ABI (Application Binary Interface), 262–63
    dual-boot installation restrictions, 74
fsck(8) tool, 300, 303–4, 305, 318
fsize fragment, 55
fstab file system, 270
fstype column, 55
FTP (File Transfer Protocol), 36, 66
    configuring proxy application, 390
    installing from, 35, 246–48
    Logging feature, 391
    login.conf variables affecting, 128
    not loging in via, 270
    options, 128
    proxy PF rules, 391
ftp(1) program, 255–56
ftpchroot directory, 270
ftpchroot FTP-affecting login.conf variable, 128
ftpd_flags, 95
ftp-dir FTP-affecting login.conf variable, 128
ftplist file, 36
ftp-proxy(8), 390
ftpusers file, 270

I

-i flag, 420
i386 platform, 32, 42
ICMP codes, 13, 368–69, 375
ICMP (Internet Control Message
    Protocol), 155
ICMP states, 379–80
ICMP types, 375
ICMP-type keyword, 375
ICMP unreachable message, 369
ID numbers, 119, 279
id(1) command, 123
IDE controller, 33
IDE drive, 52, 203
identd_flags, 95
ifconfig -a command, 62–63
ifconfig(8) program, 161–62, 176
ignorenologin environment setting, 128
"in" keyword, 354, 369
inbound load balancing, 394–95
INDEX file, 241, 242
index line, 243
index, search, 276
inet6 flag, 161
inetd server, 95
inetd(8) daemon, 271–73
inetd.conf, 271–73
info level, 290
info line, 243
information sources, multiple, 290–91
infrastructure directory, 241
inodes, 300
inserts entry, 411
inspection options, 380
inspection, stateful, 378–81
INSTALL file, 252
Install option, 51
install program, 51–52
installation media, 65–67
installation sets, custom, 69
installed software, upgrading, 338
installer, *51*
installing
    bootstrap tools, 329
    kernel, 217, 234–35
    multiple operating systems, 71–85
        boot managers, 84–85
        disklabel on multiboot
            systems, 81–82
        dual-boot installation
            restrictions, 73–75
        dual-boot install overview, 72
        fdisk options, 80–81
        hard disk geometry, 75–76

        installing from a foreign file
            system partition, 82–83
        MBR partitions, 72–73
        using fdisk during, 76–80
    packages, 245–48
    ports, 98, 253, 253–55
    source code, 98
    updated base software, 329–32
    Windows 2000, 74
    Windows XP, 73, 74
Installing message, 253
installing OpenBSD, 47–70
    booting, 50–51
    creating partitions, 53–58
    custom installation sets and scripts,
        69
    disk setup, 52–53
    disklabel operations, 59–61
    distribution sets, 68–69
    final disk configuration, 61
    final installation steps, 69–70
    from foreign file system partition,
        82–83
    hardware setup, 48
    install program, 51–52
    installation media, 65–67
    making boot floppy, 49–50
    network setup, 62–65
    preparations before, 31–46, 31–46
        choosing method, 37–38
        disk sectors, 46
        distribution sets, 38–40
        getting OpenBSD, 34–37
        hardware, 32–34
        multiple OS partitioning, 45
        OpenBSD Release, 37
        partitioning, 40–41
        standalone partitioning, 41–45
    root password, 65
    subsequent disks, 59
/install.site shell script, 69
integrated program configuration,
    91–92
integrity check, filesystem, 268
interactively users, 115–16
interface, 163
    configuring, 160–61
    matching, 370
    packet filtering, 378
interface name, 160
internal firewall, 163
internal network, 162, 163
Internet
    finding program on, 35
    hardware crypto support, 27

Y

yppasswdd_flags variable, 98
ypserv_flags variable, 98

Z

z command, 60
-z flag, 412

HACKING
The Art of Exploitation

by JON ERICKSON

A comprehensive introduction to exploitation techniques and creative problem-solving methods known as "hacking." Explains technical aspects of hacking such as stack based overflows, heap based overflows, string exploits, return-into-libc, shellcode, and cryptographic attacks on 802.11b.

2003, 400 PP., $39.95 ($59.95 CDN)
ISBN 1-59327-007-0

THE BOOK OF OPENOFFICE.ORG
Your Guide to the Free Microsoft Compatible Office Suite

by AUTHOR TBA

This book is the complete guide to using this remarkably powerful and stable office suite. Practical and task-based, it includes coverage of installation, working with documents and spreadsheets, creating presentations and databases, using the draw utility, and much more. Clear and straightforward examples make it easy to switch from MS Office to OpenOffice.org.

2003, 432 PP., $34.95 ($52.95 CDN)
ISBN 1-886411-98-0

ABSOLUTE BSD
The Ultimate Guide to FreeBSD

by MICHAEL W. LUCAS

FreeBSD, the powerful, flexible, and free UNIX-based operating system, is the preferred server for many enterprises. This definitive guide covers installation, networking, security, network services, system performance, kernel tweaking, file systems, SMP, upgrading, crash debugging, and much more.

"One of the Top Ten Books of 2002." — *;login*

2002, 616 PP., $39.95 ($61.95 CDN)
ISBN 1-886411-74-3

THE BOOK OF WEBMIN
...or How I Learned to Stop Worrying and Love UNIX

by JOE COOPER

Shows you how to use Webmin, the web-based systems administration software suite, to manage your UNIX systems with ease—even if you are unfamiliar with the command line. Step-by-step tutorials show how to accomplish nearly every service and task needed to maintain a UNIX system including how to configure popular services like Apache, BIND, Squid, and Sendmail, plus manage features like network configuration, disk configuration, users and groups.

2003, 368 PP., $34.95 ($49.95 CDN)
ISBN 1-886411-92-1

CRACKPROOF YOUR SOFTWARE
The Best Ways to Protect Your Software Against Crackers

by PAVOL CERVEN

This essential resource for software developers highlights the weak points in software protection, shows how crackers break common protection schemes, and describes how to defend against them. CD-ROM contains compression and encoding software, debuggers and anti-debugging tricks, and practical protection demonstrations.

2002, 272 PP., $34.95 ($52.95 CDN)
ISBN 1-886411-79-4

PHONE:

1 (800) 420-7240 OR
(415) 863-9900
MONDAY THROUGH FRIDAY,
9 A.M. TO 5 P.M. (PST)

FAX:

(415) 863-9950
24 HOURS A DAY,
7 DAYS A WEEK

EMAIL:

SALES@NOSTARCH.COM

WEB:

HTTP://WWW.NOSTARCH.COM

MAIL:

NO STARCH PRESS
555 DE HARO STREET, SUITE 250
SAN FRANCISCO, CA 94107
USA

UPDATES

Visit **http://www.nostarch.com/openbsd.htm** for updates, errata, and other information.